# LAW & BANKING

## *Principles*

JAMES C. CONBOY, JR.

EDUCATION POLICY & DEVELOPMENT

AMERICAN BANKERS ASSOCIATION

1120 Connecticut Avenue, N.W.
Washington, D.C. 20036

This publication is designed to provide accurate and authoritative information in regard to the subject matter covered. It is sold with the understanding that the publisher is not engaged in rendering legal, accounting, or other professional service. If legal advice or other expert assistance is required, the services of a competent professional person should be sought.

—*From a Declaration of Principles jointly adopted by a Committee of the American Bar Association and a Committee of Publishers and Associations.*

© 1990 by the American Bankers Association

All rights reserved. This book may not be reproduced in whole or in part in any form whatsoever without permission from the publisher.

Printed in the United States of America

*Library of Congress Cataloging-in-Publication Data*

Conboy, James C.
  Law & banking : principles / James C. Conboy, Jr.
    p. cm.
  ISBN 0-89982-362-9
  1. Banking law—United States.  I. American Institute of Banking.
  II. Title.   III. Title: Law and banking.
KF974.C65   1990
346.73'082—dc20
[347.30682]
                                              90-341
                                                CIP

# Contents

Preface  v

CHAPTER 1  Sources of Law  1
CHAPTER 2  Banking Law in Action  19
CHAPTER 3  Torts and Crimes  41
CHAPTER 4  Legal Entities  59
CHAPTER 5  Contracts  129
CHAPTER 6  Real and Personal Property  203
CHAPTER 7  Bankruptcy  265
CHAPTER 8  Federal Regulations Governing Consumer Lending, Privacy, and Electronic Fund Transfers  303

Answers to Questions for Review and Discussion  379
Glossary  389
Index  413

# List of Figures

FIGURE 1   Model Disclosure Form   *309*
FIGURE 2   Sample Disclosure Form for Installment Loans   *312*
FIGURE 3   G–10(A)—Applications and Solicitations Model Form (Credit Cards)   *313*
FIGURE 4   Sample Loan Program Disclosure   *314*

# *Preface*

In today's world, it is extremely difficult for people to function without some knowledge of the law that governs many of their day-to-day activities, from making a will to opening a savings account to acquiring a building permit. For banks and their employees a knowledge of law is critical, since their activities without exception are governed by extremely technical laws and regulations enforced not only by courts but, more frequently, by state and federal regulatory agencies.

In terms of government control, banks lie somewhere between a corner grocery store and a utility that provides services such as power or water. The grocery business is open to anyone with enough cash either to buy an already existing store or open a new one, and prospers or declines without much government intervention. Utilities, however, are subject to a great amount of regulation. Government agencies usually approve their rates, often subsidize them, and, through licensing laws, preclude competitors to protect specific market areas. Thus, many grocery stores can serve an area, but only one utility can provide electricity for that same area.

Banks, like utilities, are exposed to limited competition from other banks because of state and federal laws that govern the establishment of new banks and the relocation and branching of existing banks, but they are given greater control over what they charge customers. And like utilities, banks come within the jurisdiction of various government regulatory agencies, depending on the type and particular functions of the bank being regulated. This book will discuss bank regulation and regulators, including the Comptroller of the Currency, the Federal Reserve Board, the Federal Deposit Insurance Corporation, and state banking authorities.

Chapter 1 discusses the sources of law, including common, statutory, and uniform laws; constitutions; and regulations. Chapter 2 discusses the role of regulators and courts in banking, specifically their role as moderators and enforcers of the laws governing banks. Chapter 3 defines torts and crimes and their relationship to each other and discusses particular torts and crimes applicable to banking.

While certain laws and regulations apply only to banks, banks must also transact business within a legal environment common to all individuals and entities within the United States. A bank's transaction with a customer that is a corporation will differ little from the dealings a corner grocery store or utility company has with the same corporation, as far as the rights and responsibilities of the corporation are concerned. As an introduction to "legal entities," chapter 4 discusses sole proprietorships, partnerships, corporations, governments, estates, trusts, and other legal entities with which banks transact business. Since banks also deal with third persons who act as agents, chapter 4 includes a discussion of agency law.

Nearly every banking transaction is a contract. Promissory notes, security agreements, negotiable instruments, savings account passbooks, and employee pension programs all involve contractual relationships. Chapter 5 sets forth the basic elements required to form a contract. The chapter not only discusses how individuals and entities form contracts but also what laws govern the performance of contracts, including the Uniform Commercial Code and common law.

As lenders, banks continually encounter questions about the legal technicalities of property interests. In evaluating customers' financial statements, permitting withdrawals from joint savings accounts, and properly securing loans, banks must determine property ownership. Chapter 6 discusses the acquisition and forms of ownership of personal property. The chapter also deals with similar issues relating to real property, including the use of real property as collateral in mortgage law.

Chapter 7 discusses the liquidation and rehabilitation procedures for a debtor under federal bankruptcy law and the effect of those procedures on banks as creditors. Chapter 8 covers areas of law that were either nonexistent or in their formative stages when *Law and Banking* was originally released in 1971. Laws reviewed in this chapter include the Truth in Lending Act, Fair Credit Billing Act, Consumer Leasing Act, Equal Credit Opportunity Act, Real Estate Settlement Procedures Act, Electronic Fund Transfer Act, Right to Financial Privacy Act, Fair Credit Reporting Act, and Fair Debt Collection

Practices Act. Chapter 8 also covers the Credit Practices Rule.

*Law and Banking: Principles* is a basic introduction to its subject. Hundreds of statutes, court decisions, and legal treatises have been written covering the topics included in this book. The goal of this text is not to make the student an expert in banking law, but rather to make bankers aware of law-related areas in their day-to-day work and to enable them to recognize legal problems when they arise. Recognizing a legal problem is often more important than solving it, particularly if the recognition occurs before the problem becomes serious.

In conjunction with *Law and Banking: Principles*, the American Bankers Association is publishing *Law and Banking: Applications*. Both books reflect the continued efforts of the American Bankers Association to provide up-to-date education for its members.

Craig Smith, the author of *Law and Banking: Applications*, has provided a text that covers such subjects as commercial paper, holder-in-due-course liability, bank collections, check losses, letters of credit, secured transactions, and legal implications of commercial lending.

As with the previous editions of *Law and Banking* by such legal authorities as Dean William D. Hawkland, the intent of these texts is to provide useful information to bankers that they can use in their day-to-day banking careers. Further, the texts attempt to provide the rationale behind the laws and regulations discussed. Thus, while each volume stands on its own as a resource for the areas of law it covers, the American Bankers Association intends the volumes to provide an introduction to the unique position of banks in the U.S. legal system.

# Acknowledgments

Personally, I have been delighted to have participated in the revision of *Law and Banking: Principles*, and my thanks go to the American Bankers Association for that opportunity.

As with the previous edition, my secretary, Phyllis Yeck, has given a great deal of time to manuscript preparation and often ignored the scheduled end of the workday to complete the additional workload caused by the text.

Many thanks to my wife and fellow lawyer, Susan, who demonstrated her superb ability for detail in editing and source-checking the text.

My partners and associates, including Lloyd Fell, Kathy Lieder, Mike Stack, Larry Hanson, Linda Throne, David Barton, and Susan Conboy, were very much appreciated during the text's preparation, particularly when they willingly helped me with other tasks so that I could write.

In the preface to previous editions, I noted the contribution my tenure at Citizens National Bank of Cheboygan made to my development as a bank lawyer. That relationship and tutelage continues, as does my appreciation to Lyle McKinley, the bank's now-retired president.

In addition, I extend my sincere appreciation to those who devoted considerable time and energy to reviewing the content of this workbook and who provided invaluable suggestions for improvement. Special thanks to

Josephine A. Bednarz
Assistant Vice President
  Security Department
Key Bank of Western New
  York, N.A.
Buffalo, New York

Gerald L. Blanchard
Senior Vice President/Senior
  Counsel
The Citizens and Southern
  Corporation
Atlanta, Georgia

Nancy L. Cahill
Attorney
Ellis & Li
Seattle, Washington

Keith R. Fisher
Of Counsel
Hogan & Hartson
Washington, D.C.

Steven N. Klein
Attorney
Schwartz & Freeman
Chicago, Illinois

David L. Mackey
Assistant Vice President and
 Commercial Loan Officer
Star Bank, N.A., Eastern
 Indiana
Connersville, Indiana

David C. Sharman
Senior Vice President
NCNB Texas National Bank
Dallas, Texas

Donald G. Smith
Auditor
Central National Bank of
 Howard County
Kokomo, Indiana

My wife, Susan, and my children, Ryan, Becky, and Brendan, once again gave me the encouragement to complete this book. I very much hope that it will enhance the careers of bankers around the country.

James C. Conboy, Jr.
CONBOY, FELL, STACK, LIEDER & HANSON

# 1

## Sources of Law

After studying this chapter, you will be able to

- describe sources of law governing individuals and entities in the United States
- discuss the development of the Uniform Commercial Code
- differentiate between common law, statutory law, constitutions, and regulations

Law is a society's basic set of rules that define and govern many aspects of its members' conduct. Because it not only defines proper conduct but enforces it against those who transgress, law goes beyond society's norms for acceptable social behavior. Enforcement, perceived or actual, is what sets law apart from manners, ethics, diplomacy, and other standards for behavior imposed on individuals by society or segments within society.

While law may have as its origin society's definition of proper behavior, it differs from those rules because its infraction can lead to punitive measures by the state or wronged individuals, whereas violation of the rules of proper behavior leads only to social ostracism. For example, spitting on public sidewalks is considered offensive behavior that may result in public criticism. If that is insufficient to stop the practice, it may become the subject of a law prohibiting such conduct.

The pervasive intrusion of law into many aspects of behavior in the United States parallels the growth of the nation's industrial economy. An agrarian society that has a small, nontransient population and a simple economy has little need for a complicated legal system. The number of U.S. laws has grown in proportion to the industrialization of the nation, the movement of the populace to cities, and the transient nature of society. One example of this growth can be seen in the increase in laws and regulations governing waste disposal. In the eighteenth century, farmers disposed of their production waste on their own property. No laws existed regarding the manner of such disposal. Today, myriad laws and regulations govern every aspect of waste disposal, including its packaging, processing, and location.

Laws also reflect society's changing attitudes about what role, if any, government should play in protecting individuals within it. Thus, over the years child labor, welfare, occupational safety, and federal deposit insurance laws were passed. Today, since many have criticized the extent to which government does control the lives and economics of the populace, the role of government is being reexamined. This reexamination has resulted in the repeal or relaxation of regulations governing such industries as the airlines, trucking, and banking. An example of bank deregulation can be seen in Regulation Q (12 C.F.R. § 217). To assure that banks were not compelled to compete detrimentally in payment of interest on deposits, the Federal Reserve Board adopted Regulation Q to set maximum ceilings on rates banks could pay on such deposits. As part of the movement toward bank deregulation, the ceiling on rates in Regulation Q was fully repealed in 1986.

However, since 1986 the thrift industry crisis has led to increased emphasis on regulation of financial institutions. The enactment of the Financial Institutions Reform, Recovery and Enforcement Act of 1989 (FIRREA) represents a retreat from deregulation.

Law takes many forms and within the United States has many origins. These origins include federal and state common law, statutory law, constitutions, and regulations.

## COMMON LAW

The oldest source of U.S. law is **common law**, which originated among the jurists in England, from the fall of Roman authority until after the Norman invasion of 1066. During this period few, if any, legislative or executive bodies enacted any written or statutory laws. Instead, customs that had evolved over centuries dictated relationships between people. In making their decisions when disputes arose among people, judges relied on these customs. When no custom existed with which to settle a dispute, judges based their decisions upon the prevailing ethical, social, and political principles of their time. After making decisions based on such principles, judges would reuse the same decision to settle other disputes involving similar facts.

The following is an example of how the common law can develop by the practice of **stare decisis**. This is the policy of following rules laid down in previous judicial decisions as long as they do not contradict ordinary principles of justice.

*Case for Discussion*

**BURDEN, INJURED PARTY v. BANK**

### Facts
Customer Burden has harassed Teller Ryan every day for 30 years. While making a deposit, Burden shouts at Ryan, "Of all the stupid tellers I've ever dealt with, you, tinselmouth, are the stupidest." After 30 years of smiling in response to Burden's insults, that day Ryan pulls a gun and shoots him.

Saying it is responsible for Ryan's action, Burden sues the bank. The bank asserts that it is only responsible for its employees when they act within the scope of their duties, and Ryan's duties do not include shooting customers.

### Decision
The trial judge notes that the question has never arisen before and rules that a bank is liable as a matter of law for whatever a bank employee does to a customer on bank premises. On appeal, the state supreme court affirms the trial judge and publishes its opinion.

### Facts
A year later, virtually the same incident occurs at another bank. Again, the injured party sues the bank.

### Decision
The trial judge in this case rules that the bank should not be held liable as a matter of law, because the shooting was beyond the scope of an

employee's duty and the bank could not have prevented it.

On appeal, the state supreme court reverses the second judge. Once it is established by the highest court in a state, a rule of law binds all judges in subsequent cases where the same kinds of facts are present.

### Questions for Discussion
1. What are the main advantages of following the doctrine of stare decisis?
2. Under what conditions would it be appropriate for a court to depart from legal precedent?

---

*[Margin note: New York State does not recognize common-law marriage.]*

Thus developed the doctrine of stare decisis within the common law—that is, courts should normally follow the decisions of cases involving similar facts. By repeatedly recognizing their own and other judges' decisions, the judiciary of medieval England developed the continuity of decisions known as the common law. Once other judges begin to use and commonly refer to another judge's decision, it becomes a principle of law and part of the common law.

Common-law marriage is an excellent example of the influence of common law. At some point in medieval English history, a man and woman lived together by mutual agreement but without having their relationship solemnized by either a religious or a secular official. Then perhaps the man died and left the woman with children who needed support. A judge, realizing that unless the man's property could be passed to the woman and children they would become burdens to society, decided that because of their relationship the man and woman were legally husband and wife and thus she and the children could inherit his property. Once the principle of common-law marriage was established, other judges used it as a basis for ordering support for common-law wives and their children deserted by common-law husbands, as well as for finding a common-law spouse who married another without first obtaining a divorce a bigamist.

Over the centuries, judge-made common law developed into a sophisticated group of laws in England. A particular spur to this development was the eventual practice of reporting court decisions in written form. As a result, judges throughout the country could more easily refer to them.

With the growth of the British empire came the export of English common law. By the American Revolution in 1776, the colonies were well acquainted with and relied upon common law extensively in their courts. After the Revolution, the states continued to rely on English common law and continue to do so still, but statutes or decisions of American courts have modified or reversed much of the earlier common law.

The ability of a court to modify or reverse prior common law is as much a part of the common law as stare decisis. Normally, only the highest court in a jurisdiction has the power to reverse or modify existing common law and will do so only where a change is needed because society itself has changed and the existing common law is antiquated. In 1880, a court might have recognized that horse-drawn vehicles had the right-of-way over motor-propelled vehicles, because at that time the former were necessary to everyday commerce while the latter were little more than toys of the wealthy. Today, a court would recognize the priority of motor-propelled over horse-drawn vehicles because of the change in their importance to society.

## STATUTORY LAW

Common law is less significant to the twentieth-century United States than it was to medieval England or the United States in 1800 because of the great importance of **statutory law**. Statutes are passed by municipal, county, and state legislative bodies and the U.S. Congress. Unlike the common law, which is determined by judges, statutes are passed by the elected representatives of the federal, state, or local jurisdiction. Because greater credence is given to the authority of elected representatives, statutory laws that conflict with common laws override and supersede them. For example, in 1956, a state legislature passed a statute declaring that from that time forward, common-law marriages would not be recognized as valid in the state. This statutory law effectively repealed the common law.

While statutory laws override judge-made common law, they also provide a great opportunity for further judicial decisions, an opportunity that results from the need for courts to interpret or construe statutes. Statutes may be written in an ambiguous fashion or with gaps in the scope of their coverage. Courts have the power to decide ambiguities and fill in such gaps, thereby reflecting the legislative intent. One situation in which the courts determined the legislative intent of a banking statute involved clarifying the meaning of "branch bank" under the McFadden Act.

The U.S. Congress passed a statute defining a branch bank to be any branch place of business at which deposits are received, or checks paid, or money lent (McFadden Act, 12 U.S.C. § 36(f)). Many years after passage of the statute, technology developed unmanned customer-bank computer terminals (CBCTs) located far from manned bank offices, which could receive deposits, dispense money either as loans or withdrawals from accounts, and, at the request of a customer using a precoded identification card inserted in the CBCT, transfer funds between accounts.

National banks began setting up CBCTs without receiving branch approval from their regulatory agency. Finally, a lawsuit was brought that requested the courts to find that CBCTs were branches under the McFadden Act. A court interpreted the statute, found CBCTs were branches, and ordered national banks to seek branch approval before opening such terminals. *Independent Bankers Association of America (IBAA) v. Smith*, 534 F.2d 921 (D.C. Cir. 1976).

As stated, statutory law is the product of municipal, county, and state legislatures and the U.S. Congress. The impetus for legislation may be members of a legislative body itself or interest groups representing particular aspects of society, which lobby for enactment of particular bills. Such groups may be as informal as a few people with a shared interest or may be a large trade association, such as the American Bankers Association, which represents thousands of people and entities. These interest groups may form around one issue. For example, in recent years, many individuals have become concerned about what they perceive as lax laws regarding drunk drivers. They have formed groups that have successfully lobbied many state legislatures for stiffer drunk-driving laws. Alternatively, interest groups may be concerned with all issues affecting one industry. For example, the American Bankers Association, which represents the nation's commercial banks, proposes legislation helpful to its members, reacts to bills potentially harmful to its members, and generally makes its views on banking known to the U.S. Congress and state legislatures.

Usually, groups advocate the adoption of legislation to benefit themselves or the individuals they represent. Others support legislation for what they perceive as the common good of society, which can include such objectives as removing drunk drivers from the nation's roads or making the wheels of commerce turn more easily.

Because the United States has a federal system, 50 state legislatures, the legislatures of the territories and the Commonwealth of Puerto Rico, the City Council of Washington, D.C., and the U.S. Congress all make laws. There is no assurance that laws passed by the various legislative bodies will be uniform, and certainly uniformity is no requirement and may not even be desirable for certain types of legislation.

---

EXAMPLE ■ In state X, a rural state where cattle ranching is a primary industry, the law requires motorists to be observant of cattle wandering free on roads. If motorists strike any of Farmer Ernst's animals, they are held liable for the damage done to them. In state A, a heavily populated industrialized state, Farmer Brown, whose cattle wander onto a road, will be held liable for any damages they cause if a motorist hits them.

---

While article IV of the U.S. Constitution requires each state to give "full faith and credit" to the laws of other states, no constitutional or other requirement exists that laws must be uniform among the states. This lack of uniformity will become most apparent in the discussion in chapter 6 on real property. Because of the differences from state to state in both statutory and common law, the method by which real property is acquired, spouses' rights in each other's real property, and methods of mortgaging real property vary widely among the states.

## UNIFORM LAWS

Lack of uniform laws among the states has led to problems, especially for those entities including banks that deal across state boundaries. An entity engaged in interstate transactions must be aware of the laws affecting its operations in each state in which it does business.

Recognition of the desirability of uniform state laws has received attention from several groups, including the National Conference of Commissioners on Uniform State Laws. This group has drafted numerous uniform laws that it then encourages various states to enact. Among the uniform laws proposed by the National Conference have been the Uniform Commercial Code, the Uniform Consumer Credit Code, Uniform Disposition of Unclaimed Property Act, Uniform Fraudulent Conveyance Act, Uniform Gifts to Minors Act, and Uniform Partnership Act.

The most significant uniform act proposed by the National Conference has been the **Uniform Commercial Code (UCC)**, which covers commercial transactions involving personal property.

**Uniform Commercial Code**

After 1900, with more railroads, faster communication, and more sophisticated recordkeeping procedures, all of which greatly expanded interstate commerce, the necessity within the states for uniform statutes governing commercial transactions became apparent. Between 1890 and 1910, the National Conference, made up of individuals from all the states, thoroughly reviewed the status of commercial laws within the United States and the necessity for conformity. This review led them to draft the Uniform Negotiable Instruments Act, Uniform Stock Transfer Act, and Uniform Sales Act. These acts were adopted in many states, with the Negotiable Instruments Act being enacted in all the states admitted to the Union at the time.

In the 1930s, the commissioners began to envision even further uniformity of laws affecting commerce in response to the growing need for uniform commercial law. The commissioners' goal became not a revision of the various uniform laws but rather the development of one code whose scope would include all commercial law. Then in 1943, the American Law Institute joined the commissioners to assist in the project. In 1951, the conference and the institute finished their project and the American Bar Association approved the text later that year. The official publication was made available the next year and entitled the "Uniform Commercial Code, Official Draft: Text and Comments Edition 1952."

In 1953, Pennsylvania was the first state to enact the UCC as part of its statutes. Since that time, the UCC has been revised several times, most recently in 1989 with the addition of article 4A (Wire Transfers). Some version of the UCC is now effective in 49 states, the District of Columbia, and the Virgin Islands. Although Louisiana has not adopted the entire UCC, it has enacted article 9 effective July 1, 1989, and incorporated many other provisions in its commercial laws.

While the UCC generally has achieved its goal of introducing uniformity in commercial transactions throughout the United States, there are often significant differences in the versions adopted by each state because many states have added to or deleted from the text as drafted by the commissioners. For example, the 1972 version of the UCC states that the county where the debtor lives is the proper place to file documents to perfect a security interest for some types of collateral. Although New Hampshire adopted the 1972 version of the UCC, it substituted "town" for "county" in its statute. While this example represents a minor change, many states have made more significant substitutions, additions, and deletions that must be reviewed by a party doing business in those states.

Another reason for variations in the UCC among the states is court interpretations. While those who drafted the UCC generally created clear and concise provisions, various courts have disagreed over the meanings of certain words and phrases. As a result, identical provisions may be applied differently in different states. This can be seen, for example, in the application of UCC article 9.

Article 9 provides that if a debtor is in default, a creditor may repossess any collateral the debtor used to secure the loan. If any part of the debt is left after disposing of the collateral, creditors normally sue for the balance (deficiency). The article requires the creditor to reasonably notify the debtor of the disposition of the collateral and to conduct a commercially reasonable sale. If the creditor fails to comply with the requirements, some courts adopt the "absolute bar" approach, denying the creditor any deficiency. *First State Bank v. Hallett*, 291 Ark. 37, 722 S.W.2d 555 (1987). Other courts follow the "setoff" approach, reducing the noncomplying creditor's deficiency judgment by any damages the debtor can prove. *Gulf Homes, Inc. v. Goubeaux*, 136 Ariz. 33, 664 P.2d 183 (1983).

Still other courts adopt the "rebuttable presumption" approach, requiring the noncomplying creditor to prove that the fair market value of the collateral was less than the debt before the court will award a deficiency judgment. *Connecticut Bank and Trust Co. v. Incendy*, 207 Conn. 15, 540 A.2d 32 (1988). Finally, the Utah Supreme Court recently acknowledged that its state courts had adopted all three approaches on various occasions, but that the question remained open in that state. *Cottam v. Heppner*, 9 U.C.C. Rep. Serv. 2d 805 (1989).

The UCC contains articles entitled "Sales," "Leases," "Commercial Paper," "Bank Deposits and Collections," "Letters of Credit," "Bulk Transfers," "Warehouse Receipts, Bills of Lading and Other Documents of Title," "Investment Securities," "Secured Transactions; Sales of Accounts and Chattel Paper," along with articles addressing general provisions.

In addition to the National Conference of Commissioners on Uniform State Laws, other groups, including the American Bar Association, have proffered several model acts, including the Model Business Corporation Act.

## CONSTITUTIONS

**Constitutions** in the United States exist at both the state and federal levels of government. Constitutions are the fundamental laws of the nation and the states, no other man-made law supersedes them, and any law conflicting with them is considered void or "unconstitutional." Unlike statutes, constitutions are not usually created by legislatures (though some may be amended by legislatures). Instead, a convention is called for the purpose of drafting a constitution which, once drafted, is placed before the voters for ratification or rejection.

Courts determine when statutory or common law conflicts with a constitution. If a court finds a conflict, the law is ruled to be of no effect and need not be obeyed. An example of an unconstitutional statute would be one establishing a tax to raise funds for a particular religion. Courts have declared such statutes unconstitutional because they violate the First Amendment to the U.S. Constitution and similar provisions of state constitutions.

# FEDERAL VERSUS STATE STATUTES AND CONSTITUTIONS

The United States has a political system composed of both national and state constitutions, executives, legislatures, and judiciaries. Occasionally, conflicts arise between these two spheres of authority, which must be resolved. To a great extent, the U.S. Constitution delineates the division of governmental responsibilities between the federal and state government. Specifically, the federal government has the exclusive power to

- declare war and make peace
- maintain armed forces
- make treaties and otherwise conduct foreign relations
- regulate foreign and interstate commerce
- levy and collect taxes
- establish post offices and post roads
- coin money and regulate its value
- fix uniform standards of weights and measures
- borrow on the credit of the United States
- grant patents and copyrights
- establish a federal court system
- regulate bankruptcy
- regulate naturalization

All of these powers are set forth in article I, section 8, of the U.S. Constitution. In addition, section 8 gives Congress the power to enact all laws "necessary and proper for carrying into execution the foregoing powers. . . ." Powers that the federal government has exercised under the "necessary and proper" clause of the Constitution include regulation of labor-management relations and river and harbor improvement, to name but two of the hundreds of powers commonly called the "implied powers."

The federal government also has "inherent powers," which are powers that all sovereign national governments exercise, including the power to regulate immigration, acquire territory, recognize foreign governments, and protect the nation against internal subversion.

Recognition of the federal government's implied and inherent powers has led to greatly expanded federal authority, as the courts and Congress have expanded the definitions of those powers since the Constitution was originally adopted.

The Tenth Amendment to the U.S. Constitution provides that state governments may exercise such powers not specifically delegated by the Constitution to the federal government and not otherwise denied to the state governments. In addition, the federal government and state governments exercise "concurrent powers." Among the powers shared by both state and federal governments are the powers to tax, define and punish crimes, and condemn private property for public use.

Banking law exemplifies the duality of government in the United States. Federal law prohibits payment of interest on demand accounts, but state law governs demand deposit contracts. State law also governs bank insurance activities and branching. Both state and federal laws govern bank chartering and interest rates charged by banks for money loaned, and both federal and state regulators conduct examinations of banks.

The above constitutional allocations of powers and responsibilities between the federal and state governments are themselves sources of further law. Congress and the state legislatures have enacted numerous statutes to implement the powers and responsibilities entrusted to them in the U.S. Constitution. For example, in article I, section 8, of the U.S. Constitution, Congress is given the power to raise, support, and maintain an army and navy. To fulfill that obligation, Congress through a statute has provided for the draft during wartime, although nowhere in the Constitution is the Congress given specific power to draft citizens for military service. The Constitution is the supreme law of the land and all other law, whether state constitutions, common law, or statutory law, is inferior to it.

In a federal system such as that of the United States, which has a federal constitution, federal statutes, state constitutions, and state and local statutes, it is particularly important to know the relative rank given to the different constitutions and laws. Because the U.S. Constitution is the supreme law of the land, any statute—whether enacted by Congress or by a state or local legislature—is unconstitutional and void if it conflicts with this Constitution. Next in rank comes law enacted by Congress pursuant to the powers given it by the federal Constitution. Whenever Congress acts under a constitutional grant of power, the states are precluded from legislating on that subject if the intent of Congress was to preempt such use of state legislative powers. Laws so passed by Congress are superior to state constitutions and state laws.

Within the limits of each particular state, the state constitution is next in rank. A state legislature cannot enact a law that counters any provisions of the state constitution, even though such a law might not violate the federal Constitution. In other words, a state constitution outranks a state statute. Usually, the ordinances enacted by municipalities occupy the lowest rank in the hierarchy of laws.

## REGULATIONS

A discussion about sources of law, particularly in a text for bankers, is incomplete without addressing regulatory law. Most laws that banks must observe are regulatory. **Regulations** are neither common law nor statutes but written rules, usually drafted by administrative agencies of the executive branches of the federal and state governments. The Federal Reserve Board, the Comptroller of the Currency, and the Federal Deposit Insurance Corporation have issued most of the regulations discussed in this book.

Regulatory law has its origins in the early English attempt to limit the power of bureaucrats. Agents of the Crown, such as sheriffs, were originally liable to citizens damaged by agent conduct that was outside the scope of their authority. Thus, if an official unlawfully trespassed on an individual's property or assaulted a person outside the scope of the official's authority, the individual could resort to the courts. However, in response to their perceived need for governmental discretion, courts created defenses that led to the now well-accepted doctrine of sovereign immunity, which limited the liability of government in a direct action against it. (**Sovereign immunity** is a doctrine holding that without its consent a government entity is immune from suit.) Instead of such direct action against officials, the courts permitted the issuing of writs to control officials' actions. **Writs of mandamus, prohibition,** and **certiorari** were used to compel, prohibit, or cause review of officials' actions.

These writs were available to Americans both before and after the Revolution. One of the earliest and most influential cases involving a writ was *Marbury v. Madison* (1803). In this case, William Marbury requested that the Supreme Court issue a writ of mandamus ordering Secretary of State Madison to deliver to him a commission as justice of the peace, a position to which he had been appointed by the previous administration but which had by neglect not been delivered to him before that administration's term was over.

The Court denied Marbury's request by finding that the Judiciary Act of 1789, which authorized such writs, was unconstitutional. *Marbury v. Madison* remains a landmark in American constitutional law because it is the first case in which the Supreme Court held a law of Congress void.

In addition to writs, individuals also used the courts' injunctive power to prohibit or force action by agents of the government. If an individual was subjected to treatment by an official that the individual believed was outside the scope of the official's power, the individual could request that a court issue an injunction to restrain the official from such conduct.

Typically a hearing that afforded all sides an opportunity to be heard preceded court issuance of writs and injunctions. Given the agrarian nature of the economy, the small population of the country, and the minimal contact most people had with government officials in the early days of the Republic, such hearings were apparently adequate to handle most grievances against government officials. However, by the last half of the nineteenth century, with the industrialization and overall expansion of the country and government's increased intrusion into the private sector, recourse to the courts for perceived official wrongs became a clumsy, time-consuming process.

**Regulatory Agencies**

By regulating railroads and other monopolies, states began the process of change that led to increased regulation. The federal government began its large-scale regulatory function with the creation of the Interstate Commerce Commission in 1887. Thereafter the federal government, both by executive and congressional actions, created numerous regulatory agencies, including the Federal Trade Commission, which is charged with the responsibility to prohibit "unfair methods of competition." The private sector reacted to these regulatory efforts of government with repeated pleas to the courts to prohibit or limit such actions by writ or injunction.

The courts and legislative bodies reacted to the private sector's pleas and established judicial review of regulators' decisions based on statutory procedures and constitutional requirements for due process. The courts found that, since many regulatory decisions constituted deprivation of property rights by the government, aggrieved citizens were entitled to a judicial review of regulators' decisions to assure their rights of due process under the Constitution were protected.

Close judicial scrutiny of regulatory agencies' decisions was common from the early days of the twentieth century through the New Deal era. The Federal Reserve Act of 1913 set up the Federal Reserve System. With the New Deal came the Securities and Exchange Commission, National Labor Relations Board, Federal Communications System, Civil Aeronautics Board, Federal Deposit Insurance Corporation, and many other organizations created to regulate the nation's economic markets. The private sector vigorously opposed this regulatory expansion and was initially successful in its attacks on these agencies in the courts. However, that success was not long-lived due to the Supreme Court's upholding not only the formation of the agencies but also the independence of their decision-making process from judicial review. Judicial review was not eliminated but rather made to recognize the agencies' expertise to make decisions within the scope of their authority. *Switchmen's Union of North America v. National Mediation Board*, 320 U.S. 297 (1943).

## Administrative Procedure Act

In 1946 Congress passed the Administrative Procedure Act (5 U.S.C. § 551) which many states have emulated. The purpose of the act was to bring some uniformity to federal agency rulemaking. The act sets forth procedural steps agencies must observe in formulating regulations, including publishing proposed rules in the Federal Register, making available to the public documents and other evidence upon which proposed rules are based; opening agency meetings to the public; providing public opportunity to comment on proposed rules; and, in some cases, providing evidentiary hearings before administrative law judges prior to rulemaking. These requirements are meant to provide "due process" to administrative law procedures to assure compliance with the Fifth Amendment to the U.S. Constitution.

The Administrative Procedure Act also encompasses the scope of judicial review of agency decisions. Those standards for review codified existing law, added new law, and included review standards such as the following:

- In formulating its rule, did the regulatory agency comply with relevant statutes?

- Was the agency's action arbitrary, capricious, or an abuse of its discretion?

- If the regulation was preceded by an evidentiary hearing, were the agency's conclusions of fact upon which its decision was based supported by "substantial evidence" in the hearing record?

The aim of those involved in passage of the Administrative Procedure Act was to work a compromise between those wanting unfettered regulatory authority and those wanting judicial review of every regulatory action. The latter were typically the businesses being regulated, whether banks, airlines, or radio stations. Beginning in the 1960s, a third force entered the process: consumer interests. In their reviews, courts began permitting input from these interests on the basis that such rules also affect consumers.

Based on their belief that most regulatory agencies had grown so close to the industries they regulated that they lost objectivity, public interest groups advocated a return to stricter and more formal judicial review of agency decisions. Courts have favorably responded to these demands through specific decisions requiring agencies to document their decisions more fully and implement more formal procedures that will afford greater public input.

Given the extent of regulations to which banks are subjected from both federal and state governments, regulation as a source of law is more important in everyday banking transactions than either statutory or judicial law.

## CONCLUSION

Law is never fixed in time. As with all other aspects of society, it continually evolves to reflect movements within the populace. In the United States, law has evolved into a complicated set of rules that are the product of judges, legislators, and regulators who abide by and formulate the common law, statutes, and regulations.

The evolution of law in the United States has paralleled the changes that have occurred in this country since its independence from Great Britain. As industry and technology have replaced agriculture and cities have replaced small towns as centers of population, so too has a complicated legal system replaced the informal arbitration of disputes between people. Law now pervades every aspect of an individual's life, from health regulations governing sanitary conditions in a delivery room to the disposition of human remains.

In the United States, legislation is not the product of a despotic government imposing its will on people but is a reflection of their desires or at least the desires of the most assertive elements of the populace, who make their wishes known through their elected representatives or through special interest groups to which they belong.

Perhaps the most unique phenomenon within the U.S. legal system in the twentieth century has been the onslaught of regulations drafted and enforced by entities not elected by the nation's citizens. While the authority to draft regulations is based on statutes, the perceived need for technicality in regulations requires expertise and time beyond the abilities of legislators, who by statute delegate regulatory and supervisory authority to the agencies.

**Questions for Review and Discussion**

1. What effect can a legislative body have on the common law?
2. What forces cause passage of statutes by legislative bodies?
3. Are all laws passed by state legislatures on a particular subject uniform?

4. How do constitutions differ from statutes?

5. What is a federal system and how in particular does it affect the banking industry?

6. Regulations originally represented an attempt to limit the abuses of government officials. Explain.

# 2

# Banking Law in Action

After studying this chapter, you will be able to

- discuss the history of bank regulation, as well as the regulation of bank holding companies and branching
- identify the various agencies that regulate banks
- describe the functions of bank regulators
- discuss the court system, its functions in society, and its role as an enforcer of laws affecting banks

## HISTORICAL BACKGROUND

Government regulation of banking is based upon the crucial role the industry plays in the nation's economy. The importance of this role was recognized in the country's infancy with the establishment in 1791 of the Bank of the United States, which the federal government owned and operated. At about the same time, banks were being formed within the separate states, pursuant to state laws. In the case of *McCulloch v. Maryland*, 17 U.S. 316 (1819), the U.S. Supreme Court established the authority of the federal government to create and operate a national banking system without state interference. Holding that the state of Maryland could not tax a branch of the Bank of the United States located in Baltimore, the Court thus assured the system of separate national and state banks.

Because President Andrew Jackson believed that the federal government should not own and operate banks, the Bank of the United States dissolved in 1836, leaving states in complete control of the banking system. During that period little, if any, control was exercised over banks even by state governments, and banks opened, operated, and closed much the same as grocery stores and auto dealerships do today. That period of little or no bank regulation led to complete lack of uniformity in the issuance of currency, with over a thousand state banks printing their own notes. It led also to many bank failures, with depositors losing millions of dollars.

By 1863, the effect of the Civil War on the economy greatly increased the financial problems created by the lack of a national regulatory scheme for banks. In 1863 and 1864, Congress passed the National Bank Act, creating a system for chartering national banks. Unlike the Bank of the United States, the national banks permitted by the new act were to be privately owned and operated but regulated by the federal government. Passage of the National Bank Act brought uniformity to currency and other positive economic benefits. The act authorized national banks to issue notes secured by the deposit of federal obligations with the U.S. Treasury. This provided both a uniform national currency and an investment vehicle for federal securities that helped finance the Civil War.

State banks continued to operate with little federal control. In 1913, however, Congress passed the Federal Reserve Act, which established the **Federal Reserve System** to encourage cooperation between banks. State banks were permitted but not required to join the system, although state banks that did join were then subject to some federal authority, along with supervision by their state governments.

Between 1913 and 1933, there existed national banks, state banks that were members of the Federal Reserve System, and state banks that were not members of the system. The federal government did not regulate the latter. The Banking Act of 1933 created the **Federal Deposit Insurance Corporation (FDIC)** to protect at least part of the savings of bank customers. The FDIC is also the federal regulator of those state banks that are not members of the Federal Reserve System but whose deposits are insured by it. With the passage of the Financial Institutions Reform, Recovery and Enforcement Act of 1989 (FIRREA), the role of the FDIC was greatly expanded. In addition to insuring deposits of banks, the FDIC replaced the Federal Savings and Loan Insurance Corporation (FSLIC) as the insurer of the nation's thrift deposits and acquired receivership and conservatorship powers over failed thrifts.

The Federal Reserve Board is the federal regulator of state banks that are members of the Federal Reserve System. The **Office of the Comptroller of the Currency**, which is part of the U.S. Treasury, regulates national banks. State agencies do not regulate the banking activities of national banks but do regulate state banks, whether or not they are members of the Federal Reserve.

---

EXAMPLE ■ Acme State Bank of Lansing, Michigan, is a member of the Federal Reserve System. As such, the bank lies within the regulatory jurisdiction of both the Federal Reserve System and the Michigan Financial Institutions Bureau.

First National Bank, located in Grand Rapids, Michigan, comes within the regulatory jurisdiction of the Office of the Comptroller of the Currency. The Michigan Financial Institutions Bureau exercises no jurisdiction over the bank.

Citizens State Bank, located in Kalamazoo, Michigan, is not a member of the Federal Reserve System, but its deposits are insured by the FDIC. The bank thus falls within the regulatory jurisdiction of the FDIC and the Michigan Financial Institutions Bureau.

*N4's Banks are required to be members of the fed.*

---

## FUNCTIONS OF BANK REGULATORS

The previous section mentioned the four main government regulators of banks: the Comptroller of the Currency, the Federal Reserve Board, the FDIC, and state banking agencies. The following discussion summarizes the responsibilities of those four agencies within the scheme of bank regulation.

## Power to Charter

The ultimate control any legislature or government agency has over a business is the power to decide whether the business will exist and, if the business already exists, whether its existence will be terminated. In banking, the power to decide whether a bank may come into existence is the authority to decide whether a bank charter will be granted.

Only the Comptroller of the Currency and state banking regulatory agencies possess the power to grant a bank charter. If individuals wish to establish a national bank, they must seek their charter from the Comptroller of the Currency. Individuals wishing to obtain a state bank charter must secure it from a state banking agency. The Federal Reserve Board and the FDIC do not have the power to grant bank charters.

Whether individuals wish to obtain a charter for a national or a state bank, the qualifications it must meet before a charter will be granted are similar and relate to the following aspects of the proposed bank:

- minimum capital structure

- earnings prospects

- ability to serve the convenience and needs of the community in which it will be located

- prospective directors, officers, key employees, and investors, particularly their character and banking experience

Once a national bank is chartered, it is required to become a member of the Federal Reserve System and its deposits qualify for insurance under the authority of the FDIC. Banks that acquire their charters under state law and wish to become members of the Federal Reserve System or have their deposits insured by the FDIC must make separate application to those governmental authorities. While a state bank may elect to stay outside the Federal Reserve System but obtain deposit insurance, it cannot request membership in the system without deposit insurance. Membership in the Federal Reserve System and qualification for deposit insurance may require a state bank to give more proof of financial soundness than its state's chartering laws require. On the other hand, some states will not grant a charter to proposed banks that do not qualify for federal deposit insurance.

What the Comptroller of the Currency and state banking authorities have the power to give, they also have the power to take away. But revocation of bank charters happens infrequently. However, when a bank engages in unsafe or unsound practices, becomes insolvent, or violates provisions of the National Bank Act or state banking laws, its chartering authority—whether the Comptroller of the Currency or the state banking agency—may revoke its charter and thus terminate its existence.

Since charter revocation is such a severe measure with possible dire consequences not only for a bank and its employees but also for the community in which the bank is located, the federal and state governments have legislated other measures that can be taken short of charter revocation, thereby leaving a bank in operation but assuring its compliance with regulatory requirements.

Among these measures is the FDIC's power to terminate deposit insurance. When an insured bank or director engages in unsafe or unsound practices, the FDIC may invoke this power. Once the FDIC determines that an insured bank is committing an unsafe or unsound practice, it gives the bank a notice requiring corrective action within a certain period. If the corrective action does not satisfy the FDIC, it can issue an order for the termination of insurance and publish a copy of the order in a newspaper in the bank's locale. Notice of the termination must be sent to the bank's depositors, whose deposits as of the date of the notice will cease to be insured within two years. Once a state bank loses its insured status, it no longer qualifies for membership in the Federal Reserve System. A national bank losing its insured status is subject to direct control by the FDIC through the receivership provisions of the federal statutes creating the FDIC. The actions taken by the FDIC to notify depositors and publish notice of the termination of insurance would no doubt cause the public to lose confidence in such a bank and to withdraw their deposits. Thus, the practical effect of any bank's involuntarily losing its insured status is the termination of its business.

Short of revoking a charter and terminating deposit insurance, the banking regulatory agencies have "cease-and-desist powers" that permit them to proceed against the directors, officers, employees, or agents of banks. Statutes also permit the agencies to proceed against other persons participating in the affairs of banks who are, or will be, engaging in unsafe or unsound practices or who have violated, or are about to violate, any law, rule, regulation, condition, or agreement between a bank and its supervisory agency. A cease-and-desist order issued by a regulatory agency prohibits the bank or individual to whom it is addressed from engaging in a particular activity or practice. Along with cease-and-desist powers, the federal regulatory agencies have the power to remove or suspend directors, officers, employees, and other persons or prohibit them from conducting bank business. The passage of FIRREA in 1989 has greatly enhanced the federal agencies' already impressive enforcement powers.

Regulatory agencies may impose fines for any violation of any law or regulation, including unsafe or unsound practices and breaches of fiduciary duties. Fines of $1,000 per day to $1,000,000 per day may be levied depending on the type of violation and the intent of the perpetrator.

While the legislation authorizing cease-and-desist and removal orders provides for judicial review of the orders issued by banking regulatory agencies, courts are reluctant to overturn such orders and usually the agencies' positions prevail.

## Bank Examinations

The Comptroller of the Currency, the Federal Reserve Board, the FDIC, and state banking agencies all conduct bank examinations that help them carry out their responsibilities of bank supervision. The Financial Institutions Examination Council, which was created by Congress in 1978 (12 U.S.C. § 3301), established for the federal banking agencies uniform principles and standards for examinations. Traditionally, the purpose of the examinations has been to assess the financial condition of banks in order to assure their financial safety and soundness. Safety and soundness are determined by reviewing a bank's internal operations and policies, services offered to the public, balance sheet, loan portfolio, and trust operation (if any).

In addition to the examination of a bank's financial "safety and soundness," each federal banking regulatory agency has been conducting consumer examinations since the early to mid-1970s to assure bank compliance with such acts as Truth in Lending, Equal Credit Opportunity, Real Estate Settlement Procedures, Fair Housing, Community Reinvestment, Home Mortgage Disclosure, Equal Employment Opportunity, and Bank Secrecy.

Once an examination of a bank is completed, the examiners present a written report of the bank's condition to its board of directors. The report contains the examiners' summary of the bank's problems with recommendations or instructions for solving the problems. Reports normally review and comment on a bank's capital, loan portfolio, management, branches (if any), and compliance with consumer legislation.

Normally banks will comply voluntarily with recommendations or instructions set forth in examination reports. However, if a bank refuses or fails to cure such problems, the federal banking regulatory agencies can use the disciplinary powers discussed earlier.

---

**EXAMPLE** ■ Several examination reports were critical of a bank's practice of permitting its chief stockholder to overdraw his checking account in amounts equaling thousands of dollars, thereby giving him interest-free, short-term loans. After the bank ignored several warnings, its regulatory agency issued a cease-and-desist order prohibiting the bank from entering into any credit or loan transactions with the stockholder, his relatives, or his business associates. Courts upheld the regulator's order based upon its power to correct practices that are "unsafe or unsound" or violate law. *Groos National Bank v. Comptroller of the Currency*, 573 F.2d 889 (5th Cir. 1978).

---

**Specific Application of Regulations**

Banking regulations cover mergers, sale of bank stock, political activities, trust operations, change in control, establishment of branches and foreign offices, investments, and liquidation. Banks are also affected by regulations under the Bank Holding Company Act.

*Bank Holding Companies*

In 1956, Congress passed the Bank Holding Company Act (12 U.S.C. §§ 1841–49). The purpose of the act is to regulate companies that own or control banks. If XYZ Corporation owns 50 percent of the shares of First National Bank and 75 percent of the shares of Annapolis State Bank, under the federal Bank Holding Company Act, XYZ Corporation is a bank holding company.

The purpose of regulating **bank holding companies** is to limit their activities to financial matters, prevent undue concentration of banking within a limited number of companies, prevent unsafe activities, and regulate their nonbanking activities. These purposes are achieved by Federal Reserve regulations that provide for examinations, fines for violations, and prior approval for a change in holding company control, and by cease-and-desist powers.

Bank holding companies generally are permitted to engage in nonbanking business activities to the extent that they relate to the financial services of banks. These activities have included such services as investment advising, leasing personal and real property, providing data-processing services, operating insurance agencies, and providing management consulting advice and advertising services. All these services may be available to banks both within and outside the holding company.

States may prohibit the existence of bank holding companies within their boundaries. If states do permit their existence, they may impose further state restrictions on them in addition to those imposed by the federal Bank Holding Company Act.

Bank holding companies have been popular in states that forbid statewide branching because of the ability of such companies to operate statewide, with their various owned or controlled banks located over a wide geographic area within the state.

One-bank holding companies are also included within the scope of the Bank Holding Company Act. Their popularity in recent years is due mainly to favorable income tax treatment and their creation of a market for a bank's stock. Without this market, independent banks often have been forced to affiliate with bank holding companies or become part of another bank's statewide branching system because of their shareholders' sale of stock to holding companies.

## *Branching*

Most businesses in the United States can establish themselves wherever and whenever they please. If the corner grocery store becomes a success, it may create a chain of stores that can open anywhere within the state of its original location and cross state boundaries with little governmental interference. Ultimately, such a business could open and operate overseas markets, again with little interference from the

U.S. government. However, as with utilities, both federal and state laws have restricted a bank's ability to open new locations or branches.

Reasons for bank branching restrictions have included legislative desire to assure that existing banks will succeed, that local public financial needs will be served, and that the overall monetary system will be protected, which unlimited competition among banks has been perceived to threaten. In this era of great pressure for interstate banking, Congress and state legislatures are scrutinizing each of these reasons for branching restrictions.

State law primarily controls the ability of a bank to branch. State-chartered banks are entirely within the control of state legislatures regarding the ability to branch, while national banks, as a result of the 1927 McFadden Act (12 U.S.C. § 36), have the same right to branch as the state banks in the state in which they are located.

Recently national banks have successfully argued that their ability to emulate branching powers of state "banks" includes thrift institutions in those states where thrifts have powers nearly identical to banks. *Department of Banking and Consumer Finance v. Clarke*, 809 F.2d 266 (5th Cir. 1987), *cert. denied*, 483 U.S. 1010 (1987).

While the ability to branch is based upon state law, specific branch approval is within the jurisdiction of the chief regulatory agency of the bank seeking a branch. Thus, state banks seek approval of proposed branches from state banking authorities, while national banks require approval from the Comptroller of the Currency to open branches. Capital adequacy and other requirements for a branch may differ between a state banking agency and the Comptroller of the Currency.

The McFadden Act defines a branch as a "branch bank, branch office, branch agency, additional office, or any branch place of business located in any State or Territory of the United States or in the District of Columbia at which deposits are received, or checks paid, or money lent." This definition is applicable only to national banks. States may adopt, and have adopted, their own definition of "branch." As a result, in some states the operation of an off-premise electronic funds transfer terminal may be a branch for a national bank but not for a state bank. In such a situation, a national bank would need to seek approval for a branch before it operated an electronic funds transfer terminal, while a state bank would not need approval of its state banking authority.

# THE COURT SYSTEM

While the Comptroller of the Currency, the Federal Reserve Board, the FDIC, and state banking agencies are the day-to-day regulators of banks, courts are playing an ever-increasing role in banking. This role is attributable to many factors, including the need to interpret laws and regulations when banks and regulatory agencies assert differing interpretations. Courts also help enforce criminal laws relating to banks and review regulatory enforcement actions and civil cases involving banks as litigants.

## Federal Court System

The U.S. Constitution provides for a federal judicial system which is authorized to decide the following types of cases: (1) cases arising under the federal Constitution, the laws of Congress, and treaties; (2) cases affecting ambassadors and public ministers; (3) cases of admiralty; and (4) controversies between two or more states and between citizens of different states.

---

*Case for Discussion*

**NORTHEAST BANCORP, INC. v. FEDERAL RESERVE SYSTEM**

### Facts

The Bank Holding Company Act of 1956 requires bank holding companies to obtain approval from the Federal Reserve Board before acquiring banks. Under this act, the Federal Reserve Board is prohibited from approving applications by bank holding companies to acquire banks in states other than the one in which the holding company is incorporated, unless such acquisitions are permitted under the laws of those states.

Connecticut and Massachusetts both have statutes that allow bank holding companies from other states to acquire banks within their borders. However, these statutes limit such acquisitions to bank holding companies in states in the New England region that have reciprocal statutes—that is, Connecticut, Massachusetts, Maine, New Hampshire, Rhode Island, and Vermont.

In recent years, the Federal Reserve Board has approved several acquisitions and mergers across state boundaries by bank holding companies in Connecticut and Massachusetts. Northeast Bancorp challenged these actions by the Federal Reserve Board, arguing before the Supreme Court that the Bank Holding Company Act did not give the Federal Reserve the authority to approve interstate banking. In support of Northeast Bancorp, Citicorp further contended that the state statutes limiting acquisitions to holding companies within a specific geographic region were discriminatory and therefore unconstitutional.

### Decision
In June 1985, the Supreme Court ruled in favor of the Federal Reserve Board, thereby permitting interstate mergers and acquisitions by bank holding companies under the state statutes described above. The Court stated that the Bank Holding Company Act clearly intended to allow states to lift the federal prohibition against interstate banking. The Court further stated that it was not discriminatory or unconstitutional for the New England states to prohibit out-of-region bank holding companies from acquiring banks within their borders. *Northeast Bancorp, Inc. v. Board of Governors of the Federal Reserve System*, 472 U.S. 159 (1985).

### Questions for Discussion
1. Why was this case appropriate for consideration by the U.S. Supreme Court?
2. Who was the plaintiff in this case?
3. What factors did the Court consider in deciding this case?

---

The U.S. Supreme Court is the only federal court established by the Constitution, but article III, section 1 of the Constitution permits Congress to create inferior federal courts, which Congress has done by establishing federal district courts and courts of appeal.

Federal courts created pursuant to other constitutional provisions are usually called "legislative courts," which are specialized and limited by statute and constitution. Examples of legislative courts include territorial courts, the court of claims, the court of customs and patent appeals, the tax courts, and various military tribunals.

## District Courts

For purposes of judicial administration, the United States is divided into districts. Each state constitutes at least one district and no district includes territory in more than one state. A federal district court serves each district and, in addition, federal district courts are located in the District of Columbia, Guam, Puerto Rico, and the U.S. Virgin Islands.

District courts are the principal trial courts of the federal system. They are empowered to hear a broad range of civil and criminal cases within the scope of article III, section 2 of the Constitution. Most civil cases involve federal statutes or diversity of citizenship (with the plaintiff living in one state and the defendant in another). Criminal cases involve federal crimes, such as robbery of FDIC-insured banks and violations of the narcotic, tax, and interstate gambling laws.

Many cases have arisen in which the federal district court has concurrent jurisdiction with a state court. In many situations where concurrent jurisdiction exists, if a party wants a case tried in federal court, that party may do so no matter what the other party desires. Congressional enactments, for example, permit the defendant to remove the case to the federal district court in many situations, the two most important of which are when the action arises under federal law, and when a diversity of citizenship exists and the matter in controversy exceeds $50,000. Removal is permitted even when a case is before a state court that is fully competent to hear it. However, cases that are properly before the federal district courts may not usually be removed to the state courts.

---

EXAMPLE ■ Juan Rodriguez, a resident of California, is involved in an auto accident in Idaho with Fred Small, a resident of that state. Small sues Rodriguez for $51,000 in the Idaho state courts. Whether or not Small agreed, Rodriguez would be able to remove the matter to federal district court.

---

*Courts of Appeal*  The federal system has 12 courts of appeal, one for each of 11 federal circuits and one for the District of Columbia. The courts of appeal have no original jurisdiction and are strictly appellate tribunals. Although their principal function is to review the work of the district courts, they also review decisions of many federal administrative agencies. Courts of appeal usually have six or more judges, but rotating panels of three judges normally conduct hearings so that a greater workload is possible.

## *Supreme Court*

The Supreme Court of the United States is the court of last resort in the federal system. It also has original jurisdiction in a few extraordinary situations, such as civil actions when a state is a party, and when actions are brought against ambassadors or other public ministers.

The only method of obtaining the Supreme Court's consent to review a case is by "writ of certiorari," issued after the parties have exhausted their remedies in the courts of appeal in the federal system or the courts of last resort in the state system. The Supreme Court has absolute discretion to grant or deny a writ or petition of certiorari. Far more petitions are denied than are granted and the Supreme Court has said that it will grant the writ of certiorari "only where there are special and important reasons."

In a limited number of cases, one can reach the Supreme Court by appeal (as contrasted with certiorari). Appeals are "a matter of right" and the court has no discretion with respect to them; that is, if an appeal is proper, the Supreme Court must take the case. Appeals are proper when a state's court of last resort has found a federal statute or treaty to be unconstitutional or when it has upheld the constitutionality of a state statute that is being challenged as a violation of the federal Constitution or a federal statute.

---

**EXAMPLE** ■ The state in which Third National Bank is located enacted a statute prohibiting all banks within the state from charging more than 7 percent simple interest on any type of loan. The bank subsequently makes a loan at 11 percent simple interest, based upon a provision in the National Banking Act permitting banks to charge that rate for that particular loan. A usury suit results and the state's supreme court decides that the state law is valid and applicable to the loan. The U.S. Supreme Court could hear the matter because a state statute is being challenged as a violation of a federal statute.

---

31  *Banking Law in Action*

Finally, a case may come before the Supreme Court upon certification of a federal court of appeal. This device, used infrequently and designed to facilitate the work of the intermediate appellate courts, permits the appellate court to seek instructions from the Supreme Court on how a question of law should be properly decided.

**State Court System**

Each state has established a system of courts that usually includes a **court of general jurisdiction**, some **courts of limited jurisdiction**, and one or more **courts of appellate jurisdiction**. These courts differ somewhat from state to state, so the following descriptions are general and do not describe the actual court system of any particular state.

*Courts of General Jurisdiction*
(Supreme Court NYS)

Courts of general jurisdiction are courts of original jurisdiction. Matters within their jurisdiction are tried first in these courts.

In addition to being courts of original jurisdiction, courts of general jurisdiction must also have unlimited jurisdiction; that is, they can hear any case regardless of the amount of money or subject matter. However, many courts that would otherwise be courts of unlimited jurisdiction are prohibited from hearing matters in which the amount involved is less than an amount determined by statute.

---

EXAMPLE ■ The circuit courts in Michigan may not hear legal controversies involving less than $10,000. Henry Gross owes Frank Snider $9,000 and refuses to pay. Both Gross and Snider are residents of Michigan. Snider starts a lawsuit in circuit court against Gross to collect his money. Gross could successfully challenge the jurisdiction of the circuit court because it cannot hear legal matters where the disputed amount is less than $10,000. The case would have to be heard in a state district court, which hears cases involving amounts of less than $10,000.

---

*Courts of Limited Jurisdiction*

Statutes or state constitutions permit courts of limited jurisdiction to entertain only certain cases, usually according to subject matter, amount of money in dispute, or the type of relief sought. In the previous example, the Michigan circuit court would be a court of limited jurisdiction since it cannot take any legal matter involving a claim of $10,000 or less. Courts of limited jurisdiction include small claims courts; courts of the justice of the peace; magistrate's courts; city, county, and district courts; family, surrogate, probate, and orphan's courts; and courts of claims.

## SMALL CLAIMS COURTS

These courts usually have the most limited jurisdiction of any system. The states created them to provide a system for dealing with disputes that involve relatively small amounts of money and would otherwise go unresolved or would be resolved only through a more formal and expensive procedure. To keep small claims courts simple, attorneys usually are not entitled to appear in court to represent clients, no one is entitled to a jury, and formal rules of evidence are relaxed to let people present their sides of disputes without much interruption.

Small claims courts are civil courts and hear no criminal matters. They usually have a jurisdictional limit of $1,500 or less and are typically used to collect debts for under that amount.

*Handwritten margin notes: "No separate small claims court in NYS. Covered under city, town or village courts." and "In NYS city, town or village courts have criminal jurisdiction."*

---

**EXAMPLE** ■ Sam Fell owes a $600 balance on a promissory note to Joan Lieder. Lieder does not wish to incur the expense of hiring an attorney to collect a debt of that size, so she files her claim against Fell in small claims court.

---

In many states, to further the objective of simplicity, the decisions of small claims courts cannot be appealed. Thus, in the previous example, if Lieder lost her debt action against Fell, she could not appeal the decision.

## JUSTICE OF THE PEACE AND MAGISTRATE'S COURTS

Before small claims courts were created, justice of the peace courts were the state courts most often involved in civil matters concerning limited amounts of money. These courts also exercise jurisdiction over lesser criminal matters, including traffic offenses. Some states have

*Handwritten margin note: "Now called justice courts"*

33  *Banking Law in Action*

abolished justice of the peace courts and turned their civil functions over to small claims courts.

Magistrate's courts are those overseen by a court officer who may not be required to be an attorney (although many justices of the peace are attorneys) but is experienced in legal practices and principles. Where these courts exist, they vary in jurisdiction, but in some states their jurisdiction is limited to traffic matters.

Appeals from decisions of the justice of the peace and magistrate's courts go to a higher-level trial court, which serves as an appellate court for this purpose.

CITY, COUNTY, AND DISTRICT COURTS

City, county, and district courts, where they exist, have jurisdictions that usually are confined to civil disputes involving no more than $10,000 and criminal matters involving misdemeanors (crimes whose maximum sentence is usually less than one year of imprisonment).

Judges, who generally are lawyers, preside over these courts. They are courts of record (recorded transcripts of their proceedings are kept), following rules of evidence. Lawyers usually represent parties involved with matters in these courts.

Appeals from these courts may go before a higher-level trial court, which serves as an appellate court to review the decisions of these courts.

FAMILY COURTS

Family courts are limited in their jurisdiction to cases involving the family, such as divorce, child support, paternity, custody, adoption, family offenses, and juvenile delinquency. Usually these courts are courts of record and are presided over by a legally trained judge, who also may have training or expertise in one or more disciplines related to the family, such as sociology, psychology, social work, or theology.

SURROGATE, PROBATE, AND ORPHAN'S COURTS

Most states have established courts whose jurisdiction is limited to the affairs of decedents. These courts probate wills and provide for the distribution of a decedent's estate. Many states call these courts "probate courts," but the terms "surrogate courts" and "orphan's courts" are also used. In some states, these courts are family courts as well. Normally these courts are courts of record and are presided over by a legally trained judge, who may adopt informal or formal procedures, depending on the type of action being heard.

Appeals from family, surrogate, probate, and orphan's courts often go to those state courts whose only function is to hear appeals. In some states, however, courts that are considered higher-level trial courts will hear appeals from these courts' decisions.

## COURTS OF CLAIMS

Individuals cannot sue their government unless it permits itself to be sued through constitutional or statutory authorization. If in a particular situation no authority is provided for a suit against a government, the government's defense is "sovereign immunity."

---

**EXAMPLE** ■ Sam Gleason was driving his auto when it hit a pothole in a street maintained by the city of Vallance. Gleason was injured and his car was damaged. The laws of the state in which Vallance is located have no provision for suits against cities for damages caused by poorly maintained streets. If Gleason sues the city of Vallance, the city may raise "sovereign immunity" as a defense and Gleason will lose. However, if state law gives up sovereign immunity as a defense for a situation such as this, the suit may proceed.

---

Many states that have surrendered sovereign immunity have established a court of claims to hear cases in which private claims against the state or its agencies are asserted. The establishment of a court of claims is usually a limited waiver of sovereign immunity. In effect, the state says that it is willing to be sued to the extent that the court of claims has jurisdiction. Thus, the jurisdiction of the court of claims will vary from state to state, depending on the willingness of the state involved to be sued for its own wrongdoing and breaches. Some states have not established these courts.

Appeals from these courts usually go directly to an appellate court, whose entire function is to hear appeals.

## Courts Having Concurrent Jurisdiction

Some cases may fall within the jurisdiction of more than one court. In such a situation, those courts have **concurrent jurisdiction**. Most cases may involve courts having concurrent jurisdiction because usually both the court of general jurisdiction and at least one court of limited jurisdiction will be competent to hear the matter. In a small claim, for example, a plaintiff may have the choice of starting an action before a justice of the peace, a small claims court, a county court, or the court of general jurisdiction, all of which would have concurrent jurisdiction. If only one court were competent to hear the case, it would have "exclusive jurisdiction."

## Appellate Courts

Each state has at least one court that hears appeals from the trial courts, which are the courts of original jurisdiction. In some states, two levels of **appellate courts** exist: intermediate appellate courts and courts of last resort. In other states, there is only one appellate court, which is usually called the supreme court of the state. Intermediate appellate courts are often called courts of appeal, but names vary among the states. For example, in New York the supreme court is a trial court of general jurisdiction and the court of appeals is a court of last resort. The intermediate appellate court in New York is called the appellate division of the supreme court, and the court of last resort is called the court of appeals. In Illinois, on the other hand, the trial court of general jurisdiction is called the circuit court, the intermediate appellate court is called the appellate court, and the court of ast resort is called the supreme court of Illinois.

The function of appellate courts is to review decisions of the courts of original jurisdiction to determine whether those courts made any errors of law that actually or potentially injured the party bringing the appeal, who is called the "appellant." The party responding to the appeal is the "appellee." In states with two levels of appellate courts, the appellant normally is required to appeal first to the intermediate appellate court. In a few cases, the appellant may appeal from the court of original jurisdiction directly to the court of last resort. These extraordinary cases usually involve extreme situations, such as the imposition of the death penalty or a holding that a state statute is unconstitutional.

In making an appeal, the appellant must allege that the court of original jurisdiction committed an error that adversely affected his or her case. The alleged error must also be one of "law," not "fact."

**EXAMPLE** ■ Peter Bacon brings a lawsuit against Harbor National Bank for violation of the federal Truth in Lending Act. After hearing the evidence, the jury decides that Bacon did not use the subject loan's proceeds for personal, family, or household purposes and that thus the statute was inapplicable.

Whether the proceeds of a loan are used for personal, family, or household purposes is a question of fact. A jury (or judge sitting without a jury) decides questions of fact and generally an appellate court is not permitted on appeal to substitute its own opinion of the facts for that of the judge or jury.

The record, however, may show that the jury's or judge's finding was not supported by the facts; that is, the record may show that as a matter of law no reasonable person could make the factual findings that the jury made in deciding the case for one party and against the other. In such a case, the appellant usually moves the trial judge to enter judgment for the appellant "notwithstanding the verdict." If the judge denies this motion, he or she has made an error of law, which is subject to review on appeal.

**EXAMPLE** ■ Fred Snow brings a lawsuit against Green State Bank for a violation of the federal Truth in Lending Act. In this case, the judge decides that the bank did violate the act. However, the judge does not permit a judgment against the bank, because Snow admitted he suffered no actual damages.

Under the Truth in Lending Act, a plaintiff need only show a violation of the act to be entitled to damages, whether or not the plaintiff suffered actual harm (see chapter 8). The judge in this matter made an error of law that could be corrected on appeal. No new evidence is presented on the appeal, and the appellate court usually makes its decision based on the verbatim record of the trial court proceedings. The appellate courts, therefore, do not call witnesses or use a jury. The lawyers for the appellant and appellee argue the law of the case to the judges. In addition to this oral argument, the lawyers usually submit "briefs," which are written documents that outline the arguments and the legal precedents that the lawyers feel should govern the case.

The appellate courts usually do one of four things. First, they can affirm the judgment of the lower court. By doing so, an appellate court expresses its belief that the lower court has not committed an error of law or, at least, that any error of law was not sufficiently substantial to have prejudiced the appellant. In this event, the lower court's decision stands.

Second, an appellate court can reverse the judgment of the lower court. Here the appellate court has found a serious error of law. It thus orders that the appellee shall be declared the losing party in the trial court and the appellant shall be given a favorable judgment.

Third, an appellate court can remand the case. Here the appellate court finds a serious error of law but is unwilling to reverse the judgment. It therefore remands the case for a new trial. This means that the case is sent back to the court of original jurisdiction to be tried again in conformity with the opinion that the appellate court has rendered.

Fourth, an appellate court can modify the judgment. Here the appellate court has found a serious error that has not resulted in the wrong person's being given the judgment but in an error in the judgment itself. For example, an error of law may result in a plaintiff's receiving a judgment of $50,000, where only $10,000 is indicated. In such a case, the appellate court may modify the judgment for the plaintiff to allow recovery of only $10,000.

The decision of an appellate court is a final decision, unless a higher appellate court exists in the state in which the matter was tried. In that case, the decision of the intermediate appellate court may be appealed to the state's highest appellate court. Laws concerning the legal basis for appeal vary considerably among the states. The decision of a state supreme court is usually final and cannot be appealed except in situations where an issue of federal law is involved. In that case a state supreme court's decision can be appealed to the federal court.

## CONCLUSION

Political battles early in the nation's history resulted in the federal government withdrawing from the idea of operating its own bank. However, banks in the private sector have experienced and continue to experience considerable federal and state government regulation. The Comptroller of the Currency, the Federal Reserve Board, the FDIC, and state banking agencies all carry out the banking laws of government. These regulators enforce not only banking laws passed by Congress and the state legislators but also their own banking regulations promulgated under legislative authority. The powers of these regulators are "cradle to grave," that is, from the chartering to liquidation of a bank.

The U.S. court system is of paramount importance to banks. Ultimately, if regulators are unsuccessful in enforcing banking laws with their various powers, they can seek court enforcement. Banks likewise can resort to the courts to fend off regulators they feel have overstepped their authority. Being involved in myriad commercial activities, banks are also continually suing and being sued.

As with the legislative structure in this country, the court system reflects the duality of federalism, with separate federal and state court systems and levels of trial and appellate courts within each system.

## Questions for Review and Discussion

1. What was the Bank of the United States?
2. What statute enables national banks to be chartered?
3. What two functions does the FDIC serve?
4. What authority does the Comptroller of the Currency have over state-chartered banks?
5. May a bank refuse an examination from a regulatory agency having authority over it?
6. May any company own a bank?
7. If a bank wishes to establish a branch, does it need to comply with state law?

8. May the U.S. Supreme Court hear any case it wishes? Explain why or why not.

9. In which courts are attorneys usually not permitted to represent people?

10. What doctrine would probably protect a local, state, or federal government from suit?

# 3

## Torts and Crimes

After studying this chapter, you will be able to

■ state the definitions of torts and crimes and describe their differences

■ determine different types of torts applicable to banks

■ discuss various types of crimes bankers encounter

■ discuss the responsibilities of banks to make criminal referrals

Banks play a central role in facilitating the flow of money within the U.S. economy. In performing this role, banks are frequently subjected to wrongful acts committed by individuals or entities who, for their own benefit, strive to interfere with normal financial transactions. Those wrongful acts usually constitute torts and/or crimes.

A basic understanding of the similarities and differences between a tort and a crime is essential to bank employees. A tort is a breach of duty that one owes to another member of society; a crime is an injury to society at large. Many acts that constitute crimes are also wrongs that amount to torts.

**EXAMPLE** ■ If Johnson robs First National Bank, she has committed the tort of conversion or trespass and also the crime of larceny. When Johnson is prosecuted for the crime, a district attorney or prosecutor will bring an action on behalf of society called the *People v. Johnson.* If Johnson is convicted, she may be punished by fine and/or imprisonment. Since the outcome of the criminal action has no effect upon the tort, First National may sue Johnson in a civil (as opposed to a criminal) suit for conversion or trespass called *First National Bank v. Johnson.* If she is found liable for the tort, she will be required to pay First National Bank damages equal at least to the amount of money she stole. No double jeopardy is involved in this situation, because the two trials involve different parties and distinct wrongs. Thus, Johnson's one act constitutes both a tort and a crime, since it involves both a breach of her duty to another person and to society at large.

---

The crime of larceny is not identical to the tort of conversion or trespass. A finding of innocence on the larceny charge does not preclude a finding that Johnson did commit the tort of conversion or trespass. Similarly, when a wrongful act is both a tort and a crime, a finding of liability for commission of a tort does not automatically constitute a guilty finding for a crime. This is because the burden of proof for crimes is not the same as that for torts.

To establish the guilt of an individual charged with a crime, the prosecutor must establish guilt beyond a reasonable doubt. In a tort case, the burden is on the plaintiff to establish the defendant's liability by a preponderance of the evidence (more likely than not). The difference between these two burdens of proof is apparent in their definitions. In criminal cases

[a] reasonable doubt is a fair, honest doubt growing out of the evidence or lack of evidence in this case or growing out of any reasonable or legitimate inferences drawn from the evidence or the lack of evidence. It is not merely an imaginary doubt or a flimsy, fanciful doubt or a doubt based upon the mere possibility of the innocence of the defendant or a doubt based upon sympathy, but rather it is a fair, honest doubt based upon reason and common sense. It is a state of mind which would cause you to hesitate in making an important

decision in your own personal life. By stating that the prosecution must prove guilt beyond a reasonable doubt, . . . there must be such evidence that causes you to have a firm conviction to a moral certainty of the truth of the charge here made against this defendant. (Michigan Criminal Jury Instruction, 3:1:04.)

Given the presumption of innocence to which all those accused of crimes are entitled, reasonable doubt is a heavy burden. The burden of proof in civil cases is defined as follows:

[T]he evidence must satisfy you that the proposition on which that party has the burden of proof has been established by evidence which outweighs the evidence against it. (Michigan Standard Jury Instructions—Civil—2d edition, 16.01.)

## TORTS

A tort consists of an injury done to a person through the violation of a duty that the law imposes in favor of that person. A tort may consist of an injury to a person's property, physical person, family, reputation, business or social relationships, or to some other interest that the law recognizes as susceptible to legal injury.

Torts usually are caused intentionally or through the negligent conduct of the wrongdoer, called the **tortfeasor.** Some situations involve "strict liability," where, for reasons of social policy, one may be a tortfeasor even without intentionally or negligently inflicting an injury on another. Cases of strict liability usually involve situations in which the action is hazardous and harm is foreseeable if anything goes amiss, even though the tortfeasor is careful and intends to injure no one.

---

EXAMPLE ■ Taylor kept a wild tiger in her garage. Although Taylor acted carefully, kept the tiger chained at all times, and intended no one to be injured by the animal, the tiger escaped one night and inflicted serious injuries on Donovan. In this situation, Donovan can hold Taylor liable. (Most likely, Taylor also faces criminal prosecution if her community or state has enacted an ordinance or statute prohibiting citizens from keeping wild animals.)

---

Although many different kinds of torts could conceivably involve a bank, those torts of particular concern to bankers include negligence, fraud or deceit, and defamation.

**Negligence**    The most common tort is **negligence.** While one tends to think of automobile accidents when the tort of negligence is mentioned, the concept of negligence is much broader than this and sets standards of conduct for all phases of society, including the operation of a bank. A banker who runs a bank negligently, like any other negligent person, must pay damages to anyone who has suffered an injury as the result of such carelessness.

The tort of negligence is based on the assumption that each member of society has a duty to every other member to act as a reasonable person would act under similar circumstances. For example, if Brown fails to act reasonably and that failure is the proximate cause of Smith's injury, Smith may recover damages in a negligence tort action, unless Brown has a good defense. Defenses to negligence actions include issues of "assumption of the risk" or "contributory negligence."

Negligent behavior alone does not give rise to a tort action. The defendant's failure to act as a reasonable person under the circumstances must have resulted in a loss to the plaintiff, and the defendant's negligence must also be the proximate cause of the loss. For the "proximate cause" limitation to be satisfied, some courts have said that the defendant's negligence must have been the cause in fact or a substantial factor in bringing about the loss.

Even if the defendant's failure to act as a reasonable person has proximately caused the plaintiff a loss, the plaintiff may be unable to recover if he or she assumed the risk or was also guilty of negligence (called "contributory negligence").

---

EXAMPLE ■ Francine Edwards has filed a complaint in State X for malpractice against Dr. O'Connor alleging that he did not make a timely diagnosis of her cancer, causing her to have an amputation that early diagnosis would have prevented. State X follows the traditional (now minority) rule barring recovery by a plaintiff who was contributorily negligent, as long as the defendant was not grossly negligent. O'Connor answered the complaint by saying Edwards was negligent in failing to follow his recommended treatment as quickly as possible, thereby contributing to the damage. Even if Edwards proves her case, O'Connor will not be liable if he can prove Edwards was contributorily negligent.

---

A majority of states have adopted the standard of "comparative negligence." In such states, if Edwards proved O'Connor was negligent, she would receive damages, but they would be reduced by an amount a judge or jury felt was attributable to her own negligence. In other words, if the judge or jury found Edwards was damaged in an amount equal to $500,000 but her own negligence contributed to $200,000 of these damages, she would receive $300,000.

## Fraud or Deceit

A common type of tort that is frequently committed in business is fraud or deceit. **Fraud** is a tort that may result in damages to compensate the defrauded party for any injury caused by the fraud.

---

EXAMPLE ■ In his application to Peoples State Bank for $50,000, Douglas Harrison listed nonexistent assets. The bank would not have made the loan if the true state of Harrison's assets had been known. Upon discovery of the fraud, the bank took action to accelerate the debt and sued Harrison for fraud.

---

The tort of fraud is more commonly called the tort of **deceit**. It has five essential elements:

■ a false representation of a material fact made by one person, *A* to another, *B*

- knowledge by *A* that the representation is false
- communication of the representation to *B* with the intention that *B* should rely on the representation when acting upon it
- justifiable reliance by *B* in the truth of the representation
- substantial damage to *B*, proximately caused by reliance on *A's* false representation

All of these elements must be present before the action of deceit is present.

As with many torts, the underlying conduct will not only be a tort but also a crime. Providing a false loan application to a bank is a crime that can result in a fine of up to $5,000, a prison sentence of up to two years, or both (18 U.S.C. § 1014). In addition, the Bankruptcy Code, 11 U.S.C. § 523(a)(2), specifically provides that fraudulently incurred insolvency is not dischargeable.

In addition, the federal bank fraud statute provides that

(a) Whoever knowingly executes, or attempts to execute, a scheme or artifice—
(1) to defraud a federally chartered or insured financial institution; or
(2) to obtain any of the moneys, funds, credits, assets, securities or other property owned by or under the custody or control of a federally chartered or insured financial institution by means of false or fraudulent pretenses, representations, or promises, shall be fined not more than $10,000, or imprisoned not more than five years, or both (18 U.S.C. § 1344).

## Defamation

The tort of **defamation** covers both libel and slander. **Slander** springs from an injury caused to one's reputation by an oral defamatory statement, while **libel** is written defamation. Libelous and slanderous statements are those that tend to expose a person to hatred, contempt, or ridicule, or that injure the person in his or her office or business.

EXAMPLE ■ Jerry Day told Jim Brown that Alice Jones had filed for bankruptcy. Because Day knew this statement was untrue, it was slanderous.

To constitute either slander or libel, the defendant must publish the defamatory statement. This means that the maker of the statement must utter it or bring it to the notice of someone other than the defamed person.

EXAMPLE ■ Jerry Day said to Alice Jones, "I hear you have filed for bankruptcy." No one else was present when Day made this remark. In this case, the statement was not slanderous because it was not published.

Some defamatory statements are not grounds for a lawsuit because they are made under privileged circumstances. The U.S. Supreme Court has ruled that a democratic form of government requires that free speech be strongly protected with respect to statements made about public officials, public figures, and matters of public concern. Under this ruling, it is difficult to defame a public official unless a statement is proven both false and malicious.

EXAMPLE ■ Jacobs was running for public office against O'Donnell. During the campaign, Jacobs falsely charged that O'Donnell was a "blundering idiot and not competent to hold the office she seeks." O'Donnell sued for slander.

While O'Donnell might derive some political advantage in bringing this lawsuit, she cannot win it. Jacobs is privileged to make these statements. In the view of the Supreme Court, if he did not have this privilege, the U.S. democratic processes would be harmed.

The truth of an otherwise defamatory statement can be a defense to an action for libel or slander. Certain factors may also mitigate damages, without constituting a complete defense. They are

■ retraction

- evidence of the defamed person's bad reputation before the defamatory statement

- good faith and absence of malice of the person making the defamatory statement

---

## Case for Discussion

### THE LUNCHEON PITCH

Brad Jordan, a young, aggressive, commercial loan officer for First Friendly National Bank, began a year ago to approach Tony Cuisine, a successful local restaurateur, who was a long-time customer of rival Big City Federal Bank. Jordan had succeeded in attracting some small loan activity from Cuisine, mostly personal loans unrelated to the business. Jordan began pressing Cuisine to seek larger loans and to become a First Friendly customer.

During a meeting over lunch, Jordan made his pitch. Cuisine was complaining about Big City and also confided that his business, although still profitable, was in trouble. Jordan, seeing an opportunity to sell First Friendly's congenial image, told Cuisine that he had talked with a dozen businessmen in the past month who also complained about the attitude of Big City Federal's loan officers. Also, he pointed out that First Friendly had an experienced staff and a solid credit department and worked in partnership with customers to assist in business planning. "If you become a First Friendly customer," he told Cuisine, "I can assure you that you will be pleased."

Cuisine said he would think it over. The next day he called Jordan. After that brief talk, he made arrangements to pay off his loans at Big City and to transfer all of his loans and accounts to First Friendly. Two days after the papers were signed, Cuisine called Friendly for an appointment to discuss his business problems. Jordan was not in the office and his secretary told Cuisine that she did not expect him until the following day. On the following day, Jordan called Cuisine, who said that he needed to talk to him because the state unemployment tax bureau was claiming he owed back payments from 1983. Also, two of Cuisine's suppliers had advised him that his credit was no longer good because of his slow payment.

Jordan set up a meeting for the following week. The day before the meeting, however, he was called out of town on an important problem loan. He had his secretary call Cuisine to advise him that the meeting would have to be rescheduled.

When Jordan returned to First Friendly the following morning, two telephone messages were waiting for him. One was from Cuisine's attorney who advised that he was commencing legal action against First Friendly. The other was from Rockwell Moder, corporate counsel, who wanted to talk to him about a call from Big City Federal's attorney concerning slanderous statements.

Jordan was upset. Should he be?

*Sanchez-Corea v. Bank of America,* 701 P.2d 826 (1985).

## CRIMES

As stated earlier, crimes unlike torts are injuries to society at large. Among the crimes that bankers may encounter are larceny, embezzlement, bribery, and money laundering.

**Larceny**

Larceny is the crime of taking and carrying away of the personal property of another with the intent to steal it. If the property taken has a sufficiently high value, the crime is grand larceny—a felony. (The amount required to constitute grand larceny varies among the states.) If the property is of lesser value, the crime is petty, or petit, larceny—a misdemeanor.

**Embezzlement**

Embezzlement is the crime of fraudulent conversion or misappropriation of money or property that is already in the custody of the wrongdoer by virtue of his or her employment.

EXAMPLE ■ Van Ry, a bank courier, took for his own use $5,000 of the bank's money he was transporting for the bank. Van Ry is guilty of embezzlement.

Misappropriation of funds is a form of embezzlement often associated with banks. To establish an embezzlement or misappropriation of funds necessary to convict an individual who deprives a bank of its funds, the prosecutor (the People) must establish that

- the accused had a specified relationship to the bank such as an officer, director, employer, or agent

- the accused willingly misapplied specified assets of the bank or assets entrusted to the bank's custody

- the accused acted with intent to injure or defraud the bank

If these criteria are established, the accused may be convicted and fined up to $5,000, receive five years in jail, or both if the amount involved exceeded $100. Any lesser amount would result in a fine of up to $1,000, one year in prison, or both (18 U.S.C. § 656).

The federal misapplication and embezzlement statutes have been the basis for conviction of directors who declared an illegal dividend, bank officers who paid customers' overdrafts, bank officers who overdrew on their own accounts, bank officers who knowingly lent money to people incapable of paying it back, and bank officers who made unauthorized loans (18 U.S.C. §§ 656 and 657).

## Bribery

The Bank Bribery Act makes the following actions felonies punishable by a fine of not more than $5,000 or three times the value of anything offered, asked, given, received, or to be given or received, whichever is greater; by a prison term of not more than five years; or both. This statute applies to

(a) Whoever—
(1) corruptly gives, offers, or promises anything of value to any person, with intent to influence or reward an officer, director, employee, agent, or attorney of a financial institution in connection with any business or transaction of such institution; or
(2) as an officer, director, employee, agent, or attorney of a financial institution, corruptly solicits or demands for the benefit of any person, or corruptly accepts or agrees to accept, anything of value from any person, intending to be influenced or rewarded in connection with any business or transaction of such institution. . . .

If the value of the "anything" involved does not exceed $100, the penalty is a fine of no more than $1,000, a jail term of no more than one year, or both (18 U.S.C. § 215).

While traditional bribery statutes find criminal liability only where favorable treatment is conditioned upon the actual or promised receipt of a bribe, this statute prohibits a bank employee from receiving gratuities for any bank-related decisions or activity; that is, there is no need to prove that the bank or third party would not have completed the transaction without the gratuity.

The act also mandates that the federal banking agencies issue guidelines to assist officers, directors, employees, agents, and attorneys of banks to comply with the act. The agencies have issued nearly identical guidelines (52 Fed. Reg. 46061, Dec 4, 1987 (OCC); 52 Fed. Reg. 39277, Oct 21, 1987 (FRB); 52 Fed. Reg. 43939, Nov 17, 1987 (FDIC)).

In their guidelines, the regulatory agencies encourage banks and holding companies to adopt internal codes of conduct or written policies explaining the general prohibitions of the Bank Bribery Act. A bank's code of conduct should prohibit any employee from soliciting or accepting anything of value from anyone in connection with the business of the bank. The bank should also require any employee who receives or is offered something of value from a customer beyond what is authorized in the bank's code of conduct to make full disclosure to a designated bank official.

In general, there is no violation of the Bank Bribery Act if

- the acceptance of an item is based on family or personal relationships existing independently of any business of the institution

- the benefit is available to the general public under the same conditions on which it is available to the bank official

- the benefit would be paid for by the institution as a reasonable business expense if not paid for by another party

*Procedures*   The regulatory agencies have urged banks to establish procedures that will ensure compliance with the Bank Bribery Act as follows:

- Banks should maintain a copy of their code of conduct.

- Banks should require from employees a written acknowledgment of and agreement to comply with that code.

- Banks should maintain contemporaneous written reports of disclosures made by employees in connection with the code of conduct or policy.

The regulatory agencies also have encouraged all banks to adopt in their codes of conduct a range of internally acceptable dollar amounts for various benefits that employees may receive from those doing or seeking to do business with the bank.

Each agency recommends that banks require such disclosures and that management review the disclosures to determine whether the items offered or accepted are reasonable or will pose any threat to the integrity of the bank. The Comptroller of the Currency, the FDIC, and the Federal Reserve Board further advise banks that an offer of anything of value beyond the limits set by the bank's policies, even if not accepted, will be a violation of the law if it relates to bank business and is made with corrupt intent.

EXAMPLE ■ ABC Corporation applies for a $500,000 loan at West National Bank and simultaneously pays for the bank president's trip to Sunshine Resort for a weekend. Both the corporation and the bank president could be found guilty of violating the Bank Bribery Act.

## Money Laundering

In 1970 Congress passed the Currency and Foreign Transaction Reporting Act, commonly referred to as the Bank Secrecy Act. Since 1970 the act has been amended a number of times to strengthen its use by law enforcement officials in the prosecution of criminal activity (31 U.S.C. § 5311). In addition to the act, the United States Secretary of the Treasury has issued implementing regulations that are enforced by the Treasury and federal bank regulatory agencies (31 C.F.R. § 103).

The act has received a great deal of attention since 1985 when the federal government began vigorous enforcement of its provisions as part of the national war on drugs. The government has used it as a tool against "money laundering," that is, the transferring of cash from illegal activities through accounts to conceal the source of the cash.

**EXAMPLES** ■ Joe Smith takes the proceeds of his day's cocaine sales, $25,000 in cash, to People's State Bank and purchases two money orders. Smith then takes the money orders, one for $12,000, one for $13,000, and deposits the money in accounts he has at two separate banks.

■ George Jones wishes to avoid paying tax on the income received in his restaurant business. He deposits one half of his week's receipts, $12,000 in cash, in a bank account he keeps in a separate town under an assumed name.

To enable detection of these types of activities, the Bank Secrecy Act and its implementing regulations require banks to complete and file certain reports with the Internal Revenue Service (IRS) (12 U.S.C. § 1818(s)). One statute states

When a domestic financial institution is involved in a transaction for the payment, receipt, or transfer of United States coins or currency (or other monetary instruments the Secretary of the Treasury prescribes), in an amount, denomination, or amount and denomination, or under circumstances the Secretary prescribes by regulation, the institution and any other participant in the transaction the Secretary may prescribe shall file a report on the transaction at the time and in the way the Secretary prescribes. A participant acting for another person shall make the report as the agent or bailee of the person and identify the person for whom the transaction is being made (31 U.S.C. § 5313).

At the present time, the amount designated by the Secretary of the Treasury is "more than $10,000.00" (31 C.F.R. § 103.22). The report is referred to as a **currency transaction report** (CTR). The $10,000 figure refers to activity within one day.

**EXAMPLE** ■ On January 5, Judy Long deposits $20,000 in cash at Big Bank—$9,000 at its main office, $4,000 at its south branch, and $7,000 at its north branch. The bank is required to file a CTR.

In addition to CTRs, the regulations also require the filing of reports on transactions involving "monetary instruments" across international boundaries in amounts in excess of $10,000 or the equivalent in foreign currency (31 C.F.R. § 103.23).

The act and regulations also require recordkeeping regarding certain loans, transfers of funds, certificates of deposit, deposit accounts, checks and drafts, and other transactions in excess of $10,000 (31 C.F.R. §§ 103.33 and 103.34).

Banks are required by regulation to have a written policy that conforms to the Bank Secrecy Act and includes the designation of an individual or individuals responsible for coordinating and monitoring daily compliance (12 C.F.R. §§ 21.21, 208.14, and 326.8).

Violations of the Bank Secrecy Act have serious consequences for banks, directors, officers, and employees. Criminal and/or civil penalties exist for failure to file or properly complete CTRs, and for evading reporting requirements, including violations when no intent is involved.

## Criminal Referral

Typically, one who witnesses a crime has no responsibility to either intercede to prevent it or to report it to authorities. Exceptions exist for certain individuals whose jobs put them into contact with potential crimes. For example, many states have laws requiring individuals who encounter suspected child abuse in the course of their employment to report their suspicions to authorities.

Banks also have a duty to report criminal activity. Each of the federal bank regulatory agencies has adopted similar criminal referral procedures that require banks to report known or suspected crimes involving the bank.

If a bank employee, officer, director, or shareholder is suspected of criminal activity, a criminal referral must be made regardless of the amount involved. If the suspect is not a bank employee, officer, director, or shareholder, or if no suspect is known, the necessity to report is based on the amount of loss to the bank.

Failure to file a criminal referral, if willful or careless, can subject a bank's officers, its directors, or both to civil money penalties.

If a criminal referral is warranted, it is made on a prescribed form to the bank's federal regulatory agency, the Federal Bureau of Investigation, and to a United States Attorney. Depending on the nature of the crime, reports to the IRS and U.S. Secret Service may also be required. If the suspected activity could also be a state crime, the referral may also include the appropriate state or local prosecuting authority.

---

**EXAMPLE** ■ During an internal audit at Fourth National Bank, it is discovered that Laura Throne, a teller, deposited $500 in her own checking account the same day her teller account was $500 short. Throne has been with the bank for 20 years, and members of her family are excellent bank customers. The bank's president confronts Throne who admits the theft. Throne is permitted to make immediate restitution and to resign. No further action is taken.

The bank's president has violated the criminal referral reporting requirements, exposing himself and the bank to civil money penalties.

---

Exceptions to the referral requirements do exist for robberies, burglaries, and for lost or missing securities. These exceptions are only provided because they are regulated elsewhere. The Comptroller of the Currency requires that banks keep on file records of all attempted and committed crimes of robbery, burglary, and nonemployee larceny (12 C.F.R. § 21.5(c)). The FDIC has a similar requirement (12 C.F.R. § 326.5(c)), as does the Federal Reserve Board (12 C.F.R. § 216.5(b)). The Securities and Exchange Commission has its own reporting requirements (17 C.F.R. § 240.17(f-1)) regarding the report of all lost and missing securities.

Other crimes involving banks include wrongful certification of checks (18 U.S.C. § 1004); making false entries in books, reports, or statements (18 U.S.C. § 1005); and making improper or prohibited loans, including loans exceeding a bank's loan limits.

---

**EXAMPLE** ■ Larry Earl, an officer of Acme National Bank, is asked by Kay Thompson to certify a $5,000 check drawn on her account at the bank. Earl reviews the account and determines that it has collected funds of $1,000. After receiving assurances from Thompson that she will deposit funds to cover the check the following week, Earl certifies the check.

Earl could be convicted of wrongful certification of a check, which is a violation of 18 U.S.C. § 1004. He could be sentenced to up to five years in jail and fined up to $5,000. To convict Earl, no intent to defraud the bank is necessary. *U.S. v. Giordano,* 489 F.2d 327 (2d Cir. 1973).

---

## CONCLUSION

Commission of a tort or crime may arise out of one act, but violate two separate duties. A crime is an individual's breach of a duty to society as defined by law. A tort is a breach of a legally defined duty one individual owes another. The government in its representation of society as the wronged party prosecutes individuals accused of crimes. Torts do not involve the government but instead are litigated between the individuals involved.

Because of the crucial role banks play in the nation's economy, protection of their assets from wrongdoing is a particular goal of criminal law. Wrongful conduct that might be only a tort in another business is often also a crime if it involves a bank. To avoid committing crimes in even seemingly innocent activities, bank directors, officers, employees, and agents must carefully comply with banking law and regulation.

**Questions for Review and Discussion**

1. Whom does a tort harm?

2. To sue someone for negligence, is it necessary to show only a wrongful act?

3. List the five essential elements of the tort of deceit.

4. What is publication and why is it necessary in a defamation action?

5. What is the difference between larceny and embezzlement?

6. To be convicted of bribery under federal law, must a banker have specifically agreed to furnish something of value in return for the bribe?

7. What is a currency transaction report?

8. Must a bank report suspected criminal activity?

# Legal Entities

After studying this chapter, you will be able to

- identify the various entities with which banks do business, including individuals, sole proprietorships, agents, partnerships, corporations, governments, estates, trusts, sureties, and guarantors
- determine the importance of distinguishing between these entities for banks
- discuss the manner in which banks should deal with each entity

Every day banks deal with tens of thousands of customers throughout the United States. Most of those customers are individuals doing business with banks for their own reasons, in connection with their personal accounts or loan requests. However, many individuals dealing with banks do so as agents of legal entities that may be partnerships, corporations, government entities, estates, trusts, associations, and others. Understanding these legal entities can help a bank avoid financial losses and serious legal problems.

## INDIVIDUAL CUSTOMERS

Whether they are cashing paychecks, depositing money in savings accounts, purchasing certificates of deposit, making loan payments, or requesting loans, most customers do business with banks as individuals. As discussed more thoroughly in chapter 5, as long as a bank is satisfed that its customer has the capacity to contract, it is not liable for that individual's banking decisions.

---

EXAMPLE ■ Maria Renaldo withdraws $20,000 from her savings account at Third State Bank and invests the money in Blue Sky Corporation's stock, which soon becomes valueless.

In such a situation, Third State Bank has no liability for Renaldo's loss. She had the power to open a savings account in her own name and withdraw funds from it for whatever purposes she wished, with no obligation on the bank's part to assure that she used her money wisely.

---

When a bank transacts business with individuals, probably the most troublesome area involves married couples.

---

EXAMPLE ■ One Friday, Joe Smite receives his paycheck and leaves it on his dresser. His wife, Mae, endorses the check with her own name, "Mae Smite," and cashes the check at Centerville State Bank. Although the bank realizes Joe Smite's endorsement does not appear on the check, it negotiates the check because Joe and Mae are married. Mae takes the cash and leaves Joe. Joe then demands that the bank pay him an amount equal to that of his check.

In this situation, the bank will probably lose. A marital relationship does not in and of itself give one spouse the right to act for another. Spouses are separate legal entities and banks should do business with them as such.

---

*[handwritten note: In NYS there is no implied authority.]*

One defense the bank in the preceding example could advance is that of "implied authority," discussed in the section on agents in this chapter. (See the subsection entitled "Agent's Authority to Act for Principal.") However, "implied authority" arises not from the marital relationship but from the couple's past course of conduct, as discussed in the section on agents.

## SOLE PROPRIETORSHIPS

The law recognizes as **sole proprietorships** people who own and operate businesses individually. A sole proprietorship is perhaps the simplest form of business organization. The shoe store owned and operated by one person is a sole proprietorship, as is an insurance agency that is owned and operated by an individual insurance agent. Use of employees and others to assist in a business does not affect an individual's status as a sole proprietor, as long as only one person owns the business.

---

EXAMPLE ■ Sam Small owns and operates a milk route. His business assets include his milk truck and a typewriter he uses for business correspondence. His annual gross sales are $30,000.

George Big is the owner of a dairy farm, a pasteurizing operation, and a bottling plant, all of which he uses to sell milk to consumers, individual distributors like Sam Small, and grocery stores. His annual gross sales are $1 million and he employs 100 people.

Both Sam Small and George Big have sole proprietorships. Differences in gross sales and in number of operations and employees do not legally require different types of business organizations.

---

A bank dealing with a sole proprietorship may transact business in the same way it does with any other individual, unless the owner of the sole proprietorship operates his or her business under an "assumed name." An assumed name is nothing more than the use of a name other than the owner's to operate a business. For example, if Sam Small calls his milk delivery business "Sunshine Company" and George Big conducts business as "Centerville Dairy Products," they both operate under assumed names.

Many states require those who use assumed names in operating a business to file an "assumed-name certificate" with either a local or state office. This certificate is available for anyone to review in order to determine the true name of the owner of a particular business. Further, by filing the certificate, the user of the assumed name is protected from the possibility of another person's use of the same name in the same location.

When a bank transacts business with a sole proprietorship or other entity using an assumed name, it is wise to require that an account be opened only in the names of the individuals involved. The bank can also note the assumed name on the account, for example, Samuel Brown d/b/a (doing business as) "Acme Cleaners." In addition, the bank may ask for a copy of the assumed-name certificate before an account is opened or any business is transacted. In this way, the bank can avoid confusion, particularly where the account is opened in the assumed name and not the actual owner's name. This procedure may also alert the businessperson regarding the need to file the certificate if it has not already been done, thus protecting the assumed name and avoiding the civil and criminal liabilities that exist in some states for operating a business under an assumed name without filing a certificate.

---

EXAMPLE ■ Jack Cohen operates "Charlie's Record Shop" in Hartland, Michigan. Because he has not filed an assumed-name certificate, he could be subject to a fine of $25 to $100 or up to 30 days imprisonment in the county jail or both (Mich. Comp. Laws § 445.5).

---

## AGENTS

In addition to dealing with individuals transacting their own personal or business matters, banks also do business with individuals representing others. **Agency** signifies the legal relationship established when one person represents or acts for another. An **agent** represents or has authority to represent another person in transactions with third persons. The person represented is known as the **principal.**

A person may act for or represent another in two different ways. He or she may be employed to do ministerial work for another, subject to orders about details and methods used and without authority to affect the principal's legal relationships with third parties. In this case, the employee is given the special name servant and the principal is known as the master.

---

EXAMPLE ■ Charlie Coyne is treasurer for the Daltan Swim Club. One of his assigned tasks is making bank deposits, but he does not have the right to sign checks. In this example, Charlie Coyne is an agent for the swim club but only for a ministerial task not affecting his principal's legal relationship with the bank or with other third parties.

---

On the other hand, a principal may give an agent the authority to make contracts or engage in other business with third parties that definitely affect the principal's legal relationship with those third parties.

---

EXAMPLE ■ Centerville Corporation employs Vince Smith as financial vice president. Part of his job includes negotiating loans with banks and he is empowered to sign promissory notes on the corporation's behalf.

---

These two examples illustrate the wide range between the "master-servant" relationship of Charlie Coyne and the Daltan Swim Club and the "principal-agent" relationship of Vince Smith and Centerville Corporation. The master and principal determine the extent of the relationship. While both Coyne and Smith are agents, Coyne's representation of the Daltan Swim Club is much more limited than Smith's powers on behalf of Centerville Corporation.

---

EXAMPLE ■ Charlie Coyne applied to Acme National Bank for a loan to Centerville Corporation. The bank denied the loan request because Coyne had no authority to make the request.

Had Vince Smith made the loan request, the bank could have approved the loan, let Smith sign a promissory note on behalf of Centerville Corporation, and if the loan had gone into default, sued Centerville Corporation. This is because the cornerstone of agency law is the liability of the principal or master for the authorized acts of the servant or agent. Of course, before making the loan, the bank should have assured itself that Smith actually had the authority that he claimed to have.

---

A third kind of agency relationship looks much like the master-servant or principal-agent relationships but does not make the employer liable for the acts of the third person. This relationship involves the third person as an independent contractor. The difference in the independent contractor relationship lies in the control retained over the physical conduct of the person performing the service.

Although this distinction may seem clear, in some situations it is difficult to apply to the particular facts. However, a servant or agent is subject to the employer's direction, while an independent contractor is obligated to produce a result and is free to choose a particular method to achieve that result.

---

EXAMPLE ■ Citizens National Bank decided to paint the exteriors of its main office and one of its branch offices. The bank requested its maintenance man, Stewart, to paint the branch and hired Harry Jones, Inc., to paint the main office. Stewart is a servant or agent of Citizens National Bank, while Jones is an independent contractor.

Both Stewart and Jones entered into a contract with Paint Supply Company to buy paint for the job. Since Jones is an independent contractor, Citizens is not liable for payment for his paint. However, since Stewart is its agent, Citizens must pay for the paint received by Stewart.

## Creation of the Agency Relationship

Agency relationships are created every day everywhere in the United States. Every time someone finds a job or is given greater responsibilities in his or her present job, an agency relationship is created or expanded. No special form is required for the appointment of an agent or servant. An oral contract of agency is often as effective as a written one. Some state statutes and courts require certain agency relationships to be created by written contract, for example, hiring a real estate broker to sell and transfer real estate.

**EXAMPLE** ■ Marietta State Bank orally hired John Avery, a real estate broker, to sell real estate it owned. The bank orally agreed to pay Avery a 6 percent commission from any sale he made.

In those states where statutes or court decisions require real estate listing agreements to be in writing, Avery would be unable to collect his commission if he sold the bank's property and it refused to pay him voluntarily.

*[handwritten note: Not true in NYS. Can be oral.]*

Powers of attorney authorizing attorneys-in-fact to convey real estate must also be in writing, and state statutes usually set forth the specifics of such appointments. A **power of attorney** is a written document whereby a principal specifically appoints an agent, usually called an **attorney-in-fact,** to perform all or any specific acts the principal could do, including the power to withdraw from accounts, execute notes, convey real and personal property, and endorse negotiable instruments. A bank concerned about the authority of an agent to perform a particular act for a principal should require a power of attorney specifying the agent's authority.

Anyone desiring to be a principal who has the legal capacity to act alone can enter into an agency relationship.

---

EXAMPLE ■ Jimmy Murdoch, an individual suffering from a mental illness and for whom a guardian has been appointed, has a checking account. He wishes to have his brother Mark's name added to the account in order to permit Mark to act occasionally on his behalf.

Because Jimmy is the ward of a legally appointed guardian, he is legally incapable of entering into contracts and thus cannot engage an agent to undertake acts on his behalf that he cannot perform himself. If Mark Murdoch were the owner of the checking account, he could have his brother Jimmy's name added to the account. Since an agent acts not for him- or herself but for a principal, it is not necessary that the agent have the legal capacity to contract.

---

**Agent's Authority to Act for Principal**

An agent has authority to act for his or her principal only to the extent of the authority given by the principal.

---

EXAMPLE ■ Acme State Bank employs Donald Rose as a loan officer. The maximum amount the bank permits him to loan a customer without another loan officer's approval is $25,000. Thus, in making loans, Rose's authority to act as the bank's agent is limited to $25,000.

One day, Rose's good friend Fred Abel comes to the bank and requests a $30,000 loan for construction equipment from Rose. From past transactions, Abel knows of Rose's lending limit of $25,000. Because no other officer is available at the time of Abel's request, Rose approves the loan himself and asks Abel to return the next day when the promissory note and money will be ready for him. Abel leaves the bank and signs a contract for the equipment. The next day, Rose tells Abel he cannot make the loan after all, based on his superior's orders. Abel sues the bank and requests the court to order it to make the loan.

Abel wins and loses. The court orders the bank to loan him $25,000, not $30,000. The reason is that Rose as the bank's agent had no ability to bind the bank to a loan exceeding $25,000 and Abel was aware of the extent of Rose's authority.

---

Two kinds of agent authority exist: actual and apparent. Actual authority, in turn, has two forms—express and implied. Express authority is actual authority to perform the act in question. Therefore, a principal is bound by agent actions that he or she expressly authorized. Implied authority, on the other hand, is a form of actual authority, but it can involve a situation where the principal denies that the agent was authorized to perform the act in question. The authority may be implied, however, from the nature of the transaction, the custom of the trade, prior dealings, or other conduct from which the agent reasonably could believe that the principal intended the agent to perform the act. In other words, implied authority includes those actions a person must take to effectuate an actual authority. For example, if an agent is authorized to apply for and obtain a loan, then he or she has the implied authority to sign all required documents.

---

EXAMPLE ■ Lois Lane is a loan officer with Metropolis National Bank. The bank never imposed a lending limit on Lane or any of its other loan officers. They were simply told to use good judgment. Clark Kent requested a loan for $20,000, which Lane approved. She told Kent to return the following day for the funds and execution of a promissory note. Kent had borrowed like sums from the bank in the past, and Lane regularly approved loans of that size. Kent returned the next day and the bank's president informed him that the loan for $20,000 could not be made and that that amount exceeded Lane's authority. Kent sued the bank and demanded the $20,000 loan.

The courts would probably decide that Lane had the implied authority to make the $20,000 loan and, if this were the case,

Metropolis National Bank would be bound by her action. That the bank did not give Lane a specific lending limit does not preclude the finding of actual authority on her part to make the $20,000 loan. That authority can be implied from the context of the transaction, Kent's past dealings with Lane, and Lane's previous loans to other customers.

---

Apparent authority, unlike actual authority, is not expressly given, nor can it be implied from the circumstances. As its name indicates, apparent authority is the authority that a third person reasonably thinks the agent has, based on the conduct of the principal, which must create the appearance of authority. If a third person relies on this apparent authority, the principal is bound even though there was no intent to give such appearance of authority.

---

**EXAMPLE** ■ The facts are the same as in the earlier example of Donald Rose and Fred Abel, except that in this case, Abel has never dealt with Rose and has no idea of his lending limit when Rose agrees to Abel's $30,000 loan request, which is $5,000 over Rose's lending limit.

In this case, Abel would probably win his suit against the bank because of Rose's position with the bank as a loan officer and the public's general unfamiliarity with the lending limits of loan officers, which vary from officer to officer. The court could find that Rose had apparent authority to make the loan, since the bank, by giving Rose the title of loan officer and not informing its customers of loan officers' lending limits, created the appearance that Rose could approve a loan of $30,000. Thus, the bank could be required to complete the loan by the appearance it created. However, Rose may be liable to the bank for any loss resulting from his failure to stay within the bounds of his actual authority.

---

As already stated, a principal is not bound by agent action unless it is within the agent's actual or apparent authority. However, if a principal ratifies an agent's act, the principal becomes bound for the act. Ratification occurs when the principal consents to acts done on the principal's behalf by an agent without actual or apparent authority. Ratification may be express or it may be implied from the circumstances, when the principal knowingly keeps or takes the benefits of the agent's unauthorized act.

---

EXAMPLE ■ John Romero, a loan officer for Merci State Bank, has a lending limit of $40,000. Frank Wong requests a loan of $50,000 from Romero, who approves it. Wong is aware of Romero's lending limit. The next day, Wong returns to the bank for the funds, which he receives after executing a promissory note. Between the time of Romero's approval of the loan and Wong's return, the bank's president reprimands Romero for exceeding his limit but does approve or "ratify" his loan approval.

---

Ratification is a technical concept that requires the following elements:

■ The act must have been done purportedly on behalf of the principal. (A principal cannot ratify and adopt an act that the agent did on the agent's own behalf.)

■ Ratification of an unauthorized act cannot be partial. The principal may not ratify favorable parts of a single transaction and refuse to be bound by other parts.

■ Unless the principal has full knowledge of the material facts of the transaction, there can be no ratification.

■ The principal must have existed when the act was done. For instance, a corporation cannot ratify an act that was done on its behalf at a time when the corporation did not yet exist.

■ The principal cannot ratify the act if the third party has already canceled it.

**Delegation of Authority**  If an agent is hired or appointed to perform a certain task or job, it must be done personally and ordinarily cannot be delegated to another, unless the principal makes an express or implied agreement to the delegation.

**Imputed Knowledge**  Not only is the principal bound when his or her agent acts with actual or apparent authority or upon ratification, but the principal is bound by all knowledge that the agent acquires while so acting. This doctrine—known as the doctrine of imputed knowledge—is based on the idea that the principal and the agent are in law deemed to be one person. Facts known by the agent, therefore, are said to be known by the principal.

---

EXAMPLE ■ The cashier of a bank knew that a certain customer of the bank had been declared mentally incompetent, which under applicable state law meant the person could not handle his own affairs. Checks drawn by the customer were presented to a teller of the bank who did not know of his status as a mental incompetent. The teller paid them.

The bank cannot charge these checks to the customer's account. The bank had imputed knowledge of the customer's status and thus should not have paid his checks.

---

**Liability**  The creation of an agency relationship may expose principals and agents to certain liabilities, including the liabilities of principals to third persons, principals to agents, and agents to principals.

*Liability of Principals to Third Persons*  In addition to binding principals to agreements made within the agents' actual or apparent authority or by ratification, agents may also expose their principals to tort liability by their actions. (Chapter 3 discusses torts.)

If an agent (including an employee) commits a tort while acting within his or her authority and on behalf of his or her principal, both the principal and the agent will be liable for the damages caused by the agent's tort.

EXAMPLE ■ As a result of his negligence while driving, Joe Neale, a bank employee, runs down a pedestrian, causing substantial injuries. Neale is driving his employer's car on bank business when the accident occurs.

Because Neale was acting within the scope of his employment, the pedestrian may sue both the bank and Neale, jointly or separately. If the pedestrian obtains a joint judgment, it may be collected in full from either Neale or the bank, or both may share in the amount paid.

UNAUTHORIZED ACTS

An agent purporting to act on behalf of a principal warrants to third persons his or her authority to act in a particular transaction. If the agent lacks that authority, he or she becomes personally liable for breach of warranty of authority on the contract.

EXAMPLE ■ Joe Hanson, a manufacturer's representative for Widget, Inc., agrees to sell 4,000 widgets to Acme Industries for $8,000. Widget, Inc., had agreed Hanson could sell its widgets for no less than $3 per unit and it refuses to honor Acme's order. Hanson will be personally liable for the $4,000 difference.

AUTHORIZED ACTS

If the agent acting on behalf of a principal discloses both his or her representative capacity and the principal's name, the agent is not liable to the third person on the contract if the action in question was authorized. In this case, the contract is deemed to be between the principal and the third person, and the agent has no rights or responsibilities with regard to it.

EXAMPLE ■ Loan officer Nancy Petrullo approves a loan within her loan limit to George Ward, but subsequently the bank refuses to make the loan unless the borrower agrees to a higher interest rate than Petrullo authorized.

The borrower can sue the bank but not Petrullo. When he made the loan request, the borrower knew he was dealing with an agent and knew the principal's identity.

---

However, often at the principal's direction, an agent may conceal that he or she is acting for a principal. In the previous example, the agent has authority to make a deal on behalf of a principal, but the third party is unaware of this situation. To protect the third party in such a case, the law holds the agent liable on the contract to the third party. Additionally, after discovery of the principal's existence, the third party can hold the principal liable. In most states, however, the third party is forced to elect which of the two parties—the agent or the undisclosed principal—to hold liable. Once the election has been made, the other party is discharged from liability to the third party.

## Liability of Principals to Agents

The agent has two rights against the principal:

- a right to compensation, unless the understanding is that the agent is to receive no compensation

- a right to reimbursement for advances made and to indemnity for losses sustained in the scope of employment

Clearly, if the principal has agreed to pay the agent a salary or commission, the agent has enforceable contractual rights. Occasionally, an agent will agree to work for no compensation, removing any right to payment for wages.

An agent is entitled to reimbursement or indemnity for all expenses incurred within the scope of employment and for all liability incurred because of the execution of actual authority. As discussed earlier, an agent may be held personally liable when the principal is undisclosed. In such a situation, if the principal directed that his or her existence should be undisclosed, the agent can collect from the principal any loss suffered by the agent in carrying out this plan.

An agent who commits a tort, on the other hand, has no action against the principal, even in situations where the principal is also liable. A tort is seldom expressly authorized and, even if it were, it would be against social policy to allow the agent to be exonerated by recovering the loss from the principal.

## Liability of Agents to Principals

A fiduciary relationship, obligating the agent to act with utmost good faith and loyalty in all dealings undertaken on the principal's behalf, exists between agent and principal. The law also requires the agent to act with a certain degree of diligence and skill. Failure to meet any of these duties exposes the agent to liability for the ensuing loss to the principal.

The principal has a right to have the agent render reasonably diligent, careful, and skillful service. The amount of skill that the principal can fairly demand from the agent depends upon the character of the contract between the two parties and the circumstances that surround the particular relationship. When a bank hires a vice president with a graduate degree and 10 years of banking experience, for example, it has a right to expect greater skill than when it hires a teller just graduating from high school. The amount of compensation paid to the employee frequently determines the amount of skill the employer is entitled to expect.

**EXAMPLE** ■ Cotoctin State Bank hires Herman Wendal, an ex-bank examiner, as its vice president and pays him a large salary. Wendal carelessly approves the cashing of a large check drawn on an account with insufficient funds. When the bank cannot collect the funds from the drawer of the check, it discharges Wendal and successfully sues him.

The principal also has a right to have the agent obey instructions and act within the limits of the agent's authority. If the agent exceeds his or her actual authority, causing loss to the principal, the agent is liable to the principal for that loss.

The agent owes a duty of loyalty or fidelity to the principal. One of the most common violations of this duty occurs when one person undertakes to act as agent for two separate parties to a transaction. In this case, the agent is liable to both principals for the losses caused them.

## Termination of Agency

If the parties have agreed that the agency shall end at a certain time, the arrival of that time will terminate the agency. If third parties are not informed of the termination and have dealt previously with the agent, however, under the principle of apparent authority, the principal may be liable to those third parties on subsequent contracts made by the agent.

Even though a principal may contract with an agent for a particular period of service, a principal may revoke the agency at any time. The principal, however, may have to pay damages for breach of contract or compensate the agent at the contract rate for the unexpired period of the terminated contract.

If the agency has no designated period, either the principal or the agent may terminate it at any time. An important exception to this rule is that a principal may not terminate an "agency coupled with an interest." This exists when the principal gives the agent a power (for example, power of sale) as a security interest in property to protect an interest of the agent (for example, debt owed to agent by principal). Some states, however, treat such an arrangement as a secured transaction, which can be revoked upon redemption.

---

EXAMPLE ■ McFee loaned money to Ferrigan. As security for repayment, Ferrigan puts McFee in possession of his car and authorizes him to sell it and keep enough proceeds from the sale to pay the loan. Ferrigan subsequently wants to revoke McFee's power to sell the car. McFee has an agency coupled with an interest, which cannot be revoked.

---

Many courts, however, now regard an agency coupled with an interest as a mere security device, better handled under the law of secured transactions than under the law of agency. These courts would give Ferrigan the right to redemption—that is, the right to get his car back after he repays the loan to McFee. In these courts, the agency could be revoked by satisfaction of the "interest" that made it irrevocable.

Based on constitutional principles outlawing slavery and peonage, the rule that an agent may renounce employment at any time is firmly established. The renunciation, of course, may breach a contract of employment, for which the agent will be liable in damages. Finally, the operation of law upon the occurrence of a certain event may also terminate a contract of agency. The destruction of the subject matter of the agency, for example, terminates the agency relationship on grounds of impossibility, as does the death of either the principal or agent.

## PARTNERSHIP CUSTOMERS

After sole proprietorships, partnerships are probably the most common type of legal entity with which banks do business. A **partnership** is a legal entity composed of two or more persons who as co-owners carry on a business for profit.

---

EXAMPLE ■ Mary Quince and Toby Adams both operated competing sole proprietorship shoe stores in Burlington for years. Finally they joined forces, each bringing to their new business the assets and debts of their sole proprietorships, with the agreement that they would evenly share the profits of the new business.

By taking this action, Quince and Adams formed a partnership. They are co-owners of assets with the purpose of using those assets to make and split a profit between them. Had Quince simply sold her shoe store's assets to Adams and gone to work for Adams at an hourly wage, no partnership would have been created. If instead they sold their assets to purchase a cottage together for their families' use in the summer, they also would not be partners because, while they jointly own an asset, they did not acquire it to make a profit.

---

## Uniform Partnership Act

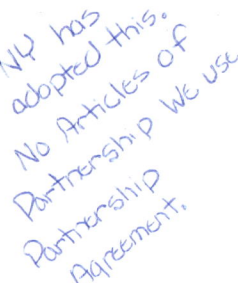

*NY has adopted this. No Articles of Partnership we use Partnership Agreement.*

As chapter 1 explains, the National Conference of Commissioners on Uniform State Laws has drafted numerous model statutes, including the Uniform Commercial Code (UCC), for the various states to consider. The **Uniform Partnership Act,** which has been adopted with some variation in every state but Louisiana, and is in effect in the District of Columbia and the Virgin Islands but not Puerto Rico, is one of those model statutes. However, as with the UCC, states are free to amend the model statute and have done so with their own unique variations. Before adoption of the Uniform Partnership Act, common law governed partnerships and developed many rules that the model statute absorbed.

## Formation of Partnerships

Partnerships can be formed with or without formal, written agreements. They can also be formed by **estoppel.** For legal purposes, estoppel binds a person who, by conduct, statement, or silent acquiescence, knowingly misleads another to act or fail to act, causing injury because of the other's good faith reliance on the person's misrepresentation.

---

EXAMPLE ■ Thomas and Agnes Chappell, husband and wife, started a clothing store. They both work in the store, make business decisions jointly, and take a salary from the business. The business is operated as "Chappell's Clothing Emporium." There are no written agreements between them.

The Chappells have a partnership, assuming the state they are located within has adopted the Uniform Partnership Act.

---

## *Formation of Partnerships by Written Agreement*

Although partnerships can be formed without formal agreements, as with any legal arrangement between parties, it is best to formalize a partnership, beginning with a document that sets forth the agreement of the parties entering into the partnership. Such a document is called **articles of partnership.** Articles of partnership, or partnership agreements, usually have provisions for the following matters:

■ the nature, name, and place of business

- the dates when the relationship is to begin and end
- the amount of capital contributed by each partner and the form in which and the time when it will be contributed (where partners contribute property other than money, its value in money should also be stated)
- each partner's share in the profits and losses
- each partner's interest in the partnership (otherwise it is presumed that the interests of all partners are equal, notwithstanding that their contributions may have been unequal)
- each partner's powers and duties
- the time when accountings shall be had
- the amount and the time when each partner shall be entitled to draw from the partnership
- any partner's receipt of a salary (in the absence of any provision for salary, each is presumed to depend on the profits, if any, as compensation for time and services)

A bank doing business with a partnership should request a copy of its articles of partnership or partnership agreement and refer to them particularly when the partnership wishes to establish accounts or borrow money.

---

**EXAMPLE** ■ Kashe, Wiley, and Greene have a partnership agreement, which specifies that bank loans into which the partnership enters require all of their signatures. Greene went into Taloosca State Bank to request a loan of $10,000 to the partnership and asked that he alone sign the promissory note on the partnership's behalf. A review of the articles of partnership by the bank would end a potential problem before it started. The bank would then advise Greene that it could not make such a loan, because it would not conform to the articles' requirements that all partners sign promissory notes.

---

## Formation of Partnerships by Estoppel

Under both the common law and the Uniform Partnership Act, partnerships can also be established by estoppel. A partnership by estoppel is created whenever two or more parties, by written or oral representations or conduct, represent themselves as a partnership to others who rely on that representation (for example, by granting credit) to their detriment.

---

## Case for Discussion

### DEALER AND SOUTHWESTERN NATIONAL BANK v. CASH

#### Facts

Daisy Cash and Joe Mellon operate a fruit-and-flower stand. A sign out front reads "Cash and Mellon, Partners." However, Cash and Mellon have signed no formal articles of partnership or partnership agreement.

Occasionally, the business needs working capital, which it borrows from Southwestern National Bank. Cash and Mellon individually always sign the business promissory notes with "partner" noted after the name of the one signing the note.

Mellon becomes dissatisifed with his lot in life, borrows $15,000 from Southwestern National Bank (which is within the normal range of the business loans), and leaves for Mexico for a life of ease. When the loan is not repaid, Southwestern National Bank sues Daisy Cash. She claims she is not liable because no formal partnership agreement exists between her and Mellon.

In addition, before Mellon leaves he also orders a new car from a dealer 500 miles from his business, with whom neither he nor Cash have ever dealt. Although he does not identify the business, he represents to the dealer that the car will be used in his business. Mellon picks up the automobile, gives cash as a down payment, and promises that his business will pay the balance within 14 days.

When the balance remains unpaid and Mellon and the car have disappeared, the dealer sues Cash. Again, she claims she is not liable, because she and Mellon are not partners and no formal partnership agreement exists between them.

#### Decisions

In this situation, Cash will probably both win and lose. Her business arrangement with Mellon created a partnership by estoppel and, with it, the individual liability of each partner for the debts of the partnership. Southwestern National Bank made the loan based on the outward representations of Cash and Mellon to the world that they were a partnership, as well as on their past practice of signing loans individually as partners. Thus, the court will probably hold Cash liable for Mellon's bank loan.

However, Cash will probably not be held liable for the balance of the car payment because when the dealer extended credit to Mellon he relied on no representations by Cash or Mellon that they were partners.

### Questions for Discussion
1. What proof would the bank need to submit to the court that Cash and Mellon represented themselves to the bank as a partnership?
2. When doing business with partnerships formed by estoppel, what safeguards should a bank maintain to protect itself against potential losses?
3. How would the circumstances in the case have to vary for Cash to be liable for Mellon's car payment as well as his bank loan?

---

The existence of a partnership by estoppel is decided on a case-by-case basis. A creditor arguing that two or more other parties are partners by estoppel must demonstrate that it extended credit based on representations made specifically to it or made publicly. As the case above illustrates, one party might be able to prove that a partnership exists, while another party might not.

## Partners' Authority

For banks, a vital aspect of dealing with the public is correctly assessing an individual or entity's legal authority to undertake a certain banking transaction. Tellers face this challenge in nearly every transaction they handle, from reviewing check endorsements to ensure proper presentment to reviewing savings account withdrawal slips to ensure authorized withdrawals.

Individual partners transact business daily on behalf of their partnerships, from ordering and selling goods to buying or leasing real estate, borrowing money, or creating deposit accounts. Because of the numerous decisions a partnership may make every day, the law does not require every decision to have the approval of every partner. Such a procedure would probably not be too difficult for a 2-person fruit-and-flower-stand partnership but would quickly halt the business of a 100-person law partnership with offices in several states. For partnerships to function on a day-to-day basis, section 9 of the Uniform Partnership Act provides

Every partner is an agent of the partnership for the purpose of its business, and the act of every partner, including the execution in the partnership name of any instrument, for apparently carrying on in the usual way the business of the partnership of which he is a member, binds the partnership, unless the partner so acting has in fact no authority to act for the partnership in the particular matter, and the person with whom he is dealing has knowledge of the fact that he has no such authority.

Although this section appears to be clear and concise, a careful analysis is required to fully understand its meaning and effect.

First, the statute declares every partner to be an agent of the partnership. Thus, the first determination is whether the individual representing the partnership is a "partner." A simple check of the articles of partnership or partnership agreement will reveal whether the person is a partner. If the bank does not have a copy of the articles of agreement, it may ask the purported partner to produce it. The bank might also check with the secretary of state for the state in which the partnership does business or with the county clerk in the county where the partnership does business to determine whether a certificate of partnership is on file. Many states require the filing of such a certificate, which will reveal the names and addresses of the partnership's partners, and its purpose for, and terms of, existence.

---

**EXAMPLE** ■ Chuck West requests a loan of $10,000 from State Bank for 90 days for Acme Company, a partnership that is a long-time customer of the bank and whose loan history includes short-term loans between $5,000 and $15,000. While the bank is familiar with the partnership, it has never dealt with West before.

If the bank makes the loan and subsequently learns that West is not a partner, the bank will be unable to seek repayment from the partnership. If West is a partner, then he is an "agent" of the partnership and, pursuant to the law of agency, will probably have the authority to bind the partnership to the terms of the loan, including, of course, its repayment.

As a partner and thus an agent of Acme Company, West's ability to act for the partnership, secure a loan, or conduct other business is not unlimited. An important restriction is whether the business a partner transacts is within the "usual way" of the partnership's business. West sought funds in an amount that had been borrowed by the partnership before on numerous occasions and for the usual period of time. Thus, his request was within the "usual way" of the partnership's course of business.

---

A second factor in analyzing partnership authority concerns the articles of partnership. A partner may act in the usual way of the partnership's business and still not be able to bind the partnership to the transaction undertaken on the partnership's behalf. This situation usually arises because of limitations in the articles of partnership.

---

EXAMPLE ■ Acme Company's articles of partnership state that three of the partnership's five partners must sign any loan agreement for the company. Larry Marx requests $12,000 for the partnership from State Bank for 90 days and is the only partner who executes the note on the partnership's behalf. Marx obtains the loan proceeds and leaves the country. State Bank has a copy of the partnership's articles but did not review them before it granted the loan request.

State Bank cannot require Acme Company to pay off the loan because, by possessing a copy of the articles, it was aware that Marx alone had no authority to bind the company to the terms of the note.

---

In the preceding example, if the bank had not had a copy of the articles of partnership or otherwise had no knowledge of the limitation of Marx's authority, the bank could enforce the loan against Acme

Company if it were a "trading partnership." Trading partnerships are those in the business of buying and selling for profit. Partners in a trading partnership have implied power to borrow money for the partnership. Partners in a "nontrading" partnership, such as partners in a law firm, have no implied power to borrow money unless it is needed in the transaction of their business.

In addition to the usual way of doing business requirement and the articles of partnership limitations, the Uniform Partnership Act also prohibits certain acts relating to partnerships unless all the partners approve the acts or have abandoned the business. These acts include

- assigning the partnership's property in trust for creditors or on the assignee's promise to pay the partnership's debts
- disposing of the goodwill of the business
- doing any other act that would make it impossible to carry on the ordinary business of the partnership
- confessing a judgment
- submitting a partnership claim or liability to arbitration

## Partnership Assets

Partners own partnership property as "tenants in partnership." Like joint tenancy or tenancy in common, a **tenancy in partnership** is a form of owning property by more than one individual. The elements of a tenancy in partnership are defined by section 25 of the Uniform Partnership Act as follows:

- Each partner has an equal right to possess specific partnership property for partnership purposes.
- A partner's right in that property is not assignable unless connected with the assignment of rights of all the partners.
- A partner's right in specific partnership property is not subject to attachment (including garnishment) for a partner's individual debts and cannot be claimed under homestead or exemption laws.
- When a partner dies, the partnership property vests in the surviving partners and no interest passes to the deceased partner's heirs, unless the deceased was the last surviving partner.

- A partner's right in specific partnership property is not subject to dower, curtesy, or allowances to widows, heirs, or next of kin.

Agreement between the partners can modify any of the above elements, but if no modifications exist, the partners are tenants in partnership with the above limitations on their personal interest in the partnership property.

The purpose of creating a tenancy in partnership is to give partnerships the ability to continue ownership and the use of their assets despite the financial difficulties of any one partner.

---

EXAMPLES
- Tom Ernst, a partner in Acme Company, has a $40,000 judgment against him resulting from a debt unrelated to his association with Acme Company. The judgment creditor secures a writ of garnishment from the court, which is served on State Bank. Ernst has no accounts at State Bank, but Acme Company has a demand account with $60,000 in it, which it needs for day-to-day business.

  State Bank is required to disclose any property it holds of the debtor Ernst, but should not disclose the $60,000 in Acme Company's account or withdraw the funds, because the company's property is not subject to garnishments arising out of judgments against individual partners.

- Widget Machine Company has five partners, five machines, and a profit and surplus for the year of $500,000.

  No one of the partners has any individual interest in or right to any of the machines, but each has a right to $100,000, which is his or her share of the profit and surplus generated by the machines.

---

Of particular interest to banks is the inability of a partner to assign his or her interest in partnership property as security or collateral for individual debts.

---

EXAMPLE
- Samantha Jones is a partner in a construction business that owns

equipment worth $5 million, generating a current year's income of $500,000. Jones applies for a $50,000 loan from First National Bank and offers as security her interest in the partnership equipment.

In this example, First National Bank should refuse to take the security offered, because, upon a default, it could not repossess any of the partnership equipment. However, the bank could take an assignment of Jones's interest in business profits and surplus, which it could claim upon a default in Jones's loan.

## Partnership Contributions, Income, Losses, and Management

Section 18 of the Uniform Partnership Act provides that, unless the partners of a partnership agree otherwise (usually in their articles of partnership), they will share equally in the profits and surplus of the partnership. (Profits and surplus are funds left after the partnership pays its liabilities.) The Uniform Partnership Act mandates the equal division of the profits and surplus no matter what contributions individual partners have made. Such contributions are usually advanced by individual partners to start up the partnership's business or to maintain it when income is low.

EXAMPLE ■ Jose, Peter, and William decide to start a soybean-processing business. Jose contributes $200,000 in cash to start up the business. Peter and William each contribute $100,000. The business succeeds and, at the end of the first year, its profits and surplus after payment of all its liabilities except partners' contributions are $1 million.

According to the Uniform Partnership Act and because their articles of partnership or other agreements do not provide otherwise, the three partners must divide the $1 million as follows: $400,000 to Jose, $300,000 to Peter, and $300,000 to William. These payments would pay each of the partner's initial contribution plus his equal share of the partnership's profits and surplus. By agreement, the partners could have divided profits and surplus in proportion to their contributions, which many partnerships do. In that case, payments would have been

$500,000 to Jose, $250,000 to Peter, and $250,000 to William.

Knowledge of how a partnership's profits and surplus are divided is important to a bank extending a loan to any one partner.

EXAMPLE ■ Phyllis O'Connor, a partner in a three-person partnership, requested a $50,000 loan from Third State Bank and agreed to give as collateral her interest in the profits and surplus of the partnership. She showed the bank the partnership's financial statements for a previous year, when profits and surplus were $210,000.

To decide whether to make the loan, the bank should review the partnership's articles of partnership and other agreements to determine the percentage of partnership profits and surplus to which O'Connor is entitled. If these documents are silent about partner division of profit and surplus, then the law requires equal division assuming equal contribution, namely $70,000 to each partner.

Another feature of partnerships is a partner's personal liability for losses sustained by the partnership. A partner's personal liability is in proportion to his or her share of profits. For example, if a partner's share of profits and surplus is 33.3 percent, that partner would be personally liable to the other partners for that percentage of the partnership's losses.

EXAMPLE ■ A three-person partnership had $60,000 in liabilities it could not pay. Their articles of partnership stipulated equal division of profit and surplus. Each of the partners contributed $20,000 of personal funds to pay the liabilities.

Section 18 of the Uniform Partnership Act requires partners to share losses in the same proportion as they share profits and surplus, unless the partners agree otherwise.

---

EXAMPLE ■ A partnership composed of Francesca, Sven, and Riley has articles of partnership wherein it is agreed Francesca shall receive 50 percent of the profits and surplus and Sven and Riley will each receive 25 percent. The articles are silent about losses. In the previous year, the partnership lost $100,000.

In this example, Francesca would be personally liable to the partners for $50,000 of the loss and her two partners would each be personally liable to the partners for $25,000 of the loss.

---

As long as partners abide by the Uniform Partnership Act or agreements among themselves about personal liability for payment of the partnership's losses, no problems should develop. But what happens in situations in which a partner refuses or is unable to pay his or her share of a liability?

---

EXAMPLE ■ In the previous example, Francesca is unable to pay any part of the $100,000 loss. The creditors demand payment in full from Sven and Riley. Since partners are jointly liable for all of a partnership's losses, Sven and Riley will have to pay the entire $100,000 loss.

---

If any part of a loss results from tortious conduct of the partnership, such as negligence, fraud, or embezzlement, partner liability is both "joint" and "joint and several." The difference between "joint" and "joint and several" liabilty is illustrated in the following example.

---

EXAMPLE ■ Of the $100,000 loss suffered by the Francesca, Sven, and Riley partnership, $60,000 resulted from a debt owed Centerville Bank and $40,000 from a claim stemming from an accident Riley caused while driving the partnership's car on business for the partnership. In this situation, the partners are jointly liable for the $60,000 debt and jointly and severally liable for the $40,000 debt.

---

If the partnership does not pay the contract debt, Centerville Bank will have to sue the partnership, because the liability is joint and no suit could be started solely against any one of the partners. But the individual claiming the $40,000 debt because of Riley's negligence can sue both the partnership and/or each of the partners individually, because they are jointly and severally liable for that debt. (The term "severally" means distinct, apart from the others.)

---

EXAMPLE ■ After investigation, Polaski, the party harmed in the accident with Riley, determines that the partnership has no assets, Francesca cannot be found, and Riley has no assets. He decides to sue only Sven for the $40,000 damages he suffered. Polaski's attempt to collect the debt from Sven alone is proper because Sven is severally liable for the debt, as well as jointly liable with Francesca and Riley. However, because the partners are only jointly liable for the debt to Centerville Bank, the bank must take its legal action against all three partners doing business as a partnership.

The importance of the difference between the suits brought by Polaski and Centerville Bank becomes clear once the judgments are entered. Upon obtaining a judgment, Polaski can proceed directly against Sven's personal assets to satisfy his judgment for $40,000. In some states, Centerville Bank, after obtaining its judgment against the partnership, must first proceed against the partnership to collect its judgment of $60,000. If it is unable to collect its judgment from the partnership's "property," Centerville Bank may then proceed against the partners' individual assets. Partnership "assets" include its property and the partners' contributions necessary for the payment of partnership liabilities.

---

As with profits, surplus, and losses, the Uniform Partnership Act or an agreement between the parties controls the management of partnerships. The Uniform Partnership Act provides for a majority of the partners to make the managerial decisions on ordinary matters, unless an agreement between the partners states otherwise.

---

EXAMPLE ■ Widget Company is a partnership with five partners. Its articles of partnership require four partners to consent to any managerial decision. Three of the partners request an $80,000 loan for the partnership from Third National Bank, which has a copy of Widget's articles of partnership in the partnership credit file. Relying on the Uniform Partnership Act, Third National makes the loan. Subsequently, the loan goes into default, the partnership goes out of business, and none of the three partners who executed the loan documents has any personal assets with which to pay the loan. The bank sues the two partners who neither made the loan application nor signed the loan documents.

Unless Third National can prove that the two partners knew of the loan, were aware of the partnership's use of the funds, and consented to such use, the two partners will not be liable for the debt. In this partnership, three partners could not bind the partnership to a debt, and this limitation was apparent in the articles of partnership, a copy of which the bank had.

---

Under the Uniform Partnership Act and by agreement, partnership management is not affected by either the proportion of profits and surplus a partner has a right to receive or by the proportion of losses a partner is obligated to pay.

---

EXAMPLE ■ Grady, Centille, and Ford created a partnership. Their initial investment was $600,000—$400,000 from Grady, $100,000 from Centille, and $100,000 from Ford. The articles of partnership divided the profits, surplus, and losses of the partnership in the same proportions as the initial investment—two-thirds to Grady and one-sixth each to Centille and Ford. The articles did not mention the number of partners required to make decisions. In this situation, the Uniform Partnership Act would mandate that a majority of the partners, two, could make decisions on ordinary matters for the partnership.

## Limited Partnerships

Probably the most discouraging element of partnership law is the personal liability that can be incurred for a partner's acts. This concern for personal liability is particularly appropriate where a partner's role is limited to investment, with no active managerial role.

To avoid personal liability, many people entering a business form a corporation. (Later, this chapter will discuss the corporate "shield" that protects shareholders from personal liability.) Sometimes, however, incorporating is not advantageous to a business enterprise for tax and other reasons. In those situations, the business may want to take the form of a "limited partnership."

The object of a **limited partnership** is to enable one or more individuals to invest money in a partnership business without being exposed to liability for partnership debts beyond the amount of their investments.

In most states, the Uniform Limited Partnership Act or some variation of it governs limited partnerships. Article 3, section 303 of the Uniform Limited Partnership Act (amended 1985) provides that a limited partner is not liable for the limited partnership obligations unless one or more of the following conditions exist:

■ He or she is also a general partner.

■ He or she participates in the control of the business. (Under this provision, liability of the limited partner only extends to persons who transact business with the limited partnership and reasonably believe, based on the limited partner's conduct, that he or she is a general partner.)

- The limited partner knowingly permits his or her name to be used in the limited partnership's name. (Liability of the limited partner extends to any creditor who makes loans without actual knowledge that the limited partner is not a general partner.)

To qualify as a limited partnership under the Uniform Limited Partnership Act, one must file a certificate of limited partnership in the office of the state's secretary of state. This certificate must state

- the name of the limited partnership (which must include the words "limited partnership")
- the office address and name and address of the agent for service of process
- the name and business address of each general partner
- the latest date upon which the limited partnership is to dissolve
- any other matters the general partners determine to include

The certificate is a public record and is considered "constructive" notice to the world that the partnership is a limited partnership and that the persons designated are general partners.

## Case for Discussion

### WEST SIDE BANK v. MARTINEZ

#### Facts

Agnes Page applies for a loan at West Side Bank for $100,000. She plans to use the loan in Myriad Gadgets International, a manufacturing business she owns with Thomas Martinez as a partnership. Martinez is a long-standing customer of the bank and has great personal wealth.

The bank makes the loan because it believes that, even if the partnership cannot repay the loan, Martinez's personal liability for the partnership debt assures payment. Page, however, fails to inform the bank that Martinez is a limited partner. The bank also fails to check the public record where a certificate of limited partnership is on file.

Later, the loan is not repaid, neither the partnership nor Page has any funds, and the bank demands payment from Martinez. He refuses and the bank sues him.

### Decision

The court would probably decide that Martinez does not have to pay the loan. As a limited partner in Myriad Gadgets, he has no personal liability for the business. If the bank had checked the public records where certificates of limited partnership are recorded, it could have avoided the loss.

West Side Bank might be able to salvage the situation if it could show that, despite his status as a limited partner, Martinez took part in the control of the business, making the bank reasonably believe he was a general partner. West Side Bank could then hold Martinez personally liable for the loan made to the partnership, which the bank could not otherwise collect. Under those circumstances, because of his activity in the business, Martinez would have forfeited the protection of his status as a limited partner.

### Questions for Discussion

1. Describe at least two ways the bank could prove that Martinez took part in the control of the business.
2. What steps should banks always take to determine a partner's liability for partnership debts?

---

## CORPORATIONS

A **corporation** is an entity legally separate from the people who own, manage, and work for it, to a much greater extent than sole proprietorships or partnerships. Unlike a sole proprietorship or partnership, a corporation is considered a separate legal person. It has the rights and responsibilities of an individual person, including buying and selling property, entering into contracts (such as deposit and loan agreements with banks), being sued and suing in courts, and even being convicted of a crime.

---

**EXAMPLE** ■ David Wolf borrowed $15,000 at First City Bank, a banking corporation, and was charged 30 percent interest. The criminal usury rate in the state in which the bank is located is 25 percent.

In this situation, the bank itself could be charged with criminal usury. While the corporation could not, of course, be imprisoned for the crime, it could be fined.

## Limited Liability

Probably the best known reason for operating a business as a corporation is the limited liability it affords its owners. The owners of a corporation are called shareholders and they usually have no liability beyond the investment they initially make in the corporation to purchase their shares.

EXAMPLE ■ Donald Hall purchases 85 shares of Gimmick, Inc., for $850. One year later, owing its creditors $3,000, the corporation goes out of business. While Hall looses his $850 investment, he is not personally liable to the corporation's creditors for any of the $3,000 in debts owed them.

Comparing this situation with a similar scenario involving a sole proprietorship or a partnership, one can clearly see the liability protection offered by a corporation.

EXAMPLES ■ Sam Johnson operated XYZ Company, a sole proprietorship he had purchased for $850. Within one year, the business failed, owing its creditors $3,000. Johnson not only lost his $850 purchase price but also had to pay the $3,000 debt personally.

■ Frank O'Hare operated a partnership with his brother Pat, in which he invested $850 at its inception. The business failed, owing its creditors $3,000, and Pat had no money. Frank lost his $850 investment and also had to pay the $3,000 debt personally.

While incorporation offers limited liability to a corporation's shareholders, directors, and officers, that limitation is not absolute. Courts have the power to disregard the separate personality of a corporation and hold its shareholders, officers, and directors personally liable if they abuse the corporate form.

If those dealing with a corporation demand the personal guarantee of corporate debt, the protection afforded by the corporate form will also be lost. Such demands are common, particularly by those dealing with corporations regularly, such as banks.

In addition to limited liability, other equally important reasons for incorporating involve tax planning; ability to raise capital; perpetual life if desired, unaffected by the death of a firm member; and ease of transferring ownership.

As stated, shareholders of a corporation typically enjoy significant limitations on personal liability for corporate obligations. However, principal stockholders of a bank may be exposed to greater personal liability than shareholders of other corporations. Shareholders directly or indirectly controlling five or more percent of a bank's stock are, for many purposes, considered "insiders" with fiduciary resonsibilities to the bank and its other shareholders.

## Organization of a Corporation

Once an individual or group decides to conduct a business as a corporation, the first step is to consult the laws of the state in which the business is to be incorporated. The Committee on Corporate Laws of the American Bar Association has drafted a Model Business Corporation Act and proposed it to the states for adoption, but it has not been as widely adopted in total as either the Uniform Commercial Code or the Uniform Partnership Act. Thus, state laws governing corporations vary more from state to state than those governing commercial transactions or partnerships.

Despite state variations in the laws governing corporations, in many respects these laws are similar. The first requirement for organizing a corporation is to draft corporate articles of incorporation and file them with the proper state authorities. Although some state laws require other details, **articles of incorporation** usually furnish the following information:

[handwritten note: Not in NYS. We have a certificate of incorporation.]

- the name of the corporation

- the name and address of each incorporator

- the broad purposes or objectives of the corporation

- the street address of its principal office and the name of its registered agent
- the length of time it is to last
- the number of shares the corporation is authorized to issue
- the par value of its common stock
- a statement about the preferred stock, if any is to be issued

*[Handwritten note: Most of the time in NYS - the attorney who files certificate is the incorporator.]*

Incorporators are the individuals wishing to start a corporation, and often they compose a corporation's first board of directors. Generally, the incorporators must sign the articles of incorporation. Once the articles have been drafted and signed, they are then filed in a public office, the identity of which varies from state to state.

Officials of the office where the articles are filed review them for compliance with state law. If the articles are approved, the state usually issues a certificate of incorporation or charter. The incorporators then hold their first meeting to elect directors and adopt bylaws for the conduct of the corporation's internal affairs. After the directors have appointed the necessary officers and agents, the corporation generally can transact business, although some state laws provide that corporations cannot begin business until a certain portion of the capital has been paid into the corporate treasury in cash.

Banks dealing with customers claiming to do business as corporations should assure themselves that such is the case. Many banks have unwittingly helped dishonest individuals who request a corporate checking account and issue checks without sufficient funds on deposit. Such individuals rely on the "official" look of a corporate check to lull payees into accepting checks they would not otherwise take.

---

EXAMPLE ■ With a deposit of $400, Dennis Huntley establishes a checking account in the name of "Conglomerate Enterprises Corporation" at First National Bank and orders the bank's most impressive checks. Within a month, the bank returns checks totaling $25,000, drawn on the account without sufficient funds.

Had the bank required Huntley to provide a copy of his "corporation's" articles and certificate of incorporation, he would not have been able to do so, and the checking account would never have been set up.

**Stock**  Once a corporation receives its certificates of incorporation and holds its first meeting, it may issue stock to its incorporators. **Stock** is nothing more than a document certifying that its holder owns an interest in a corporation.

EXAMPLE ■ Pete, George, Henry, and Victor incorporated a business whose articles indicated the corporation had 50,000 shares. Each of the incorporators subscribed to 12,500 shares and each was issued one certificate representing 12,500 shares of the corporation.

To become a stockholder in a corporation, a person must either subscribe to its stock (purchase stock when the corporation first issues it) or purchase outstanding stock (stock that has already been issued to another subscriber).

*Close Corporations*  Issuance of stock is a relatively simple transaction if the corporation is a "close" and not a "publicly held" corporation. A **close corporation** is one whose stock is not generally traded in the securities markets, such as the New York or American Stock Exchanges. Often, the shareholders of a close corporation consist of the management of the corporation, with perhaps only one or two shareholders who are investors.

EXAMPLE ■ Tom Jones is an inventor who has developed a new method for producing wrenches. His brother-in-law, Herb Harris, is willing to invest in Jones's invention. They form a corporation called "Nu-Wrench, Inc.," and issue stock to themselves and their wives. No stock is sold to anyone other than Jones, Harris, and their spouses.

---

While most close corporations are small enterprises, a number of large corporations whose stock is held by a few shareholders and not traded in securities markets do exist. Members of the Ford family exclusively owned stock in the Ford Motor Company until the company went "public" in 1955.

As long as the transactions are isolated and few in number, a close corporation may sell its stock with little concern for state or federal securities laws and regulations.

---

EXAMPLE ■ The facts are the same as in the previous example. Nu-Wrench, Inc., does very well and soon needs an additional manager. Sam Baker is hired and, as part of his compensation, receives 100 shares of the corporation.

---

In their dealings with close corporations (which make up most of the corporations in the United States), banks must be aware that incorporation does not make a business any more creditworthy than one that is not incorporated. In fact, because of the limited liability of a corporation's stockholders, officers, and directors, a corporation's creditworthiness may be more suspect than that of a sole proprietorship or partnership.

Personal guaranties and cosignatures are the methods most banks use to overcome the problem of security in lending to close corporations with limited assets or income. This chapter discusses both topics more fully under the sections entitled "Sureties" and "Guaranties," but the following example illustrates the use of the terms.

---

EXAMPLE ■ James Brothers, Inc., applies to Third State Bank for a $50,000 capital improvement loan. The bank reviews the loan application and notes that the business is relatively new and its assets and income are relatively small. The bank also reviews the personal financial statements of the corporation's only shareholders, Andrew and William James, and notes that individually they have sizeable amounts of assets and income.

In this example, the bank would no doubt deny the corporation's loan application but would make a counteroffer to lend the corporation the money if the James brothers either cosigned the loan with the corporation or personally guaranteed the loan, thus making their personal assets and income available to the bank if the corporation could not repay the debt.

---

Most banks have the principal shareholders, officers, and directors cosign or personally guarantee loans to closely held corporations. In fact, in most situations involving loans to close corporations, the failure to obtain such cosignatures or personal guaranties may be considered an unsound banking practice. At one time, it was common practice for banks to require the spouses of such individuals to guarantee close corporate debt. However, as more fully discussed in chapter 8, such a requirement now could well be a violation of the Equal Credit Opportunity Act.

*Publicly Held Corporations*

Corporations wishing to expand their operations often sell large amounts of their stock to raise money for such expansion.

---

EXAMPLE ■ Toys Unlimited, Inc., is a close corporation. Its stock is owned entirely by three shareholders who are also the officers and directors of the corporation. Toys Unlimited finds that the demand for its products has outstripped its ability to produce them, and it must expand.

The shareholders initially talk to several banks about loans to pay the cost of the expansion but find the loan terms unacceptable, especially the requirement that the loan be on an installment basis with payments to begin almost immediately.

The corporation then considers selling shares of stock to the general public to raise money and decides to sell 49 percent of the authorized shares of the company and keep 51 percent. The corporation can use the money from the stock for the expansion, no interest will be due, and the company will not have to pay dividends until it makes a profit. Thus, Toys Unlimited, Inc., is transformed from a close corporation to a publicly held corporation.

---

Any time a corporation sells its shares publicly, it brings itself within federal and/or state securities laws and regulations designed to protect the stock-buying public.

State laws and regulations that regulate the issuance and sale of securities are labeled **blue-sky laws** and, like federal law, were drafted to assure that those purchasing stock receive more than "blue sky" for their money. Blue-sky legislation requires corporations and securities dealers acting on their behalf to file with the state an application for permission to sell the stock. This application must contain detailed information about the nature and powers of the issuing company, its properties, business, and stock issues. The proper state authority, which grants permission to sell stock upon certain conditions, then examines the application. If securities are sold without complying with the law, the seller can incur severe penalties, including the voiding of the sales of the securities, fines, and imprisonment.

The **Securities Act of 1933** regulates the issuance and sale of securities. This act does not forbid the issuance of any particular type of stock but merely requires the issuer to make truthful disclosures of all the relevant facts in an approved registration statement. The act applies whenever a public offering of a substantial amount of securities will be sold in interstate commerce or sent through the mail. The prospectus used in selling stock to investors must fully disclose all relevant facts.

A seller cannot solicit prospective purchasers, except orally, until they have received the required prospectus. A **prospectus** is a detailed statement that describes the securities to be sold and the corporation issuing them, and contains other required information to help the public make an intelligent decision about purchasing the stock.

The **Securities Exchange Act of 1934** protects investors in corporate securities. This act regulates the exchanges, such as the New York and Chicago Stock Exchanges, where securities are bought and sold. Under this act, any corporation whose securities are listed on any of these exchanges must provide annual reports to the Securities and Exchange Commission. The purpose of the reports is to ensure that both the commission and the investing public have adequate information on the nature of the securities handled on the exchange.

Once a corporation becomes publicly held, banks deal with it more as a truly separate entity from its shareholders than when dealing with a close corporation. **Publicly held corporations** usually have sufficient assets and income to justify loans without personal guaranties by their shareholders, officers, or directors. Since their interests are limited to those of investors, few shareholders of publicly held corporations become involved in the management of such corporations.

## *Stock Transfers*

Whether a corporation is closely or publicly held, its stock is usually subject to transfer. A stock certificate generally has a form printed on its back, detailing the parties to the transfer or sale. The form often looks like this:

FOR VALUE RECEIVED, _____ hereby sell, assign, and transfer unto _____, _____ shares of Common Stock represented by the within Certificate, and do hereby appoint _____ attorney to transfer the said shares on the books of the within named Corporation with full power of substitution in the premises.

Dated: \_\_\_\_\_, 19\_\_

In presence of:

_____  _____

In making a sale, the present owner or transferor usually signs at the bottom, leaving blank the space for the new owner or assignee. The new owner may fill his or her name in this blank, thereby obtaining the right to the new stock certificate. On the other hand, the new owner, without filling in this space, may sell the certificate. In that case, the buyer can complete the blank and acquire the new certificate.

When the form on the back of the stock certificate is completed, the new owner sends the certificate to the corporation that issued it. Usually the corporation has delegated the job of handling its stock transfers to a transfer agent, often a bank. This agent receives the stock certificate, cancels it, and issues a new certificate in the name of the assignee whose name appears in the appropriate space on the back of the original certificate. The assignee's name is then registered on the corporation's books and the prior owner's name is deleted.

Although registration of the new holder's name on the corporation's books is unnecessary to pass title of the stock certificate to that person, the new owner is not entitled to be treated as a stockholder by the corporation until this registration occurs. In other words, without notice of any changes, the corporation must assume that only those people registered on its books are its stockholders, entitled to receive stockholders' notices and dividends and to vote the shares.

Article 8 of the Uniform Commercial Code governs the transfer of publicly traded securities. The article also regulates the issuance, purchase, and registration of such securities in most states.

## *Bank Holding Companies*

As mentioned in chapter 2, virtually all banks in the United States are corporations chartered by either a state or the federal government and owned by shareholders. However, a shareholder itself can be a corporation. Under the federal Bank Holding Company Act, any corporation that owns more than 25 percent of a bank's stock is a **bank holding company** (12 U.S.C. § 1841). When a bank holding company purchases the shares of a bank that bank is referred to as a **subsidiary** of the holding company. A bank holding company, under federal law, can have one or many subsidiary banks. In a multibank holding company the individual banks are referred to as **affiliates** of each other.

## Shareholders

The shareholders of a corporation have certain rights and responsibilities, including attending and voting at shareholder meetings and receiving dividends.

### *Shareholder Meetings*

In general, shareholders cannot act for the corporation except at shareholder meetings, at which their business is normally limited to electing directors, adopting and amending bylaws, amending articles, and hearing official reports on the condition of the corporation. An individual shareholder—even a majority shareholder—normally cannot bind the corporation to any transaction simply because he or she is a shareholder.

---

EXAMPLE ■ Ken Sawyer owns 98 percent of the shares of the Star Tool Corporation but is neither an officer nor a director of the corporation. Without the board's approval or any officer's consent, he applied for and received a loan from New Local Bank for this corporation. He also executed a promissory note on behalf of the corporation but used the proceeds for his own benefit.

Star Tool Corporation is not liable for repayment of the debt because Sawyer, as a mere shareholder, does not have authority to act for it. The corporation is a legal entity separate and apart from Sawyer, and is controlled by a board of directors and officers, not Sawyer. New Local Bank could have avoided the problem if it had required a corporate borrowing resolution from the corporation. Such a resolution is usually passed by a corporation's board of directors, and it specifies who may sign loan documents on the corporation's behalf. The resolution may then be kept in the corporation's loan files at the various banks with which it does business.

---

## Shareholder Rights

In addition to attending and voting at shareholder meetings, shareholders have other rights. From a shareholder's point of view, the most important is the right to receive dividends. **Dividends** are that portion of a corporation's profits paid to its shareholders. Dividends are not payable except when the corporation has profits or a surplus and its directors decide that dividends should be declared. Although the corporation may have a surplus out of which it clearly could and perhaps ought to pay dividends, a stockholder has no absolute right to payment until the directors declare a dividend. If directors unreasonably withhold a dividend, shareholders can take certain legal steps to force the board to declare a dividend. However, court-ordered dividends are difficult to obtain because courts are reluctant to replace managerial decisions of a board with their own.

To prevail upon a court to order a corporation to pay dividends, shareholders must prove that the corporation is accumulating earnings beyond those necessary to meet the reasonable requirements of the business. Proof can be obtained only by a close inspection of a corporation's financial records. A shareholder has the right to inspect the corporation's books, provided the request is made in good faith for inspection at a reasonable time and place. In exercising this right, the shareholder cannot unduly harass those conducting the corporation's business.

**Ultra vires acts** are those beyond the scope of the corporation as set forth in its articles of incorporation. Shareholders have the right to restrain ultra vires acts to protect a corporation from the wrongful acts of its officers or directors.

---

**EXAMPLE** ■ Developers, Inc., is a corporation whose articles of incorporation limit its scope to the acquisition, development, and sale of residential real estate. Several years after its incorporation, corporate officers recommend that the corporation purchase a business that manufactures space industry components. Its board of directors agrees.

The shareholders of Developers, Inc., have a right to demand that the corporation not make the business purchase because it is beyond the scope of the corporation and, thus, is an ultra vires act.

---

In addition to requiring that a corporation stay within the scope of authority set forth in its articles of incorporation, shareholders have the right to bring suits on the corporation's behalf against officers or directors who abuse their responsibilities to the corporation. Shareholders can also recover monetary damages from officers or directors whose abuses have caused losses to the corporation.

EXAMPLE ■ Northwestern State Bank foreclosed on a hunting lodge, to which it acquired title as a result of the foreclosure. The lodge was appraised at $500,000. The balance on its mortgage was $350,000. Without offering the lodge for public sale after acquiring title to it, the bank's board of directors voted to sell the lodge to five of its members for $350,000. John Lyon, a shareholder who was not a member of the board, heard of the transaction and began a suit for $150,000 in the bank's name against the board members as individuals. John Lyon has brought what is commonly called a shareholder derivative suit, which would probably succeed.

## *Shareholder Liability*

One of the most attractive aspects of a business operated as a corporation is that shareholders are not liable for corporate obligations. This aspect is especially appealing to individuals who wish to invest in a business but have no intention of taking an active part in its management. These individuals are willing to risk a limited amount of money on the management skills of others but are unwilling to risk their entire financial worth.

EXAMPLE ■ Gene Rous, a wealthy banker, is interested in helping his son Ron start a business. Gene invests $20,000 in the business and emphatically tells Ron that this will be the limit of his investment. In return for the investment, Ron gives Gene 100 shares of the corporation's 200 shares of stock and retains the other half. The business flounders and, without paying $50,000 in corporation debts, Ron leaves for Timbuktu. The corporation's creditors demand payment from Gene.

As a shareholder, Gene has no liability for the corporation's debts. If corporate assets existed, they would first be used to pay creditors of the business and then its shareholders.

While shareholders usually are not held personally liable for a corporation's debts, exceptional situations do arise when, because of wrongful conduct, the "corporate veil" is pierced and shareholders become personally liable for corporate debts. Such liability can arise when a corporation is underfunded, when a corporate entity is used to evade an obligation or statute to perpetrate a fraud or commit an injustice, or when its identity as a separate entity has been ignored.

**EXAMPLE** To avoid personal liability for potential negligence cases and liability insurance premiums, Abdul Mousavi, a cab owner, set up a corporation and sold his cab to the corporation. Mousavi filed the corporation's articles with the state in which the business was located but thereafter treated the cab business as a sole proprietorship. He set up no separate books for the corporation, treated its income as his own, never issued stock, held no annual meetings, and never filed corporate tax returns. Mousavi's cab was involved in an accident and a pedestrian was severely injured as a result of Mousavi's negligence. The pedestrian sued Mousavi personally.

A court would very likely pierce the corporate veil and hold Mousavi personally liable for the damages suffered by the pedestrian because he never treated the corporation as a separate entity and created it solely to avoid his responsibility to others.

## Board of Directors

Most corporations have a board of directors whose responsibilities include establishing corporate policy, approving major transactions, and appointing and supervising corporate officers, who in turn have day-to-day responsibility for the corporation.

A few states permit corporations to exist without a board of directors or officers, leaving management of the corporation to the shareholders. Corporations taking advantage of such statutes are those whose shares are all owned by one or a small number of shareholders who, without the statute, would be the corporation's directors and officers, as well as its shareholders.

As mentioned, most corporations have a board of directors elected by the corporation's shareholders. In electing directors, shareholders usually vote their shares either one-share, one-vote, or by cumulative voting. Statutes or articles of incorporation often prescribe cumulative voting for directors to assure minority representation on a corporation's board of directors. This method of voting permits each stockholder to have as many votes as shares of stock owned, multiplied by the number of directors to be elected at the meeting. The stockholder may cast all votes for one candidate or divide them among the candidates in any amount desired. If five directors are to be elected, a stockholder may concentrate votes on one or two of the five candidates but is not compelled to vote for each.

EXAMPLE ■ First National Bank has 100,000 outstanding shares; 60,000 shares are owned by one stockholder, and the other 40,000 shares are owned by various other shareholders. The shareholders are to elect five directors. The shareholder with 60,000 shares will have 300,000 votes, while the remaining shareholders will have a total of 200,000 votes. Under cumulative voting, a shareholder may give any one or more candidates any portion of his or her total votes.

In this example, the minority shareholders, if they vote together, will assure themselves of two seats on the corporation's board of directors. By concentrating their votes on two board seats, the minority shareholders can vote 100,000 for each and thus assure their election. A one-share, one-vote system would preclude minority representation on the board since the majority shareholder would be able to vote 60,000 shares for each of the five candidates while the minority shareholders could vote only 40,000 for each board seat.

While most states leave the decision whether to use cumulative voting to each corporation, national banks must allow shareholders the ability to elect their directors by cumulative voting (12 U.S.C. § 61).

Once elected to a corporation's board of directors, a board member has power over the corporation's officers only to the extent that the board takes action as a group.

**EXAMPLES** ■ Judith Churchill is elected to New London State Bank's board of directors. The day after her election she informs the bank's head teller that he is fired.

Churchill has no authority to fire the head teller or anyone else or, for that matter, to take any individual action regarding the bank unless the board as a whole specifically delegates a particular power to her. In this example, had Churchill fired the head teller at the board's request, the action would have been valid.

■ Phyllis Yates, a director of Pottery Producers, Inc., requests a loan for the corporation from New Rochelle State Bank, which the bank agrees to make. Yates takes the loan proceeds and leaves the country. When Pottery Producers, Inc., refuses to pay off the loan the bank sues the company.

Unless Yates received the authority to borrow money for the corporation by board action, the bank will lose its suit. A director acting individually has no authority to bind a corporation to any transaction. If the bank could show that the corporation knowingly used the money, then the bank could argue that Yate's activities on the corporation's behalf were ratified, and the corporation would be liable for the debt. If the bank could also show that over many years Yates had borrowed money on the corporation's behalf which it repaid, the bank might succeed based on the implied agency agreement between Yates and the corporation.

---

Boards of directors often appoint committees that meet separately to consider matters that require more detailed review than time permits the full board. Typically, such committees make recommendations to the full board, which is responsible for final decisions. Bank board committees often include the following committees:

*Audit Committee.* This committee evaluates management's compliance with board policy, laws, and regulations by reviewing reports of inside and outside auditors and bank regulatory examiners.

*Loan Committee.* This committee formulates and monitors compliance with policy, laws, and regulations applicable to loans, including lending limits and insider loan restrictions. It also reviews loan requests referred by management, particularly requests for amounts beyond the loan officer's lending limit.

*Investment/Asset-Liability Committee.* This committee assures management's compliance with board investment policy. It also examines portfolio diversification, asset quality, liquidity, and profitability.

*Trust Committee.* This committee oversees the trust department to assure compliance with the laws and regulations governing trusts and reviews the types of services to be offered, investment procedures, and fees.

In addition to the above, other committees can be appointed by the board on a permanent ot temporary basis, depending on board needs.

*Duties and Responsibilities of Directors*

Directors of corporations, and particularly of banks, have extremely responsible positions. Failure to meet those responsibilities can result in removal from the board and personal liability. Perhaps a board's most important duty is appointing officers who are qualified to manage the corporation's business. Directors need not, and probably should not, involve themselves in the day-to-day operation of corporations, but they must be aware of and approve major transactions.

---

EXAMPLE ■ Jonesville State Bank permits its loan officers to approve loans up to $40,000 without board approval; loans over that amount must have board approval.

---

To supervise a corporation properly, directors must spend enough time to become familiar with its business and ongoing financial condition. Larger corporations, including banks, employ both internal and outside auditors to continually monitor the corporation's financial condition for the board of directors.

Directors establish a corporation's policy and objectives, which its officers and employees then follow. Corporate policy and objectives on such topics as profit planning, budgeting, and personnel policies are needed for any size corporation. Directors are also responsible for a corporation's compliance with the laws and regulations governing the business in which the corporation is engaged.

Directors must avoid self-serving practices, including the use of corporate assets for personal gain, competition with the corporation for personal gain, excessive compensation, appropriation of corporate opportunity, and failure to be loyal to the corporation.

---

**EXAMPLE** ■ At a board meeting, Donald Green, a director, learns that the bank is considering purchasing property for a branch office. Green quickly negotiates the purchase for his own use. By using inside information, Green has seized a corporate opportunity for his own benefit and could be removed from the board for such a self-serving action.

---

The **duty of loyalty,** which Green violated, is a requirement of directors under common law and many state statutes. In addition, directors have a fiduciary relationship with a corporation and must exercise the duty of due care. This duty has been defined by courts as the duty to exercise the care of a reasonable and prudent person in a similar situation. A violation of the duty of care is well illustrated in the Comptroller of the Currency's volume, *The Director's Book,* as follows:

A bank director learns that the bank's senior loan officer has made repeated loans to a corporate customer greatly exceeding the bank's lending limit. The director confronts the officer about the matter and receives an assurance that the officer will take care of it and that it will not happen again. The director later learns that the corporate customer has received a sizable new loan from the bank, approved by the same lending officer. The director, relying on the senior loan officer's earlier assurances, does nothing. The director's failure to seek reliable confirmation that the loan was within the bank's lending limit would likely be a breach of the director's duty of care which, if violations occurred causing losses, could result in personal liability to the director.

In addition to common law duties, bank directors are subject to myriad statutory and regulatory requirements.

## Liability of Directors

Directors are not directly liable to the stockholders for their misdeeds but rather to the corporation. If directors who are wrongdoers control the corporation so that it will not sue for a loss or injury to itself, the stockholders may institute proceedings against the directors. In such an action, called a shareholder derivative suit, the shareholders demand redress for the corporation, not for themselves, and whatever they recover is for the corporation's benefit.

In managing the corporation's affairs, directors are allowed considerable discretion. Others may question their actions in the exercise of that discretion, but directors nevertheless cannot be held liable if their actions involved no fraud, illegality, or conflict of interest, and they acted in good faith and with reasonable diligence. Nor are they liable if their timidity prevented them from entering into ventures that would have provided profits for the corporation. Directors are bound to exercise reasonable care and judgment in the conduct of corporate business. If they have been negligent in guarding the corporation's welfare, they may be liable for damages directly traceable to such negligence.

A creditor may hold directors liable for failing to pay debts and declaring a dividend while the corporation is insolvent. Likewise, if the directors make false reports to inflate the corporation's financial standing to secure credit that the corporation could not otherwise have obtained, a creditor who was meant to and did act on such a report could hold the directors personally liable.

Personal liability of a bank director is much greater than that of the typical corporate director. This liability has been even further expanded with the passage of the Financial Institutions Reform, Recovery and Enforcement Act of 1989 (FIRREA).

By obtaining liability insurance for their officers and directors, corporations often protect them from lawsuits arising out of their positions with the corporations. These policies will repay corporations for reimbursement of directors' and officers' legal costs defending lawsuits that resulted from their work for the corporations. However, corporations generally can reimburse or indemnify their directors or officers only when their conduct has been proper or a court orders payment. Thus, insurance companies have provided policies that directly pay officers and directors when there will be no corporate reimbursement.

---

**EXAMPLE** ■ State banking authorities charge Jack Van, a vice president for Mid-State Bank, with criminal misapplication of funds. In defending his action in a state criminal court where he is found not guilty, he incurs $20,000 in legal fees.

If Mid-State Bank has liability insurance for its directors and officers, the policy will pay $20,000 to the bank, which then may properly pay Van for costs incurred in the matter. However, if the court found Van guilty and did not order indemnification because there were no mitigating circumstances, the bank could not make the payment to Van and the insurance company would not pay the bank. In such a case, an insurance policy that would pay Van directly could cover his costs.

---

## Corporate Officers

Along with boards of directors, most corporations have officers, although a few states do permit shareholders to manage corporations without a board or officers. The directors of a corporation appoint its officers in conformity with the articles of incorporation and bylaws. If the bylaws do not spell out the officer's powers, the directors may prescribe such powers.

The president of most corporations is usually a member of its board of directors and, in the case of national banks, the president is required to be a director (12 U.S.C. § 76). Usually the president has power to execute contracts, deeds, and other documents. A president cannot, however, transact business outside the corporation's ordinary business without specific authority from the board.

---

**EXAMPLE** ■ In its ordinary course of business, XYZ Corporation buys and sells real estate. Francesca Orlano, its president, executes deeds to parcels of corporate property on an almost daily basis without the board's approval.

The president of Fourth National Bank, Susan Hay, executes a deed conveying the bank's main office to John Jones without the board's approval.

The deeds executed by Orlano, president of XYZ Corporation, are valid and binding on the corporation since selling real estate is part of the ordinary course of the corporation's business. The deed executed by Susan Hay is invalid and not binding on Fourth National, since selling real estate is not within the ordinary course of a bank's business.

---

Although most corporations are required by law to have a president, the appointment of vice presidents is within the discretion of the board of directors. While presidents have inherent authority to transact the day-to-day business of a corporation, vice presidents have no more authority than is expressly granted by corporate bylaws or board resolutions. Normally the vice president takes the president's place when the president is absent. In large corporations, vice presidents often preside over a special department of the business. Such corporations often have several vice presidents, known as first vice president, second vice president, and so forth.

In addition to requiring a president, many state statutes require a corporation to appoint a secretary, who must be a person other than the president and must keep the records of the meetings of the directors and stockholders. The secretary also oversees the transfer of the stock certificates on the corporation's books.

A corporation's treasurer administers the corporate funds, bank account, securities, and general assets. The books are kept under the treasurer's supervision, and the treasurer usually countersigns the corporate obligations including contracts, checks and notes. The treasurer also endorses for deposit or collection the checks payable to the corporation.

Many banking corporations do not have a secretary or treasurer and instead combine their functions in the office of cashier. A bank's cashier is the financial manager of the bank, entrusted with the institution's funds and securities. The cashier may also oversee the bank's books, payments, and receipts.

## GOVERNMENTS

Banks do business with various government entities who may be both depositors and borrowers. These entities are separate and distinct legal personalities apart from the elected officials and employees who act on their behalf.

In dealing with such entities, banks must be extremely careful to ascertain that the proposed transactions are within the power not only of the individual representing the entity, but also within the scope of the entity's authority as granted by a state constitution or statute or a municipality's charter. If either of those basic elements is missing, the transaction could easily be declared void and unenforceable.

---

**EXAMPLE** ■ Jon Ernst, a road equipment salesperson, sold an $18,000 power grader to the township of Farmville. He made the sale on a conditional sales contract signed by the town's clerk. Subsequently, Farmville failed to make any payments for the grader. After making repeated demands for payment, Ernst informed the township that the company intended to repossess the grader and to sue for the balance of the debt. He then belatedly discovered that Farmville had no legal authority to enter into a contract for the purchase of road repair equipment and the clerk had no authority to sign documents on the township's behalf.

---

## ESTATES

The term **estate** is defined as the right, title, or interest that a person has in any property, to be distinguished from the property itself.

## Estates of Deceased Persons

When a person who owns real or personal property dies, the property normally will become subject to court administration. Courts administering such estates are often separate from other courts and, depending on the particular state, may be known as probate, surrogate, or orphan's courts.

Courts administer a deceased person's property to ensure that such property is assembled, administered, and distributed as the law directs.

EXAMPLE ■ Ted Johnson, a single man, owns as sole proprietor a hardware business employing 25 people. He also owns a car and a boat and has $50,000 in savings. He dies suddenly of a heart attack.

Upon Johnson's death, all his property comes within the jurisdiction of the court in his state that handles deceased persons' estates. If Johnson left a will, the estate is "testate"; if he left no will, the estate in "intestate."

One of the first steps the court will take is to appoint an **executor** or **administrator** (if a woman is appointed, the titles are often executrix or administratrix) to oversee the estate throughout the **probate** procedure. Many states now use the term **personal representative.** If Johnson left a will, he probably nominated a person or entity (such as a bank trust department) to be named personal representative of his estate. If Johnson left no will, the court will appoint a personal representative or administrator, usually basing its decision on the recommendation of the family of the deceased or an interested party.

The court will issue **letters testamentary** (to an executor) or **letters of administration** (to an administrator), or **letters of authority** (to a personal representative). These legal documents evidence the authority of the appointed person or entity to act on behalf of the estate.

EXAMPLE ■ The facts are the same as in the previous example. However, Fred Johnson, Ted Johnson's brother, was appointed administrator of his brother's estate, since Ted left no will.

Upon his appointment, which would normally occur shortly after the decedent's death, Fred Johnson could assume control of Ted's business, use the savings account to support the business if necessary, and generally control Ted's assets as Ted had done during his lifetime.

Realizing that the hardware business needed funds to meet an upcoming payroll and to purchase merchandise, Fred went to First State Bank where Ted had his savings. By producing the letters of administration, Fred was able to withdraw $10,000 from Ted's account and transfer the balance of the savings into a new account created by the bank and labeled "Ted Johnson Estate Account."

---

An executor, administrator, or personal representative will administer an estate until all the deceased person's affairs, including payment of debts and collection of money due, are completed.

---

EXAMPLE ■ Fred Johnson and the lawyer he retained to probate Ted's estate determined that Lee Do Thi owed Ted $25,000, based on a promissory note they found among Ted's records. They contacted Lee Do Thi who refused to pay.

An executor, administrator, or personal representative has the power and the responsibility to collect money owed decedents. In this situation the estate of Ted Johnson would bring a lawsuit against Lee Do Thi for $25,000.

---

An executor, administrator, or personal representative is also responsible for paying the decedent's debts from the assets of the estate. In many states, the law provides that a notice of the decedent's death be published in a newspaper. This notice should set forth a date by which those having claims against the decedent must submit notice of their claims to the court.

**EXAMPLE** ■ At the time of his death on May 30, 1989, Ted Johnson owed First State Bank $15,000 on an unsecured promissory note. After receiving his letters of administration, Fred Johnson complied with state law and published in the town's newspaper a notice stating that Ted Johnson had died and that anyone with a claim against him had to file a notice of claim by September 1, 1989. After reading the notice on June 15, 1989, Linda Lawson, vice president of First State Bank, filed a notice of claim with the probate court.

Assuming that Ted Johnson's estate has sufficient assets, First State Bank will be fully paid its $15,000 claim before the estate is closed, as will all other creditors who file a notice of claim.

After all the assets of a decedent's estate have been taken into account and claims received and paid, an estate may be closed and the assets may be distributed to those persons named in the decedent's will or, if no will exists, to the decedent's heirs. The property of the estate may then be converted to cash to pay the claims or to obey the request of the heirs.

**EXAMPLE** ■ After a full accounting, including collection of the estate's assets and allowance of claims against it, the administrator, Fred Johnson, finds the claims total $200,000, while the cash amounts to $40,000. To raise cash to pay the claims, Fred arranges for the sale of the decedent's automobile, boat, and hardware business, for a total of $560,000. From these funds Fred, with the court's permission, pays the claims, leaving a balance of $400,000 in cash.

Once debts have been paid, including applicable federal and state taxes and administrative fees, Ted's heirs will receive the balance of the estate.

**EXAMPLE** ■ If Ted Johnson has no will, the court will determine his heirs according to a state statute on descent and distribution. In most states, the heirs of Ted Johnson are as follows (in order of succession):

- children
- grandchildren
- parents
- brothers and sisters
- grandparents, nieces, and nephews

If Ted Johnson had a will, his estate probably would be distributed to those named in the will, whether they were related to him or not. However, in some states, a spouse and minor children cannot be excluded. The spouse and any minor children must receive a specified minimum amount, unless a valid prenuptial agreement exists, in which case the spouse may be excluded from the distribution.

In summary, when a person dies, his or her property becomes an "estate" subject to a court's administration. Until a court terminates and distributes the property interests to the proper persons, the estate continues to have the right to buy and sell property, borrow money, create accounts, sue, and be sued. Banks dealing with individuals or entities who are executors, administrators, or personal representatives must assure themselves that any transactions entered into are within the powers granted by the courts. Further, banks must realize that an individual or entity authorized to act on behalf of an estate assumes no personal liability in doing so, as long as the acts are within the powers granted by the court.

**EXAMPLE** ■ Teri Cambridge is the executrix of her late sister's estate. To pay certain claims, Cambridge, as executrix, signs a promissory note on behalf of the estate for $50,000 to First State Bank. The note becomes delinquent. The bank demands payment and is informed that, because certain stock held by the estate has suffered a severe decline in value, the assets are insufficient to pay the debt. The bank sues the estate and Cambridge. In this situation, the bank will lose in its action against Cambridge, because she did not cosign the note or personally guarantee it.

## Estates of Persons Subject to Guardianship

Besides transactions with decedents' estates, banks also deal with estates of persons subject to guardianship. A **guardian** is a person who has legal authority to care for the person and/or estate of someone who is incompetent. The incompetent person is usually called a **ward** or **legally incapacitated person**.

A ward's property is the estate, and a guardian administers that estate for the ward's benefit according to the requirements of state law. Because of the authority a guardian has over a ward's estate, the appointment and conduct of a guardian are under a court's supervision, unless the relationship between the guardian and the ward is one of parent and child. In that case, a **guardianship by nature** or **natural guardianship** is recognized by law and no court appointment is necessary during a child's minority.

EXAMPLE ▪ Jake Kelly has two daughters, ages 15 and 23. The oldest is mentally retarded to the extent that she is unable to manage her own affairs. Kelly also cares for the 10-year-old son of a deceased friend, who lives with him.

Kelly is the natural guardian of his 15-year-old child because the child is a minor. However, because his 23-year-old child is not a minor, he will need a court appointment to become her guardian. Kelly will also need a court appointment to become guardian of the 10-year-old child living with him if he wishes to administer that child's person and estate.

Once a guardian is appointed, that appointment will continue until the minor ward becomes an adult at an age determined by state law or, if the ward is not a minor, until the guardian dies, resigns, or is removed.

Guardians can be appointed to care for both a ward's person and estate; to protect a ward more fully, some courts prefer separate appointments. In some states, the person appointed to administer the ward's finances is called a **conservator.** Banks and others dealing with a ward's assets must verify that the person transacting business for a ward is a guardian of the ward's estate and not merely a guardian of the ward's person.

EXAMPLE ■ After informing the bank he was Charles Tobin's guardian, a claim he substantiated by showing the bank letters of guardianship, Frank Lee withdrew $10,000 from Charles Tobin's savings account. However, Lee was guardian of Tobin's person only, as stated in the guardianship letters.

The bank is liable to Tobin for the $10,000 withdrawal to which Lee had no right, since his guardianship extended only to Tobin's person, not to his estate.

To avoid the bank's situation in this example, a bank doing business with a guardian should obtain a copy of the court-ordered appointment. A further protection would be to insist that a court officer countersign withdrawals from a guardian's account, if the court would agree to such a procedure.

Guardians of wards' estates are fiduciaries, required to manage estates with the utmost good faith and competence and to avoid promoting their own interests.

EXAMPLE ■ Rob Klein, guardian of the estate of Hortense Harper, realizes that his ward needs more funds to assure proper care so he decides to sell her jewelry. Klein sells the jewelry and buys several pieces for his wife at prices well below their value. Through self-dealing, Klein has abused his fiduciary duty to Harper and, as a result, could be removed as guardian and made to pay fair value for his ward's jewelry.

---

Guardians of wards' estates have the right and responsibility to manage those estates. In that capacity and typically upon court approval, guardians can buy and sell property, invest, open and close bank accounts for the estate, and take any other action the ward could for the estate, as long as the action taken is the result of reasonable diligence and prudence.

Guardians may also invest their wards' funds and are not personally liable for losses suffered by their wards' estates, as long as the losses occurred despite the guardians' diligent and prudent actions. Guardians in these situations must carefully review applicable statutes since many states restrict their investments into particular types of accounts and stocks.

---

**EXAMPLE** ■ On the advice of a reputable investment adviser, Laureen Smith, guardian of the estate of Nancy Houle, purchased stock in Fancy Foods, Inc., with the intent of producing dividend income for the estate. Under the applicable statute, the stock was acceptable for investment purposes. The stock not only paid no dividends but had also depreciated in value by 50 percent when Smith finally sold it. As a result, the estate suffered a loss of $20,000.

Smith would not be personally liable for the loss since it occurred despite her diligent and prudent behavior.

---

In summary, a guardian must deal with a ward's estate as a fiduciary, exercising diligence and prudence. Likewise, those transacting business with a guardian must verify the extent of authority claimed by the guardian before approving and completing the transaction.

# TRUSTS

In the broadest legal sense, a **trust** is a legal relationship in which one person (the **trustee**) holds title to property and can keep or use the property for the benefit of another (the **beneficiary**). An **express trust** is intentionally created in a writing, deed, or will of the settlor. A **settlor** is an individual or legal entity having legal title to real or personal property that is conveyed to a trust at the time of its creation or in the future.

When a trust is created, the settlor usually names a trustee. A trustee may be an individual or legal entity, such as a bank with trust powers. A trustee is a fiduciary whose responsibilities regarding property of the trust are similar to those of guardians toward assets they manage for wards.

The typical trusts with which banks do business are those created for estate planning and are either "inter vivos" or "testamentary" trusts. An **inter vivos** trust is created during the lifetime of its settlor, who usually conveys real or personal property to the trust at the time of its creation and from time to time thereafter until the settlor's death.

A **testamentary trust** is created by a settlor's will and becomes effective only upon the settlor's death.

---

**EXAMPLE** ■ Ralph Wheat creates an inter vivos trust into which he conveys $100,000 worth of stock. The dividends from those stocks are designated for the benefit of his oldest son who is disabled. The trustee is Fred Dixon, a long-time friend of Wheat.

Wheat also executes a will with provisions for the creation of a testamentary trust, into which all the assets he possesses at death will go and which in turn will be used to support his wife. Upon her death, the trust will terminate and its assets will be divided among all of Wheat's children. The trustee will be Rural State Bank of Littletown.

In a trust, legal ownership of property is separated from its beneficial enjoyment. The stock whose dividends will be used for the benefit of Wheat's disabled son will be legally owned by Fred Dixon as trustee. The assets owned by Wheat at death will be used for his wife's benefit, but their legal title will be held by Rural State Bank as trustee.

---

In creating trusts, settlors can impose conditions and limitations on trustee administration of trust assets. By naming him- or herself as trustee of an inter vivos trust, a settlor can have the ultimate ability to control the administration of trust assets.

---

EXAMPLE ■ Tobias Bell conveys all his assets to himself as trustee of the "Tobias Bell Trust," with provisions in the trust agreement providing that as trustee he shall administer the trust for his own benefit during his lifetime and, upon his death, the remaining assets shall be divided equally among his children. As settlor, Bell also reserves the power to revoke the trust at any time during his life.

---

This trust example is often called a "revocable living trust." Its main benefit is the avoidance of court administration of a settlor's estate since, at death, the trust immediately conveys the assets to the beneficiaries named in the trust. Without the trust, assets would remain legally titled in the settlor's name and would have to be administered by the court.

While the settlor's control over the administration of a trust is perfectly legal, too much control—including the settlor's being the trustee—will deprive the settlor of tax advantages many settlors desire when creating trusts.

Trustees are fiduciaries, charged with the duty to make prudent decisions on trust management. In addition, trustees must observe the conditions placed upon them within the trust instruments, by state statutes, and by court decisions on trust management.

---

EXAMPLE ■ Secure Trust Company is the trustee for the Lawrence Howe Trust. The trustee wishes to invest $500,000 of trust assets in the stock of Wonder Chemicals, Inc., which is a safe, secure, blue-chip investment. However, in drafting the trust agreement, Mr. Howe had his lawyer add a provision that no trust assets could be invested in the stock of Wonder Chemicals, Inc., because Howe did not approve of its products.

Despite the stock's potential as a good, safe investment, the trustee could not purchase it, since Secure Trust Company had to observe the conditions of the trust.

---

If a trustee finds that conditions in a trust are so restrictive that they impair the trustee's ability to manage its assets, a trustee may resign and have a substitute trustee appointed.

Since prudent persons consider banks safe places for funds, trustees properly exercise their fiduciary responsibilities when they deposit trust funds in banks. When the trust agreement or state law permits the trustee to place the assets in more permanent investments with higher yields than bank deposits, trust deposits in banks are usually of short duration. However, a bank that knowingly receives trust deposits has no duty to report apparently lengthy deposit periods.

---

**EXAMPLE** ■ In 1960, Joe Lyon became trustee of a testamentary trust. The beneficiaries of the trust were the deceased settlor's minor children. Lyon deposited the trust assets, $1 million, in a bank savings account at an annual yield of 5 percent. As the trust provided, the trust terminated and was distributed in 1980 when the youngest of the settlor's children reached 21 years of age. Alleging the assets had not been properly invested, the children sued Lyon and the bank.

Since a court would probably find that Lyon was not prudent in attending to the investment of trust assets, Lyon may be personally liable to the beneficiaries. However, a beneficiary suit against the bank would fail. Since the bank is not a trustee, it owes no duty to the trust to ensure proper investments.

---

In addition to receiving deposits into trust funds, banks may also lend funds to trusts. This can occur when part of a trust's assets is a business that occasionally requires additional capital to operate.

---

**EXAMPLE** ■ Sam Hiker is trustee for a trust having a summer resort business among its assets. During the winter, money is needed for utilities and other maintenance expenses. As trustee, Hiker borrows the necessary funds from a bank and signs a promissory note that requires payment in full on the following September 1.

---

Unless a trust agreement states otherwise, the power to borrow money to operate a trust's business is implied by law. A bank doing business with a trustee should review the underlying trust agreement to be certain that the trustee is not acting contrary to the agreement. Further, when dealing with a trustee, a bank must realize that any notes or other documents the trustee properly signs in that capacity do not bind the trustee personally to their terms.

If their chartering authority grants them trust powers, banks may act as trustees. National banks receive trust powers from the Comptroller of the Currency, while state banks receive trust powers from the various state banking authorities.

Settlors often prefer banks as trustees because, in addition to the common law and statutory duties impressed on all trustees, regulatory agencies add additional requirements to banks' fiduciary responsibilities. Trust departments at banks are subject to separate examinations by their regulatory agencies, which focus on their trust investments, avoidance of self-promotion, trust officers' qualifications, proper supervision of trust departments by boards of directors, and compliance with recordkeeping for trust departments.

## SURETIES

Borrowers unable to obtain credit based on their own creditworthiness often turn to sureties to enhance their credit applications. **Sureties** are persons who agree to be equally responsible for the debt of a borrower ("principal debtor"). A true surety agreement constitutes a surety's promise to pay the debt personally when it becomes due without a precondition that the creditor first look to the principal debtor for payment.

---

EXAMPLE ■ Frank Stroman borrows $1,000 from Five Streams State Bank. Joe Anderson agrees to be a surety. When the note matures on February 1, the bank can demand payment from Anderson without first presenting the note to Stroman for payment.

---

As with any contract, consideration must support a contract of suretyship. However, that benefit need not go directly to the surety; consideration received by the principal debtor is sufficient.

The presence of a surety does not, however, relieve the principal debtor from the debt. In the above example, Anderson would be entitled to seek reimbursement from Stroman for the money he paid to the bank.

Once a surety pays a principal debtor's obligation, he or she is entitled to an assignment of the creditor's rights against the principal debtor and can pursue the debtor to the same extent as an unpaid creditor; that is, the surety is **subrogated** to the rights of the creditor.

**Suretyship Defenses**

Because creditors owe sureties the duty of continuous good faith, creditors seeking payment from sureties may encounter "suretyship defenses" asserted by them. These defenses arise from creditor conduct that increases the risk the surety originally assumed. For example, if a creditor—without the surety's approval—agrees with the principal debtor to increase the debt and extend the time of its maturity, or agrees to release collateral, the surety is discharged from his or her obligation. Further, a creditor cannot discharge a principal debtor from his payment obligation without also discharging the surety.

EXAMPLE ■ Joan Bear borrows $10,000 from Cheboygan State Bank and secures the debt with equipment. Sam Cobb agrees to be a surety for the loan. Bear asks and the bank agrees to release the collateral without Cobb's approval. Cobb's duty as a surety is discharged because the bank increased his risk.

In some states, statutes specify what acts will discharge a surety from his or her obligations.

In addition to, or instead of, personally pledging to repay a debtor's obligation, a surety can secure with collateral the promise to repay the debt.

EXAMPLE ■ Sam Brown borrows $10,000 from State Bank. Joe Green enters into a suretyship contract with the bank and puts up machinery as collateral, but he makes no personal promise to pay.

Sureties usually will be discharged from their obligation if any material alteration is made in the principal's obligation. Such material changes include an agreement by the principal debtor to a higher interest than required by the original note, a time extension for repayment of the debt, and formal agreement to forbear from collection of the debt.

Although a formal agreement for forbearance between a creditor and principal debtor will discharge a surety, passive forbearance usually will not. However, in some states, a creditor's refusal to sue a defaulting debtor after a surety's request for the suit will result in a discharge.

A creditor's release of a principal's security without a surety's consent usually discharges a surety. However, a surety is not discharged when a creditor simply refuses to pursue security if the principal defaults. This is because the surety can pay the debt, acquire the creditor's rights to the collateral, and then repossess and sell the collateral.

Sureties may, of course, waive their defenses in their underlying suretyship agreement or as events occur that would otherwise discharge them from their obligations. Typical suretyship agreements (and guaranty agreements, discussed in the next section) drafted by creditors will contain provisions permitting them to take certain actions without losing their ability to pursue a surety (or a guaranty).

**EXAMPLE** ■ Susan Hay enters into a surety agreement for the benefit of John Farr, who has borrowed $100,000 from Fifth National Bank. Farr secures the debt with machinery from his business. The agreement signed by Hay permits the bank to release collateral without affecting the surety's obligation upon a default.

Because of the agreement, if Farr wants to sell the machinery and the bank agrees, he may do so and the bank may consent without jeopardizing the suretyship agreement.

## GUARANTIES

Guaranties differ from sureties. While a surety is a debtor from the inception of the contract, a guarantor is bound only when the principal is unable to pay or perform the contract. A contract of guaranty may require a guarantor to perform immediately upon the principal's default, without prior notice to the guarantor or demand on the principal.

**EXAMPLE** ■ George Jones borrows $2,000 from Reserve National Bank. Joe Smite agrees to be a guarantor. The contract of guaranty requires immediate payment by the guarantor upon the principal's default, and disclaims the need for prior notice to the guarantor or prior demand from the principal. When the note matures, the bank presents it to Smite, the guarantor, for payment. Smite refuses to pay it because the bank has not yet demanded payment from Jones.

In this situation, Smite has to pay the note. He became personally liable for the debt upon Jones's default. Under the guaranty agreement, the bank is not obligated to seek payment from Jones as a condition to its demand on Smite.

---

The written documents evidencing a surety's or guarantor's agreement to repay a debt often blur the distinction between a surety and a guaranty. Such written documents and the circumstances surrounding them override the labels applied to the agreements. Thus, a document entitled "guaranty" might well be a suretyship agreement.

## CONCLUSION

This chapter illustrates that banks must deal with many different kinds of legal entities. Those entities include individual customers, sole proprietorships, agents, partnerships formed both by written agreement and estoppel, closely and publicly held corporations, governments, estates of both deceased persons and those subject to guardianships, trusts, sureties, and guarantors. By clearly understanding the differences between these entities, banks can avoid potentially serious legal problems and continue to maintain smooth relations with each type of customer.

**Questions for Review and Discussion**

1. In what ways should a bank do business differently with a sole proprietorship than with a corporation?

2. An agent's authority can be actual or apparent. Explain the difference by giving an example of each. In the example of actual authority, use facts giving rise to implied authority.

3. Describe the difference between a partnership and a limited partnership.

4. What is the difference between an intestate and a testate estate?

5. Discuss the importance of thoroughly checking the authority of a government entity before dealing with it.

6. How does the guardian of a person differ from the guardian of a person's estate?

7. Can a settlor, trustee, and beneficiary be one and the same?

# 5

## Contracts

After studying this chapter, you will be able to

- identify the elements of a contract, including the necessity for legal capacity, legal objective, mutual assent, and consideration
- explain the statute of frauds and its application
- describe the parol evidence rule and its application
- identify rules used to interpret contracts
- discuss the performance of contracts
- define third-party beneficiaries
- distinguish between the various forms of damages for failure to perform a contract
- discuss the concept of quasi contract

Common law defines a **contract** in simple terms as a legally enforceable agreement between two or more persons containing a promise or mutual promises to perform or refrain from performing a specific act.

Contracts are created between two or more persons—that is, legal entities—for numerous types of transactions, including those dealing with real property, personal property, and services. Article 2 of the Uniform Commercial Code (UCC) governs contracts relating to the sale of goods, while most other contracts continue to be subject to common-law principles.

Section 2–105 of the UCC defines **goods** as "all things (including specially manufactured goods) which are movable at the time of identification to the contract for sale. . . ." Thus, article 2 of the UCC governs transactions where, by contract, a seller transfers the ownership of goods to a buyer for a price. Such contracts may relate to goods presently for sale or those to be sold in the future.

---

EXAMPLE ■ Jane Smith goes into a retail store and purchases a shovel. At the same time she orders a refrigerator, which will be delivered to her at a later date. Smith's purchase of the shovel involves a present sale of goods, while her order for a refrigerator is a contract for purchase of goods in the future. Both contracts come within article 2 of the UCC.

---

Contracts not involving goods usually involve real estate or services and such contracts are not governed by the UCC, which is concerned only with personal property.

---

EXAMPLE ■ Barber signs a purchase agreement for MacNamara's 40-acre parcel of land and an agreement with Franks to build a house on the real estate. Neither of these contracts is within the scope of the UCC. The agreement with MacNamara involves real estate and the agreement with Franks involves services.

---

Article 2 of the UCC governs contracts relating to the sale of vending machines, which are "goods," while common law governs a contract providing for maintenance of the machine.

Although article 2 has developed a body of contract law separate from common law, many of its principles parallel common law. The following discussion of contract law will highlight article 2 of the UCC only where its provisions about goods differ from the common-law principles of contract law.

# ELEMENTS OF A CONTRACT

Essentially, a contract exists only when four criteria are met:

- The parties have the legal capacity to enter into a contractual agreement.
- The contract's objective is legal.
- The parties mutually assent to the contract.
- Each party provides consideration.

**Legal Capacity**   To create a legally binding contract, the parties must have the legal capacity to bind themselves to the contract when they enter into it. Over the centuries, the law has classified certain categories of people as either incapable of binding themselves to a contract or, if capable, able also to unilaterally disaffirm their contracts. These categories are composed of people perceived by society as unable to represent or protect their own interests. If individuals fall within these categories, they will be unable to enter into legally binding contracts, despite their otherwise "actual capacity" to understand the ramifications of the contracts. Categories of legally incapacitated persons include infants, the mentally ill or defective, and the intoxicated.

*Infants*   For purposes of contract law, **infants** are individuals who have not reached their "majority." Under common law, an infant was anyone under 21 years of age. Most states have now set by statute the age of minority to be under 18 years of age.

Because of the inexperience of infants and their potential susceptibility to others' control, the law has developed prohibitions regarding enforcement of contracts with minors. While minors are free to enter into contracts, they are also free to disaffirm them under most circumstances; that is, such contracts are voidable.

This means that infants have the choice of enforcing or disaffirming contracts against others. **Disaffirmance** is an action whereby a person who lacks contractual capacity voids or repudiates a contract at will. However, if an infant disaffirms a contract, any property acquired under the contract is returned to the other party. If the infant has consumed or dissipated the property, the other party to the contract

131   *Contracts*

will be without a remedy, unless the principles of quasi contract apply (as discussed later in this chapter).

Upon disaffirmance, even if an infant has nothing left to return, the other party must restore to the infant anything received from the infant pursuant to the contract. If, for example, an infant gives a bank a lien on an automobile as collateral for a $5,000 loan, the bank will be required to discharge the lien even though no payments have been made. Clearly, doing business with a person who is legally an infant can have perilous consequences.

If an individual chooses to disaffirm a contract based on infancy, it must be done while the individual is still an infant or within a reasonable time after reaching the age of majority.

---

**EXAMPLE** ■ Third State Bank lent Sally Smith $1,500 when she was 17 years of age to be repaid in 24 monthly installments under terms of a promissory note. Under applicable state law, Sally is an infant until she reaches age 18. Six months after she becomes 18, Sally notifies the bank that she wishes to disaffirm the promissory note, claiming the right to do so because of her infancy when she executed the note. Smith will be required to pay the balance due under the note and will not be entitled to a return of payments if a court finds the six-month period to have been an "unreasonable time" in which to disaffirm a contract after reaching her majority.

---

An individual who continues to perform a contract made during infancy for a reasonable time after reaching the age of majority is said to have ratified the contract. **Ratification**, for purposes of contract law, means conduct by a person consistent with the existence of a contract. Smith's continued payment of installments due under her promissory note with Third State Bank was an act consistent with the terms of her contract with the bank. Once Smith ratified the contract, she waived her power of avoidance, making the contract enforceable against her.

State or federal law may, of course, vary the principles governing infants' contracts and may deprive infants of their power of avoidance.

An infant's contracts for enlistment in the armed forces, insurance, and bail have been held enforceable based on specific state or federal statutes. Contracts made by married infants may also be enforceable if, by state statute, an infant's power to avoid a contract is nullified upon marriage. In addition, section 207 of article 3 of the UCC states that negotiation of instruments is not impaired because an infant who made the negotiation may avoid it. Contracts that infants enter under judicial authority or with their guardian's approval are enforceable, despite their infancy.

Under the principles of **quasi contract**, an infant can be held liable, even during infancy, for the reasonable value of "necessaries" furnished under contract. **Necessaries** include items required for the existence of an infant. However, what is necessary for one infant may not be so for the next. Except for such things as reasonable amounts of food, shelter, clothing, and medical care, what is a necessary will depend on the individual infant's situation in life, wealth, or parents' wealth.

While an infant can be forced to pay for necessaries, only their "reasonable value" must be paid. If the contract price for an item exceeds the item's reasonable value, an infant can disaffirm the difference and either escape liability for the excess or recover the excess.

---

**EXAMPLE** ■ Larry Jones was 16 years of age and far from home when he engaged a physician to perform certain medical services reasonably needed for his health. The doctor told him the services would cost $1,000 and Jones agreed to pay that amount. The doctor performed the services to Jones's satisfaction, but his attorney was later able to show that the reasonable value of the services was only $250.

If Jones disaffirmed the contract, the doctor would be limited in his recovery to $250.

---

Things already available to an infant are not considered necessaries. In the example above, if Jones lived with his parents who paid his medical expenses, he could successfully avoid any liability to the physician.

A bank or other lender who loans an infant money to purchase necessaries may enforce the infant's promise to repay the loan only if the lender can demonstrate that the infant in fact did use the loan proceeds to purchase necessaries. Further, an infant found liable to a lender need repay only an amount equal to the reasonable value of the necessaries purchased with the loan proceeds. In the preceding example, if Jones had borrowed $1,000 to pay the doctor's fee, he would have been liable for repayment of only $250, since that was the "reasonable value" of the services. The lender would not be able to recover the balance of $750 from Jones.

In summary, lenders and others are well advised not to contract with infants at all, even if they allege the need for necessaries. No laws, including the federal Equal Credit Opportunity Act (discussed in chapter 8), require anyone to do business with infants, even if the transaction involves necessaries. Those who decide to deal with infants should insist upon sureties, such as guarantors or cosigners, who will assure performance of the infant's obligation if the infant disaffirms the contractual obligation. An alternative to securing a cosigner or guarantor for an infant's contract is, of course, to deal with an infant's guardian (see chapter 4).

An infant who misrepresents his or her age to obtain a loan or other contractual benefit is said by some courts to be estopped or prohibited from later disaffirming a contract based on infancy. Those courts which apply **estoppel** with regard to infants' contracts usually do so only when (1) the infant is old enough to exercise discretion, (2) the infant's conduct is intentionally fraudulent, and (3) the other party to the contract has in good faith detrimentally relied on the infant's misrepresentation.

---

**EXAMPLE** ■ Ralph White, age 20, realizes that in his state those not yet 21 are considered infants able to disaffirm contracts. With this knowledge, White borrows $3,000 from First National Bank. The bank relies on White's loan application, which lists his age as 22. After receiving the funds, White disaffirms his promise to repay the loan, the bank sues White, and he raises his infancy as a defense. In many states, a court faced with this situation would declare that White was estopped from raising the defense of infancy and enforce his promise to repay the loan.

---

An infant allowed to avoid a contract despite age misrepresentation, however, is subject to an action for fraud and deceit.

## Mental Illness or Defect

Those who suffer from a mental illness or defect fall within one of two categories regarding the legal capacity to contract. The first includes those for whom a court has appointed a guardian. In these situations, the person suffering from the mental illness or defect is referred to as a **ward** or legally incapacitated person. (Chapter 4 discusses the legal relationship between a guardian and a ward and the ability of the former to act on the latter's behalf.)

A ward has no capacity to incur contractual obligations. It is a nearly universal rule of law that the appointment of the guardian serves to immunize the ward from contractual obligations. Any agreement into which a ward enters is an absolutely **void**, not a voidable, contract. The basis for this rule is that, upon appointment of a guardian, all of a ward's property, interests, and power then vest in the guardian, who has the sole power to contract in the ward's name for the ward's benefit. The next example illustrates the difference between void and voidable contracts.

---

**EXAMPLE** ■ Phil Pappas, age 16, signs a promissory note to Peoples' State Bank for $3,000 to be paid in 90 days. On the same day, Charles Lee, also 16, signs a promissory note to the same bank for $4,000. However, the day before Lee signed this note, Mary Lehan was appointed his guardian because of his mental illness.

The promissory note signed by Pappas is legally voidable; that is, it is enforceable until Phil disaffirms it. The promissory note signed by Lee, on the other hand, is not enforceable. Furthermore, because a guardian has been appointed, Charles does not need to take any action to disaffirm the note.

---

135    *Contracts*

Whether a person entering into an agreement with a ward knows of the legal incapacity is irrelevant to the validity of the agreement as a contract because the agreement is void with or without such knowledge.

Unlike an infant, a ward who enters into an agreement for necessaries cannot personally be held liable, because the agreement is not a contract. However, a guardian is liable for the ward's necessaries out of the property of the ward's estate. If a guardian chooses not to ratify a ward's agreement as a contract, the guardian must return any remaining consideration received by the ward. If the ward has consumed or dissipated the property, the person supplying the goods will be without a remedy except for the possibility of recovering the "reasonable value" of any items deemed necessaries.

---

**EXAMPLE** ▪ Roger Wagner, while a ward, entered into an agreement for the purchase of an automobile. After learning of the transaction, his guardian refused to approve it and demanded a return of the purchase price, because Roger had smashed the car and destroyed most of its value. When his demand produced no result, the guardian sued.

The court ruled that the guardian was entitled to a return of the full purchase price. If the court had determined the car to be a necessary, however, the guardian would have been obligated to pay its "reasonable value." However, because the car was not considered to be a necessary in this situation, the guardian was able to recover its full purchase price by simply returning the car.

---

If the reason for a guardianship ends, judicial decree ordinarily terminates the guardianship. In this event, the ward regains the capacity to make a contract. Occasionally, however, when the ward recovers from mental illness, the guardian simply abandons the guardianship without any formality. Although technically the guardianship is still legally operative in this situation, evidence cannot be regarded as conclusive that the ward has no contractual capacity. Instead, the court may examine the abandoned guardianship to see whether the ward has acquired the capacity to make contracts.

A guardian has the power to ratify an agreement made by the ward. If such ratification occurs, the agreement will be a contract and enforceable against the ward's estate.

The second category of individuals with mental illness or defects within contract law includes those who have no guardians, either because no guardian was sought or because the court reviewing the guardianship petition did not find the illness or defect sufficiently severe to require the appointment of a guardian.

A person who is mentally incompetent through illness or defect may avoid contracts even though no guardian has been appointed to care for his or her person or estate. When no guardian has been appointed, however, there is no objective determination that the party does in fact lack mental competence. Thus, the law of mental competence largely revolves around efforts to establish standards of competence, burdens of proof, and means of reconciling the protection of innocent suppliers of goods, services, and credit with the protection of people who cannot care for themselves.

In defining the standard of competency, the law now holds that a person is incompetent when unable to understand in a reasonable manner the nature and consequences of the transaction at hand. Consequently, there is a wide variety of types and degrees of mental incompetency. In some instances, a person may be incompetent to enter into any transaction. In others, the person may be lucid most of the time and only occasionally disabled. Thus, the rule relates to the particular transaction at hand. When no guardian has been appointed, full contractual capacity exists in any case, unless the mental illness or defect has affected the particular transaction. The burden of proving incompetency is on the party attempting to void the contract.

---

**EXAMPLE** ■ Brendan O'Malley signed a promissory note for $10,000 on October 15, 1985, payable to First Citizens' Bank. He immediately gave away the loan proceeds to strangers for no apparent reason. On December 1, 1985, upon petition of his brother, Michael, a court declared Brendan to be mentally incompetent and appointed Michael his guardian. Shortly thereafter, the note became due and the bank sued to collect it. Michael refused payment, asserting Brendan's mental incompetency as a defense.

In this situation, the burden is on the guardian to prove that on October 15, 1985, his ward was incompetent and that the contract is therefore voidable (as opposed to void, which would have been the case had Brendan been a ward when the promissory note was executed).

---

If a transaction is voided on grounds of mental incompetency, what should be done to protect the other innocent party to the contract? The considerations involved in this situation are different from those in situations involving infants. Someone doing business with an infant can confirm by checking identification that he or she is dealing with a person who may have a limited capacity to make a contract. But someone dealing with a mentally incompetent person may not be aware of that person's incompetence because that person may show no outward signs of it. Therefore, somewhat different rules have evolved to address the contractual obligations of the mentally incompetent.

Mentally incompetent people may disaffirm contracts only upon "equitable terms." When someone dealing with a mentally incompetent person knows or should know of the disability, the courts find no special equities and generally treat the matter as they would in the case of infancy. However, when someone dealing with an incompetent person does not know and cannot reasonably be expected to know of the disability, the courts generally permit disaffirmance only where the competent person is able to make restitution for the value of the goods consumed or dissipated. In both cases, of course, the incompetent person must pay for necessaries.

---

**EXAMPLE** ■ Becky Lake, while mentally incompetent and not under guardianship, bought an automobile from John Swift on credit for a price of $6,000. Swift was unaware of Lake's mental illness. A short time later, Sam Rogers, with full knowledge of Lake's mental condition, bought the car from her for $2,000 in cash. Lake then dissipated the $2,000 at the race track and now wants to disaffirm all her obligations and contracts.

She may disaffirm the transaction with Rogers and get her car back, even though she is unable to return any part of the money Rogers paid her. She may also disaffirm her transaction with Swift but only if she returns the car to Swift and pays him for its use.

---

If the mentally incompetent person regains full mental capacity, he or she may disaffirm all contracts made while incompetent, within the limitations indicated earlier. As in the case of infancy, failure to disaffirm a contract within a reasonable time after the recovery may operate as a ratification that will make the contract enforceable.

*Intoxication*  People judged mentally incompetent by reason of alcoholism or drug addiction and for whom guardians have been appointed fall within the law that applies to other mentally incompetent people. Thus, their ability to contract is the same as that discussed in the section titled "Mental Illness or Defect." The discussion in this section, however, deals with those who are inebriated or under the influence of drugs and for whom no guardian has been appointed.

Early common law provided no defense against the enforcement of a contract on the grounds of intoxication when the contract was executed. Current law, however, holds that contracts made while a person is under the influence of drugs or alcohol are voidable if the condition was so excessive that it rendered the individual incapable of comprehending the nature and effect of the contract. If the party dealing with the substance abuser was or should have been aware of the individual's inability to understand the nature and consequence of the transaction, the substance abuser's defense will be greatly enhanced.

---

EXAMPLE ■ On Saturday morning, Robert Dow applied in person for a loan from Second State Bank while in a state of obvious intoxication.

The loan was granted on a 30-day promissory note. Dow left the bank and immediately passed the money out among strangers.

On the same Saturday morning, Peter O'Brian called the same bank to request a transfer of money from his savings account to the account of Richard Paine. Although O'Brian did not slur his speech, he was actually very intoxicated when he made the request.

By the following Monday, both Dow and O'Brian were sober and attempted to disaffirm their contractual transactions with Second State Bank. Dow will have a much easier time convincing a court of his legal incapacity than O'Brian. The burden is on the inebriated person to prove that the intoxication was so excessive that he or she was incapable of comprehending the nature of the contract. In addition, many courts require the person to prove that the other party to the contract was aware of the intoxication.

---

Upon becoming sober, the person previously under the influence of alcohol or drugs must promptly disaffirm the contracts made while incapacitated or run the risk of ratification. Usually, the courts will not permit a disaffirmance on grounds of intoxication unless an offer is made to restore the consideration received. If the consideration has been dissipated during the period of intoxication, however, some courts permit disaffirmance without restitution if restitution cannot be given. Disaffirmance will also be allowed if it can be demonstrated that the other party actually knew that the person was under the influence of alcohol or drugs when entering into the contract.

## Legality of Objective

Along with the required legal capacity of the parties to contract, another essential element of any contract is that its objective or purpose be legal. If the objective or performance of an agreement is illegal, the "contract" is unenforceable. The most egregious example of an illegal agreement is a pact to commit murder. Other categories of illegal agreements include

- agreements in unreasonable restraint of trade

- agreements harmful to the public interest, the administration of justice, and the marriage relationship
- wagering agreements
- agreements rendered illegal by statute, such as usury, licensing, and Sunday contract statutes

*Contracts in Unreasonable Restraint of Trade*

Because a cornerstone of capitalism is competition, the common law and American statutory law have developed prohibitions against making contracts whose objective is the unreasonable restraint of trade. Examples include agreements that completely prohibit a person from exercising a trade, business, or profession, as well as those that fix minimum prices, divide sales territories, limit production, or pool profits.

---

EXAMPLE ■ George Webber sells his restaurant to Ed Charles and, as part of the sales contract, Webber agrees not to operate a restaurant anywhere for the rest of his life. Five years after the sale, Webber opens a restaurant in a location 1,000 miles from the one he sold to Charles. Charles sues Webber to enforce the provision of the contract forbidding Webber to operate a restaurant. Charles would lose the suit because the contract's provision is an unreasonable restraint on trade.

Suppose the contract provided that Webber would not operate a restaurant for two years within 10 miles of the one sold. If Webber violated this limited prohibition on competition, Charles probably could enforce the restriction.

---

A promise not to compete is valid if its purpose is to protect a property right and if the restraint of trade is reasonable with respect to its territory, time, and subject matter.

Agreements not to compete are made not only by people selling their businesses, but also by people buying property and promising not to use it to compete with the seller, and by retiring partners or employees promising not to compete with their former firms and employers. As with restrictions on the right of sellers of businesses to operate competing businesses, the validity and enforceability of these other agreements often depend on the time, territory, and subject matter of the restrictions they contain.

Unless otherwise permitted by statute, combination and monopoly contracts for the purpose of eliminating competition are also unenforceable restraints on trade.

---

**EXAMPLE** ■ First National Bank of Smithville and Howard State Bank have their offices in adjoining counties. The two banks sign a contract providing that they will not make loans to or take deposits from individuals residing in the county in which the other is located. First National violates the agreement and Howard State Bank begins suit to enforce the agreement.

Howard State Bank will lose its suit, since the agreement is an unenforceable restraint on trade. Further, the banks and their directors and officers could face state and federal civil and criminal penalties under antitrust laws.

---

Certain businesses, such as utilities and transportation companies, may be monopolies under statutory authority, based on the premise that competition in these areas may harm the public interest.

*Agreements Harmful to the Public Interest*

Agreements that disrupt or subvert the workings of government are, of course, illegal and unenforceable. Included in this category of illegal agreements are provisions for

■ payment of bribes to elected officials for their votes

■ payment for appointment to public office

■ payment to procure government contracts by corrupt methods

■ payment to private citizens in violation of public duty

■ payment to public officials for performing duties they are required by law to perform

142   *Law & Banking: Principles*

**EXAMPLE** ■ Tom Rodriguez, a banker, is particularly interested in a vote coming before his state's legislature on elimination of usury. He agrees to pay State Senator Earl George $10,000 if the senator votes yes for the bill. George votes yes, but Rodriguez refuses to pay him.

Alice Cocoran agrees to contribute $1,000 to a political action committee that is composed of bankers who contribute their members' pooled funds to the campaigns of legislators who are friendly to banks or who they hope will become so. Cocoran then refuses to pay the contribution.

Senator George will be unable to enforce his agreement with Rodriguez since it was a promise to pay a bribe, which is an illegal agreement. Cocoran's promise to contribute to a political action committee is a contract and probably enforceable, since the committee's contributions to legislators are not specifically directed at a particular vote the legislators will cast nor are they directed at obtaining any other promise to support a particular issue.

*Agreements to Defraud or Injure Third Persons*

In addition to "murder for hire" agreements, other unenforceable pacts to harm others include agreements to

■ defraud third parties

■ induce another to breach a contract with a third party

■ defraud creditors

■ induce a fiduciary to violate his or her duties

**EXAMPLE** ■ Ralph Simmons is a trustee for an estate. He is promised $100,000 if he invests $2 million of the trust estate in a speculative land venture promoted by Stan Nelson. Simmons makes the investment but Nelson refuses to pay him the $100,000. Simmons cannot enforce the agreement because it produces a conflict between his personal interests and his fiduciary duty to the trust.

*Agreements Harmful to the Administration of Justice*

Examples of agreements harmful to the administration of justice include the following:

- an agreement not to prosecute a crime in return for a payment
- an agreement that induces a witness to give perjured testimony
- an agreement to compensate a juror made by anyone other than the court
- an agreement between an attorney and client precluding settlement on any terms, resulting in protracted litigation

Depending upon state law, a bank's promise not to initiate criminal proceedings in return for payment of a civil debt may or may not be valid. At one time, for example, an agreement to arbitrate all future disputes that might arise under a contract was said to be an illegal interference in the court's jurisdiction. Today, courts do not have exclusive jurisdiction over the resolution of all disputes and this change in the government's philosophy has served to validate arbitration agreements.

*Agreements Harmful to the Marriage Relationship*

An agreement that completely limits the freedom of a person to marry or not to marry or to choose a partner in marriage is illegal. However, an agreement not to marry for a reasonable, limited time is legal. Agreements to end a marriage or to regulate the duties of the married parties are illegal, but an agreement for immediate separation is not.

EXAMPLE
- John Paul promises to pay Sean Mack $10,000 if Mack's daughter, Jean, will marry Paul. The promise is illegal, even though Mack may give his daughter a choice in the matter. Because Mack stands to gain financially by the agreement, pressure is exerted on his daughter and limits her choice. Though

perhaps slight, this limitation on her choice through a contract is not allowed.

In another situation, Mr. and Mrs. Isaiah Young entered into a contract whereby Mr. Young agreed to pay his wife an allowance and she promised to keep their home neat and clean. The agreement is illegal and unenforceable as a contract.

---

While courts typically state that such agreements harm the marriage relationship, an equally valid reason is the reluctance of most courts to interfere in matters deemed private.

General restraints on marriage made for a limited time and for a lawful purpose have been sustained.

---

EXAMPLE ■ David Stone promises his 21-year-old daughter a trip around the world if she promises not to get married until she receives her master's degree. She so promises.

Stone's promise is a contract. Although it restrains marriage, the restraint is reasonably limited in time and has a valid objective.

---

*Wagering Agreements*  A wagering agreement is one in which each party takes the risk of being required to give something for nothing upon the happening of an uncertain event.

---

EXAMPLE ■ Joe, Sam, and Jim each bet $500 that they will draw the best poker hand, and the one with the best hand will win all the money. This is a wagering agreement. One of these men will receive $1,500 for giving $500, and the other two will give a total of $1,000 and receive nothing. The identity of the winner will depend on an uncertain event (that is, drawing the best poker hand).

All gambling and other betting transactions are wagering agreements and are enforceable as contracts only in those states that permit them by statute. The enforceability of a lottery agreement as a contract will depend on state law, which generally prohibits lotteries unless they are licensed by the state. This prohibition extends even to those lotteries whose proceeds are for charitable or civic purposes.

*Agreements Rendered Illegal by Licensing and Other Statutes*

Many states have statutes requiring that certain trades, occupations, and professions be practiced only by those licensed by the state. These statutes usually provide that anyone engaging in such trades, occupations, or professions without a license may not enforce an agreement relating to such a business.

---

EXAMPLE ■ Felix Benson entered into a contract to build a home for Enrico Garcia. The contract called for Benson to be paid $45,000 upon completion of the house. Benson is not a licensed builder as required by the state in which he does business. If Garcia refuses to pay Benson, Benson will probably be without a legal remedy.

---

While many states have repealed statutes that hold agreements made on Sunday void, many still have such statutes. Thus, before executing an agreement on a Sunday, the parties to a contract should determine what their particular state law provides.

*Usurious Agreements*

**Interest** is money charged as compensation for the loan of money or for **forbearance** (refraining) from collecting money owed. **Usury** is the collection of interest in an amount that exceeds the maximum permitted by statute.

Whether the interest required under a loan contract is considered usurious depends upon the applicable state constitution, federal statute, or state statute to which a particular type of loan is subject. Usury provisions vary from state to state and many usury statutes base their rates on either the type of lender, borrower, or loan involved. Thus, in many states, loans made to businesses may carry a higher interest rate than consumer loans, and the rates charged by financial institutions may exceed the rates permitted to private parties.

---

**EXAMPLE** ■ Tom Stanley wants to borrow $40,000. In the state in which he resides, statutes provide that if the loan is for business purposes, the borrower can be charged up to 15 percent per year by a private individual. However, if Stanley plans to put up real estate as collateral, he may be charged 18 percent per year by a private individual or a bank, since that is the maximum rate permitted for mortgages in his state. If Stanley's loan is unsecured and for consumer purposes—that is, for personal, household, or family purposes—the law specifies that the interest charged may not exceed 7 percent per year.

---

While a few states have one maximum rate for all types of loans, most do not. Thus, the law must be carefully reviewed for each type of loan under consideration. In addition to maximum interest rates, statutes may also govern such items as application, commitment, and loan-processing fees, as well as service charges, late fees, term of loans, and prepayment penalties.

FEDERAL LAW AND USURY

The maximum interest rates available to banks traditionally have been governed by state law. Even rates for national banks were tied primarily to state rates. The National Banking Act provides that a national bank may charge rates available to lenders in the state where the bank is located (12 U.S.C. § 85). The ability of national banks to use the rates permitted to other state lenders located in the same state has become known as the "most-favored-lender" doctrine.

---

**EXAMPLE** ■ Peoples' National Bank is located within a state where state-chartered credit unions are permitted to charge 18 percent per year and the state's banking code limits the rate for the same loans to 14 percent. As a result of the most-favored-lender doctrine within the National Banking Act, Peoples' National Bank may charge 18 percent per year.

---

The National Banking Act also permits a national bank to avoid state law entirely and charge up to 1 percent above the discount rate on 90-day commercial paper in effect at the district Federal Reserve bank. Thus, if the applicable discount rate is 9 percent, a national bank can charge 10 percent on any of its loans regardless of the usury laws of the state in which it is located (12 U.S.C. § 85).

In 1980, Congress passed the **Depository Institutions Deregulation and Monetary Control Act (DIDMCA) (Pub. L. No. 96-221)**, sections of which gave the benefits of the most-favored-lender doctrine to state-chartered banks, credit unions, savings and loan associations, and federal savings and loan associations. However, the legislatures or voters of the states may repeal at any time the sections of DIDMCA granting the most-favored-lender doctrine to these financial institutions. DIDMCA also granted these financial institutions the right enjoyed by national banks to charge 1 percent above the discount rate on 90-day commercial paper in effect at the district Federal Reserve bank.

Another section of DIDMCA preempted state interest-rate statutes for loans made to finance residential housing (Pub. L. No. 96-501, 12 U.S.C. § 1735f-7). A bank wishing to rely on DIDMCA for justification of an interest rate should carefully review the act's requirements and the expiration dates of its various sections, and should be certain that its state has not repealed the relevant provisions.

PENALTIES FOR USURY

A loan whose interest rate is usurious—exceeds the maximum permitted by law—is unenforceable because its objective, the collection of excessive interest, is illegal. However, the penalty for usury will depend upon the specific state or federal law violated. In some states, the penalty is limited to forfeiture of the excess interest. In other states, all interest is forfeited. In still others, all or a portion of a usurious loan's principal as well as interest is forfeited.

If a national bank is liable for usury, the following federal penalty will be assessed:

> The taking, receiving, reserving, or charging a rate of interest greater than is allowed [by section 85 of this title] when knowingly done, shall be deemed a forfeiture of the entire interest which the note, bill, or other evidence of debt carries with it, or which has been agreed to be paid thereon. In case the greater rate of interest has been paid, the person by whom it has been paid, or his legal representatives, may recover back, in an action in the nature of an action of debt, twice the amount of the interest thus paid from the association taking or receiving the same: provided such action is commenced within 2 years from the time the usurious transaction occurred (12 U.S.C. § 86).

State banks relying on DIDMCA as justification for a usurious loan are subject to a usury penalty similar to the one to which national banks are subject.

## Mutual Assent or Agreement

If people have the legal capacity to enter into a contract whose objective is legal, their next requirement is mutual assent. In an attempt to explain mutual assent, some courts have referred to it as a requirement that a "meeting of the minds" occur before a contract can be created. However, this explanation of mutual assent is oversimplified, because there is no way to determine what a person is thinking. If the validity of contracts depended on an actual meeting of minds, anyone desiring to avoid contractual responsibilities would simply maintain that the agreement as asserted by the other party was not what he or she had in mind when it was made.

"Meeting of the minds" or mutual assent is determined solely by what people communicate to each other rather than what their thoughts may have been. Not only must mutual assent be based on a person's actual conduct but, in most cases, it must also be communicated to the other party or parties.

---

**EXAMPLE** ■ Larry Grady made an offer to Jerry Newmann. Newmann told several people that he had accepted the offer, but he did not communicate his decision to Grady.

No contract exists between these two parties. Although a meeting of their minds may have actually occurred and their words and conduct—rather than their thoughts—may show objectively that they concur on the terms of the agreement, no contract exists because Newmann did not communicate to Grady his determination to accept it. While it would be possible in this case to say that Newmann manifested his assent to accept the contract but failed to communicate that manifestation to Grady, most courts lump the two matters together and say simply that in this case no manifestation of mutual assent was made.

---

Thus, as a practical rule, courts require the objective manifestation of mutual assent to include a communication showing agreement on the terms of the contract.

The UCC has reduced the requirement for mutual assent to a statute that governs the sale of goods:

A contract for sale of goods may be made in any manner sufficient to show agreement, including conduct by both parties which recognizes the existence of such a contract (U.C.C. § 2–204(1)).

The objective manifestation of mutual assent does not occur only through written or spoken words, although it usually does. Conduct may also convey clearly what is meant in a particular situation, and many contracts have been formed through a manifestation of assent that is partly by written or spoken words and partly by acts or conduct.

---

**EXAMPLE** ■ Sam Biggs, a regular customer, enters Harry Parker's grocery store. Parker is busy waiting on a customer and Biggs is in a hurry. He holds up a melon so Parker can see it. Parker sees it and nods his head, and Biggs leaves the store with the melon.

In this situation, a contract exists under which Biggs acquires the ownership of the melon and Parker acquires the right to collect the price for it. The parties' conduct manifests the required mutual assent. The manifestation of mutual assent arises through the process of one party making an offer and the other party accepting it.

## Offer and Acceptance

Mutual assent, then, usually involves an offer made by one person (called the **offeror**) and its acceptance by another person (called the **offeree**). An **offer** is a promise conditioned upon something to be done by the offeree. The condition may be the performance of or forbearance from an act, in which case the offer is said to be "unilateral." Conversely, the condition may be the giving of a return promise, in which case the offer is said to be "bilateral."

Once the offeror makes an offer to the offeree, the latter by accepting it has the ability to bind the offeror to a contract. The acceptance occurs when the offeree satisfies all the conditions of the offer. Until the acceptance does occur, however, the offeror is generally free to revoke the offer, eliminating the offeree's ability to accept the offer and thus form a contract. In addition, under common law, the offeree can reject the offer, eliminating his or her power of acceptance.

EXAMPLE ■ First Security Bank offers 7 percent on its passbook savings accounts to customers who deposit money in such accounts. This offer is unilateral; that is, it is conditioned upon an act. In this case, the act is the deposit of funds. Once the customers (the offerees) make their deposits, acceptance occurs and a contract is created.

A promise to perform an act is not the act itself. Thus, in the preceding example, if a customer merely promises to deposit funds, that would not constitute acceptance under the terms of the offer, since acceptance must conform with those terms.

EXAMPLE ■ State Bank agrees to loan Elaine Davis $2,000 if she will promise to repay it in 90 days and make that promise in the form of a promissory note. In this case, the bank's offer is bilateral; that is, it is conditioned upon a promise to be made by the offeree, Davis. Once she signs the promissory note, acceptance occurs and a contract is created.

---

Since parties must be free to negotiate the terms of contracts, the law protects parties from having those negotiations become a contract before they are completed. General statements expressing a willingness to bargain without extending a specific commitment do not constitute offers.

---

EXAMPLE ■ Deborah Deane says to Lydia Shaw, "I would be interested in selling you my house if you would offer me $90,000 for it." Shaw replies, "I accept."

No contract exists between these two parties, because Deane's statement is not an offer. It does not show that she promises to sell the house if Shaw promises to pay the price. Rather, it is a mere request that Shaw make an offer to her. In short, Deane does not want to be the offeror. She wants to be the offeree and is stating the kind of offer that she would entertain seriously and probably accept. Deane's statement, therefore, would be legally classified as a preliminary negotiation and not an offer.

---

Advertisements, catalogs, and circulars containing price quotations also are not offers. These communications are considered invitations for, rather than actual, offers.

---

EXAMPLE ■ Acton National Bank decided to set aside $100,000 for auto loans to qualified applicants. The availability of the loans was advertised on the radio and in local newspapers. Loan demand was greater than expected and available funds were exhausted within a few days. Albert Maxon came into the bank a few days after the last of the funds were lent and, although he was otherwise qualified, the bank rejected his application. If Maxon sues the bank alleging breach of contract, he will lose. The advertisement was the bank's invitation to the general public to make offers for the auto loans. Maxon's application was an offer, not an acceptance. The offer was rejected and no contract was created.

---

Once an offer is made, an acceptance is required before a contract is created. Acceptance occurs when the conditions stated in the offer have been satisfied.

Generally, only the person to whom the offer is addressed may accept it. This proposition is sometimes stated in terms of a condition that limits acceptance to the offeree.

---

EXAMPLE ■ Anderson offers to sell his house to Greene for $100,000. Carson writes Anderson, "I accept your offer." No contract exists between Carson and Anderson because Carson has no power to accept the offer. The promise in Anderson's offer ran only in favor of Greene. Some courts state that one condition of Anderson's offer is that the acceptance must come only from Greene.

---

Of course, an offer by its terms may run to a class of people or to anyone aware of the offer. The offeror then must determine who shall have the power of acceptance—a single person, a class of people, or anyone who learns of the offer.

---

EXAMPLE ■ Bob Calvin publishes an offer of reward in a newspaper, promising to pay $500 to anyone who finds and returns his ring to him by a given day. This general offer gives a power of acceptance to any person who learns of it.

---

To be effective, an offer must be communicated to the offeree; the offeree can then accept the terms of the offer by communicating his or her mutual assent to the terms offered.

---

EXAMPLE ■ Bob Calvin publishes an offer of reward in a newspaper, promising to pay $500 to anyone who finds and returns his ring to him by a given day. In ignorance of the offer of reward, a garbage collector finds and returns the ring to Calvin within the time limit.

No contract exists between these two parties and the garbage collector is not entitled to the reward. The acceptance must be in response to the offer and a response to an offer is impossible when the offer has not been communicated.

---

The acceptance, of course, must occur within the time limit stated in the offer. If no time limit is stated, the acceptance must be made within a "reasonable time." Circumstances, the usage of the trade, and the special facts of the particular case are relevant in determining whether a reasonable time has elapsed.

Under common law, an acceptance must comply exactly with the specific requirements of an offer.

---

EXAMPLE ■ Patrick Flinn offers to sell his house to Mary Curtis for $80,000. Curtis responds, "I accept at a price of $75,000."

No acceptance has occurred in this situation. Curtis's response is a rejection that terminates Flinn's offer. As a result, Curtis could not later accept the offer at $80,000 unless Flinn reinstated it. Curtis's response, however, is not only a rejection but also a counteroffer to buy the house at $75,000. By accepting this counteroffer, Flinn could make a contract.

---

The UCC, however, provides that where an offer to purchase or sell goods is made, the buyer or seller offeree may accept some of the offeror's terms and substitute other terms for those rejected or may accept all the offeror's terms but propose additional terms:

A definite and seasonable expression of acceptance or a written confirmation which is sent within a reasonable time operates as an acceptance even though it states terms additional to or different from those offered or agreed upon, unless acceptance is expressly made conditional on assent to the additional or different terms (U.C.C. § 2–207(1)).

The additional terms proposed by the offeree to the offeror do not become part of the contract unless the offeror specifically accepts them. But if both the parties are "merchants," the additional or substitute terms will become part of the contract unless (1) the offeror expressly limits acceptance to the terms offered, (2) they materially alter the contract, or (3) notification of objection to the additional terms has already been given or is given within a reasonable time after notice of them is received (U.C.C. § 2–207(2)). The UCC defines **merchant** as

a person who deals in goods of the kind or otherwise by his occupation holds himself out as having knowledge or skill peculiar to the practices or goods involved in the transaction or to whom such knowledge or skill may be attributed by his employment of an agent or broker or other intermediary who by his occupation holds himself out as having such knowledge or skill (U.C.C. § 2–104(1)).

---

EXAMPLE ■ Bob Brooke and Frank Golden are both merchants. Brooke offers to sell Golden 1,000 widgets for $2,000. Brooke's offer does not expressly limit acceptance to the terms offered. Golden responds by agreeing to purchase 1,010 widgets for $2,000. Brooke does not reply.

Under the UCC, a valid sales contract has been formed for

1,010 widgets for $2,000. Since Brooke was a merchant doing business with a merchant, his silence was acceptance of the additional terms. Had the parties not both been merchants or had the additional terms materially altered Brooke's offer, the additional terms would not have become part of the contract.

*Revocation*  Normally an offer may be revoked any time before it is accepted. The revocation, however, is not effective until the offeree receives it. Further, a revocation cannot be made after the offer is accepted, because an acceptance terminates the offer and results in a contract. However, three exceptions apply to the general rule that an offer may be revoked any time before acceptance. The first concerns options. The second concerns offers to enter into unilateral contracts, when the offeree has begun but not completed the required performance at the time of the purported revocation. The third involves offers by merchants to buy or sell goods.

OPTIONS

A promise to keep an offer open, supported by consideration, creates an option, which the offeror cannot revoke during its stated period.

EXAMPLE ■ Barclay offers to sell his house to Fulton for $90,000 and also says, "I will agree to keep this offer open for 15 days if you will pay me $500." Fulton pays $500 in response to this proposition. Fulton has not accepted the offer to buy the house, but he has accepted the offer to keep the offer open. A collateral contract called an option is thus created, which obligates Barclay to keep the offer open for Fulton for 15 days.

UNILATERAL CONTRACTS

When an offer is made to enter into a unilateral contract and the offeree has started performance, the offeror loses the power of revocation.

However, in this situation, no contract is formed until the offeree performs the act required by the offer.

**EXAMPLE** ■ Cecil Caxton offers to pay Albrush $5,000 if Albrush will paint Caxton's house. When Albrush finishes half of the job, Caxton tells him the offer is revoked.

This case involves an offer to enter into a unilateral contract because the offeror requests an act, rather than a promise, from the offeree. The contract is not formed until the offeree does the act requested. Thus, Albrush does not accept the offer until he completely paints the house. In the interest of fairness, however, the rule has evolved that Albrush, by beginning his performance, bars Caxton's right to revoke. This rule is an exception to the principle that a person can always revoke an offer before acceptance.

MERCHANTS' OFFERS

Under the UCC, if a merchant signs a written offer to buy or sell goods and gives assurances in the writing that the offer will be held open, the offer is not revocable during the period stated in the writing, which cannot be more than three months, or if no time is stated, for a "reasonable time." No separate option payment is required to keep the offer irrevocably open.

## *Other Methods of Terminating Offers*

In addition to revocation, an offer may be terminated in a number of other ways. The most obvious terminating event is a lapse of time or the failure to comply with a condition of the offer.

**EXAMPLE** ■ Lopez offers Connors $80,000 for his business upon the condition that the offer be accepted within 60 days. Once the 60 days pass, the offer will end and Connors will be unable to accept it.

In addition to terminating events stated in the offer itself, the courts have listed other events that terminate an offer. Those events include the offeree's rejection of the offer; the offeror's death; an event that deprives the offeror of the legal capacity to make a contract; the death or destruction of a person or thing essential for the performance of the proposed contract; or the supervening legal prohibition of the proposed contract.

---

**EXAMPLES** ■ Gary Adam makes an offer to purchase three acres from Peter Case. The next day, Adam dies. Even if Case wishes to accept the offer, he will be unable to do so because Adam's death terminated the offer.

After Adam's death, Lee Owen makes an offer to buy Case's three acres. Before Case can decide whether to accept it, an accident renders Owen mentally impaired, and a guardian is subsequently appointed for him. Thus, Owen's legal capacity to enter into a contract is terminated and, with it, his offer.

■ Darian National Bank offers to purchase a competing bank from its shareholders. Before acceptance of the offer, the state in which the banks are located enacts unit bank legislation prohibiting banks from having more than one office. The offer is terminated since its essential purpose has become illegal.

---

While rejections terminate offers, they may also produce counteroffers that may be accepted and result in contracts.

---

**EXAMPLE** ■ Marwick applies to Third National Bank for a $50,000 loan to be repaid with interest in one year. The bank does not wish to wait that long for payment so it rejects Marwick's application (which is an offer) and counteroffers to make the loan if Marwick pays interest monthly, with the principal due in full in one year. Marwick accepts the offer and a contract is created.

---

# Consideration

Legal capacity to contract, an objective that is legal, and mutual assent do not themselves create a contract. In addition, a valid contract must also meet the requirement of **consideration**; that is, all parties to the contract must provide something of value. A promise is unenforceable as a contract unless consideration has been given for it. The law therefore divides promises into two basic categories: gratuitous promises and promises of consideration. Gratuitous promises are unenforceable as contracts. Promises of consideration may be enforceable as contracts if the requested promise is rendered.

EXAMPLE ■ Tom Tinker promises Sue Ingram that he will repair her watch free of charge. He afterward refuses to do so. Ingram sues. The courts will rule in favor of Tinker because no consideration was given for Tinker's promise, which did not request anything in exchange. Thus, Tinker's promise was gratuitous.

Suppose instead that Ingram promises to pay Tinker $100 if he will promise to fix her watch. In this case, consideration has been given for both promises.

Where a **bilateral contract** exists, there is "mutuality of obligation"; that is, both parties, by their promises to perform or forbear from an act, create and are bound to a contract. Where a **unilateral contract** exists, there is no mutuality of obligation, since the promisor is bound only if the promisee actually performs or forbears from an act. Forbearance, or refraining from doing something a promisee had a legal right to do or not to do, is a form of consideration.

**Legal detriment** involves the sacrifice of a legal right or interest. It may be an act, a forbearance, or a promise. Legal benefit arises when an individual requests and receives from another either the performance of or forbearance from an act, or a promise to perform or forbear from an act.

EXAMPLE ■ A father writes to his son, "I will give you $5,000 if you refrain from smoking until you are 21 years of age." The son refrains.

The son may enforce his father's promise. In refraining from doing what he had a legal right to do, the son suffered a legal detriment and thus should be paid the agreed price for the promise. Refraining from smoking in response to his father's promise is a legal detriment even though it may have physically benefited the son.

---

Thus, legal detriment is not measured by any resulting benefit, but by the sacrifice of a legal right to act or refrain from acting. Legal detriment becomes consideration only if it is requested by the promisor.

---

EXAMPLE ■ John Penn promised Mary Spark that he would give her $6,000 at Christmas. Relying on the promise, Spark bought a car on credit for $6,000. Penn did not make the gift at Christmas and Spark sued.

The courts would rule in favor of Penn, because no consideration was given for his promise to make the gift. Although Spark relied on the promise and did something she was not legally obligated to do—namely, buy the car—this act is not legal detriment because Penn did not request the purchase. Therefore, the purchase did not furnish consideration for his promise. Stated differently, Spark cannot seriously claim that her purchase was a price she paid for Penn's promise, since he never asked her to buy the car.

---

A gift upon condition is also not consideration given for a contract.

---

EXAMPLE ■ Sara Carson said to Joe Walsh, a homeless man shivering in the cold a few blocks from her house, "Walk with me to my house, and I will give you an overcoat." Walsh walked with Carson to her house but made a remark that convinced her that he would not be sufficiently grateful for the coat. She therefore refused to give him the coat. Is Walsh legally entitled to it?

No. No consideration was given for Carson's promise. While Walsh in walking to Carson's house sustained a detriment, Carson did not ask him to do this as the price or exchange for her promise. Rather, the total transaction demonstrates that Carson was planning to make a gift and that her request to Walsh to come to her house was only so that he would be in a position to receive the gift. Thus, legally the transaction would be characterized as a conditional gift and not consideration for a contract.

---

*Adequacy of Consideration*

Consideration need not be adequate to create a contract. As with many terms, the legal definition of "adequacy" differs from its definition in day-to-day conversation. Whether the price paid for forbearance from or performance of an act is fair is not the law's concern. The law is generally concerned only with whether consideration is given and not with its amount or adequacy.

---

EXAMPLE ■ Wills deposits $100,000 in a new time account at First State Bank, which pays 1 percent interest per year. The competitive rate at other banks is 14 percent. Wills finds this out and asks to cancel the time deposit and withdraw his funds. Based on the terms of the contract, which prohibit early withdrawal, the bank refuses. A contract exists in this situation and Wills may not withdraw his funds because, in paying even minimal interest for the deposit, the bank has given consideration.

---

The refusal of courts in most situations to determine whether consideration is fair is based on the belief that people ought to be able to bargain freely in their transactions without the court's interference. Further, if parties to contracts sued whenever consideration seemed inadequate, court case loads would greatly increase.

Courts will review adequacy of consideration in situations where things of the same type are exchanged in unequal quantities, for in such situations lack of adequacy is apparent from the facts of the contract.

---

EXAMPLE ■ Hay promises immediately to pay Wiess $1 for $600. In this example, things of the same type—dollars—are exchanged in unequal quantities at the same time. This exchange does not constitute consideration. Hay could not enforce the agreement since without consideration there is no contract. More likely, this transaction would be considered an executory promise to make a gift of $599, which is not binding.

However, if payment of the larger amount is to be made at a future time, a contract can exist, but in this case it would be usurious.

---

A court will also review adequacy of consideration where such gross inadequacy exists that it renders enforcement of a contract unconscionable. No specific test for "adequacy" exists. Each case contesting adequacy will be decided on its own merits.

---

EXAMPLE ■ Knowing a parcel of land contains oil, a land speculator pays its owner $100 per acre when comparable acreage is selling for $50,000 per acre. In such a case, a court could find that no contract exists because of the inadequacy of consideration.

---

Under the UCC, a court may declare unconscionable a contract involving the sale of goods which lacks adequacy of consideration and may then refuse to enforce the contract. The relevant provision states

If the court as a matter of law finds the contract or any clause of the contract to have been unconscionable at the time it was made, the court may refuse to enforce the contract, or it may enforce the remainder of the contract without the unconscionable clause, or it may so limit the application of any unconscionable clause as to avoid any unconscionable result (U.C.C. § 2–302(1)).

## Contracts That May Be Enforced without Consideration

While consideration is necessary to most contracts, this rule has several exceptions. Included within these exceptions are (1) promises to pay debts barred by the statute of limitations; (2) promises to pay debts discharged in bankruptcy; (3) certain promises to perform a voidable duty; (4) promises supported by promissory estoppel; and (5) modification of contracts coming within the scope of article 2 of the UCC.

---

**EXAMPLE** ■ Lindsay owed money to Hodges but the statute of limitations barred the debt. Nevertheless, Lindsay promised to pay the debt. Lindsay's promise waives the statutory bar of unenforceability of the debt and is binding, even though no consideration is given for it.

---

Courts sometimes say that moral consideration supports the promise or the statute of limitations bars only the remedy and not the right, but these are simply justifications for not insisting on the application of consideration under these circumstances. Stated another way, many courts feel that the statute of limitations is designed to protect the debtor against potential abuses when suit is brought on a very old debt. If the debtor, however, promises to pay such a debt, the potential abuses are removed and the courts feel that the doctrine of consideration should not prevent the other party to the contract from collecting on the debt. In most states, the promise to waive the statute must be in writing.

---

**EXAMPLE** ■ Lowell, who legally is an infant, makes a contract with Peale, an adult. After reaching his majority, Lowell promises to pay the debt arising under the contract. In this situation, Lowell is

163  *Contracts*

liable. The absence of consideration does not prevent this agreement from being binding.

## Case for Discussion

### CENTRAL COLLEGE v. SANTINI

#### Facts

Allen, a representative of Central College, calls at the office of Santini. He tells Santini that the college is conducting a drive to obtain $10 million for its endowment fund and that donations totaling $9,750,000 have already been subscribed. Allen then asks Santini for a subscription toward raising the balance. Santini agrees to contribute $100,000 toward the remaining balance. Later, Santini denies ever making the promise and refuses to give the college the $100,000. Central College then sues Santini.

#### Decision

Generally, courts would rule that Santini's promise to pay the money is binding. Some courts would say that Santini by his refusal to pay the money has impliedly requested the representative to obtain additional subscriptions to reach the amount needed. Since the representative in this case would be asked to do something he was not legally bound to do, he would suffer a legal detriment and thus provide consideration to support Santini's promise.

However, most courts frankly admit no consideration is given in cases such as this, because Santini did not ask Allen to do anything as a price for the subscription. But public policy calls for the enforcement of charitable subscriptions because the public is interested in the support, growth, and maintenance of charitable, religious, and educational institutions, and often their principal source of support is charitable subscriptions. Thus, in this situation, the courts would probably make an exception to the doctrine of consideration and enforce Santini's promise on the ground of "promissory estoppel."

#### Questions for Discussion

1. What steps could Allen have taken to ensure that Santini's promise of contribution was binding?
2. Describe a situation in which a bank might be involved in promissory estoppel.

**Promissory estoppel** is an equitable doctrine applied to prevent injustice. Elements of the cause of action include

- an express promise made by the promisor
- a reasonable expectation by the promisor that the promisee will rely on the promise
- a justified reliance by the promisee
- an injustice will result if the promise isn't enforced

Thus, the doctrine of promissory estoppel states that when a person reasonably relies upon a promise and changes his or her position in good faith, the promisor is estopped from using the absence of consideration as a defense to breaking the promise.

---

EXAMPLE ■ Dorset National Bank holds a mortgage on Meyer's land. The bank tells Meyer it will not foreclose for a specified time, even though he is in default. Relying on this promise, Meyer makes some improvements on the land. The bank now attempts to foreclose.

The bank's promise to Meyer prevents it from foreclosing. Although the promise is not supported by consideration, this is one of the limited situations that will be enforced under the doctrine of promissory estoppel.

---

When a contract involves the sale of goods and thus comes under the UCC, it can be modified by agreement of the parties and the modification is enforceable without additional consideration (U.C.C. § 2–209).

---

EXAMPLE ■ Home Appliances, Inc., enters into a contract with Top Products Company to buy 10,000 screws for $1,000. Subsequently the parties agree to modify the contract to provide for the purchase of

165   Contracts

10,000 screws for $900. This modification of the contract is enforceable without additional consideration.

## STATUTE OF FRAUDS

Contracts should be in writing to assure the contracting parties and any third persons with whom they are dealing that in fact an agreement exists to which all can readily refer in order to understand the parties' transaction properly. Certainly this is true of the contracts into which banks enter, since both the banks and their customers must have certainty when it comes to financial matters.

Not only does good policy require the use of written rather than oral contracts, but in many transactions the law will not enforce contracts unless they can be established by a proper writing. In 1677, the British Parliament enacted the Statute of Frauds to help prevent the use of fraud and perjury when proving contracts in court. To accomplish its purpose, the statute required that contracts governing certain types of transactions would be enforced only if a proper writing existed. Adopted in varying forms throughout the United States, the Statute of Frauds also has been interpreted through numerous court decisions.

**Contractual Promises Addressed by the Statute of Frauds**

In most states, the **statute of frauds** addresses six fundamental types of contractual promises, including

- promises made in consideration of marriage

- promises by executors, administrators, or personal representatives to pay a decedent's debts from personal funds

- promises to answer for the duty, debt, or default of another

- promises that, by their terms, cannot be performed within one year from the time they are made

- contracts for the sale of land or any interest in land

- contracts for the sale of goods above the purchase price fixed in the statute

The areas covered by the statute of frauds generally reflect concern for situations in which the parties are especially vulnerable to fraud or where the temptation to perpetrate fraud may be strong.

## *Promises Made in Consideration of Marriage*

This aspect of the statute of frauds is not as important today as it was in past centuries, when large sums of money, land, and other valuable items were pledged to newly married couples or to their families, once the couple married. However, the statute continues to require that agreements made before marriage, including antenuptial agreements regarding the division of property between spouses, must be in writing. Such agreements are common and are motivated by desires to curtail or enlarge property rights that normally arise upon a marriage.

---

EXAMPLE ■ Ruth Kind and Frank Sharp want to marry. They live in Michigan and, upon their marriage, if they do not agree otherwise, Ruth will acquire a dower interest in all Frank's real estate. Before the marriage, Ruth agrees that she will take no dower interest in Frank's real estate. Unless the agreement is contained in a proper writing, Frank will never be able to enforce it and Ruth will be able to assert dower interest in his real estate.

---

Consideration for an antenuptial agreement may be the marriage itself and no other value need be given.

Third parties may also make promises in consideration of marriage.

---

EXAMPLE ■ Justin Lane claims that Joe Duncan, the father of Ruth Duncan, promised him a job in Duncan's company and $10,000 after his upcoming marriage to Ruth. As a promise "in consideration of marriage" that falls within the meaning of the statute of frauds, this promise is unenforceable unless proved by a proper writing and signed by Duncan.

---

## Promises by Executors, Administrators, or Personal Representatives to Pay Decedents' Debts from Personal Funds

A disappointed creditor who finds that a debtor died leaving an insufficient estate to pay all of the bills may be tempted to claim that the executor, administrator, or personal representative had promised to pay the debt. To protect the deceased's representative from such claims, the statute of frauds provides that any such promise to answer for the duty, debt, or default of a decedent out of the representative's own estate must be proved by a writing to be enforceable.

**EXAMPLE** ■ Nancy Hall is the personal representative of her deceased son Don's estate. During the administration of the son's estate, his creditors contact her demanding payment. In her bereaved state and for "family honor" she orally promises that, even if the estate cannot pay the debts, she will pay them with personal funds.

After the estate is closed, many creditors remain unpaid and they sue Nancy for payment. Since her promise is not in writing, it is unenforceable under the statute of frauds.

## Promises to Answer for the Duty of Another

Similar to promises by executors, administrators, or personal representatives to pay the decedent's debts out of their own pockets, general promises to answer for the duty of another are unenforceable under the statute of frauds, unless there is a proper writing.

**EXAMPLE** ■ Lyle Lekas applies for a loan at Totterville State Bank. The bank denies his application but makes a counteroffer that, if he obtains a suitable guarantor, the loan will be made. Lyle resubmits an application indicating that his father, Lawrence, will guarantee the debt. A bank loan officer calls Lawrence and he assures her that he will guarantee the debt. The loan closes, but Lawrence's guaranty is never put into writing. Lyle defaults and the bank sues Lawrence, who readily admits the oral guaranty but refuses to pay on the basis of the statute of frauds. In this situation,

Lawrence will probably win because the guaranty was not in writing.

## Promises That, by Their Terms, Cannot Be Performed within One Year

Promises that, by their terms, cannot be performed within one year from their execution are unenforceable unless proved by a proper writing. The policy behind this provision of the statute of frauds is the desire not to leave the terms of a contract that may be performed many years after its execution to nothing more than the memory of the parties.

To bring a promise within the provisions of this section of the statute of frauds, the promise must be incapable of being performed within one year.

EXAMPLE ■ Munch promises to paint Angel's house within the next 30 days for $1,000. Since this promise, by its terms, is to be performed within one year, it can be enforced whether or not it is in writing.

Suppose instead that Munch promises to paint Angel's house for $1,000 without mentioning a completion date. Since nothing exists in the terms of the promise making Munch incapable of meeting those terms within one year, this promise is enforceable even if it is only made orally.

Thus, an oral promise need not specify a date of completion to be enforceable. As long as its performance could be undertaken within one year, an oral promise is enforceable.

However, an oral promise that, by its own terms, is not to be performed within one year is unenforceable unless proved by a proper writing.

EXAMPLE ■ On January 2, 1989, Pollack promises to paint Harbin's house in February 1990 for $1,000. Since Pollack's promise to Harbin cannot be performed by January 1, 1990, there must be a proper writing for his promise to be enforced.

## Contracts for the Sale of Land or Any Interest in Land

To be enforceable, contracts creating or transferring any interest in real estate, including land contracts, liens, leases, easements, and restrictions, must be proved by a proper writing.

EXAMPLE ■ MacKenzie orally agreed to sell Ford 20 acres of land for $20,000. MacKenzie subsequently refused to complete the transaction. The promise is unenforceable in this situation since it related to a conveyance of land and there was no proper writing.

In another situation, Citizens' Bank loaned Sova $250,000. Sova agreed to secure the loan with a mortgage on the land, but the mortgage was never put into writing. Sova defaulted on the loan and the bank began foreclosure proceedings. Sova resisted the foreclosure, based on the absence of a written mortgage. While a judgment could be rendered against Sova for the balance due on the loan at the time of her default, she also could raise the statute of frauds as a defense against the foreclosure.

## Contracts for the Sale of Goods

The section of the original Statute of Frauds requiring written proof of contracts for the sale of goods above a certain purchase price as fixed by the statute has been incorporated into the UCC:

Except as otherwise provided in this section a contract for the sale of goods for the price of $500 or more is not enforceable by way of action or defense unless there is some writing sufficient to indicate that a contract for sale has been made between the parties and signed by the party against whom enforcement is sought or by his authorized agent or broker (U.C.C. § 2–201(1)).

EXAMPLE ■ Gadgets, Inc., agrees to sell 300 products to Monopoly Corp.

for $4,000. Since the price exceeds $500, the promise is unenforceable unless there is a proper writing.

## Exceptions to the Statute of Frauds

Since passage of the original Statute of Frauds in 1677, courts and legislatures have recognized that reliance on the statute can have harsh results. In certain instances, court decisions and various statutes have provided for the enforcement of oral contracts that otherwise would be unenforceable because of the statute of frauds.

Partial performance will render enforceable (a) an oral contract for the transfer of interest in land and (b) under the UCC, an oral contract for the sale of goods for $500 or more, but only to the extent of such partial performance.

EXAMPLES
- Epstein promises to sell land to Valenti for $90,000, to be paid in installments. Relying on Epstein's promise, Valenti sells his home, takes possession of the land, builds a house on it, and over a period of two years pays Epstein all but $10,000 of the $90,000 purchase price. Suddenly, Epstein orders Valenti off the land, asserting his promise to convey the property is unenforceable based on the statute of frauds. Because Valenti's partial performance of the oral contract for the sale of land is substantial, a court could enforce the contract against Epstein.

- Franks orally agrees to buy 10,000 trinkets from Chen for $1 per trinket. Delivery of 5,000 trinkets is to be made on January 10 and the remainder on March 1. Chen makes the January 10 delivery, which Franks accepts. Franks later informs Chen he does not want the March 1 delivery and refuses to pay for the January 10 delivery.

    Since Franks received and accepted the January 10 delivery, he will have to pay for it, but he has the right to refuse the March 1 delivery. An oral contract for the sale of goods for a price of $500 or more is enforceable "with respect to goods for which payment has been made and accepted or which have been received and accepted" (U.C.C. § 2–201(3)(c)).

**Oral Promises to Lend Money**

Notwithstanding the statute of frauds, courts recently have begun to enforce oral commitments to lend money. These cases come within the "lender liability" label applied to various theories of litigation against banks based on contract, tort, and negligence law. Typically, borrowers allege that because they have relied on an oral commitment to lend money, an exception to the statute of frauds applies.

---

EXAMPLE ■ Sam Barton applies for a $300,000 loan at Third National Bank to purchase equipment for a business he intends to start. Specific terms are discussed. Linda Thorne, president of the bank, assures Barton the loan will be made; however, no written commitment is issued and no loan documents are signed. Based on this discussion, Barton pays $50,000 of his own money as a deposit on the equipment. Further, the bank advances Barton $10,000 on an unsecured term note. However, the note makes no mention of the larger loan amount. Barton informs the bank he is ready to close the loan, but Thorne states that the bank will not advance further funds. Because of Barton's reliance on Thorne's promise and what the court could perceive is the bank's partial performance, the court could find that a contract to lend does exist.

---

Given potential "lender liability" lawsuits, banks must be particularly careful to avoid the appearance of an oral commitment to lend money when no commitment is intended.

**Writings That Satisfy the Statute of Frauds**

To satisfy the requirement that a contract coming within the statute of frauds be proved by a proper writing, statutory and case law require a writing that at least sets forth the material terms of the parties' agreement and is signed by the party against whom the contract is to be enforced. Thus, the writing needed to satisfy the statute of frauds need not be a written contract. In most jurisdictions, the essential elements needed to satisfy the statute of frauds are the identity of the parties, identification of the contract's subject matter, and the consideration. Other terms of the parties' contract, such as delivery dates, time of performance, default provisions, and termination dates, may be oral. Under the UCC, proof of a contract for the sale of goods for $500 or more requires a memorandum that a contract for the sale has been made, signed by the party to be charged and specifying the quantity of goods (U.C.C. § 2–201(1)).

## PAROL EVIDENCE RULE

As the statute of frauds indicates, the law encourages contracts to be in writing. This basic policy of the law led to the common-law creation of the parol evidence rule, which has been incorporated in the laws of many states either by court decisions or statutes. The UCC has made the parol evidence rule part of article 2:

Terms with respect to which the confirmatory memoranda of the parties agree or which are otherwise set forth in a writing intended by the parties as a final expression of their agreement with respect to such terms as are included therein may not be contradicted by evidence of any prior agreement or of a contemporaneous oral agreement but may be explained or supplemented (a) by course of dealing or usage of trade (U.C.C. § 1–205) or by course of performance (U.C.C. § 2–208); and (b) by evidence of consistent additional terms unless the court finds the writing to have been intended also as a complete and exclusive statement of the terms of the agreement (U.C.C. § 2–202).

The rule holds that where parties have entered into a written contract that reflects their complete statement of the contract, no written or oral evidence of prior understandings or negotiations is admissable to contradict or vary the terms of the written contract.

---

EXAMPLE ■ Maggini offers to sell his real estate to Lux. They negotiate and agree on a purchase price of $200,000. A written purchase agreement is prepared, but it states that the purchase price is $205,000. Lux objects but executes the agreement when Maggini orally agrees that the purchase price will be $200,000. Subsequently Lux gives Maggini $200,000 but Maggini refuses to give Lux a deed and claims the purchase price is actually $205,000.

If Lux sues Maggini, he will be precluded from using evidence of the oral negotiations about the purchase price that occurred both before and during the execution of the written contract. His inability to introduce evidence of these negotiations is due to the parol evidence rule, which precludes evidence of oral agreements that contradict terms of a written contract. Nor would it help Lux had the $200,000 price been put in a writing that was written before execution of the purchase agreement, since such a writing before a contract is also precluded from consideration.

---

Under the parol evidence rule, only a writing, and not an oral agreement that is contemporaneous with a written contract may be used to contradict terms in the contract.

The parol evidence rule cannot be used to prohibit use of oral or written agreements made after a written contract that contradict the contract's terms. In the above example, had Maggini agreed after the purchase contract was signed that the price was $200,000, Lux could use evidence of that postcontract agreement to contradict the terms of the purchase agreement.

---

**EXAMPLE** ■ The facts are the same as in the previous example. The purchase contract made no mention of the condition of the building on the property, but in oral negotiations leading to execution of the purchase contract, Maggini promises to paint the building's exterior within 30 days of delivery of a deed.

If Lux needed to enforce that promise, he could introduce evidence of Maggini's oral promise to paint, since its introduction does not contradict, but only supplements, any terms in the purchase contract.

---

Several aspects about the parol evidence rule alleviate what would otherwise be harshness in the law of contracts. As has been indicated, the rule prevents a contradiction of the written contract as evidencing the intentions of the parties to the contract. Parol evidence can be introduced to show that a contract was actually made or else resulted from fraud, mistake, duress, undue influence, incapacity, or illegality. Further, parol evidence can also be used to explain ambiguous terms in a contract.

## INTERPRETING CONTRACTS

In preparing a written contract, the drafter seeks to put the intentions of the parties to the contract into words only to the extent needed to express their complete agreement. The drafter hopes that the words and phrases used will have the same meaning to all the parties and that each party will clearly understand in the same way all the rights and obligations arising from the contract. Unfortunately, that goal is not always met and, after contracts are executed, questions about their meanings arise and must be answered. To help those attempting to interpret the meanings of contracts, including lawyers and judges, the law has developed guidelines that are called primary and secondary rules of interpretation.

### Primary Rules of Interpretation

Under the primary rules of interpretation, when contracts are written, words are to be given their plain and usual meaning. This rule has three exceptions: (1) usage of the trade or locality may vary the usual meaning of words, (2) technical words ("words of art") are to be given their technical meaning, and (3) words may not be given their plain meaning if that construction contradicts the intention of the parties to the contract.

Contracts are to be interpreted to carry out the intentions of the parties to the contract. To so interpret a contract, it must be read as a whole, whether it is composed of one or many documents. Individual documents or clauses that compose a contract must be read together to discover what the parties really intended their contract to do. If the words themselves do not fully reflect the parties' intentions, the circumstances leading up to the contract may be considered to convey its meaning.

EXAMPLE ■ In the food industry, the term "tin cans" does not mean cans made of tin but those made of steel and other metals. Jones ordered 100,000 "tin cans" from Smith. Smith, by delivering cans made of steel or other metals, can perform the contract. The usage of the trade makes clear that a plain-meaning interpretation of the words "tin cans" is inappropriate.

*Case for Discussion*

**STARK v. BUDWARKER**

### Facts
Pursuant to an installment sales contract, Stark sold Budwarker a bar business. The bar was located on real estate that adjoined a municipality in which the business would be illegal. At the time of the negotiations leading to the sale of the business, both parties believed the property might be annexed to the adjoining municipality and, as a result, it was agreed in the contract that, if annexation occurred, Budwarker could transfer the bar back to Stark and owe her no further money. After execution of the contract, the municipality passed an ordinance permitting bar businesses within its boundaries. Shortly after passage of the ordinance, the municipality annexed the property on which the bar was located. Budwarker attempted to transfer the business back to Stark, who refused it and demanded that Budwarker comply with the payment terms of the contract.

### Decision
In this situation, a literal interpretation of the contract would require Stark to take back the bar and forfeit further payments. However, the intent of the parties when entering into the contract was to transfer the bar to Stark only if the bar business became illegal. Therefore, Budwarker cannot enforce the reconveyance clause, given its meaning within the entire context of the contract. (See *Stark v. Budwarker, Inc.*, 25 Mich. App. 305, 181 N.W. 2d 298 (1970).)

**Questions for Discussion**

1. Give two examples in which banks might find themselves in a situation similar to this case.
2. What defense can be raised in a case in which the literal interpretation of a contract is different from its overall intent?

---

**Secondary Rules of Interpretation**

If the meaning of the contract remains ambiguous after the primary rules of interpretation have been applied, the following secondary rules will take effect:

- An interpretation that gives a reasonable meaning to all or the main provisions of the contract will be preferred.

- A specific clause will prevail over a conflicting general clause.

- An interpretation that makes a contract legal and reasonable will be preferred over an interpretation that renders the contract illegal or harsh.

- Language will be interpreted against the drafter of the contract.

- If a conflict exists between a handwritten and a typed term, the handwritten term will prevail.

- Related writings may be interpreted together.

## PERFORMANCE OF THE CONTRACT

The parties perform their contract by doing exactly what they promised to do. The exact obligations of the parties are sometimes difficult to determine because contracts are frequently vague in their expressions of rights and duties. Through the process of interpretation, however, the courts have construed definite meanings for terms and this has resulted in some certainty regarding performance.

The concept of performance should not be confused with that of breach. A party has breached a contract only when his or her nonperformance is without excuse and thus wrongful. Moreover, the courts recognize that in some cases it would be unjust to permit the "victim" to allege and prove a complete breach after substantial performance has been tendered. But for the sake of simplicity, courts usually say that "breach" is wrongful nonperformance. Accepting this definition requires recognizing that the problems of performance also involve a determination of what circumstances excuse it and what situations require the acceptance of substantial performance plus a money allowance.

## Excuses for Nonperformance

Performance of a contract is excused only for certain reasons, including when the contract is legally impossible to carry out. In such a case, neither party may recover on the contract nor insist on the other's performance.

### Impossibility as an Excuse for Nonperformance

Legal impossibility of performance of a contract is different from personal impossibility. Legal impossibility in effect means "it cannot be done"; personal impossibility means "I cannot do it." If a person agrees to do a certain act, personal inability to do it does not excuse performance. If no one could do it, however, he or she would be excused. Common-law legal impossibility generally involves one of three situations: (1) the death or incapacity of the promisor of a contract that is personal in nature, (2) the supervening illegality of performance, or (3) the destruction of the subject matter essential to performance.

DEATH OR INCAPACITY OF THE PROMISOR OF A CONTRACT THAT IS PERSONAL IN NATURE

A contract that is personal in nature is one where a party's skill, taste, or particular knowledge is the essence of the contract.

---

EXAMPLES
- Frost agrees to sell Evans 100 cases of Scotch whiskey. He dies before delivering the whiskey. Performance is not excused. Frost's executor must deliver the whiskey because the contract is not personal in nature.

- Halstead agrees to paint a portrait of Kolchek's wife but dies before beginning the portrait. Halstead's performance is excused because the contract is personal in nature.

---

## SUPERVENING ILLEGALITY OF PERFORMANCE

Contract law does not require a person to perform criminal acts, even where those acts were not criminal when the agreement was made. In other words, an illegal performance of a contract is excused.

---

**EXAMPLE** ■ Krol agrees to sell Paine 100 cases of Scotch whiskey. Before performance, the state makes the sale of liquor illegal. In this case, Krol is excused because the contract was legal when made but a supervening law made its performance illegal.

---

## DESTRUCTION OF THE SUBJECT MATTER ESSENTIAL TO PERFORMANCE

Impracticability excuses performance of a contract, based on common law and the UCC (U.C.C. § 2–615). Impracticability exists where an individual may be unable to perform a contract due to circumstances beyond his or her control, such as war or natural disasters. In addition, impracticability exists where an individual may be able to perform, but due to an unforseen contingency, at a cost grossly greater than that anticipated by the parties when the contract was made.

---

**EXAMPLE** ■ Spencer has a contract with Orange Juicy, Inc., to provide 10,000 oranges a week to Juicy during the months of December and January. Both Spencer and Juicy contemplate that the oranges will come from Spencer's orange grove in Florida. In late November, a record frost destroys most of Spencer's crop.

Spencer must notify Juicy of his inability to completely perform the contract and will be excused for nonperformance. If

Juicy wants the remaining oranges, Spencer may be required to allocate them to Juicy.

## Other Excuses for Nonperformance

Frustration of purpose is another valid excuse from performing a contract. Under this doctrine, although the parties are able to perform, performance is excused when something happens (something the parties assumed would not happen when they made the contract) that destroys the value of the contract.

## Case for Discussion

### KRELL v. HENRY

#### Facts
The defendant agreed to hire a flat in London from the plaintiff for June 26 and 27, 1902, on which days it had been officially announced that the coronation processions of Edward VII would occur along a route that passed the flat. The defendant planned to use the flat to view the parades. King Edward VII became ill and the coronation was postponed. The defendant refused to pay the rent for the flat.

#### Decision
The court held that the defendant was excused from performing the contract. The court recognized that no impossibility was present in this situation, because the defendant could pay for the flat and the plaintiff could provide it. Rather, the court rested its decision on the fact that the value of the performance had been frustrated and destroyed—or almost totally destroyed—by an unanticipated supervening event (the king's illness), the nonoccurrence of which constituted a basic assumption of the parties in making the contract. *Krell v. Henry*, 2 K.B. 740 (1903).

#### Questions for Discussion
1. How should the plaintiff in this case have protected himself in the original contract against a frustration-of-purpose excuse for nonperformance?
2. Give an example in which a bank might have to deal with the excuse of frustration of purpose from a customer for nonperformance of a contract. Describe steps the bank could take to avoid such a development or defenses it could raise should such a development occur.

3. Give an example in which a bank itself might have to use a frustration-of-purpose excuse for its own nonperformance of a contract.

---

It is sometimes said that a party's duty to perform is excused by the nonoccurrence of a condition of the contract. Technically, such a statement is incorrect, because *no* performance is due if a term of the contract suspends it. In that case, performance is not excused—it is simply not due. For convenience, however, lawyers tend to regard conditions as part of the law of excuse. The purpose of inserting a condition in a contract is to postpone the duty of performance or to extinguish that duty under certain circumstances. Thus, a party may provide in the contract that he or she will not be bound if certain events occur. The events themselves might not provide an excuse for nonperformance and the condition, therefore, is inserted to relieve an otherwise unprotected party.

---

EXAMPLE ■ Baker applies for a loan to be secured by a real estate mortgage. Central State Bank agrees to make the loan, conditioned upon a clear title of the real estate offered as collateral. A title search is conducted and a prior lien on the property is discovered.

In this situation, Central State Bank does not have to perform the contract. Technically, its performance of the contract is not excused. Rather, it has no duty to perform the contract. Its performance in making the loan was conditioned on the happening of an event, receipt of a clear title.

---

Conditions may be created expressly or by implication and they are said to be "precedent," "concurrent," or "subsequent" in nature. A fact or event may be a condition, because the parties have so stated in the contract. Such a condition is called **express**. The intention of the parties that certain events should constitute conditions, however, may be reasonably inferred from their acts and the other terms of the contract. In this case, the resulting conditions are said to be **implied**.

Whether express or implied, a precedent condition arises when one party's performance of a contract is to precede the other party's performance. In this case, the party who is to perform first is bound to perform before the other party is required to perform. For example, it is an implied condition that when work is to be performed on one side of a contract and money to be paid on the other, the work must be done before payment is made. If the worker does not perform, he or she may be sued for breach of contract. But the employer cannot be sued for breach of contract merely for nonperformance unless the worker has already tendered performance. Thus, a precedent condition runs in favor of the employer, who is not liable until the worker first performs. The worker, on the other hand, does not enjoy a precedent condition and inactivity on his or her part will result in a breach of contract.

A concurrent condition requires the contracting parties to render performance at the same time. A contract for the sale of goods that mentions no time of payment or delivery is a common example of a situation in which concurrent conditions exist. In this situation, neither the seller nor the buyer needs to perform the contract until the other tenders performance.

---

**EXAMPLE** ■ Graham agrees to buy Drew's car and pay $3,000 cash for it and Drew agrees to sell the car on these terms. Subsequently neither Graham nor Drew does anything to perform the contract.

In this case, no breach of contract occurs. If neither Graham nor Drew does anything, it may seem that each has broken her promise. But if Graham sues Drew for not delivering the car she must first offer Drew the $3,000 before she can sue. If Drew brings the suit, she must first offer the car to Graham before the suit can begin. This situation exists because each party has conditioned (usually by implication) her own performance on the other's performance.

---

A subsequent condition is any operative fact that will extinguish a duty to make compensation for breach of contract after an event has occurred. A common example is a contractual term that suit must be brought within a stated period or liability will be discharged. Insurance contracts frequently contain terms that operate to forfeit the insured's rights unless certain actions are taken within a prescribed time. These terms are properly said to be "conditions subsequent."

## Substantial Performance

Failure to perform a contract completely may be excused for the reasons already discussed. Such a failure may also be excused at least to the extent that the party failing to complete performance will not lose all of the benefits under the contract. This is a case where substantial performance has occurred; namely, the major purpose of the contract has been performed or not defeated. The doctrine of substantial performance is applied most frequently in construction cases, primarily to prevent forfeiture.

---

EXAMPLE ■ Crane agrees to build a house for Davis for $80,000. Crane has fully completed the house, except that some defects, which can be remedied for $2,000, remain in the plastering. Crane does not have the opportunity to correct these defects because the time for performance has expired. Davis elects to stand on the contract and refuses to pay Crane on the ground that the latter has breached the plastering term of the agreement.

While Crane has not fully performed and thus breached the contract, the courts will require Davis to accept the house and pay the full price, less a money allowance of $2,000 to cure the defects. In this manner, a forfeiture is prevented.

---

If a party willfully fails to complete performance of a contract, substantial performance will be unavailable to that party as an excuse for failure to perform the contract completely.

## Third Parties' Performance of Contracts

Under certain conditions, the obligations and rights associated with contracts may be transferred to third parties. However, if a party who undertakes an obligation or receives a right under a contract is essential to its performance, then the rights or obligations cannot be transferred. The basic principle involved in such cases is that certain rights can be assigned and certain duties can be delegated.

## Assignment of Rights

Unless a contract specifically prohibits such assignment, rights of the parties to a contract can generally be assigned to third parties. However, rights cannot be assigned to third parties when such action will (1) materially change the other party's duty, (2) materially increase the burden or risk imposed by the contract, or (3) materially impair the chance of obtaining return performance.

A typical example of an assignable contract is one in which the promisor is obligated to pay money. As assignment by the promisee of the right to receive the money (an account receivable) is no imposition on the promisor, since it should not matter who is to receive the money. The assignment does not materially change the other party's duty, materially increase the risk or burden imposed by the contract, or materially impair the chance of obtaining a return performance.

On the other hand, contracts of a personal nature are usually held to be nonassignable, because the personality of the original promisee may be quite different from that of the assignee, resulting in a substantial change in the nature of performance, an increase in the risk or burden, or an impairment of the promisor's chances of obtaining a return performance.

---

**EXAMPLE** ■ Carter promised to work for Barnhart for one year. She knew Barnhart was a kindhearted and reasonable employer and one whose solvency permitted him to pay his bills as they came due. Barnhart attempted to assign his contract rights to Benedict, a financially irresponsible individual.

In this situation, the contract cannot be assigned. The assignment, permitted, would materially change Carter's situation, increase her burdens, and impair her chances of being paid.

---

Once an assignment is made, the assignee steps into the shoes of the assignor (promisee) and is entitled to all of the assignor's rights under the contract. Stated negatively, the assignee gets only the rights of the assignor and takes the contract subject to any defenses that the promisor might have against the promisee.

**EXAMPLE** ■ Jake's Auto Dealership assigns to Rapid State Bank its right to receive payments under the terms of a purchase installment contract with Weller. The car purchased by Weller proves to be defective, permitting him to set off its value against the debt he owes the dealership. The bank knows nothing of the defects and claims that its good faith status entitles it to collect the full amount due on the contract from Weller.

The bank may collect only the contract balance less the setoff from Weller. Since the bank took an assignment from the dealership, it took the contract subject to all defenses Weller has against the dealership.

---

In this example, the bank was not a holder in due course of the contract, primarily because the contract was not a negotiable instrument. Instead, the bank was an assignee subject to all defenses that may be set up against its assignor. (Chapter 2 of *Law and Banking: Applications* discusses more fully the difference between an assignee and a holder in due course.)

Normally it is assumed that, when an assignment is made, the assignor (promisee) warrants to the assignee that the claim is valid and, to the assignor's knowledge, that it is enforceable and not subject to defenses. Thus, if a promisor raises defenses against an assignee, the assignee may have an action against the assignor on the warranty for any loss that might occur.

A promisor may be unaware that the promisee has assigned contractual rights to a third person. Under this circumstance, if the promisor performs to the original promisee, the contract is discharged and the assignee has no recourse against the promisor, although there may be recourse against the promisee-assignor on the warranty. If the assignee wishes to be protected against this risk, the assignee must give the promisor notice of the assignment. After notice is given, the promisor must then tender performance to the assignee.

---

**EXAMPLE** ■ Cowley bought goods on credit from Hall for a price of $1,000.

Hall assigned his right to receive the $1,000 to White. In ignorance of this assignment, Cowley paid $1,000 to Hall, who then left town with the money. White now demands $1,000 from Cowley.

The courts would rule in favor of Cowley. Cowley may make his performance to the promisee and thereby discharge the contract, unless he is notified of an assignment. By giving notice to Cowley, White could have protected himself. In that case, it would have been up to Cowley to pay the right person, namely, White.

*Delegation of Duties*   Just as contractual rights may sometimes be assigned, contractual duties may sometimes be delegated. Generally, courts say that duties may be delegated where no substantial reason can be shown why the delegated performance will not be as satisfactory as personal performance.

EXAMPLES
- Dunn retained Wyeth to paint his portrait. Wyeth delegated the duty to Rockwell, but Dunn refused to accept Rockwell as a substitute for Wyeth.

   The contractual duty in this case cannot be delegated. Dunn has a substantial interest in having Wyeth paint his portrait. The work involves a highly personal service and Dunn should be able to select the person to do it.

- Freedman retained Reynolds to paint his house. Reynolds delegated the duty to Bryant, but Freedman refused to accept Bryant as a substitute for Reynolds.

   Unless Freedman can show that Bryant will not be as satisfactory as Reynolds, the delegation is effective. Here no personal service is involved and no particularly high skills are required. Only if Freedman could show that he had a substantial interest in having the work done by Reynolds could the delegation be defeated.

A delegation of duties does not relieve the promisor of any duty to perform or any liability for breach. This rule protects the promisee and makes the delegation of performance possible and safe in most cases.

---

EXAMPLE ■ Freedman retained Reynolds to paint his house. Reynolds delegated the duty to Bryant, who did a poor job.

Freedman has a cause of action against both Reynolds and Bryant. Reynolds cannot escape liability on the ground that he delegated the work to Bryant.

---

Often, whether or not contracts are personal in nature, they will contain clauses prohibiting assignments and/or delegations of duties. If such a prohibition is clearly stated, it will be valid in most states. The prohibitions against the sale of real estate and/or mortgage assumption that are contained in many real estate mortgages are valid in most states, but a significant minority of states hold such prohibitions void as an unreasonable restraint on alienation of real estate. (See the subsection on the conveyance of mortgaged property under the section on mortgages in chapter 6.)

The UCC recognizes both assignments and delegations as normal and permissible in contracts for the sale of goods, and only limits the ability of parties to a contract to prohibit assignment or delegation if the parties have agreed to such limits or if a duty, risk, or return performance would be materially altered (U.C.C. § 2–210).

While assignments and delegations of performance usually do not require consent of the party with whom the assignor or delegating party has contracted, novations do require such consent. Under a **novation**, a new party is substituted for one of the original parties by the agreement of all three parties, and the original contract is discharged. In this case, the person who has dropped out of the original contract has no further liability.

---

EXAMPLE ■ Peters has a mortgage on his home with First National Bank, with a balance due of $25,000. Peters wishes to sell the home without paying off the mortgage. He does not want to assign his interest in the mortgage, since he will continue to be liable for it if his purchaser fails to make payments. The bank agrees that, if Peters finds a creditworthy purchaser, it will replace the purchaser for Peters in the mortgage.

If Peters finds a creditworthy buyer who agrees to pay the mortgage as part of the purchase price, a novation will be created. If the buyer subsequently defaults under the terms of the mortgage, Peters will not be held liable.

## THIRD-PARTY BENEFICIARIES

As has been discussed, consideration necessary to create a contract may be provided to a third person who is not a party to a contract. Normally such third parties have no right to enforce a contract to which they are not a direct party. However, if parties enter into a contract with the intention of benefiting a third party, the third party will acquire rights as a "third-party beneficiary" if that third party is either a "donee beneficiary" or a "creditor beneficiary."

When the promisee in exacting a promise from the promisor plans to bestow a gift upon a third person, the latter is a **donee beneficiary** protected by a rule of law that entitles the donee to the promised performance. A donee beneficiary has all the rights of an original party to the transaction, and takes those rights subject to the defenses that the promisor has against the promisee. Since the promisee is no longer entitled to the promisor's performance, the promisee's action against the promisor in a donee beneficiary case is usually limited to an action for specific performance, a remedy designed to force the promisor to perform for the donee beneficiary.

EXAMPLE ■ Meredith promises to give Lamont his used power lawn mower in return for Lamont's promise to give $150 to Ellis. After Meredith has delivered the lawn mower to Lamont pursuant to this agreement, Lamont refuses to pay the money to Ellis. Ellis sues Lamont.

The courts will decide in favor of Ellis. Although Ellis was not an original party to the contract, he is a third-party donee beneficiary, since the promisee, Meredith, made the contract to bestow a gift ($150) on Ellis. Thus, the donee beneficiary may sue the promisor for the performance promised. Meredith also would have an action against Lamont for specific performance designed to force Lamont to perform for Ellis.

---

Where a promisee owes a debt to a third party and secures the promisor's promise to satisfy that debt, the third party becomes a **creditor beneficiary** capable of enforcing that promise against the promisor.

---

EXAMPLE ■ Walsh sells his landscaping business to Stone for $30,000 plus Stone's assumption of the debts of the business, which total $20,000, including $12,000 owed Marquette State Bank. After completing the sale, Walsh leaves the country. Subsequently, Stone fails to make a payment due to the bank.

---

Because the bank is a third-party creditor beneficiary of the contract between Walsh and Stone, it may enforce the contract against Stone.

In addition, if it wished, it could sue Walsh but could actually collect the debt from only one of the parties.

---

## Case for Discussion

**BANK v. RAILWAY COMPANY**

### Facts

Locke wanted to enter into a construction contract with Railway Company. To finance the contract, Locke borrowed funds from the bank. As security for the loan, Locke assigned his interest in the contract to the bank—an assignment recognized by Railway.

In the contract, Railway bound itself to pay Locke for certain work completed at an agreed rate. The contract also provided that on completion of the work and "after the contractor has furnished written evidence that he has fully paid all amounts that may be due from him to *any and all persons* who may have performed labor or furnished materials or supplies to the contractor in connection with the work, the Railway Company shall pay to the contractor the full amount earned under the contract, less payments previously made."

In due time, Locke complied with this contract. However, two contractors that furnished Locke with materials were never paid. In addition, the bank was never fully paid. Locke owed approximately $700 to the contractors and $2,200 to the bank. In turn, Railway still owed Locke approximately $2,200 on the contract, which the bank demanded under the assignment of contract to be paid. In addition, before the bank demanded payment, the two contractors failed to file a lien against Railway.

The contractors claim that Railway is under no duty to pay the bank until Locke complies with the exact letter of the contract. The contractors base their claim on that section of the contract that requires Locke to give notice to Railway of any debts due for material or supplies, even though the contractors were not parties to the contract.

### Decision

The court rules in favor of the bank. The court states that the contract must be interpreted in its entirety and its language given the full meaning intended by the parties to the contract. Thus, to isolate one paragraph and construe it in favor of the suppliers would be improper. In light of the full contract, the intent of that clause was not to protect those who are not parties to the contract but to protect the Railway Company against those who might claim liens against it.

The court further states that a person not a party to a contract may enforce it if it appears that it was made for his or her benefit. Parties are presumed to contract for themselves and a contract will not be construed as having been made for the benefit of a third person unless it clearly appears that such was the contracting parties' intention. This case does not show such an intention for the contractors. *Citizens National Bank in Abilene v. Texas & Pacific Railway Company*, 150 S.W.2d 1003, *cert. denied* 314 U.S. 656 (1941).

### Questions for Discussion

1. Explain the rights and duties of parties to contracts when the contract is assigned.
2. Define a third-party beneficiary.
3. When the judges in this case spoke of giving a "full-meaning interpretation" to this contract, what did they mean?
4. How could the contract have been rewritten to protect the contractors?

## REMEDIES

When any party to a contract fails to perform its contractual obligation, the other parties are entitled to be put in as favorable a position as they would have enjoyed had the contract been performed. Courts can obtain this position for "aggrieved parties" by either ordering the delinquent party to specifically perform the contract or by awarding the aggrieved parties monetary damages.

### Specific Performance

Courts do not consider specific performance as a viable remedy for breach of contract because of the difficulty of actually forcing a party to undertake contractual obligations. The assumption here is that if a party is forced to specifically perform on a contract, the resulting product or service may be below accepted standards. The effect would be to place the wronged party in no better (and perhaps worse) a situation than existed before the contract was made.

**EXAMPLE** ■ Duval agrees to build a house for Anderson but subsequently refuses to carry out the agreement. Anderson is entitled to monetary damages to put him in the same economic position he would have enjoyed had Duval built the house. The court will probably not decree specific performance, because if Duval is reluctant to build the house and the court required him to perform, he might do a poor job.

Only when monetary damages are inadequate will the courts order specific performance as a remedy for breach of contract.

## Damages

Statute and case decisions divide damages into six categories:

- compensatory
- consequential or special
- punitive or exemplary
- incidental
- nominal
- liquidated

The UCC specifically provides for compensatory, consequential, punitive, incidental, and liquidated damages for the various types of breaches of contracts for the sale of goods.

## Compensatory Damages

**Compensatory damages** are those that place the plaintiff in the same economic position as if the breach had not occurred. Usually, compensatory damages are computed by measuring the difference between the value of the promised performance and the plaintiff's cost to perform.

---

EXAMPLE ■ Knudsen agrees to sell and deliver 2,500 bushels of potatoes to Costello for $5,000. Costello wrongfully refuses to accept Knudsen's tender of delivery.

If Knudsen sues Costello for damages, he is entitled to recover that amount of money by which the contract price ($5,000) exceeds the market price at the time Costello should have accepted delivery. If the market price was then $4,750, Knudsen is entitled to $250 damages, together with any incidental damages but less expenses saved in consequence of the breach. If Knudsen is awarded the compensatory damages, he will have $250 in cash plus the potatoes, which are worth $4,750 on the open market. Thus, Knudsen has the equivalent of $5,000, which places him in about the same position he would have enjoyed had the breach not occurred. In addition, he will recover his court costs from Costello. However, in suing Costello, Knudsen must bear the cost of his own attorney's fees unless the contract provided otherwise.

---

In the United States, even if they win the suit, parties to lawsuits normally pay their own attorneys' fees. The most common exceptions to this rule are when a victorious party to a lawsuit has sued under the provisions of a statute that provides that the losing party shall pay the attorney's fees of the successful party, or when a contract that is the subject of a lawsuit provides for attorney's fees. Provisions for such fees are often found in consumer protection statutes, such as the federal Truth in Lending and Equal Credit Opportunity Acts.

*Consequential or Special Damages*

**Consequential** or **special damages** are those that accrue because of some special or unusual circumstance surrounding the particular contractual relationship of the parties. In undertaking commitments, a promisor is said to have intended to assume only the risks that normally result from breach of contract. If a promisor knows or should be aware of special circumstances that indicate a greater than normal loss for a breach, liability for consequential damages may result. In this case, a promisor is said to have assumed the risk of the unusual loss as a consequence of a breach.

Special or consequential damages may include loss of employment, business credit, or customers, which result indirectly from a breach of contract. These losses may be recovered in addition to compensatory damages if it can be proven that they were foreseeable when the contract was made.

---

**EXAMPLE** ■ Nashville County State Bank gave Hermans a commitment letter wherein it contracted to loan her $40,000 to purchase a piece of property on which she had an option. In her application, Hermans disclosed that she wished to buy the property for resale to another party who had offered her $55,000 for the property. The bank breached its commitment contract and refused to lend Hermans the money.

As long as Hermans can prove that the bank had no legitimate reason for breaching its contract, Hermans could receive $15,000 in consequential damages if she were able to show that her agreement to purchase land fell through because of the bank's promise and subsequent failure to loan her the $40,000.

*Punitive or Exemplary Damages*

**Punitive** or **exemplary damages** are those in excess of compensation for loss, awarded to punish a party. They are seldom awarded in contract cases but frequently apply to tort cases. Such damages are normally awarded for intentional wrongs.

*Incidental Damages*

**Incidental damages** include expenses incurred by the aggrieved party as a result of the breach of contract.

EXAMPLE ■ Veblen agreed to sell 2,000 bushels of potatoes to Erwin, who later refused to accept delivery. As a result, Veblen was forced to store the potatoes and hire a commission agent to resell them. He sues Erwin for compensatory damages and also for the cost of storage, the commission agent's fee, and the cost of the lawsuit. In this situation, Veblen may collect as incidental damages the cost of storage, the commission agent's fee, and the court costs. He may not, however, collect his lawyer's fee, unless the contract provided otherwise.

*Nominal Damages*

Every breach of contract entitles the aggrieved party to damages. As a result of this principle, the aggrieved party is permitted **nominal damages** in those cases in which there is no monetary loss or the loss is too speculative to be recoverable. As the name implies, nominal damages are a token amount (for example, a few dollars) given to show the world that the plaintiff—although unable to show monetary loss—is correct in the contention that the defendant wrongfully invaded his or her interest (for example, walked over the plaintiff's land). Nominal damages give the plaintiff a moral—but expensive—victory, since the plaintiff will probably have to pay attorney's fees.

## Liquidated Damages

Frequently the parties to a contract wish to minimize the uncertainties attending the determination of damages. Accordingly, they will agree in advance on the amount of damages that will be recoverable in case of breach. Damages recovered under such an agreement are called **liquidated damages**. A liquidated-damages clause in a contract is enforceable if the amount is reasonable, but if unreasonable, the courts will ignore it and award damages just as if the liquidation clause did not exist in the contract.

EXAMPLE ■ Cobb agreed to build a house for Frick for $50,000. The contract contained a clause that Cobb would pay Frick $500 for each day the house was unfinished after a set date. Cobb was 30 days late in finishing the house. Frick demanded the house and $15,000 in liquidated damages.

In this situation, the liquidated-damages clause is too harsh and the courts would not enforce it. It is unreasonable in light of the cost of the house, the anticipated actual harm caused by the breach, the difficulties of proof, and the inconvenience of otherwise obtaining an adequate remedy. Since the liquidated-damages clause in this case is unreasonable, the court would compute damages without reference to it.

## Limitation of Damages

Once a contract has been breached, an aggrieved party cannot stand by and not at least attempt to lessen the damages. In fact, the aggrieved party is bound to do all that is reasonable to keep the amount of the damage as small as possible. This doctrine, known as "the doctrine of avoidable consequence" or the "doctrine of mitigating damages," was not developed to favor defendants but rather to prevent unnecessary economic waste. To the extent that the aggrieved party fails to mitigate damages, he or she is penalized by not being permitted to recover them.

EXAMPLE ■ Foremost National Bank leased a building from Arbut, which it used as a branch office. With six months remaining on its lease, the bank vacated the premises without cause. Despite the desirability of the building as rental property and several inquiries by potential lessees, Arbut took no action to rent the building after the bank moved out. Because Arbut did nothing to avoid the damages caused by the bank's breach of its lease, he may not be entitled to any damages or may at least not be entitled to the equivalent of six months' rent.

## QUASI CONTRACTS

Over the centuries, English courts were faced with many situations in which the law provided no remedy for people who had been wronged because their grievances did not fit into a particular remedy provided by the strict common-law rules. To provide remedies for these wrongs, courts of chancery developed, paralleling the common-law courts. Chancery courts were not compelled to follow hard-and-fast rules and were able to deal equitably with matters before them. Thus, the legal system known as equity developed. Today in the United States, the courts of law and equity have been merged into one judicial system, but the principles of law and equity continue in the courts.

Quasi contract law developed in the courts of equity out of a need to give aggrieved parties relief against unjust enrichment. **Quasi contract** is a legal obligation arising out of the receipt of a benefit for which there has been no actual promise to pay, but the retention of which without giving consideration would be unjust. Not every enrichment is an "unjust enrichment" and not every injustice results in enrichment. Only where these two components come together may relief be ordered under quasi contract.

EXAMPLE ■ Terry Lang goes to Peoples Bank and requests a withdrawal of $400 from her savings account. Later that day she and the bank realize that a teller made a mistake and gave her $450. The bank asks Lang for the difference, which she refuses to pay, indicating she has no contractual obligation to pay the money. In this example, Lang's retention of the $50 would constitute unjust enrichment and, while she made no actual promise to repay the money, equity would impose such a promise upon her in the form of a quasi contract to prevent unjust enrichment.

---

However, not every benefit received by an individual who does not request it gives rise to unjust enrichment.

---

EXAMPLE ■ A painter agrees to paint the house located at 20 Oak Street. By mistake, he paints the house at 20 Elm Street. The occupant of 20 Elm Street is out of town when his house is mistakenly painted and he knows nothing of it. Later he refuses to pay for the work and the painter sues him for breach of a quasi contract.

The painter cannot recover in this situation. His painting may have enriched the owner of 20 Elm Street, but the enrichment is not one that is considered unjust, since the occupant of 20 Elm Street never requested that his house be painted nor did he knowingly receive the benefit. Had he been home when the painting occurred and stood by without saying anything, his enrichment would have been unjust and the painter's suit would have been successful under quasi contract.

---

**Situations Having Quasi-Contractual Relief**

Common situations involving unjust enrichment which give rise to quasi-contractual relief include

- contracts that have become impossible to perform

- contracts in which the defendant's performance is unenforceable

- situations in which benefits have been conferred under compulsion

- situations in which the parties, laboring under a mutual mistake of fact, have conferred benefits

- situations in which benefits are conferred during an emergency

*Impossibility of Performance*

For purposes of the law, impossibility is a valid excuse for nonperformance of a contract either when the promisor of a personal services contract dies or becomes incapacitated or when an element necessary to the performance of a contract is destroyed. If advance payment is made for a performance that becomes impossible, that payment can be recovered under quasi contract.

---

EXAMPLES
- Linda Lane, a recording artist, entered into a personal-appearance contract with a nightclub. On the day she was to perform, she broke her leg and was unable to fulfill her contract. Because the contract was for Lane's personal services and cannot be performed by another person, she is legally excused from performing based on impossibility. Her failure to appear would not breach her contract with the nightclub. If Lane had received any money in advance of her performance, she would have to return it. Otherwise, under quasi contract, she would be "unjustly enriched."

- A gasoline distributor contracted to furnish Jack's Service Station with gas at a set price for three years. Within two years, the price that the distributor was paying for gas exceeded the price specified in the contract with Jack's. Relying on the UCC (§ 2–615), the distributor refused to deliver further gas and Jack's Service Station sued. The outcome of this suit would depend on whether the court finds the rise in the cost of gas to have been foreseeable when the contract was signed.

---

Courts are extremely reluctant to excuse performance based on a rise in costs to one party, since such an excuse could easily be abused, especially in inflationary times.

*Promisor's Unenforceable Performance*

Contracts in which a promisor's performance is unenforceable usually arise in situations where statute or case law provides the promisor with a defense for nonperformance, such as an oral promise that fails to meet the statute of frauds. Under quasi contract, if a promisor's performance of a contract is unenforceable, the promisee can recover any unjust enrichment gained by the promisor in connection with the contract.

EXAMPLE ■ Keys orally agrees to sell real estate to Scott and takes a deposit of $1,000. Since the real estate purchase agreement is not proved by a proper writing, it cannot be enforced; that is, Scott cannot sue Keys to make him complete the purchase. However, Scott can recover his $1,000 under quasi contract since Keys's retention of the deposit would be an unjust enrichment.

*Benefits Given under Compulsion*   When a benefit has been received as the result of duress, its value may be recovered under quasi contract.

EXAMPLE ■ A water company charges a rate that Fraser believes to be excessive and unwarranted under the company's franchise. However, to continue to receive water, Fraser must pay the rate demanded by the company. He pays under protest. In this situation, Fraser may recover if he shows that the charge was illegal.

*Mutual Mistakes of Fact*   When parties negotiate an agreement that is prevented from becoming a contract due to a mutual mistake of fact, anything either one has given the other can be recovered in quasi contract.

EXAMPLE ■ Fitch received $500 from Clemens for a cow named Betsy. Unknown to either party, Betsy died before the agreement was made. No contract exists in this situation, because there is no subject matter upon which the parties can agree. Clemens can recover the $500 in quasi contract.

Mutual mistakes of fact often occur when money is paid to the wrong person or too much money is paid to the right person. In these cases, the error can be corrected through the doctrine of quasi contract.

EXAMPLE ■ Dale agrees to pay Emmett $10 a bushel for fruit. Both parties erroneously assume that Emmett has delivered 100 bushels of fruit to Dale and Dale sends a check for $1,000 to Emmett. In fact, Emmett has delivered only 60 bushels of fruit. In this situation, Dale can recover the overpayment in quasi contract.

*Benefits Given During an Emergency*

When a person receives a benefit during an emergency, the law is divided as to whether the person giving the benefit may demand payment for the value of the benefit. Normally, the courts presume that the benefits were conferred gratuitously and the gift prevents the defendant's enrichment from being characterized as "unjust." Under this presumption, no action in quasi contract will hold up in court.

EXAMPLE ■ While staying at a hotel, Watkins becomes seriously ill and the hotel's proprietor calls a physician. When she arrives, Watkins is unconscious. She treats Watkins and later sends him a bill. In most states, those who receive medical treatment under such circumstances would be liable in quasi contract; in some states, however, the courts would hold that the service had been volunteered and that no recovery could be had.

**Situations Having No Quasi-Contractual Relief**

When a contract is unenforceable because its performance would be an illegal act, quasi contract will probably provide no relief.

EXAMPLE ■ Churchill gives a bookie, Sheldon, $3,000 to bet on a horse race.

Sheldon forgets to place the bet and as a result Churchill loses $9,000. If gambling is illegal in the state in which the bet is placed, Churchill would be prevented from suing Sheldon for the loss and probably would even be unable to recover the $3,000 bet. This denial would occur because the courts do not want to aid those who have violated the law and they also do not want criminal law to be circumvented by the use of quasi contracts.

## CONCLUSION

Contract law encompasses virtually all legal relationships not otherwise within the scope of tort or criminal law. A contract can be as simple as a deposit account agreement between a bank and an individual customer or as complex as a multibillion-dollar merger agreement between giant corporations.

Notwithstanding the complexity of particular transactions, contracts are formed, performed, and breached according to the same basic legal principles. Parties to any contract must have the legal capacity to enter into the contract, their objective in doing so must be legal, they must mutually assent to the contract, and consideration must be given for it.

Once a contract has been negotiated, the statute of frauds may require it to be in writing if it comes within the prescribed categories discussed in this chapter.

The parol evidence rule was formulated to provide certainty in interpreting written contracts. The parties to a contract are bound by the content of their written word and they are not permitted to offer contradictory understandings of negotiations that occurred before the written contract's execution.

While the parol evidence rule, where applicable, eliminates reference to prior negotiations when interpreting written contracts, it does not eliminate the need to interpret the actual words of a written contract. To that end, the law has developed both primary and secondary interpretive rules for written contracts.

If a contract is performed fully according to its terms as mutually interpreted by all parties to it, problems do not arise. Unfortunately, not all contracts are so performed and the law has developed rules delineating what constitutes adequate and inadequate performance. Further, nonperformance of a contract may be excused if its objective is impossible to achieve. If lack of performance is not excused, the injured party may be entitled to one or more of the following types of damages: compensatory, consequential or special, punitive or exemplary, incidental, nominal, or liquidated.

## Questions for Review and Discussion

1. If a party is legally disabled but the disability is not outwardly manifested, will the party nevertheless be excused from performing the contract?

2. If two parties execute a contract, why should the law be able to set it aside for lack of a legal objective?

3. If after entering into a contract a party indicates he or she did not understand it, is the party bound to it?

4. If a person obviously agreed to pay too much for a product or service, will the law excuse payment?

5. Is there ever a situation where an oral contract for the sale of land may be enforced?

6. Does the parol evidence rule prohibit one party to a contract from explaining his or her understanding of a term in the contract?

7. Does the intent of a party who fails to perform his or her contractual obligations affect the type of damages that may be awarded to the other party?

# Real and Personal Property

After studying this chapter, you will be able to

- define real and personal property
- describe how real and personal property are acquired
- explain bailments, including safe deposit boxes and leases
- differentiate the various interests in real estate

For legal purposes, all property is divided into two broad classifications: real property and personal property. **Real property** is land and anything permanently affixed to it, including buildings and standing trees. **Personal property** includes all property that is not real property and is usually defined as objects that are movable or intangible.

At different times, a particular item can be either real or personal property. Mobile homes are a good example of property that can move between the two classifications of property.

---

EXAMPLE ■ Fred Thomas purchases land and moves onto it a mobile home, in which he establishes his residence. When Thomas purchases his mobile home, it is personal property and continues to be so after he moves it onto the land. However, if Thomas takes steps to affix the mobile home to his land, it could become real property since his actions might cause the home to become immovable. Such steps could include removing the home's axles and wheels and placing the home on a permanent foundation. Once Thomas affixes the home to the land, it becomes real property unless state law holds otherwise.

---

Although the distinction between immovable and movable belongings correctly separates real from personal property, the difference between the two can be more complicated. Real property can be converted into personal property by severance, while personal property can be converted into real property by attaching it to land. Thus, standing timber is real property, but when cut it becomes personal property. If it is used in the construction of a house, it once again becomes real property.

This distinction between real and personal property is particularly important to banks, because the procedures secured creditors use to protect their interests in security (collateral) for loans differ depending on whether the property is real or personal. State mortgage law defines the procedures creditors should use to secure loans with real property. Article 9 of the Uniform Commercial Code (UCC) describes the procedures to secure loans with most personal property.

## PERSONAL PROPERTY

Determining who owns real property in the United States is usually an uncomplicated matter because land registration records are kept in virtually every county in the country. Thus, ownership of real property is usually described in terms of title to real property.

Before the enactment of the UCC, statutes and court decisions in most states defined personal property titles and determined ownership of personal property. Any individual deemed to have title to personal property could use it as collateral, transfer it by gift, leave it to heirs, or otherwise dispose of it. However, in drafting the articles in the UCC on sales (article 2) and secured transactions (article 9), the National Conference of Commissioners replaced "title" as a legal concept, substituting more specific rules to govern the transfer of ownership from seller to buyer and the rights of debtor and creditor in secured transactions (U.C.C. §§ 2–401 and 9–202).

The UCC continues to recognize title where goods are held by warehousemen or carriers. Article 7 of the UCC governs the ownership and possessory rights of warehousemen and carriers and those that deal with them. Most of these rights are settled by who has possession of "documents of title," which identify the goods and usually are either bills of lading or warehouse receipts. (This chapter will discuss article 7 and documents of title later in connection with bailments.)

The concept of title also remains important in situations involving product liability, negligence, and criminal law.

---

**EXAMPLE** ■ Van Hipple received $4,000 for a car from Ted Poe. Poe took possession of the car and within a few hours used it as security for a loan from Tower National Bank. At the end of the day, he was involved in a car accident because of his own negligence. A bill of sale and title to the car were not executed until a few days after its purchase.

In this example, article 9 governs Poe's use of the car as security for a loan without reference to any other state statute governing title. However, the ability of any party harmed in the accident to sue Hipple, as well as Poe, may be determined by who had title at the time of the accident. The state in which the accident occurred may have title laws that find that Hipple, as title holder, is liable for the damage caused by Poe.

---

## Acquisition of Personal Property

Personal property may be acquired in many ways. The most common methods of acquisition are

■ production

■ purchase

■ taking possession

■ finding

■ confusion

205  *Real and Personal Property*

- accession
- gift
- inheritance

To a banker, determining how an individual acquired or will acquire an item of personal property is important in ascertaining whether the individual's right to the item is sufficient for it to be listed as an asset (when determining the individual's net worth) and in ascertaining whether the item is available as collateral (when securing a loan).

EXAMPLE ■ Janet Ostwald finds a diamond worth $100,000 on the street. Later she applies for a loan at Podunk National Bank and lists the value of the diamond as part of her net worth. Further, Ostwald offers to use the diamond as collateral for the loan. If Ostwald's acquisition of the diamond is later defeated by a third party, Podunk National Bank will lose its collateral and Ostwald's financial statement will prove to be erroneous.

*Production*   Unlike real property, new items of personal property are produced all the time. Production of personal property usually occurs by "accession," "commingling," or "processing." **Accession** occurs when one item of personal property is installed or affixed to another item of personal property.

EXAMPLE ■ Ryan Hay owns a used car lot. He has two cars on the lot; one has a bad motor but good body, and the other has a worthless body but a good motor. He installs the good motor in the car with the good body. In this example, accession has occurred to produce a new item of personal property.

Accession does not destroy the identity of the separate items of personal property that have been joined to produce the final product. In the preceding example, the car body and motor continue to be identifiable after they are joined in one product. This is not the case when items of personal property are commingled or processed.

---

EXAMPLE ■ Farmer Beck sells flour to Gamble Bakery, which adds yeast, sugar, shortening, and milk to the flour to make bread. Flour and the other ingredients are commingled or processed to produce a single product in which none of the component parts is separately identifiable.

---

Thus, production is a means not only of acquiring, but also of creating, new types of personal property.

*Purchase* — Purchase is probably the most common form of acquiring personal property and needs little explanation. The law controlling the sale of most items of personal property is in article 2 of the UCC (discussed in chapter 5).

*Taking Possession* — Taking possession is another form of acquiring personal property. This form of acquisition can occur as either adverse or nonadverse possession.

### ADVERSE POSSESSION

*[handwritten margin note: Not a NYS concept for Personal property. We use the abandoned property law.]*

Acquiring personal property by taking possession is similar to acquiring real property by **adverse possession**. To acquire personal property by taking possession, the possession must be open, actual, exclusive, hostile, or adverse, and must continue for a period prescribed by state law.

---

EXAMPLE ■ At the time of her mother's death, Sue Harper removed a piano from her parents' home, even though her mother's will left the piano to her brother Fred. Fred was aware of Sue's act, knew where she had taken the piano, and did nothing to enforce his demands that she return it to him. Depending upon individual state law, if enough years go by, Sue will acquire the piano by adverse possession.

---

Some states require that the one taking possession do so under some claim of title. Thus, in those states, a thief could never acquire title by adverse possession. In the example above, if Harper claimed the piano under a will made prior to the will that awarded it to her brother and if Harper also alleged that the second will was invalid when she took the piano, this would probably satisfy the requirement for some claim of title.

NONADVERSE POSSESSION

Taking possession is also used as a method to acquire personal property that is unowned. Wild animals and abandoned property are the most common examples of unowned property that one may acquire by taking possession.

Abandonment is the absolute, voluntary, and intentional relinquishment of property—a total desertion by its owner. The difference between an owner abandoning property and selling or giving it away is the absence of any buyer or donee.

---

**EXAMPLE** ■ Farnum State Bank repossesses a car in which it discovers clothing and tools. These items are removed and the car is sold according to the law. The bank notifies its debtor of the items found in the car. However, the debtor fails to retrieve the items and refuses to accept them even when a bank employee delivers them to his home. The owner has abandoned his clothing and tools in this situation. While originally they were taken from their owner without his consent, his refusal to take them back when they were offered indicates a voluntary, absolute, and intentional relinquishment.

---

Abandonment of personal property does not automatically result in its acquisition by the person who takes possession. To become the owner of abandoned property, that person must possess it with the intention of owning it. In the preceding example, the bank may throw away the abandoned clothes and tools, never becoming their owner. Alternatively, the bank may take possession of the abandoned items, become their owner, and sell, use, or do anything else with the property that it wishes.

## Finding

To a limited extent, acquiring personal property by "finding" it was discussed in the context of abandonment. Unlike abandoned property, however, lost property becomes the finder's property free from claims of ownership from everyone except the true owner. Since the owner of lost property has never voluntarily or intentionally relinquished control, the owner's rights in it continue. Nor can the finder's adverse possession of the lost property cut off those rights, since a critical element of adverse possession is the owner's knowledge of the identity of the possessor and the location of the property.

---

**EXAMPLE** ■ Lopez lost her watch. Ramsay found the watch but did not know who owned it. Subsequently, Ramsay lost the watch and Gould found it. Gould knew that Ramsay had lost the watch but nevertheless insisted on keeping it. Ramsay may recover the watch from Gould, because he owns it free of any claims to it except for a claim by Lopez, the original owner.

A finder of lost property who knows the identity of the person who lost it and yet keeps it is guilty of **conversion**. In the preceding example, Gould is guilty of conversion against Ramsay, but Ramsay is not guilty of conversion against Lopez.

---

*[Handwritten note: In NYS these things are treated the same.]*

The law in most states distinguishes between lost and mislaid property. Property is lost when its owner accidentally drops it. It is mislaid when its owner places it in a particular place and then forgets its location. As has been discussed, the finder of lost property acquires rights superior to those of everyone except the true owner. However, in many states, the finder of mislaid property acquires no rights. In these states, mislaid property belongs to the owner of the land or building in which it is found, subject, of course, to the rights of the true owner. This rule is based on the policy that the law should encourage the possibility that the true owner may find the misplaced goods. If those goods are in the hands of the owner of that land or building, the true owner's chances of recovery are improved over situations that allow the finder to prevail.

---

EXAMPLE ■ Collins left her camera on the counter of a clothing store. Johnson, a man from another state, found it there and claimed it. In many states, the owner of the clothing store would own the camera, subject to Collins's claim as the true owner. If the law permitted Johnson a superior right to that of the store owner, Collins's chances of recovering the camera would decrease.

---

Some states, however, make no distinction between lost and misplaced goods. In these states, the courts have often said that the distinction is impossible to administer because the line dividing lost and misplaced goods is not a sharp one.

Finally, many states and cities have enacted special statutes and ordinances to regulate a finder's acquisition of lost personal property. Usually, these statutes and ordinances require the finder to report the finding to the police if its value exceeds a certain amount or to deposit the lost property with the city's property clerk. If the true owner does not claim the lost property within a specific time, the finder is then permitted to keep it.

## *Confusion*

**Confusion** occurs when goods belonging to two or more people are inseparably intermixed. If the intermixture results from the willful and tortious act of one of the owners, that owner forfeits his or her interest and the innocent party becomes the owner of the entire mass. If one of the parties innocently, or a third party either innocently or tortiously, causes the intermixture, the original owners become common owners of the new mass and hold a fractional interest based on the proportion that each contributed originally to the mass.

---

**EXAMPLE** ■ Clarke and Duffy each owned 1,000 chickens but neither could identify his birds. Duffy willfully and tortiously caused the two flocks of chickens to be joined into a new flock of 2,000 chickens.

Under these circumstances, Clarke is entitled to all the chickens. This is necessary to protect Clarke's property rights in his chickens. Since he cannot identify his 1,000 chickens, the only way the law can make certain that he does not lose his rights in them or any part of them is to give him all the chickens. Clarke thus acquires 1,000 chickens through the doctrine of confusion.

If Duffy had innocently intermixed the chickens, Clarke and Duffy would become co-owners of the new flock of 2,000 chickens and each would have a 50 percent interest in the whole. In that situation, to give the entire flock to Clarke would work a harsh forfeiture against Duffy for circumstances in which he was innocent.

---

*Accession*  For purposes of acquiring personal property, accession is much like confusion. As such, it involves a forfeiture by a wrongdoer to protect the property rights of an innocent party. In receiving this protection, the innocent party acquires new ownership. Thus, **accession** occurs when one person wrongfully appropriates another's property and then improves it. Under the principles that a person is not permitted to profit by his or her own wrongs and an innocent person cannot be made a debtor against his or her own consent, the law in this situation gives the improved property back to the innocent party. In the process, the original owner acquires new ownership.

---

**EXAMPLE** ■ Patch steals a canvas belonging to Hadley and uses it to create a painting. In this situation, Hadley is entitled to the painting. If the decision were otherwise, one of two legal principles would be violated. The law does not let Patch profit by his own wrong and thus prevents him from keeping the painting. Nor does the law force an innocent party to become a debtor and so does not require Hadley to pay for recovering the canvas.

Together, the principles that a person is not permitted to profit by wrongdoing and that a nonconsenting innocent person cannot be made a debtor underlie the doctrine of accession.

**EXAMPLE** ■ Patch accidentally takes a canvas that belongs to Hadley and creates a painting. In this case, Hadley has an option. He may sue Patch for conversion and collect the value of the canvas or he may recover the painting but pay Patch for the value of the improvement to the canvas.

Thus, the doctrine of accession does not result in a forfeiture against an innocent party.

In some states, the doctrine of accession will not be invoked if the value of the improved property is so out of proportion to the value of the original property that the forfeiture "shocks the conscience."

**EXAMPLE** ■ Patch steals Hadley's canvas, which is worth only $3, and creates a painting worth $50,000. Some courts would not permit Hadley to recover the painting because such a result would "shock the conscience." Rather, Patch would have to pay punitive damages, perhaps $100, for stealing the canvas. In this manner, Patch is punished for his wrongdoing and Hadley is more than adequately compensated for his stolen canvas.

## Gift

For legal purposes, a **gift** is a voluntary transfer of property by one person, known as the **donor**, to another person, the **donee**, who gives no consideration for it.

Gifts are divided into two classifications: gifts inter vivos and gifts causa mortis. A **gift inter vivos** is a gift completed during the donor's lifetime and, once completed, it is irrevocable. To be complete, the inter vivos gift requires donative intent, delivery, and acceptance. A **gift causa mortis** is a gift made in contemplation of immediate death or death from a present illness. A gift causa mortis requires donative intent, delivery, acceptance, and the donor's death from the contemplated injury or disease.

### DONATIVE INTENT

The donor must have a present intent to make the gift; that is, a present desire to relinquish control and dominion over the item(s) given to the donee must exist.

---

EXAMPLE ■ Peter Martin delivers an antique watch to his nephew and asks him to keep the watch safe for him. Martin tells his nephew the watch will be his upon Martin's death. Shortly thereafter, Martin dies, his will is read, and it specifies that the watch is to go to Martin's son. In this situation, the nephew did not receive the watch as a gift because when it was delivered, Martin had no present donative intent.

---

### DELIVERY

Delivery sufficient to satisfy requirements for a gift may be actual, constructive, or symbolic. To be complete, delivery must give to the donee, and remove from the donor, control and dominion over the property.

---

EXAMPLE ■ Thelma Gwynne tells her son Richard that she wants him to have the funds in her savings account as a gift, but she fails to deliver the account's passbook to him or take any action to transfer the funds to him. In this situation, delivery of the gift is incomplete because Gwynne continues to be able to exercise control over the account.

---

While actual delivery is preferred to satisfy the delivery requirement for gifts, constructive or symbolic delivery is sufficient. Constructive delivery occurs when, instead of delivering the gift itself, the owner delivers something representing the gift, such as a deed.

---

EXAMPLE ■ Jeff Mellon deeded his farm to his son Pete as a gift. Since land cannot be physically delivered to a donee, a deed is constructive delivery and satisfies the delivery requirement for gifts.

---

In addition to land, personal property of considerable bulk or located at some distance from the parties is often subject to constructive delivery.

---

EXAMPLE ■ Freda Farmer wishes to give jewelry that is in a safe deposit box in a distant city to her niece, Sally. Farmer gives Sally the keys to the safe deposit box. In this situation, delivery of the keys is constructive or symbolic delivery.

---

ACCEPTANCE

Acceptance by the donee is a necessary element of a gift and, without it, no gift will have been given. As long as a gift benefits the donee, acceptance will be presumed even if the donee is unaware of the gift when it is delivered.

**EXAMPLE** ■ Ann Harper established a savings account in Jeff Stack's name and deposited $10,000 into it without telling him anything about the account. Harper was not an owner of the account and, when she deposited the money, she fully intended that it be a present gift to Stack. She made that quite clear to the bank employee who set up the account.

In this situation, Stack's acceptance will be presumed and it will be sufficient if he expresses his acceptance once he learns of the account, even if that does not occur until after Harper's death.

*Case for Discussion*

**CLAY v. BRIDEWELL**

**Facts**

Henry Clay was a divorcé with three children. The children, all adults, were close to their mother and hostile to Clay because of the divorce. A year or so after his marriage dissolved, Clay began seeing Betty Bridewell, who had never been married. They became steady companions and, on several occasions, Clay proposed marriage. Bridewell declined these proposals because her mother, who lived with her, was ill and Bridewell felt obligated to care for her.

One day, while driving, Clay had a heart attack. Fortunately, another driver saw what happened and rushed him to a nearby hospital. Learning of this, Bridewell went immediately to visit her friend. At the hospital, Clay wrote a check for $10,000 payable to Bridewell and gave it to her. He said she was his best friend and the $10,000 was a gift. Bridewell, surprised and pleased, thanked him and put the check in her purse. Clay died that evening. About noon of the next day, Bridewell deposited the check for collection at her bank. The check took the usual course for collection and in two days Clay's bank paid it.

Shortly thereafter, Clay's children, as heirs of his estate, filed a lawsuit against Bridewell, claiming ownership of the $10,000 in the checking account. The children contended that the gift of $10,000 was not a valid inter vivos gift, since the bank did not pay it until after Clay's death.

## Decision

The court ruled in favor of the Clay children and stated that a valid inter vivos gift requires donative intent, delivery, and acceptance. Mere delivery of a donor's personal check does not in itself constitute a valid gift. The donor may place a stop payment against the check at any time before it is presented for payment. In addition, if death occurs before the payor bank pays the check, the gift is revoked. In this case, the check was not presented to the drawee bank and either accepted or paid until after Clay's death. Because it lacked complete delivery, the gift was therefore ineffectual and revoked by Clay's death.

## Questions for Discussion

1. What should Clay have done to ensure that the money was a valid inter vivos gift?
2. What could Bridewell have done to ensure that the money was a valid inter vivos gift?
3. What steps can banks take to protect themselves in situations like this?

---

IN CONTEMPLATION OF DEATH

To establish a gift causa mortis, the elements of donative intent, delivery, and acceptance must be present. In addition, the donor must make the gift in contemplation of death from an existing disease or peril and death must result from that disease or peril.

---

**EXAMPLE** ■ About to undergo a delicate heart operation, John Arbut delivers stock valued at $100,000 to Fred Baker, who accepts it. Arbut recovers from the operation and demands return of the stock.

If Arbut can show that he made the delivery in contemplation of his own death, he will be entitled to a return of the stock because without his death, the gift was incomplete. Further, if Arbut is killed in an auto accident before the operation takes place, a gift causa mortis would be incomplete since he died of a cause he did not contemplate.

All personal property can be the subject of gifts inter vivos or causa mortis, but real property can be the subject only of gifts inter vivos.

---

**EXAMPLE** ■ Knowing he has a terminal illness, John Dokes delivers a deed to his home to John Moore. Subsequently, Dokes dies of the illness and his family contests the gift. Unless Moore can show that Dokes would have made the gift despite the knowledge that he was dying—that is, that it was a gift inter vivos—it will be set aside and the real estate will go to Dokes's heirs since real estate cannot be the subject of a gift causa mortis.

---

## *Inheritance*

Personal property also may be acquired by **inheritance**. An inheritance may be the result of a will or, if a deceased person had no will, the result of state law governing intestate estates.

Whether particular property is real or personal is unimportant if a will specifies the person to whom it is bequeathed. However, if an individual dies without a will, many states have descent and distribution statutes controlling the disposition of inherited property that treat personal and real property differently.

## **Bailments**

Rights in personal and real property include the rights of possession and ownership. Two different people can hold these rights simultaneously.

A **bailment** exists when the ownership of personal property is in one person, known as the **bailor**, and the right of possession is in another person, known as the **bailee**. In many states, the relationship between a bank and a customer with a safe deposit box is a bailment.

Many transactions in everyday life are bailments. Bailments occur, for example, every time one person delivers goods to another for some specific purpose. That purpose may be to improve the article, such as leaving a suit of clothes with a dry cleaner to be cleaned or leaving a car in a garage for repairs. The purpose may be to transport the article from one place to another, such as delivering a trunk to a railroad company.

Or the purpose may be for safekeeping, such as leaving property with a storage warehouse or placing it in a safe deposit vault.

## Bailee's Duties

All bailees must exercise care with respect to articles in their possession and must surrender those articles when the bailment ends. If a bailee's duty of care is properly performed, the bailee is not responsible to the bailor for loss or damage to the articles in his or her possession.

Based on the degree of care the bailee must exercise while possessing the bailor's personal property, the courts in many states divide bailments into three types:

- bailments for the sole benefit of the bailor

- bailments for the sole benefit of the bailee

- bailments for the mutual benefit of the bailor and bailee

Each of these types of bailment requires a different degree of care by the bailee.

In bailments for the bailor's sole benefit, bailees need exercise only slight care with respect to the bailor's articles. This kind of bailment exists when a bailee cares for personal property without charge and as an accommodation to the bailor. A bailee in this situation must act in good faith and is liable only for gross negligence.

---

**EXAMPLE** ■ Pete Franks offers to take care of Carol White's dog while Carol is on vacation. Although Franks places the dog in his fenced-in yard, the dog is stolen. Franks is not liable to White for the loss of her dog, since its loss cannot be attributed to gross negligence. If Franks had released the dog into a heavily trafficked area and it had been run over, that would probably be gross negligence and he would be liable to White for the value of the dog.

---

Bailees receiving the entire benefit of a bailment must use extraordinary care to protect the personal property in their care.

**EXAMPLE** ■ Joan Hays agrees to let Tower National Bank exhibit in its lobby without charge a valuable painting that she owns. Tower National Bank must exercise extraordinary care while the painting is in its possession. Damage to or loss of the painting attributable to even slight negligence by the bank will result in liability.

When a bailment is for the mutual benefit of both parties, the bailee is required to exercise the degree of care (often called ordinary care) that a reasonably prudent person would exercise under the circumstances. Safe deposit boxes at banks are examples of mutual benefit bailments.

### SAFE DEPOSIT BOXES

In many states, banks are bailees of **safe deposit boxes**. As the bailee, a bank receives payment in return for providing a place of safekeeping for the personal property of its customers—the bailors. Unlike most bailees, a bank is usually unaware of the type of personal property within its custody, but that does not alter the bank's required degree of care.

Unless otherwise stipulated in the contract provisions between a bank and its bailor customer, a bank must exercise ordinary care in connection with its safe deposit boxes. Ordinary care dictates the construction of the bank's building, methods of protection, and a safe deposit operation conducted in a manner appropriate to banks in such circumstances. Thus, banks must construct their buildings and have safeguard procedures that protect boxes from theft by their employees and third parties.

Contracts between bailors and bailees, which may increase or alter their common-law responsibilities to each other, govern many bailment relationships. Bailees often use such contracts to lessen the common-law degrees of care they owe to bailors. Most courts will honor such contractual limitations of liabilities unless they include disclaimer liability for willful acts by bailees.

Contracts for safe deposit boxes usually include language disclaiming the bank's liability for losses suffered by its customers, except those caused by the bank's willful conduct. In addition, such contracts address

- the ability of those representing bailors, usually called deputies, to obtain access to boxes
- termination of the bailment agreement
- the rights of joint bailors
- steps to follow upon a bailor's death
- the bank's right to set reasonable hours of access to the box and to amend the contract when and as it wishes

Banks offering safe deposit services must be aware not only of the common law of bailments for mutual benefit but also any state statutes that specifically govern safe deposit boxes.

A bank's liability for losses from safe deposit boxes usually arises out of unauthorized access to boxes. A bank that knowingly or negligently permits unauthorized access to a box that later shows a loss of content will be liable for the bailor's loss.

---

**EXAMPLE** ■ Vicky Dobbs, bailor of a safe deposit box at Harper Creek National Bank, lost her purse, which contained the key to her box and her bank statement. Harry Jones found her purse, went to her bank, and was permitted access to the box without identification, even though identification was part of the bank's written policy for access to a safe deposit box. In this situation, the bank did not exercise ordinary care for the bailor's property, nor did it abide by its own policies. Thus, the bank would be liable to Dobbs for any loss she incurred due to its negligence.

---

A bailor who fails to take possession of his or her personal property at the end of the bailment is normally considered to have abandoned the property. This is the case with safe deposit boxes whose bailors do not renew their boxes when their rental agreements expire or fail to pay rent on their boxes. However, banks must carefully observe any state statutes that govern disposition of personal property in such boxes. These statutes usually include provisions for notifying bailors that the contents of boxes will be sold at a public auction and that bailors can retrieve their property during a particular period after payment of any overdue charges.

*Bailor's Duties*     Just as bailees have responsibilities for the personal property that bailors put into their possession, bailors also have various responsibilities, depending on which of the three types of bailment is involved. If the bailment is solely for the bailor's benefit, the bailor must warrant that no defects exist in the property which will make it unsafe for the bailee.

If the bailment is for the bailee's sole benefit, the bailor's duty is very slight. The bailor is liable only for injuries resulting from defects in the bailed property of which the bailor had knowledge yet failed to give notice to the bailee, if they are of the type that the bailee will not likely notice on his or her own.

If the bailment is for the parties' mutual benefit, the bailor must reasonably inspect the property to see that it is safe for the purpose for which it is rented or otherwise bailed. The bailor is liable to the bailee for damages resulting from defects that the bailor should have discovered with such an inspection.

---

EXAMPLE ■ Walters leaves a bottle containing acid in his safe deposit box. The acid escapes from the bottle and destroys his box and several others. In this situation, Walters is liable to the bank for the damage caused by the acid.

---

**Bailee's Lien**     In those bailments where bailees are entitled to compensation for their services, they have **lien** rights in the bailed goods until they are paid for their services. Such a lien is "specific" in that it applies only to the bailed goods and it is "possessory" because its continued existence depends on the bailee's retaining possession of the bailed goods. If the bailee gives up possession, the lien is lost.

*Case for Discussion*

**EATON v. LIDDELL**

### Facts
Eaton delivers three suits of clothing to Liddell, a tailor, to be cleaned and pressed. Liddell had made one of the suits for Eaton three months earlier, but Eaton had never paid Liddell for it.

When Eaton returns to pick up his suits, Liddell announces that he will not return any of the suits until Eaton pays him for the cost of cleaning and pressing them, and for the suit he made. Eaton leaves the tailor's shop in a fit of rage and sues Liddell.

### Decision
The court rules that Liddell has a lien on Eaton's three suits for the cleaning and pressing charges and does not have to return the suits until Eaton pays these charges. However, the court also rules that Liddell cannot hold the three suits or any one of them for the price of the suit that he made. According to the court, Liddell lost his lien on the specially made suit when he delivered it to Eaton. Because this lien was "possessory," it did not revive when Eaton returned the suit to Liddell for cleaning and pressing. The court further points out that Liddell never had a lien on the other suits to assure the price of the specially made suit, because his lien on that suit was also a "specific" one.

### Questions for Discussion
1. What steps should the tailor have taken to ensure that Eaton paid for the specially made suit?
2. Describe a situation in which a bank might face a similar problem with respect to a lien on personal property.
3. What steps can banks take to avoid such problems?

---

A statute usually establishes a bank's lien on the contents of safe deposit boxes for unpaid rent. However, in the absence of such a statute, a bank usually has a common-law lien on those contents.

**Leases**  Usually, personal property leases that require the lessee to return the property to its owner, the lessor, at the end of the lease are also mutual benefit bailments.

**EXAMPLE** ■ Mary Barton enters into an agreement with Scott Rental Car to use a car for 30 days for $600. This transaction is both a bailment and a lease.

A definite difference exists between bailments and leases in certain situations involving storage of personal property.

**EXAMPLE** ■ Phyllis Marx drove her car into Third State Bank's customer parking lot. She left her keys in the car at the request of the lot's attendant, who then parked it. A short while later, the car was stolen.

Leaving a car in a parking lot may be a lease or a bailment. If the car's owner surrenders possession and the lot owner assumes possession, a bailment exists.

Because a bailment exists in this example, the question then is whether the bailee bank exercised the necessary degree of care to avoid liability. If the bank provides the lot to induce people to use its services, the bailment is one of mutual benefit. In that case the bank would need to show it exercised ordinary care in protecting the car from theft.

Suppose instead that no attendant was on duty at the lot. If Marx had parked her car and left her keys in it, a lease would exist. In this situation, the bank would have no liability, since a lessor owes a lessee no duty for goods stored in a leased space unless a written agreement expressly provides for such responsibility.

As an alternative to financing the purchase of personal property, banks lease property to their customers. These types of lease transactions normally involve industrial equipment and automobiles. Bank leasing activities take various forms, including leases involving third parties and direct leases.

EXAMPLES
- Prime Auto, Inc., leases a car to Henry Gonzalez for 24 months at $100 per month. Prime assigns its lessor's interest to Millersburg State Bank, conveys its ownership interest to the bank, and receives $2,000. Thereafter, Gonzalez makes lease payments totaling $2,400 directly to the bank.

- Acme Manufacturing, Inc., decides it needs a new $1 million machine for its plant. Following discussions, First National Bank purchases the machine and leases it to Acme Manufacturing, Inc.

Leasing as an alternative method of bank financing must meet strict statutory and regulatory requirements. Leasing for lessors, lessees, and their creditors will be subject to a significant legal development in the 1990s—the adoption in most, if not all, states of article 2A of the UCC. Bankers will need to monitor the development of this new body of law in each of the states within which they do business.

## Common Carriers and Warehousemen

Common carriers—such as truck, air, and rail transport companies that take possession of others' personal property to transport it—are bailees. In addition, **warehousemen**—those engaged in the business of storing goods for hire—are bailees. State and federal statutes specifically addressing these types of bailees govern both common carriers and warehousemen. The United States Warehouse Act (7 U.S.C. §§ 241–273) governs storage of agricultural products for interstate or foreign commerce. Common carriers engaged in interstate commerce come within the scope of the federal Bills of Lading Act (49 U.S.C. § 81) and applicable provisions of the federal Interstate Commerce Act (49 U.S.C. § 1 *et seq.*).

If other state or federal statutes do not cover goods in storage or transport and under the control of a warehouseman or common carrier, such goods will come within the UCC's article 7 (U.C.C. § 7–103). Article 7 provides for documents of title, which are issued by bailees and describe goods in their possession. These documents are accepted in the regular course of business as proof of the right of the person possessing them to receive, hold, or dispose of the documents and the goods described in them (U.C.C. § 1–201(15)). Documents of title include bills of lading, dock warrants, dock receipts, and warehouse receipts.

EXAMPLE ■ Fleetwood Company receives an order for 1,000 widgets from Worldwide, Inc., at a cost of $100,000 and ships the widgets by Acme Freight. When Acme picks up the widgets, it issues Fleetwood a bill of lading describing the goods. Fleetwood then delivers the bill of lading to Worldwide for $100,000. Worldwide presents the bill of lading to Acme, and Acme surrenders the widgets to Worldwide.

## REAL PROPERTY

While personal property usually involves objects that are movable or intangible, real property consists of land and that which is permanently attached to it. As with personal property, more than one interest in real property may exist at any one time. For purposes of U.S. law, interests in real property are divided into freehold, life, leasehold, and nonpossessory estates. These different types of interests are important not only to their owners but to anyone, including banks, who takes real property as security for loans.

EXAMPLE ■ Robin Jay offers a mortgage on his interest in Blackacre Farms as security for a loan. Pellston State Bank makes the loan secured by the mortgage. Thereafter, Jay defaults and the bank forecloses its mortgage, only to find that Jay's interest in Blackacre Farms was that of a lessee, pursuant to a lease agreement that was to expire in one year.

Because Jay's interest in Blackacre Farms was a leasehold with only a short duration, the real estate had little or no value as security for the loan to Jay. Had the bank obtained an attorney's title opinion or a commitment for mortgage title insurance, it would have understood the insignificance of Jay's interest in the real estate and not made the loan without other security.

---

Any interest in real estate may be conveyed to a lender as security for a loan. The value of a mortgage as security for a debt depends on the type of interest in real property being conveyed as security. The preceding example demonstrates an interest of little value as security. Because of the importance of mortgage law, a considerable portion of this chapter will discuss that topic.

As with any legal discussion, definitions are important and this is especially true in the area of real-property law. (The following three examples illustrate how specific terms are used.) A **grantor** is the person or entity conveying property to another, who is called the **grantee**.

---

EXAMPLE ■ Farmers' State Bank sells Greengate Farm to Phyllis Johns. In this example, Farmers' State Bank is the grantor and Johns is the grantee.

---

A person mortgaging real property in which he or she has an interest is called the **mortgagor** and the creditor is called the **mortgagee**.

---

EXAMPLE ■ After purchasing Greengate Farm from the bank, Phyllis Johns borrows money from the bank and secures the debt with a mortgage on the property. In this situation, Johns is the mortgagor and the bank is the mortgagee.

---

A person or entity who leases property is called a **lessor** or **landlord**. A person leasing property from a landlord or lessor is called a **lessee** or **tenant**.

**EXAMPLE** ■ Phyllis Johns decides to lease Greengate Farm to Howard Drake. By so doing, she becomes the lessor and Drake becomes the lessee.

## Freehold Estates

Most real estate interests lie within the **freehold estate** classification. Within that classification are **fee simple** and **fee tail estates**. All these estates may be inherited, passing from their owner to his or her heirs.

## *Fee Simple Estates*

Within the category of fee simple estates are those that are

- fee simple absolute
- fee simple conditional
- fee simple determinable

### FEE SIMPLE ABSOLUTE

Within the classification of freehold estates, most property is held as fee simple absolute estates. From a mortgagee's viewpoint, this is the most desirable kind of property to mortgage.

A **fee simple absolute** interest is the broadest interest anyone may have in real property, allowing the owner to use, abuse, exclusively possess the property, take its fruits (such as timber and crops), and dispose of it by deed or will without restriction.

**EXAMPLE** ■ Thomas Barz has a fee simple absolute title to Terra Firma, an 80-acre parcel of land. He lives on the property and uses it to graze sheep and as headquarters for his construction business. He also removes gravel and extracts oil from the property. Barz has posted the land and has often removed trespassers from it. Barz also harvests corn on 10 acres of the land. In his will, Barz leaves Terra Firma to his son.

## FEE SIMPLE CONDITIONAL OR DETERMINABLE

**Fee simple conditional** and **fee simple determinable** estates are not as widespread as fee simple absolute estates. Because owners can lose their interests in these types of estates (and thus mortgagees can lose their collateral), they are less desirable collateral from a mortgagee's view.

---

EXAMPLE ■ Astor conveyed a fee simple estate to Engels on the condition that the land should never be used for the sale of liquor and that, if it is, Astor and his heirs shall have the right to reenter and repossess it. In this situation, Engels has a fee simple conditional interest and Astor has a right of reentry. If liquor is sold on the land, Astor or his heirs may enter and reacquire the ownership of the land. The right of reentry is not automatic and Astor or his heirs could waive it through inaction. But the condition will remain on the land forever.

---

A fee simple determinable estate is like the fee simple conditional estate, except the condition (usually called a "qualification") operates automatically and requires no affirmative action (like reentry) by the party holding the executory interest. Just as the words "condition" and "reentry" are used to create the fee simple conditional estate, the fee simple determinable estate is usually created by the words "so long as."

---

EXAMPLE ■ Wulff conveys a fee simple estate in a parcel of real property to Sagebrush Public Schools, so long as the property is used for educational purposes. In this situation, Sagebrush has a fee simple determinable interest. Wulff has an interest that is called a "possibility of reverter." If the property is ever used for other than educational purposes, the estate is automatically transferred from Sagebrush back to Wulff. If Wulff, between the time he conveys the property to Sagebrush and the time the property ceases to be used for education, conveys his "possibility of reverter" to another person, the property goes to that other person when it ceases to be used for educational purposes.

## Fee Tail Estates

*Abolished in NYS*

The **fee tail estate** was developed in England to ensure that land would never cease to be family land. This estate was never popular in the United States and most states have abolished it.

EXAMPLE ■ Foley conveyed a fee tail estate to Euler "and the heirs of his body." In this situation, Euler can sell his interest in the fee tail estate, but anyone who buys it will have to return the land to Foley's children when Foley dies. These children can also sell their interest in the estate, but upon their death the land reverts to their children, and so on, forever.

## Life Estates

While property conveyed by a freehold estate is inheritable, **life estates** are never inheritable. This means, for example, that a person or other entity having a fee simple title may control disposition of the property after death if it was not conveyed while the owner was alive.

EXAMPLE ■ Vic Small deeds real property to "Chester White and his heirs." The words "his heirs" indicate that the title to the property is a fee simple title. Chester White may thereafter convey the property to whomever he wishes.

If White still has the property at the time of his death, it will go to whomever he willed it or, if he had no will, to his intestate heirs. (Intestate heirs are those relatives designated by state law to receive the decedent's property when no will was left.) Thus, if White had a will leaving all his property to his wife, the property would become hers. If he had no will, the property would be distributed to his intestate heirs, who in most states would be members of his immediate family.

Unlike fee simple estates, life estates end at death. Thus, the length of their existence is measured as the duration of someone's life.

---

EXAMPLE ■ Val Anderson conveys a parcel of real property to Dominic Forelli for his lifetime. Ten years later Forelli dies, leaving a will that passes on all his property to his wife, Alice. Alice receives no interest in the real property conveyed to Forelli by Anderson. Upon Forelli's death, his interest in the property ends and does not descend to his heirs.

---

The duration of a life estate may be measured by anyone's life, not just the life of the person to whom the property is conveyed.

---

EXAMPLE ■ The facts are the same as in previous example, except that the deed to Forelli states "to Forelli for the life of John Hile." In this situation, Forelli's interest in the property will end upon Hile's death. If Forelli dies before Hile, most state statutes permit Forelli's heirs to take the property until Hile's death.

---

When a person whose life is the measure of a life estate dies, the life estate ends and the property goes to the individual having the "remainder" interest.

**Dower** is a type of life estate. It is the interest that a married woman has in her husband's real property. Under common law, upon her husband's death, a wife becomes entitled to a life estate in a one-third interest of all the real estate her husband owned during their marriage which she did not release by joining with him in a deed of conveyance or otherwise. The dower right of the wife does not vest until her husband's death; that is, she has no right to possess one-third of his lands until his death.

Dower is thus a nonpossessory right as long as the husband remains alive. Thereafter, it becomes a possessory right. Because of dower rights, a husband cannot give an unencumbered title to real estate unless the wife joins him in the conveyance.

---

EXAMPLE ■ Herbert Jones, a married man, buys a parcel of real property. Shortly thereafter, without having his wife join in the conveyance, Jones conveys the property to Jim Nichols. Upon Jones's death, Mrs. Jones acquires a life estate in one-third of the property sold to Nichols. To protect himself, Nichols should have insisted that Mrs. Jones join in the conveyance to him to preclude her dower interest.

---

Life estates arising as a result of a dower interest are created by operation of law and not as the result of a deed or will. Under common law, married men used to enjoy a similar interest in their wives' real property. Most states abolished this interest, called the estate of **curtesy**, to permit a married woman to convey her real property without requiring her husband to join in the conveyance.

During the duration of a life estate, the tenant has exclusive possession and may use the property as he or she wishes, but must not waste it or impair the value of the remainder.

The risk of mortgaging a tenant's interest in a life estate is evident.

---

EXAMPLE ■ Fred Nerkle borrows $25,000 from First State Bank, secured by a mortgage on a 3,000-acre farm in which Nerkle has a life estate. Nerkle dies shortly thereafter. The bank will be unable to foreclose its mortgage, because its lien ended with Nerkle's death.

---

## Leasehold Estates

**Leasehold estates** are sometimes called "nonfreehold estates" and are commonly encountered in landlord-tenant law. The parties to a leasehold estate are called the lessor or landlord and the lessee or tenant. The former is usually the fee owner of the property, while the latter is the one who possesses the property during the lease period.

## Types of Leasehold Estates

Leasehold estates consist of four types:

- estate for years
- periodic estate
- estate at will
- estate at sufferance

[handwritten note: In NYS virtually the same thing.]

### ESTATE FOR YEARS

Any lease for a fixed period is an **estate for years**.

EXAMPLE ■ Hull leases Jamaica Inn to Kenny from January 1, 1990, to January 1, 1995. This lease creates an estate for years. It will end automatically on January 1, 1995.

### PERIODIC ESTATE

Unlike estates for years, which terminate automatically at the expiration of a stated term, **periodic leasehold estates** continue until the parties, by giving proper notice, end them. Unless terminated by proper notice, the periodic estate continues for another period.

EXAMPLE ■ Andrews conveys his farm to Key "month to month," beginning January 1, 1990. This is a periodic estate. By giving proper notice, either Key or Andrews can terminate the estate at the end of a period, such as February 1. If no notice is given, the lease automatically renews itself for another month, and so on.

## ESTATE AT WILL

An **estate at will** is one that the landlord or tenant may end at any time. Under special statutes widely enacted in the United States, however, notice may be required to end an estate at will. This feature gives the estate at will a duration at least equal to the time required for the notice. Statutes requiring a notice of 30 days to end an estate at will are common.

---

EXAMPLE ■ Conrad conveyed a farm to Dent for as long as Conrad wills. This is an estate at will. If the estate may be terminated at the will of one party, it may also be terminated at the will of the other. In common law, therefore, either Conrad or Dent could end the tenancy at any time. Under certain state statutes, however, notice of termination must be given.

---

## ESTATE AT SUFFERANCE

This estate is an oddity designed to protect the landlord against the dangers of adverse possession. An **estate at sufferance** gives the landlord the option of treating the holdover tenant as a trespasser and evicting him or her, or treating the tenant as a periodic tenant. If the landlord treats the tenant as a periodic tenant, the tenancy created renews the expired lease on its same terms. In such a case, the duration of the lease is year to year, unless the expired lease was for less than a year, in which case the term of the new periodic tenancy will be the same as that of the expired lease.

---

EXAMPLE ■ Joe Randalls leases a house to Al Rogers for five years. When the five years expire, Rogers remains on the land and becomes a tenant at sufferance. The doctrine of adverse possession does not run in his favor. Randalls has the option of treating Rogers as a trespasser and evicting him or treating him as a periodic tenant.

In this case, the periodic tenancy would be on a year-to-year basis, but the terms of the expired lease would otherwise apply.

*Possession, Enforcement, and Use*   Like freehold estates, leasehold estates entitle their holders to possession. A lessee's right to possess leased property exists for the duration of the lease. At the end of the lease period, the lessee has a legal obligation to surrender the property to the lessor and, if he or she fails to surrender the property, the lessor may regain the property. A lessee's right to possess the property during a lease period is exclusive and even the lessor may not interfere with that right.

EXAMPLE ■ Pat Bishop leased an apartment from Harry Blake. One day while Bishop was out, Blake entered the apartment to inspect its condition. Blake's actions violated Bishop's exclusive possessory rights. Unless the lease agreement between the parties permits a lessor access to leased property, the lessor may not enter the premises without the lessee's permission. Thus, Blake's entry into the apartment constituted trespass, for which he is liable to Bishop.

Besides exclusive possession, lessees are also entitled to "quiet enjoyment" of leased real property. Quiet enjoyment means that, during the lease period, the lessor will not disturb or evict the lessee, nor impair the lessee's enjoyment of the physical status of the property.

EXAMPLE ■ Hall Malls, Inc., leases an area within its shopping mall to Ohio Central Bank for a branch. During the lease period, Hall Malls, Inc., starts a remodeling project that will eliminate access to the branch location. In this example, the lessor will breach the lessee's right to quiet enjoyment of the leased property. Therefore, the lessee may seek not only a court injunction to prevent the lessor from restricting access to its branch but also monetary damages for any loss of business.

During a lease period, a lessee may use the leased property for any lawful purpose for which the property is fit and which does not waste or destroy the property.

EXAMPLE ■ Fanny Leppler leases a home to Hank Hicks. The home has always been used for residential purposes. Hicks opens a pool room in the house and removes several walls to accommodate his business. Since the leased property is not being used for its usual purpose and Hicks has committed waste by tearing down walls, Leppler could probably end the lease, evict Hicks, and require him to pay to restore the walls.

*Reentry*  At the end of any leasehold estate, a lessee is obligated to vacate the leased property. If a lessee breaches the conditions of the lease agreement by such acts as nonpayment of rent or waste of the property, a lessor can demand return of the property before the end of the lease term. If the lessee refuses to return the property voluntarily, the lessor may reenter the premises and take control of it. Under most state statutes, if a lessor cannot accomplish reentry peacefully, the lessor will need to resort to court proceedings. —including NYS.

NYS - you always need a court order.

EXAMPLE ■ High Point National Bank owns a house it obtained through foreclosure. The house is rented to Don Sullivan, who fails to pay the rent due the bank. Sullivan also refuses the bank's demand to quit the premises.

If the bank cannot peacefully reenter the house, it will need to seek a court order directing Sullivan to leave the house. If Sullivan refuses to obey the order, a law enforcement agency will enforce it. However, such a court order is usually rendered only after a hearing at which the lessor and lessee can present their arguments and be represented by counsel.

*Leasehold Mortgages*   A leasehold estate may be mortgaged; that is, a lease of real property may be entered into as security for a debt.

EXAMPLE ■ Henry Harper leased real property to Leon Gage for 25 years, an estate for years. Gage borrowed $30,000 from City State Bank and secured the debt with a mortgage on his leasehold estate.

Leasehold mortgages are not as secure collateral as mortgages on fee simple estates. This is because the lease will eventually end by its own terms or by default if the lessee fails to make payments or breaches other terms of the lease.

**Nonpossessory Interests in Real Property**   Freehold and leasehold estates permit their holders possession of the real property subject to their interests. However, many interests in real property do not entitle their owners to immediate possession. In these situations, their right to possession is postponed. Among the various nonpossessory interests in real property are

- dower and curtesy
- easements, profits, and licenses
- future interests

*Dower and Curtesy*   Dower and curtesy have been discussed in the earlier section of life estates. Dower and curtesy do not vest until one spouse dies. During the spouse's lifetime, dower and curtesy are nonpossessory interests.

As mentioned, many state statutes have modified or abolished dower and curtesy. In addition, in many states, special statutes governing inheritance let a surviving spouse elect whether to take a portion of the deceased spouse's real estate in fee simple absolute or to take such inheritance as the deceased spouse directed in his or her will.

EXAMPLE ■ Frank O'Hara died, leaving a wife, Maureen, and an estate that included $100,000 worth of real estate titled entirely in his name. Frank's will left $10,000 to his wife and the balance of his estate to Petula Harris. Under the applicable statutes in the state in which Frank lived, a surviving spouse can elect to take that which is left in the deceased spouse's will or one-third of the real estate. Of course, in this example, Maureen will elect to take the one-third interest in Frank's real property and forfeit the $10,000.

*Easements, Profits, and Licenses*

Nonpossessory interests in real property also include easements, profits, and licenses.

An **easement** is the right to use, not possess, the real property of another person for some limited purpose. Easements are acquired by express conveyance in a deed or will, by prescription, and by implication.

EXAMPLES ■ Mark Ranks asked the electric company to run a power line to his newly built home. The company agreed to run the line if Ranks would execute an easement agreement permitting the company's personnel to go onto the property, erect poles and lines, and maintain them in the future. This easement granted by Ranks is an express easement reduced to writing, which will be permanent unless the electric company later surrenders it to Ranks or anyone later owning the property.

■ Harry Hill and Forest Lang own two adjoining lots. For 25 years, Hill has driven over Lang's lot to reach his property, even though an alternate route existed. Hill has never asked Lang's permission to go over his property. Lang and Hill have a falling out and Lang demands that Hill cease using his lot as means of access.

In this situation, Hill has a prescriptive easement over Lang's lot which Lang cannot terminate. This type of easement is not the result of an agreement between parties. Rather, it is the result of Hill's adverse (not permissive) use of Lang's property, which was open, notorious, continuous, and for the period of prescription (usually 10 to 15 years by statute). Prescriptive easements run with the land, that is, no matter who owns Hill's and Lang's lots, the owner of the former will have an easement over the latter's lot.

■ Sunnyview Properties, Inc., owns an apartment building in which Sam Barbara rents an apartment on the third floor. Nothing in Barbara's lease agreement provides permission for him to use the hallways, stairways, and elevators to reach his apartment. However Barbara has an easement by implication to use the apartment building's hallways, stairways, and elevators to enter and leave his apartment. An implied easement does not arise as the result of an express agreement but rather as a result of the circumstances surrounding an express agreement. In this example, the agreement is the lease between the parties and the law implies that access to an apartment is granted to a lessee when he or she leases an apartment.

---

The right to take something from another's property is called a "profit a prendre" or simply a **profit**. For example, someone having a profit to take wood for heating purposes from another individual's land would be free to collect sticks and branches on that land.

A **license** is a temporary privilege to make some specific use of another person's land.

---

**EXAMPLE** ■ A repairman called to repair the roof of the White House would be a licensee. He is privileged to come onto the grounds for this job without being charged with trespass. But his presence on the grounds does not give him future rights to be there.

---

Thus, unlike an easement, a license may be terminated at any time by the owner of the property.

## Future Interests

Future interests in real property are actually present interests whose rights to possession of real property have been postponed until a particular event happens. Future interests in real property consist of

- reversions
- remainders
- possibilities of reverter
- rights of reentry
- executory interests

A **reversion** is the residue of a fee simple estate remaining in a grantor who has conveyed less than a fee simple interest to one or more parties. The grantor is entitled to possession of the real property after the outstanding estate comes to an end.

---

**EXAMPLE** ■ Meade conveys a life estate in Sunny Lake to Joyce. In this situation, Meade has a reversion and Joyce has a life estate. When Joyce dies, the land will revert to Meade. If Meade predeceases Joyce, the land will revert to Meade's heirs.

---

A **remainder** is like a reversion except that it is held by someone other than the grantor. The **remainderman** is a third party who is entitled to possession and ownership after a particular estate—less than a fee simple in quantity—comes to an end.

---

**EXAMPLE** ■ Drummond conveys "a life estate to Wilkes, remainder to Howard in fee simple." In this situation, Wilkes has a life estate, Howard has a vested remainder, and Drummond has nothing.

---

Remainders are either vested or contingent. A vested remainder is one that is certain of giving the remainderman, or his or her heirs, the property after the outstanding estate expires. A contingent remainderman, on the other hand, will not obtain the property unless certain conditions are satisfied.

---

EXAMPLE ■ Paton conveys a life estate to Sand, with a remainder to Robinson if he is 21 years of age or older when Sand dies, and otherwise to Fredericks.

In this situation, Sand has a life estate. Robinson and Fredericks each have a contingent remainder. Robinson will not acquire the land unless he is 21 years of age or older when Sand dies. Fredericks will not acquire the land unless Sand dies while Robinson is under 21 years of age. Collectively, Sand, Robinson, and Fredericks have a fee simple absolute interest. If all would join in the conveyance, they could convey such an interest.

---

To be valid under common law, contingent remainders must comply with the **rule against perpetuities**. This rule forbids postponement of the vesting of a contingent remainder beyond a period computed by a life existing at the time of a grant plus 21 years.

---

EXAMPLE ■ Sam Bilitzke executed a will in 1920 in which he provided that upon his death a parcel of real property was to become Corey's for life, with a remainder to Corey's surviving children. When Bilitzke died in 1922, Corey was living but had no children. To comply with the rule against perpetuities, the remainder must be certain to vest in Corey's children within 21 years of Bilitzke's death. Because Corey had no children when Bilitzke died, the remainder is void and Corey takes the title to the property.

---

Many states have altered the common-law rule against perpetuities. Thus, the preceding example might have a different result in those states that have made such statutory changes to this common-law rule.

The **possibility of reverter** is the interest retained by the grantor and his or her heirs after the conveyance of a fee simple determinable estate.

A contingent remainder cannot be conveyed to follow a fee simple interest, because a remainder by definition takes effect after the preceding estate comes to an end, and a fee simple interest never ends. Fee simple estates, however, can be conditioned or qualified. If the condition runs in favor of the grantor and his or her heirs, the estate is a fee simple conditional estate and the grantor and his or her heirs have a **right of reentry** to the property. If the estate is qualified by a limitation running in favor of a third person instead of the grantor, the third person has an **executory interest** in the property.

---

EXAMPLE ■ Throne conveyed Holly Oak Estate to Hanson in fee simple so long as liquor is never sold on the land and, "if it is, the land shall automatically pass to Dodge." In this situation, Hanson has a fee simple determinable interest in the property, Dodge has an executory interest in the property, and Throne has nothing.

---

## Co-Ownership of Real Property, Concurrent Estates

One person can own any of the various legal interests in real property discussed in this chapter. Such ownership, called severalty, is common throughout the United States. In addition, one or more persons may concurrently own any of the interests in real property discussed in this chapter.

---

EXAMPLES ■ Diamond and Stone convey a life estate to Harper and Mack for the life of Harper. Harper and Mack concurrently share a life estate as long as Harper lives. Diamond and Stone concurrently have a reversion interest in the property conveyed to Harper and Mack.

■ Ruby Jenkins leases a farm to Tom and Alice Eaton from February 1, 1990, to February 1, 1994. During this period, the Eatons concurrently have a leasehold estate for years.

---

241   *Real and Personal Property*

In the United States, there are four kinds of co-ownership of real property having their origin in either English common law or European civil law

- tenancy in common
- joint tenancy
- tenancy by the entirety
- community property

In addition, those states that have adopted the Uniform Partnership Act permit a "tenancy in partnership."

## Tenancy in Common

**Tenancy in common** exists when two or more people each have an undivided fractional interest in real property and each person's interest in the property descends at death to his or her heirs or according to the decedent's will. Because tenants in common have an undivided interest in property in proportion to their interest, they all have an equal right to occupy and use the property.

---

EXAMPLE ■ Fran Johnson, Marge Chappell, and Helen Hope bought a cottage as tenants in common. Later Johnson and Chappell could not get along with Hope and asked her not to use the cottage. However, as a tenant in common, Hope may use the cottage with or without their consent.

If tenants in common cannot resolve their differences about the use of their property, they may ask a court to partition the property or order its sale. In this example, partition of the property would be difficult since only one dwelling is involved and equal division among the three tenants in common would be impractical. Under the circumstances, a court would probably order a sale of the property, with the sale proceeds divided equally.

---

Once property held as a tenancy in common is partitioned, each of its former tenants in common owns a separate piece in severalty.

Tenants in common may mortgage their property interests either together or individually.

---

EXAMPLE ■ Tom Rogers and Sam Hughes own vacant acreage as tenants in common. Rogers borrows $10,000 from Third State Bank and secures the debt with a mortgage on the property.

Third State Bank has a mortgagee's interest in an undivided one-half of the property. If Rogers defaults and the bank forecloses, Rogers's interest will be sold to satisfy the debt. Any buyer at a foreclosure sale will become a tenant in common with Hughes. That buyer may then seek partition or sale of the property if he or she does not want to continue as a tenant in common with Hughes.

---

## Joint Tenancy

**Joint tenants** are like tenants in common except that they have a "right of survivorship." This means that if one joint tenant dies, the other acquires the entire interest. The interest of the deceased joint tenant does not pass to heirs or by will but passes instead to the other joint tenant. A joint tenant, however, may convey interest while alive. If a conveyance occurs, the grantee becomes a tenant in common with the other co-owner. Stated differently, a joint tenant's conveyance converts the joint tenancy into a tenancy in common.

The right of joint tenants to use the property is the same as that of tenants in common. When they possess the land, each has the right to use all the property but no right to exclude the other from doing likewise.

---

EXAMPLE ■ Mac Farmer and Alice Sommes own a 40-acre parcel of land as joint tenants. Sommes dies and, in her will, she leaves all her property to her sister, Susan. In this situation, Farmer becomes the sole owner of the acreage at the moment of Sommes's death and Susan takes no interest in the property.

---

Joint tenants may mortgage their interests in property. However, mortgagees taking a mortgage on joint tenancy property without the signatures of all owners risk losing their collateral.

EXAMPLE ■ The facts are the same as in the preceding example. Before Alice Sommes dies, she executes a mortgage upon her joint tenant's interest in the property. When Sommes dies, the mortgage ends and Farmer becomes the sole owner of the property.

If a conflict arises between joint tenants, they may seek partition of the property and, if it cannot be fairly divided, may seek its sale.

EXAMPLE ■ David Day and Fred Power own 20 vacant acres as joint tenants. Power wants to sell the property, but Day refuses to join in any sale. If Power sells his interest, the buyer would own the property as a tenant in common with Day, but Power cannot find a buyer for an undivided one-half interest in the property. Under the circumstances, Power could seek partition of the property, and, since it is vacant acreage, a court could probably divide the property evenly and give 10 acres to each owner.

## *Tenancy by the Entirety*

**A tenancy by the entirety** is basically a joint tenancy in which the two tenants are husband and wife. Like joint tenancy, this form of co-ownership carries with it a right of survivorship. In many states, however, tenancy by the entirety has one special characteristic not found in joint tenancy: the creditors of only one spouse cannot reach property held by the entirety. Only by having a claim aginst *both* the husband and wife may creditors reach such property. Further, in most states, a conveyance by one of the parties cannot destroy or convert into a tenancy in common the tenancy by the entirety. In these stages, neither the husband nor the wife alone can convey or mortgage real property held by the entirety. Only if both parties join in the deed or mortgage may a conveyance or mortgage be made.

---

**EXAMPLE** ■ Harry and Delores Harper, who are husband and wife, reside and own real property as tenants by the entirety in Michigan. Harry signs a deed conveying the property to Felix Smith. Delores signs a mortgage on the property securing a debt she owes Southern Michigan State Bank.

Neither the deed nor the mortgage are valid in Michigan. Southern Michigan State Bank may collect the debt Delores owes it but not by foreclosure of the mortgage nor any other action against the real estate, since in Michigan the creditors of only one spouse cannot reach the property of tenants by the entirety. Further, the deed signed by Harry has no effect and the property remains titled by the entirety to both Harry and Delores Harper.

---

Although many states do not recognize tenancy by the entirety, where it is recognized, it is widely used in the ownership of family homes.

*Community Property*

In some states, property acquired by a husband or wife during their marriage becomes their **community property**. Depending on the state, community property often includes many aspects of tenancy by the entirety. The rights of those with community property vary from state to state, however, so it is extremely difficult to generalize.

*Tenancy in Partnership*

In states that have adopted the Uniform Partnership Act, a concurrent estate called **tenancy in partnership** exists. Under the common law, partners owned real estate as tenants in common and thus held title to the property individually. The Uniform Partnership Act permits a partnership to hold title in the partnership's name as a tenancy in partnership. Mortgages on property held as a tenancy in partnership should be executed in the partnership's name, not in the names of the individual partners.

**Acquisition of Real Property**

Real property may be acquired by

- purchase
- gift
- will or descent
- adverse possession

*Purchase*

The owner of real property has the right to sell it. Indeed, the law has a strong policy against any restraint or **alienation** of this right and thus avoids restrictions that limit an owner's right to sell.

In most instances, the purchase of real property involves its transfer by deed plus the buyer's taking possession of it. Generally, two kinds of deeds are used in the purchase of real property: a warranty deed and a quit claim deed.

A **warranty deed** conveys the grantor's (seller's) interest in real property to the grantee (buyer). Additionally, this kind of deed guarantees that no defects exist in the title. If an outstanding interest in a third person is not specifically excepted in the warranty deed, the grantee can sue the grantor for damages in the amount of the loss suffered because of the defect in title. Usually, damages are determined by how much money is required to "buy off" the third-party claimant.

---

EXAMPLE
- Freda Kelly conveys real property to Lois Smith by warranty deed. After receiving the deed, Smith discovers a mortgage lien on the property securing a $20,000 debt. The mortgage is a defect in the title which must be removed to give Smith the clear title to which she is entitled as a result of the warranty deed. Since Smith will need $20,000 to pay off the mortgage, she is entitled to that amount from Kelly.

---

A **quit claim deed** conveys the grantor's interest in the property to the grantee but does not guarantee the title. Such a deed is used frequently in buying up outstanding claims to put together a fee simple absolute interest. In clearing title, people holding doubtful interests may be asked to sell them and these people understandably would not want to warrant that they have any title to sell.

The quit claim deed is ideally suited to cure technical defects in the title chain. But this kind of deed is not limited to clearing clouds from the title to real property. A quit claim deed can also be used in place of a warranty deed to convey real property. When it is used for this purpose, the grantor does not warrant title to the land. Instead, the deed conveys the grantor's entire "right, title, and interest" in the property.

EXAMPLE ■ Felix Allen purchased real property from Fred Hughes. Later, he discovered that Hughes was married when he conveyed the property, which is located in a state that recognizes dower rights. To assure that he has clear title to the property, Allen requests a deed from Mrs. Hughes and she agrees to give Allen a deed.

Because Mrs. Hughes's interest in the real property is not a fee simple absolute, she should give Allen a quit claim deed, which carries no warranties of title but does convey any interest a grantor has in real property. By giving Allen a quit claim deed, Mrs. Hughes extinguishes her dower interest in the property but makes no promises to Allen regarding the title to it.

Real property may also be acquired by purchase at a foreclosure sale. Once any applicable redemption period has expired as prescribed by state law, a successful bidder at a foreclosure sale will receive a deed from a sheriff or other official conducting the foreclosure sale. The title acquired at the sale extinguishes the previous owner's interests in the property.

EXAMPLE ■ John Sears owns real property encumbered by a mortgage. The mortgage goes into default and the bank forecloses. At the foreclosure sale, Ned Butler is the highest bidder. At the end of the redemption period, Butler receives a deed from the sheriff who conducted the sale. When the sheriff's deed is delivered to Butler, Sears's interest in the property ends and Butler becomes its owner.

---

Property may also be acquired at tax sales when property is sold to pay overdue taxes.

*Gift*  Real property may be given as a **gift** to a donee. For the gift to be complete, however, the donor must deliver a warranty or quit claim deed to the donee. If the deed complies with the statutory requirements of the state in which the land is located, the donee is not required to take possession of the land to complete the gift.

---

EXAMPLE ■ Attlee decides to give Seaview Farm to Eliot. Accordingly, Attlee executes a warranty deed in which Eliot is named as grantee. Attlee places this deed in his safe deposit vault and attaches to it a note stating that the deed is to be delivered to Eliot upon Attlee's death. Attlee dies and Eliot claims the land. In this situation, Attlee's gift fails for the deed's lack of delivery and Eliot does not own the land.

---

*Will or Descent*  The owner of real property who has the right to dispose of it by will must comply with the formalities established by the state in which the land is located. If the owner dies without a will, the land passes by "intestate succession"; that is, in the absence of a will, the land passes to the heirs of the deceased according to the law of descent of the state in which the land is located. If an ower of real property is a married man in a state recognizing dower rights, regardless of provisions in the owner's will for the property, his surviving wife's dower interests will preempt the will's provisions.

In some states, special statutes often give a surviving spouse (male or female) an election to take a portion (usually one-third or one-half) of the real estate in fee simple absolute or to take that portion of the estate given under the deceased person's will.

## Adverse Possession

Ownership of land may be acquired by adverse possession, a doctrine that exists because of the **statute of limitations**. The statute of limitations provides that no action may be brought to recover the possession of land after a stated number of years, which varies from 5 to 20 years depending on the state. If a person holds land so as to make the statute of limitations run against the owner, the owner will lose any remedies and rights after the statutory period has expired. To start the statute running, the adverse possessor must actually occupy the land "openly" and "hostilely." One adverse possessor's time may be added on to that of another and thus the same person need not hold the land for the entire statutory period. But the adverse possession must be continuous for the entire period.

## Case for Discussion

**THOMAS v. SAGE**

### Facts
Lily Thomas owned a farm called Flowerhill. In 1960, Danny Rose moved onto the land and began to farm it as his own, without Thomas's permission. During this time, he held the land openly.

In 1978, Rose sold his "right, title, and interest" in the land to Walter Sage by a quit claim deed. Sage immediately took the land into his possession and held it openly until 1989. At that time, Thomas brought an action to eject Sage.

### Decision
In this case, the court rules in favor of Sage. In so doing, the court states that the statute of limitations bars Thomas's action against Sage. Since Thomas cannot eject Sage from the land, Sage has acquired the ownership of it through the doctrine of adverse possession. Furthermore, the court points out that, in the running of the statute of limitations, Rose's time can be added to that of Sage and it is really the statute of limitations that gives Sage the title to Flowerhill.

### Questions for Discussion

1. Under the circumstances, what should Thomas have done to hold onto the title to her farm?

2. Why do banks need to be concerned about the statute of limitations?

3. Describe a situation in which the doctrine of adverse possession might affect a bank.

---

## Land Use

In American law, besides the limitations imposed by fee simple conditional and determinable estates, other methods exist for limiting the use of privately owned real property. Unlike the former limitations, these other limitations apply not to isolated parcels of real property but to groups of parcels. Thus, in the United States, both private restrictive covenants and local government zoning ordinances can restrict the use of real property pursuant to general plans.

### *Restrictive Covenants*

Within the limits of constitutional law, a person owning a tract of real property and selling parcels from that tract may impose, for the benefit of the remaining parcels, certain restrictions on the property.

---

**EXAMPLE** ■ Tower Heights Development Company owns 40 acres that it wishes to subdivide into 100 lots for residential purposes. To ensure that as the lots are sold they will be used only for residences, each deed that conveys the lots contains a clause stating, "The real property described herein shall be used only for residential purposes." Further, Tower Heights records a "building restriction agreement" that sets forth the residential requirement, as well as legal descriptions of all the real estate to which the restriction applies.

Restrictive covenants such as this run with the land; that is, the restriction is binding not only on the people initially purchasing lots from the original subdivider but also on all successors in title.

At one point, Tower Heights uses a deed containing the residential restrictive covenant to convey a lot to Maureen Conley. Subsequently, Conley sells the lot to Fritz Brown, who starts to build a grocery store on the lot. Brown's plans to build a grocery store violate the covenant, which is as binding on him as it was on Conley or any future owner of the lot.

Besides restricting the use of property for residential purposes, **restrictive covenants** have also been used to assure that property will not be used for religious purposes and retail outlets. However, the Supreme Court has declared unconstitutional restrictive covenants limiting the use of real property to occupancy by people of a particular race. *Shelley v. Kraemer*, 334 U.S. 1 (1948).

## *Zoning Ordinances*

While building covenants are private restrictions on the use of real property, zoning ordinances are publicly imposed restrictions on land use.

EXAMPLE ■ The Meadow City Council adopts a zoning ordinance that sets aside various areas of its municipality for certain uses, including single-family residences, multiple-family residences, retail stores, and industrial plants.

Local governments can enact zoning ordinances within the scope of their police powers, which allow actions to protect the health, safety, morals, or welfare of the public. *Village of Euclid v. Ambler Realty Co.*, 272 U.S. 365 (1926).

While zoning ordinances may restrict the future use of property, they do not affect a use that is current when an ordinance is passed.

EXAMPLE ■ The facts are the same as in the previous example. When the Meadow City Council passes its ordinance, Frank Leehan owns a dry cleaning business in an area zoned residential. In this situation, Leehan may continue to operate his business, but it will be considered a "nonconforming use." As a nonconforming use, the business will probably not be able to expand. Further, if for any reason the property ceases to be used as a dry cleaning establishment, under most zoning ordinances it could not be reestablished under a nonconforming use.

## Mortgages

As has been discussed, a **mortgage** is an interest in real property created by a written instrument as collateral for payment of a debt. At a minimum, a mortgage instrument contains the names of the mortgagor and mortgagee, a description of the real property subject to the mortgage, and a reference to the debt that the mortgage secures. One or more promissory notes usually represent a debt secured by a mortgage and, when a bank makes the loan, this is almost universally true.

The owner of the property, the **mortgagor**, remains its owner after the mortgage conveyance, but the **mortgagee** acquires a special interest in the property. This special interest allows the mortgagee to foreclose the mortgage and thus sell the real property to satisfy the debt if it goes unpaid.

EXAMPLE ■ Ann Lang owns a parcel of real estate by fee simple absolute, with an appraised value of $100,000. On August 7, 1989, Lang borrows $20,000 from Farmers Savings and Loan Association, which she secures by a mortgage on her property. A few months later Lang applies for a $10,000 loan at Valley National Bank. She again offers the real property as security.

One parcel of real property may be subject to as many mortgages as its owners and various mortgagors wish to enter. In addition, one mortgage may be collateral for many debts owed to one mortgagee.

EXAMPLE ■ Lila Axelrod owns a parcel of real property. She borrows $5,000 from Harper Hills State Bank and secures the loan with a mortgage, in which the following clause appears: "This mortgage secures all indebtedness of the mortgagor that shall at any time be due and owing to the mortgagee." Subsequently, under the same mortgage, Axelrod borrows $10,000 from the bank.

Because of the open-indebtedness language of the mortgage, it will be collateral for the $10,000 loan and all other loans Harper Hills State Bank makes to Axelrod. The clause in Axelrod's mortgage is often called a "dragnet" clause and the subsequent loans it causes to be secured by the mortgage are often called "future advances."

*Conveyance of Mortgaged Property*

The existence of a mortgage or mortgages on real property does not prevent its sale. However, many mortgages contain "due-on-sale" clauses that accelerate the entire mortgage debt if the mortgaged property is sold without the mortgagee's consent. Such a clause does not prohibit a sale but requires the mortgage debt to be fully paid when the sale occurs, unless the mortgagee consents to the conveyance. (In some states, "due-on-sale" clauses are limited or invalid.)

**EXAMPLE** ■ Herbert Bird borrows $40,000 from Posen National Bank, secured by a 20-year mortgage on his home. The mortgage contains a due-on-sale clause. Five years later, when the indebtedness has been reduced to $35,000, Bird sells the house to Linda Thorn. Unless the bank waives its right, the entire $35,000 will be due in full at the time of the sale. If Bird refuses to pay the balance, the bank may foreclose its mortgage, in which case Thorn will be left with no interest in the property.

Individuals purchasing mortgaged property take the property either "subject to" the mortgage or by assumption of the debt. Those purchasers taking property subject to an existing mortgage must recognize that their interest in the property is subordinate to that of the mortgagee, but they assume no personal liability for payment of the mortgage.

---

**EXAMPLE** ■ Donna Smith owns real property subject to a mortgage that secures a $500,000 debt to North Ellis State Bank. Smith conveys the property to Vivian Churchill by warranty deed, which states the conveyance is "subject to" the mortgage. After the sale, Smith fails to make her mortgage payments and the bank looks to Churchill for payment. She refuses.

In this situation, Churchill assumes no personal liability for Smith's debt to the bank and thus it has no cause of action against Churchill. However, unless Churchill repays the mortgage debt or somehow obtains payment for it from Smith, the bank can foreclose on the property and sell it, and Churchill will lose her interest in it.

---

Purchasers of mortgaged real property may assume an existing mortgage, in which case they are personally obligated to repay the original mortgagor's debt.

---

**EXAMPLE** ■ The facts are the same as in the previous example, except that Churchill assumes Smith's mortgage debt with North Ellis State Bank. In this situation, when Smith defaults, the bank may hold Churchill, as well as Smith, personally responsible for the balance due on Smith's mortgage debt. If payment is not forthcoming from either, the bank may then foreclose on the property.

---

Usually, when a person assumes a mortgage pursuant to the purchase of real property, that person deducts the amount of the outstanding mortgage from the sale price. Although the grantee assumes the mortgage, the grantor-mortgagor is not relieved from liability on the mortgage debt.

**EXAMPLE** ■ Arnold Chambers executed and delivered to Frank Fuller a mortgage on Luxury Mansion to secure the repayment of a $100,000 loan. Fuller recorded the mortgage in the proper place. Subsequently, Chambers agreed to sell Luxury Mansion to Sam Brown for $250,000. Brown agreed to assume the mortgage and accordingly gave Chambers $150,000 for a warranty deed on Luxury Mansion and assumed the $100,000 debt.

Brown is liable to Fuller for $100,000 under the third-party creditor beneficiary principles of contract law. Under these same principles, Chambers remains liable to Fuller for the $100,000. However, if Fuller collects the money from Chambers, Chambers has an action against Brown for the $100,000. Otherwise, in this case, if the action were not permitted, Brown would be getting Luxury Mansion for $150,000 rather than the agreed price of $250,000. Consistently, if Fuller collects the $100,000 from Brown, Brown would have no action to recover this payment against Chambers.

In addition to taking real property "subject to" or assuming an existing mortgage, a purchaser may enter into a **novation**.

**EXAMPLE** ■ Stanley Nye owns real property subject to a mortgage that secures a $300,000 debt to Merchant Bank. Nye conveys the property to Jack Lane by warranty deed, which states the conveyance is "subject to" the mortgage. When the property is conveyed, the bank agrees to release Nye from further personal liability if Lane agrees to abide by the original terms of the mortgage. In this example, a novation occurs; that is, one party to a contract is replaced by another with the consent of all the original parties. If Lane fails to abide by the terms of the original mortgage, the bank can foreclose or seek payment from Lane but cannot pursue Nye for payment because he has been released from the obligation.

## Foreclosure

Collateral for a debt is useful to a lender only after the lender takes possession of the collateral and sells it, thereby producing funds to repay the debt that the collateral secured. Article 9 of the UCC provides precise guidelines for repossessing and disposing personal property. Because similar versions of the UCC have been adopted throughout the United States, these procedures are fairly standard throughout the country. (Chapter 7 of *Law and Banking: Applications* discusses procedures secured creditors use when disposing of collateral that is personal property.) On the other hand, foreclosure procedures to dispose of real property that is collateral for debt are not uniform throughout the country. Thus, before proceeding with a foreclosure action, a bank must carefully scrutinize the appropriate state laws.

Generally, state foreclosure laws have their roots in common law. Under common law, the day on which the mortgage debt came due was called "law day." If the mortgagor failed to pay the debt on law day, the mortgagee would bring a suit to foreclose the debtor's right of redemption, disallowing any right to redeem the property. When courts spoke of foreclosing the mortgage, it was really the right of redemption that was being foreclosed or barred. As a result of the foreclosure suit, the court would usually decree a time within which the debtor might redeem the property. The decree would provide that, if the debtor failed to pay the debt within this time, the right of redemption would be forever barred or foreclosed. Thereafter, the land would belong to the mortgagee. This method of foreclosure was known as "strict" or "common-law" foreclosure.

Strict foreclosure gradually was replaced by statutes creating "judicial foreclosure" and "foreclosure by advertisement."

A judicial foreclosure permits a mortgagee to sell the mortgaged property under court supervision. This kind of foreclosure also recognizes both the mortgagor's and mortgagee's right in any surplus, and the mortgagee's right in any deficiency. Under a judicial foreclosure, the mortgagee can keep the proceeds of the sale needed to repay the mortgage debt and any surplus over this amount must be remitted to the mortgagor. However, if the proceeds are insufficient to repay the mortgage debt, the mortgagee is given a deficiency judgment for the balance.

**EXAMPLE** ■ Hicks executed and delivered to Warner a mortgage on Belleview Estate to secure the repayment of a $100,000 loan. The mortgage included a provision that Hicks would be required to pay Warner any costs incurred if Hicks defaulted on the loan. After Hicks paid $40,000 on the loan, he defaulted. Warner foreclosed the mortgage and Newton paid $200,000 for Belleview at the foreclosure sale. In this situation, Warner may keep the first $60,000 of the sale price—the amount of the debt Hicks owed to him—plus foreclosure sale costs incurred by Warner. However, he must remit the surplus to Hicks, and Newton becomes the new owner of Belleview.

If Newton had paid only $40,000 for Belleview at the foreclosure sale, Warner would be entitled to keep the entire $40,000 and obtain a deficiency judgment against Hicks for $20,000 plus Warner's costs.

Many state statutes permit nonjudicial foreclosures, which are based on a "power-of-sale" clause in a mortgage or trust deed. This clause gives a mortgagee or a trustee the power to sell the mortgaged property publicly to pay off the debt secured by the mortgage or trust deed, when a default in the terms of the mortgage occurs. This type of foreclosure is called a foreclosure by advertisement, because its statutory procedure usually requires advertising notices of sale.

**Redemption** is the mortgagor's act of redeeming real property from the purchaser at the sale, within the prescribed time after a foreclosure. Statutes that permit either judicial foreclosure or foreclosure by advertisement usually provide for redemption. However, when the foreclosures result from the use of trust deeds, many states do not provide for redemption.

**EXAMPLE** ■ Boone National Bank forecloses on mortgaged real property owned by Harold Green. The property is sold at a public sale to Mary Murray. A month after the sale, Green tenders to Murray the price she paid for the property at the sale, plus interest and the costs of the sale. As long as Green makes the tender within the redemption period provided by statute, Murray must accept it and Green will receive the property back.

---

Redemption periods are prescribed by statute and may last from one month to one year depending on the statute. In many states, mortgagors retain possession of the mortgaged real property during redemption periods and continue to be entitled to rents and profits from the property, if any. In other states, mortgagees may take possession of the property immediately after the foreclosure sale. If a mortgagor has not redeemed the property at the end of a redemption period, his or her interest in it will end.

Junior or second mortgages may also be foreclosed. **A junior mortgage** is a lien that is subordinate to the claims of the holder of a prior senior lien. If a junior mortgagee forecloses, the purchaser at the sale takes the property subject to any prior mortgages.

---

EXAMPLE ■ Ken Jackson owns a parcel of real property having a first mortgage to Vanderbilt State Bank and a second mortgage to Tom Chappell. Jackson fails to make payments due under the second mortgage and Chappell forecloses that mortgage. In this situation, anyone purchasing the property at the foreclosure sale takes it subject to the first mortgage owed Vanderbilt State Bank. The purchaser will need to keep payments on the first mortgage current or the bank could foreclose against the purchaser's interest.

---

## Mechanics' Liens

**A mechanic's lien** can arise against a landowner's real property to secure payment to a person who has performed work or furnished materials for the construction of a building on that land. The mechanic's lien was never recognized under common law. Because it is purely statutory, the exact provisions of the appropriate statute must be satisfied to create this lien. In fact, various state statutes creating mechanics' liens differ in certain details. Some limit the right to acquire a mechanic's lien to workers engaged in the construction of a building. Others extend that right to workers engaged in making repairs, alterations, improvements, or additions to an existing building.

In certain important respects, however, most of the statutes creating mechanics' liens are similar. They give a lien not only to the contractor who has actually agreed with the owner to do the required work but also to the workers and subcontractors whom the contractor may employ to complete the work. These workers have no contractual rights against the owner to compel payment of their claims. But if the workers are unpaid, they may file liens against the building which the owner must pay to release clear title on the property. Often an owner will require a contractor, before starting work, to execute a bond under which the contractor and a bonding company agree to pay all claims of workers and materialmen (suppliers). If the workers or materialmen later file a lien against the building, the owner can call upon the contractor and the bonding company to pay the claim.

For mechanics' liens to be effective, the workers or materialmen must file—within the time specified by the statute and at the proper recording office—statements of their claims and the facts upon which they are based. If no such statements are filed, no liens will arise. The purpose of the filing requirement is to protect both the owner and third persons. The owner may not know whether the workers or materialmen have been paid. However, after the claim-filing period expires, the owner can examine the records to ensure that no outstanding claims will be asserted against the building. Similarly, any one else who wants to purchase the building can also check the records to be sure of receiving a free and clear title to the property.

A mechanic's lien is a right against the property and not the owner. Therefore, the possessor of the mechanic's lien (the lienholder) cannot sue the owner for an unpaid claim but can foreclose against the building, just as if the lienholder held an unpaid mortgage. The foreclosure usually forces the owner to pay the claim to keep the building from being sold. If forced to pay, the owner may seek reimbursement from the contractor. However, in this situation, the contractor is often insolvent, which explains why the workers and materialmen have not been paid. Thus, the owner usually seeks recourse not against the contractor but against the surety bond. A **surety bond** is a guarantee usually given by a bonding company to answer for the debt, default, or miscarriage of another. The surety company binds itself to pay an obligation if the obligor defaults on the obligation.)

As another form of protection, the owner can have a term inserted into the contract entitling the owner to retain a certain amount of the money due the contractor to cover mechanics' liens. If the owner has the foresight to negotiate such a term into the contract, mechanics' liens can be paid with the retained fund.

Before loaning money secured by mortgages, banks and other creditors should ensure that no work has been done or materials delivered to the property which could result in a mechanic's lien that would take precedence over the mortgage.

---

EXAMPLE ■ Frank Bishop owns a machine shop. On February 8, 1990, Harry Smite finishes roofing Bishop's shop and bills him $10,000. On April 2, 1990, Bishop borrows $40,000 secured by a mortgage. Bishop fails to pay Smite, who then records a mechanic's lien on the property and requests, through court proceedings, an order permitting sale of the shop to pay the bill. In many states, Smite's mechanic's lien on the property will be senior to the bank's first mortgage because his lien relates back to the date when the work was finished, which preceded the mortgage date.

---

## Land Titles

The parties signing a deed, mortgage, easement, or other instrument representing an interest in real property and the parties to whom the conveyance is directed certainly know of such instruments. (An exception would be an instrument giving a gift unbeknown to the donee when it is executed, and between those parties such conveyances are binding.) However, what of third parties who have no actual knowledge of a prior conveyance? Are they bound by such instruments?

---

EXAMPLE ■ Carroll Fox owns real property that he mortgages for a loan from County National Bank. Fox later sells the same land to George

Quinn. When Fox quits making his mortgage payments, the bank begins foreclosure proceedings. In most states, if Quinn lacks either actual or constructive knowledge of the mortgage, he can stop the foreclosure proceeding and the mortgage will be of no value to the bank. Instead, the bank must pursue Fox personally for the debt.

---

By seeing the instrument or being told of its existence, a person gains knowledge of an instrument representing a prior interest in real property. In the preceding example, if Quinn saw the mortgage or was informed of its existence, he would have actual knowledge of it. If a person has actual knowledge of an instrument representing a prior interest in real property that is purchased or received as a gift, the person takes the property subject to that prior interest. Thus, if Quinn had actual knowledge of the mortgage, he would have to pay the mortgage or lose the property through foreclosure. By observing the condition of the property, a person may also gain actual knowledge of a prior interest in real property.

---

EXAMPLE ■ Felix Hope conveys residential property to Freda Lang. Before the conveyance, Lang inspects the property and notices that Fred Jones is living in the house. After receiving a deed to the property, Lang prepares to move into the house, only to find that Jones will not move out because he has four years to run on a lease agreement with Hope.

In most states, Jones would be able to complete his lease for its duration. Although no one actually told Lang about the leasehold interest in the property, she was put on notice that Jones had an interest in the property and was responsible for inquiring about that interest. Of course, Jones's leasehold interest in the property would be a breach of the covenants in the warranty deed Lang received from Hope, and Hope would be liable to Lang for damages.

While actual notice regarding land titles certainly occurs, constructive notice is much more prevalent among grantees. Constructive notice of interests in real property usually occurs through the provisions of public real property recording acts. All the states have statutes that provide for a system of registering or recording all conveyances and other instruments affecting the title to real property.

Three types of real-property recording statutes exist in the United States and all provide that, unless certain instruments affecting land titles are recorded, they are void against certain people. Those three types of land-title recording statutes are

- pure race statutes
- notice statutes
- notice race statutes

The "race" in the description of these recording statutes refers to the race between people to record instruments affecting the same real property with the appropriate public office specified by statute.

## Pure Race Statutes

In those few states with pure race public recording statutes, the only way to establish an interest in real property is to record it. Actual notice means nothing in these states. Thus, until an instrument is recorded, it has no effect.

**EXAMPLE** ■ On April 1, Conglomerate Industrial Corporation mortgages its real property to Independent State Bank, and the bank's mortgage is recorded April 10. On April 5, the corporation mortgages the same property to Ralph Fowler, who is aware of the bank's mortgage. Fowler's mortgage is recorded April 6. In this situation, Fowler's mortgage has priority over that of the bank and, if the property is ever foreclosed, Fowler will be paid before the bank.

## Notice Statutes

In states with notice public recording statutes, an unrecorded conveyance of real property is invalidated or subordinated against the rights of a subsequent bona fide purchaser. A bona fide purchaser is one who gives value for his or her interest and is without actual knowledge of any other interest.

---

EXAMPLE ■ Robert Marx sells real property to Don Hadley by warranty deed on September 3. Hadley fails to record his deed. Marx conveys the same property to Mary King, a bona fide purchaser, on October 1. In a state with a notice recording statute, King's deed has priority over Hadley's deed even if King does not record it. However, if King wishes to protect her title from any future bona fide purchasers of the real property from Marx, she must record her deed.

---

*Notice Race Statutes* (*Race Notice*) In states with notice race public recording statutes, the interest of the purchaser of real property takes priority over prior instruments if the subsequent purchaser makes the purchase without knowledge of the prior instrument and also records the instrument before the prior instrument is recorded.

---

EXAMPLE ■ Anita Hayes sells real property to Frank Schlank by warranty deed on June 6. Schlank fails to record his deed until September 1. On July 1, Hayes sells the same real property to Becky Lynn by warranty deed. Lynn is a bona fide purchaser and records her deed on July 2. In this situation, Lynn's deed has priority over Schlank's deed. Thus, Lynn takes the property and Schlank must pursue Hayes for the return of his purchase price. However, if Lynn had known of Schlank's deed when she purchased the property, Schlank's interest would be prior to hers.

## CONCLUSION

All property can be classified as either personal property (objects that are movable or intangible) or real property (land and anything permanently affixed to it).

People can acquire personal property by producing, purchasing, taking possession of, or finding it. They may also acquire it through confusion, accession, gift, or inheritance. Bailment involves a special kind of possession of personal property in which one person, the bailor, owns the property, while another person, the bailee, has the right to possess it. The relationship between a bank and a customer with a safe deposit box is an example of bailment.

People can acquire real property through purchase, gift, will or descent, and adverse possession. Once acquired, real property can be held as a freehold, life, or leasehold estate. The nonpossessory interests in real property include dower and curtesy; easements, profits, and licenses; and future interests. As another kind of interest in real property, co-ownership of real property can occur as a tenancy in common, joint tenancy, tenancy by the entirety, community property, or tenancy in partnership.

It is important for bankers to understand the difference between real and personal property, as well as the various interests in each, because the procedures they use to protect their interests in security for loans will vary depending upon which kind of property or interest in that property a customer uses for collateral.

**Questions for Review and Discussion**

1. What is the difference between real and personal property?
2. May property ever change its status from real to personal property and vice versa?
3. Name the eight ways in which personal property may be acquired.
4. Name the two classifications of gifts.
5. What type of duty does a bank owe to the holder of a safe deposit box?
6. What is a security interest in real estate called?
7. What are the characteristics of a fee simple absolute estate?
8. Discuss the desirability of a life estate for mortgages.
9. What does adverse possession of real estate accomplish?

# Bankruptcy

After studying this chapter, you will be able to

- discuss the history of bankruptcy laws in the United States
- differentiate between the liquidation and rehabilitation goals of the Bankruptcy Code
- identify a trustee's powers and responsibilities in bankruptcy
- describe creditors' rights in bankruptcy
- explain debtors' rights and duties in bankruptcy, including the right to discharge of debts under certain circumstances

## WHAT IS BANKRUPTCY?

**Bankruptcy** is the legal process by which debtors who meet certain legal tests either completely discharge or reorganize their debts. Bankruptcy is important to banks because their business is credit, and debtors can delay or extinguish the legal requirement to repay their creditors through bankruptcy.

**History of Bankruptcy**

The U.S. Constitution, specifically article 1, section 8, gives Congress the power to enact bankruptcy legislation: "Congress shall have the power . . . [t]o establish uniform laws on . . . bankruptcies throughout the United States. . . ." However, in the early days of the Republic, Congress did little with this power. In fact, until 1898, except for the years of 1800–1803 and 1841–1843, no federal statute existed on bankruptcy.

The first bankruptcy statutes gave only creditors the right to initiate bankruptcy. Under these statutes, debtors could not seek relief from their debts. The purpose of these statutes was to provide creditors with a method to obtain debtors' assets. Only with the enactment of the second bankruptcy statute in 1841 could debtors initiate bankruptcy for their own relief. With the passage of this act came the concept of a "fresh start" for debtors. In other words, the purpose of this law was to provide a new beginning for an honest but overburdened debtor.

Over time, states also passed legislation pertaining to those unable to pay their debts. These statutes included insolvency or stay acts, assignments for the benefit of creditors, and mortgage moratoriums, and were extensively used when federal bankruptcy laws did not exist. State insolvency laws, however, were not uniform and thus impeded interstate commerce because businesses crossing state lines had to deal with different relief provisions. Further, within each state, laws continued to change to reflect the pro-creditor or pro-debtor forces in power at the time.

In 1867, Congress passed a third bankruptcy act that lasted until its repeal in 1878. Movement to revive a national act developed as part of an overall push by businesses for national and uniform state laws to promote interstate commerce. After much debate, a fourth act was passed in 1898.

## Bankruptcy Reform Act of 1978

The **National Bankruptcy Act of 1898** (30 Stat. 544 (1898)) survived with few amendments through 1978, when Congress passed the **Bankruptcy Reform Act** (92 Stat. 2549 (1978)). The most significant change to the act during this period occurred with the 1938 amendments, which provided procedures for debtors' rehabilitation as an alternative to straight liquidation.

The Bankruptcy Reform Act of 1978 contains several titles. The most significant one is title I, which created the **Bankruptcy Code**. Title I became title 11 of the United States Code (USC) and sets forth all the substantive provisions of bankruptcy law today. The Bankruptcy Code itself was amended in 1984 with the enactment of the

Bankruptcy Amendments and Federal Judgeship Act of 1984 (98 Stat. 333 (1984)). As with the National Bankruptcy Act of 1898, the Bankruptcy Code provides for both liquidation and rehabilitation of a debtor.

## LIQUIDATION

Typically, liquidation is considered to be the primary relief provided by bankruptcy. **Liquidation** involves the collection of a debtor's assets (except for those that are exempt), liquidation of those assets, distribution of the proceeds from liquidation to the debtor's creditors, and discharge of the debtor's obligations. Chapter 7 of the Bankruptcy Code contains the liquidation provisions. Liquidation is sometimes also called **straight bankruptcy**.

**Voluntary and Involuntary Liquidation**

The debtor may voluntarily file a petition to initiate a liquidation proceeding (11 U.S.C. § 109(a)), or the debtor's creditors may file an involuntary petition (11 U.S.C. § 303(b)). Individuals, partnerships, corporations, and unincorporated organizations may all file voluntary petitions for bankruptcy. Government units, domestic insurance companies, banking institutions, and credit unions may not file liquidation petitions. However, they may seek bankruptcy relief under other chapters of the Bankruptcy Code or use other statutory relief procedures. In addition, creditors cannot file involuntary petitions for bankruptcy against farmers and ranchers or nonprofit organizations, such as schools, churches, and charitable organizations.

*Procedures for Involuntary Liquidation*

Under Chapter 7 of the Bankruptcy Code, a debtor's creditors may file an involuntary petition to force liquidation of the debtor's estate. The main advantage of such a petition to creditors is that the debtor's property will be distributed equally within the various classes of creditors.

Involuntary bankruptcies differ from voluntary ones only in the way they are initiated. If a prescribed number of creditors with a certain minimum debt owed them can establish that a debtor is generally not paying undisputed debts as they come due or that, within 120 days before filing, a custodian was appointed or took possession of substantially all the debtor's property, the court will usually grant a petition for involuntary bankruptcy (11 U.S.C. § 303). Once the bankruptcy is permitted, liquidation and discharge of the debts will proceed as they would in voluntary proceedings.

*Procedures for Voluntary Liquidation*

Most liquidation bankruptcies are voluntary. To initiate a voluntary liquidation, a debtor files a petition with the clerk of the appropriate federal district court. A list of all the debtor's creditors must accompany this petition. In addition, the petition must include the following items (11 U.S.C. § 521):

- a schedule listing all the debtor's assets and liabilities
- a statement of the debtor's financial affairs with a list of questions answered by the debtor
- a schedule of the debtor's current income and current expenditures

Within 30 days after filing the petition or before the meeting of creditors, whichever is earlier, a debtor with secured consumer debts must file a statement of intention regarding property subject to security interests. This will inform the creditors whether the debtor intends to claim certain property as exempt, redeem certain property, reaffirm a debt secured by the property, or surrender the property.

**Automatic Stays**

Once a debtor files a petition for bankruptcy, creditors are automatically stayed from pursuing the debtor for payment of debts (11 U.S.C. § 362). The **stay** protects not only the debtor but also the creditors, since it preserves the debtor's assets until a determination can be made as to whom they belong; that is, the stay halts any unequal distribution of assets caused by a creditor's independent actions in collecting those assets.

EXAMPLE ■ A foreclosure sale of Jensen's home is scheduled for November 5, 1990, and Peoples' Bank intends to conduct a self-help repossession of Jensen's car on the same day. At 9:00 a.m. on that day, Jensen files her petition for bankruptcy which automatically stays both the foreclosure and repossession.

---

Automatic stays, however, do not prevent certain types of debt collection, particularly actions by government agencies. Nor do the stays prevent the collection of alimony, maintenance, and support payments from debtors.

The automatic stay has caused creditors great frustration, because they have to stand by and not pursue debtors or collateral. The statement of the debtor's intention regarding property subject to security interest, which the debtor must file shortly after the petition for bankruptcy, provides some help in this situation. Even more important, however, is the code provision permitting secured creditors to seek protection for their collateral from the bankruptcy court. Such protection can be periodic cash payments by the debtor to compensate for the collateral's depreciation or the debtor's provision of additional collateral to a creditor.

## End of Stays

An automatic stay ends in several ways. Once a particular property is no longer part of the bankruptcy estate because of sale, abandonment, exemption, or otherwise, the stay ends on that particular property. Further, a judge may terminate, annul, modify, or condition the stay, or give other relief upon any interested party's motion. To lift a stay, secured creditors often assert that no equity exists in the collateral or that the property is not necessary for a reorganization, and thus nothing remains for the stay to protect. The bankruptcy judge may then require the debtor to provide adequate protection to the secured creditor by making payments during the pendency of the bankruptcy proceeding or by giving the creditor a lien on other property to cover depreciation and interest accumulation. "The principle of adequate protection reconciles the competing interests of the debtor, who needs time to reorganize free from harassing creditors, and the secured creditor, on the other hand, who is entitled to protection for its bargained-for property interest." *In re Raymond*, 99 B.R. 819, 821 (S.D. Ohio 1989). A stay also ends when a bankruptcy court issues an order of the debtor's discharge, unless proceedings for a particular property are pending in the court.

**EXAMPLE** ■ Acme State Bank has a security interest in Green's car, which the bank says is worth $3,000. The debt that the car secures has a balance of $5,000. Acme moves the court to lift the stay, since no equity exists in the collateral; that is, the value of the collateral is less than the debt it secures.

**Trustees**  Once a debtor files a Chapter 7 petition for bankruptcy, the court will appoint an interim trustee to represent the estate. A **trustee** is an officer of the bankruptcy court who represents the estate in a bankruptcy proceeding. Theoretically, anyone who can obtain a bond to secure performance of a trustee's duties may be appointed. Usually, however, each court has a pool of individuals it appoints as trustees, based on their experience and past performance.

The **estate** is a separate entity, much like a corporation, composed of the debtor's property that must be surrendered to the trustee. The trustee is empowered to pursue the debtor's property from both the debtor and third parties.

The interim trustee functions until the court calls the first meeting of the debtor's creditors as required by the Bankruptcy Code. The court must call this meeting within a reasonable time (usually 30 days) after the debtor has filed a petition (11 U.S.C. § 341). At that meeting, several important events occur. First, the debtor must appear at the meeting and submit to examination under oath, typically before the clerk of the bankruptcy court. Next, the debtor must respond to brief questioning by creditors, their attorneys, and the trustee about assets, transfers of assets, and other pertinent financial matters. The creditors may also select a permanent trustee, although they usually appoint the interim trustee.

The trustee then determines the extent of the estate and converts it into cash for eventual distribution to the creditors. To perform these duties, the trustee is given broad powers of investigation and the ability to sue to gather the debtor's assets. Some of the debtor's property is exempt from the trustee's reach (11 U.S.C. § 522). A debtor can choose between the exemptions provided by state law and federal nonbankruptcy statutes or those set forth in the Bankruptcy Code. However, any state may choose not to allow federal exemptions and thereby deprive its residents of that choice.

A debtor who chooses exemptions provided by state law can keep

- any property that under state law is exempt from attachment by unsecured creditors

- any property that is exempt under federal law other than the Bankruptcy Code

- any interest in property the debtor holds as a tenant by the entirety or as a joint tenant to the extent that creditors cannot reach that interest by judicial process under state law

---

EXAMPLE ■ A judgment is awarded against Joe Blake for $500,000. He files a bankruptcy petition in a federal district bankruptcy court in Michigan. Blake owns eight sheep and a $200,000 home with his wife as a tenant by the entirety. In Michigan, an unsecured creditor of only one spouse cannot reach either Blake's sheep or his interest in the home through judicial process. Blake also receives a pension as a retired U.S. civil servant. If Blake elects the state exemptions under Michigan law, his sheep as well as his interest in the house and his retirement pension will be exempt from liquidation by the trustee.

---

If the state in which a debtor files a petition has not disallowed federal exemptions, a debtor may alternatively choose the following code exemptions:

- up to $7,500 interest in the value of real or personal property used as a residence by the debtor or a dependent, or in a burial plot for the debtor or dependent

- up to $1,200 interest in one motor vehicle

- the debtor's interest up to $4,000 in all household goods and furnishings, clothing, appliances, books, animals, crops, or musical instruments held primarily for personal or family use by the debtor or a dependent (The exemption may not, however, exceed $200 in value in any particular item.)

- up to $500 in jewelry for personal or family use
- in addition to all other exemptions, an interest in any property, including cash, not to exceed $400 in value, plus up to $3,750 of any unused portion of the residence and burial plot exemption (This catchall provision allows the debtor to claim a total of $4,150 in property without restriction as to its type.)
- up to $750 in value in implements, tools, or professional books used in the debtor's or a dependent's trade
- any unmatured life insurance policy owned by the debtor, regardless of value or face amount, other than a credit life insurance contract
- any accrued dividends, interest, or cash surrender value of any unmatured life insurance policy of which the debtor or a dependent is the insured provided the total value of the exempt dividends, interest, or cash surrender value does not exceed $4,000
- professionally prescribed health aids for the debtor or a dependent
- certain government benefits, including Social Security; unemployment compensation; public assistance; veterans' benefits; and disability, illness, or unemployment benefits
- rights to receive income to the extent reasonably necessary for the support of the debtor and any dependent, including such income as alimony, support, or maintenance payments and payments under certain stock bonus, pension, profit sharing, annuity, or similar plan on account of illness, disability, death, age, or length of service (However, monies deposited in a Keogh plan or individual retirement account may not be exempt if the plan is established by an insider employer, is based on age or length of service, and does not qualify under the Internal Revenue Code.)
- income from certain other types of sources, including crime-victim compensation awards, certain life insurance proceeds, and personal injury awards up to $7,500

EXAMPLE ■ Fran Davis files a petition for bankruptcy and elects the federal exemptions. She owns a home worth $40,000. However, her equity in the home is $6,000 because she has a mortgage with a $34,000 balance. She also owns a car worth $10,000 and jewelry worth $400. Under federal exemptions, Fran's interest in her home, $3,100 of the value in her car, and all her jewelry are exempt. To keep her car, Fran will have to make arrangements to pay the bankruptcy trustee $6,900. The $3,100 in exempt value for the car is composed of the motor-vehicle exemption amount of $1,200, plus the unused $1,500 of the real-estate exemption and the extra $400 exemption in any property.

Except for exempt property, debtors and unsecured third parties possessing debtor's property must surrender all other property to the appointed trustee.

EXAMPLE ■ Joe Conroy has $5,000 in a savings account at First State Bank. Conroy files a petition listing this account. The trustee is entitled to these funds (11 U.S.C. § 543), unless Conroy claims the account balance as exempt under the catchall exemption, which allows a maximum of $4,150 in any type of property.

## Trustee's Powers

A debtor's estate is composed of all the debtor's legal or equitable interests in property as of the commencement of the case (11 U.S.C. § 541). After the property comes into the estate, the debtor may be permitted to exempt all or part of it. The Bankruptcy Code has complicated rules that govern the cutoff dates when property is considered to belong to the debtor and thus to be within the trustee's jurisdiction. Certainly, once a debtor files a petition, any rights in property (except for the exemptions mentioned earlier) become those of the trustee. In addition, the trustee has several methods to reach back to periods before the petition was filed and reclaim property for the estate. These powers help the trustee to maximize the size of the debtor's estate for eventual distribution to general creditors.

TRUSTEE AS HYPOTHETICAL LIEN CREDITOR

Once a petition for bankruptcy is filed, the trustee becomes a **hypothetical lien creditor** of the debtor (11 U.S.C. § 544). In other words, the trustee can act as though a state court judgment was obtained against the debtor. The laws in the state where the bankruptcy is pending determine the importance of this power. In some states, a judicial lien creditor may avoid transfers of property or debt incurred by a judgment debtor after the judgment is obtained. In other states, a judgment does not give a creditor any priority over any other unsecured creditor until the judgment creditor actually issues a levy on the property.

---

EXAMPLE ■ In state A, once a judgment is obtained against a defendant, all of that defendant's real property in the state is subject to the plaintiff's lien. In state B, to obtain a lien, a plaintiff must first obtain a writ of execution and levy on specific real property after judgment. Thus, if a judgment debtor files bankruptcy in state A, a trustee will have a lien on all the debtor's property on the filing date. But, if a judgment debtor files bankruptcy in state B, the trustee will have no such lien.

---

The trustee can most effectively use this power against unperfected security interests. As further discussed in chapter 7 of *Law and Banking: Applications*, the security interests of a debtor's secured creditors can be either perfected or unperfected, depending on whether those interests comply with the UCC's perfection requirements. A judicial lien creditor has priority over an unperfected security interest (U.C.C. 9 § 301(1)(b)).

---

EXAMPLE ■ On July 1, 1989, Second State Bank loans Everett $50,000 and takes a security interest in his inventory, pursuant to a security agreement. However, the bank fails to file its security agreement or a financing statement. Thus, its security interest remains unperfected. On September 15, 1989, Everett files a petition for bankruptcy. In this situation, the trustee will have priority and can take possession of Everett's inventory, liquidate it, and use the proceeds to repay all his creditors. The bank's claim will be that of an unsecured creditor.

---

Thus, to protect their collateral, banks and other creditors must perfect their security interests. Because trustees are obliged to assemble as much estate property as possible for distribution to the general creditors, they frequently assert challenges to secured creditors' security interests.

TRUSTEE AS HYPOTHETICAL BONA FIDE PURCHASER OF REAL ESTATE

In addition to being considered a hypothetical judicial lien creditor, the trustee is also considered a **bona fide purchaser** of real estate from the debtor on the date of the bankruptcy petition (11 U.S.C. § 544 (a)(3)). If on the date of filing the petition the debtor has transferred any real estate, evidence of which has not been perfected (usually by recording), the trustee may claim such real estate without regard to the holder of the unperfected interest.

In states where unrecorded interests in real estate do not affect the title of subsequent bona fide purchasers, trustees will take the property (unless exempt) without regard to the unrecorded party's interest.

---

EXAMPLE ■ On June 8, 1989, Peoples' National Bank lends Hay $80,000, secured by real estate. The bank's mortgage is left on the loan officer's desk while she takes a two-week vacation. On June 15, 1989, Hay's creditors file a petition for involuntary bankruptcy. The bank's mortgage is recorded on June 22, 1989. State laws provide that prior unrecorded interests in real estate do not affect the interest of a bona fide purchaser of real estate. Thus, in this situation, the bank's mortgage is worthless and its debt is unsecured for this bankruptcy.

Suppose further that, on June 1, 1989, Hay sells the real estate to Mikos who moves into the house with his family. However, Mikos fails to record his deed. State laws provide that a real estate purchaser who purchases the property with constructive knowledge of another party's interest in the real estate takes it subject to that interest. Mikos's residence on the property constitutes constructive notice and thus the interest of Mikos is senior to that of the trustee.

## TRUSTEE AS SUCCESSOR TO ACTUAL CREDITORS

The trustee is empowered to take any action the debtor's general creditors may take to bring the debtor's assets under state law (11 U.S.C. § 544(b)). In other words, the trustee "steps into the shoes" of the debtor's general creditors. Trustees usually use this power to set aside any transfers made by debtors before bankruptcy which their creditors could avoid pursuant to the fraudulent transfer acts under state law.

**EXAMPLE** ■ In 1987, Fred Moran sold real estate with a $100,000 market value to his daughter for $10,000. At the time, Moran owed Jason Simpson $500,000. Under the applicable state law, Moran's transfer was fraudulent. In 1989, without having paid Simpson, Moran filed for bankruptcy. Since Simpson had the ability under state law to set aside Moran's transfer as fraudulent, so too did the trustee. If no actual creditor had such a cause of action, neither would the trustee.

## TRUSTEE'S ABILITY TO AVOID PREFERENCES

As stated, trustees have the responsibility to collect a debtor's assets, including those to which the debtor is no longer entitled. This power is given trustees to assure greater equality of repayment among the debtor's general creditors and to dissuade debtors from "preferring" certain creditors over others in the repayment of debt.

---

EXAMPLE ■ Marcus realizes he is insolvent and considers bankruptcy. However, one of his debts is to his father in the amount of $20,000, so Marcus pays the debt with the last of his cash and a deed to vacant land he owns. Two months later, he files for bankruptcy and lists 10 creditors in his schedule. In this situation, Marcus has "preferred" one creditor, his father, over his other creditors.

---

**A preference** is a voluntary or involuntary transfer of an insolvent debtor's interest in property to or for a certain creditor's benefit, for or on account of an antecedent debt owed by the debtor, within the 90 days before filing the petition, or between 90 days and one year before that date if the recipient creditor was an "insider," that enabled the creditor to receive more than the distributive share under Chapter 7 (11 U.S.C. § 547(b)). This definition includes many transfers, the simplest of which the preceding example illustrates. The definition also includes transactions that can have adverse effects on secured creditors, such as banks.

---

EXAMPLES ■ On August 1, 1989, Perry executes a mortgage to secure an antecedent debt to Citizens' State Bank which he has been unable to pay. The mortgage is recorded on the same day. On October 10, 1989, Perry files a petition for bankruptcy. The mortgage constitutes a "transfer" of an interest in property under the definition of "preference" and, since it was made within 90 days of the filing, the trustee may avoid it and thus make Citizens' State Bank an unsecured creditor. Had the mortgage not been given to secure an "antecedent debt," the trustee could not have set it aside; that is, had the mortgage secured a new loan made August 1, 1989, no avoidance would be possible.

■ On June 8, 1989, Stack executes a security agreement granting Acme National Bank a security interest in his business equipment to secure a previously unsecured debt of $250,000. On that day, he is solvent. On July 9, 1989, a $500,000 account receivable owed him becomes worthless because of the debtor's bankruptcy. This renders Stack insolvent. On September 9, 1989, Stack himself files for bankruptcy. The trustee cannot void the June 8 transfer because on that date Stack was solvent. Under the USC, a debtor is insolvent when the sum of his or her liabilities exceeds the value of his or her nonexempt assets (11 U.S.C. § 101(31)). Further, a debtor is presumed to be insolvent on and during the 90 days immediately preceding the date of filing a bankruptcy petition (11 U.S.C. § 547(f)).

---

As established in the definition of "preference," the transferee's status as an "insider" is important if the transfer occurred between the 91st day to one year before the debtor filed the bankruptcy petition.

Whether a transferee is an **insider** depends on the debtor's status. If the debtor is an individual, an insider includes relatives, general partners, a partnership in which the debtor is a general partner, or a corporation of which the debtor is a director, officer, or person in control. If the debtor is a corporation, an insider includes directors, officers, people who control the corporation, general partners and relatives of a general partner, director, officer, or person in control of the corporation. For debtors that are partnerships, insiders include any of the general partners or their relatives, people who control the partnerships, or other partnerships in which the debtor is a partner. Any affiliates of some of these parties may also qualify as "insiders" (11 U.S.C. § 101(30)).

---

EXAMPLE ■ On April 22, 1989, XYZ, Inc., an insolvent corporation, pays off a note for $50,000 to its president, James Johns. On March 15, 1990, the corporation files its petition for bankruptcy. Since Johns is an insider and the transfer was made within one year of the petition, the trustee is entitled to a return of the $50,000 payment, which will then become available to the creditors.

## PAYMENTS IN THE ORDINARY COURSE OF BUSINESS

A trustee's ability to avoid preferences does not affect a debtor's payments made in the ordinary course of business or financial affairs (11 U.S.C. § 547 (c)(2)).

**EXAMPLE** ■ On October 7, 1989, Widget Products, Inc., paid its bolt supplier, Acme Industries, $5,000 pursuant to an invoice dated September 15, 1989, for bolts delivered on August 14, 1989, in the ordinary course of Widget's business. This payment is not an avoidable preference because Widget incurred the debt and made the payment in the ordinary course of both parties' businesses.

Other transfers that a trustee may not avoid include contemporaneous transfers for new value and transfers made by individual debtors whose debts are primarily consumer obligations, if the total value of the property affected by such transfers is less than $600 (11 U.S.C. § 547(c)(7)).

## CODE PROVISIONS REGARDING FRAUDULENT TRANSFERS

As previously mentioned, the Bankruptcy Code gives a trustee the right to step into the shoes of the debtor's actual creditors. This power gives trustees the ability to bring into the debtor's estate assets constituting fraudulent transfers under state fraudulent-conveyance acts.

The Bankruptcy Code also characterizes in its own definitions certain transfers as fraudulent and subject to the trustee's avoidance if made within one year before the filing of a bankruptcy petition (11 U.S.C. § 548). The first of such transfers are those made with the intent to defraud creditors. If a trustee can establish the debtor's intent to defraud creditors, solvency is irrelevant.

**EXAMPLE** ■ Sharon Mills gives $10,000 to her friend, Don Jones, to place it beyond her creditors' reach. Six months later, she files for bankruptcy. If the trustee can establish her intent to defraud creditors, this transfer can be avoided.

Under section 548 of the Bankruptcy Code, a trustee can also set aside a transfer for less than an asset's reasonably equivalent value if the debtor made the transfer while insolvent.

**EXAMPLE** ■ Fred Franks sells his 1989 Cadillac to his son for $2,000 when its market value is really $12,000. Nine months later, Franks files a bankruptcy petition. Whether or not Franks intended to defraud his creditors, a trustee can avoid this transfer.

A trustee may also set aside any transfers for less than a reasonably equivalent value by a debtor—whether solvent or not—with the intent to incur debt beyond his or her ability to repay it or when undercapitalized (11 U.S.C. § 548(a)(2)(B)).

*Case for Discussion*   **MINNICK v. LAFAYETTE LOAN & TRUST COMPANY**
**Facts**
On January 13, 1966, the Minnicks filed for voluntary bankruptcy. The court appointed a trustee and on March 11, 1966, the creditors met. At that time, Lafayette Loan & Trust Company filed objections to discharge of the Minnicks' debt and alleged that on December 23, 1965, the parties disposed of their home for $500 when their equity in it was $3,466. Lafayette further charged that the parties took this action to "secrete and hide" assets from the bank's and other creditors' lawful claims.

In their voluntary petition for bankruptcy, the Minnicks did state that they sold their home for $500, plus an assumption of a $7,800 mortgage. However, the bank contended that the Minnicks sold their home at a time when the value of such real estate was at least $11,000, subject to a mortgage of $7,534, with a resultant net equity of $3,466.

The referee in bankruptcy found in this case that the Minnicks had numerous debts when they sold their home and were hard pressed by their creditors. They owed $250 to the purchaser of the house and were behind in their mortgage payments. Before the purchaser, a Mr. Greives, bought the house, the Minnicks had asked him to try to sell it for $10,100. When Grieves was unsuccessful in selling the house, he offered to purchase it. The Minnicks agreed to sell the house and continued to live in it for two months, paying $100 in rent per month.

### Decision
Finding the evidence was insufficient to sustain a denial of a discharge in bankruptcy and that the Minnicks did not convey their home to defraud their creditors, the court ruled in favor of the Minnicks. According to the referee, the facts in this case did not indicate that the Minnicks were hiding assets from creditors. The Minnicks revealed the conveyance of their home to Greives and for the court to infer secret dealings would be to indulge in speculation and surmise about the Minnicks' intentions.

This case reinforces the well-accepted principle that the Bankruptcy Act was intended to allow the honest debtor a new start in life, free from debt and objections by creditors. The court ruled in this case that the act had to be construed strictly against the objectors and liberally in favor of the bankrupt parties. *Minnick v. Lafayette Loan & Trust Co.*, 392 F.2d 973 (7th Cir.), *cert. denied*, 393 U.S. 875 (1968).

### Questions for Discussion
1. What rules address a debtor's sale and transfer of property before the debtor files a petition for bankruptcy?
2. Who qualifies as an "insider" and when does the distinction matter?

---

TRANSFEREE'S LIABILITY

Once a trustee determines a voidable transfer has occurred, the trustee may pursue the transferee for return of the money, property, or value of the property (11 U.S.C. § 544(b)). If necessary, the trustee may initiate a lawsuit in the estate's name to achieve the return of such property.

## EXECUTORY CONTRACTS

Executory contracts to which the debtor is a party when the bankruptcy petition is filed become part of the estate. **Executory contracts** are contracts where both parties have yet to perform fully their obligations. A contract is not executory if either party has fully performed its obligation. Thus, a promissory note is not an executory contract, since only the payee's obligation remains unfulfilled. The trustee can either perform or reject such contracts, subject to court approval (11 U.S.C. § 365).

EXAMPLE ■ When Howard Eppler files his petition for bankruptcy, he is in the process of buying property on a land contract. The balance left on the contract is $20,000 and the market value of the property is $50,000. To protect the $30,000 in equity, the trustee in this situation chooses to perform the contract.

## Secured Creditors

As stated, trustees gather assets and assure their distribution among creditors. Unsecured creditors hold debts that are not collateralized. However, one creditor can hold both secured and unsecured claims.

EXAMPLE ■ When Frank Ford files for bankruptcy, he has both credit card debt and a mortgage with Podunk State Bank. Thus, the bank in this situation holds both a secured and unsecured claim.

Upon receiving notice of a debtor's petition, a secured creditor is automatically stayed from proceeding against the debtor or the collateral, either by self-help repossession of the collateral or litigation. The creditor's only recourse lies with the bankruptcy court and the trustee.

Whether or not a debt is secured, a creditor should first file a proof of claim with the court. Filing a proof of claim is unnecessary to preserve a security interest (11 U.S.C. § 506(d)(2)). However, such a filing is necessary if the creditor seeks a distributive share of the estate because the collateral will not satisfy the debt.

While the debtor is theoretically obligated to surrender to the trustee all property of the estate, the debtor does not do this immediately, except for liquid assets for which the trustee can easily provide care. Thus, the trustee leaves such items as cars, nonexempt household items, and real estate either with the debtor or unattended.

If a secured creditor does nothing to obtain his or her collateral and the trustee believes it is worth more than the debt it secures (that is, the debtor has equity in it), the trustee will pay the creditor its value when the trustee sells it. Under bankruptcy law, the debtor can be the purchaser of the collateral. To determine its value, the court will usually schedule a hearing.

*"Adequate Protection"*

If a secured party does not move to obtain the collateral, a trustee can use, sell, or lease property of the estate, including property that is collateral. However, before such use can occur, the trustee must notify the secured creditor who then can request a hearing at which it can object to or seek "adequate protection" from such use (11 U.S.C. § 363). This protection is particularly important for a creditor who fears that use of the collateral will depreciate its value. "Adequate protection" may include cash payment to the secured creditor equal to the collateral's loss of value or the regular monthly payment, or the trustee may grant to the creditor a lien on other property belonging to the estate.

To obtain the collateral, a creditor files a motion with the court, seeking relief from the automatic stay. Secured creditors who believe their collateral is worth less than the debt often use this option, making the collateral's retention valueless to the estate and the debtor (11 U.S.C. § 362(d)). While trustees may voluntarily abandon property that is collateral, creditors often find the motion for relief from stay a quicker procedure since, if the court does not rule on the motion within 30 days after the request for relief, the stay will automatically end to the extent requested (11 U.S.C. § 362(e)). The stay will not end, however, if within that time the court determines that the motion would probably not be granted at a subsequent hearing. To resolve issues of value, equity, and payment, the court will usually schedule a hearing within that 30-day period.

---

EXAMPLE ■ Third State Bank has a security interest in Sue Thorpe's car, which she has claimed as exempt. The car is valued at $10,000 and secures an $18,000 debt. After Thorpe files the petition for bankruptcy, she surrenders the car to the trustee. The bank then contacts the trustee and requests an abandonment. The trustee says she is too busy to deal with the request and tells the bank to wait a few months. The bank then files a motion for relief from stay. Thirty days pass without the trustee's filing of an objection or a hearing being held, so the stay is automatically lifted and the bank can proceed to repossess the car under applicable state law. Generally, if no objection is filed within 15 days, an order for relief from stay will be approved by the court.

---

*Abandonment*

**Abandonment** is the simplest method available to secured creditors desiring the return of their collateral. Under the Bankruptcy Code, trustees who believe no equity exists in the collateral, or believe its value is inconsequential, may abandon the security, releasing it from the stay with the court's permission. A secured creditor can seek such abandonment through informal discussions with the trustee or the trustee can initiate the abandonment without the secured creditor's request. Turnover of the property must be consented to by the debtor. The trustee gives notice of the intended abandonment to all interested parties and, if any objections are filed, the court must hold a hearing (11 U.S.C. § 554).

**Options Available to Debtors Under Liquidation**

During liquidation, debtors have different options available to help them resolve the situation as favorably as possible. Those options include

■ redemption of personal property

■ reaffirmation

■ setoff

With these options, however, come certain obligations and responsibilities for debtors.

## Redemption of Personal Property

Individual debtors have the right to redeem (that is, purchase) abandoned, tangible personal property from secured creditors if it is primarily for personal, family, or household use and the creditors' security interests arose from consumer debts. The debtor is obligated to pay the secured creditor's liens or the value of the property, whichever is less (11 U.S.C. § 722).

---

EXAMPLE ■ Albion National Bank has a purchase-money security interest in Larry Hoop's car, which Hoop bought to provide transportation for his family. The car is worth $12,000 and secures a debt of $15,000. By paying the bank $12,000, Hoop can redeem his car.

---

To request a **redemption**, a debtor must file a motion in the bankruptcy court and the secured creditors and others designated by the court must have an opportunity to be heard. Bankruptcy Rule 6008 also allows the trustee to initiate a motion for redemption. Typically, any dispute at such a hearing will center around the collateral's value. Since a debtor must file a statement of intention concerning redemption within 30 days of filing the bankruptcy petition or by the meeting of creditors, whichever is earlier, and perform the same within 45 days of filing the statement, a secured creditor will be alerted to the debtor's intention regarding redemption early in a bankruptcy proceeding (11 U.S.C. § 521). A debtor's right to redemption applies to both exempt and abandoned property.

---

EXAMPLE ■ Lisa George files a petition for bankruptcy. One of her assets is a lien-free car whose value is $6,000. She elects the federal exemptions, which entitle her to a $1,200 motor-vehicle exemption, and does not have any unused exemption allowance for general personal property. In this situation, Lisa may pay the trustee $4,800 and keep the vehicle.

*Reaffirmation*  Redemption requires immediate payment for the personal property being redeemed. A debtor unable to make the lump-sum payment may choose to reaffirm certain debts. In contrast to redemption, the debtor agrees in a **reaffirmation** to pay the entire debt, even if it exceeds the collateral's value. A debtor cannot force a creditor into a reaffirmation as can be done in redemption. Instead, both parties must agree to it. Reaffirmation agreements for consumer debts must meet specific requirements, including a minimum 60-day period in which the debtor may rescind the agreement. When the debtor is not represented by counsel, a hearing before the bankruptcy court is required to ensure that the debtor is fully informed of the consequences of reaffirmation (11 U.S.C. § 524).

*Setoff*  The Bankruptcy Code also recognizes the right of setoff (11 U.S.C. § 553), which is based on the existence of mutual debt between two parties. Instead of receiving an actual cash payment, one party credits the amount due against the amount owed the other party. This right can be extremely beneficial in bankruptcy, because it permits a nonfiling debtor to obtain payment that might not otherwise be received.

EXAMPLE ■ When Sam Sherwood files his petition for bankruptcy, he owes Lee Fisher $20,000 and Fisher owes him $15,000. Sherwood's estate provides 20 cents on the dollar to his unsecured creditors at the conclusion of the bankruptcy. In this situation, Fisher will end up with a $15,000 setoff (against the $20,000 owed him) and 20 percent of $5,000 for a total of $16,000 out of a $20,000 debt. Had Sherwood not owed Fisher $20,000 or the right of setoff not been available, Fisher would have lost $16,000, since he would have recovered only 20 percent of $20,000.

Banks and other institutions taking deposits and making loans may exercise the right of setoff with authorization from the court. Bank accounts represent debt owed to depositors and loans represent debt owed to banks.

---

EXAMPLE ■ When Rob Wills files his petition for bankruptcy, he has $500 on deposit in a checking account with First National and owes the bank a loan balance of $1,000. In this situation, the bank freezes the account balance, $500, and files a motion for relief from stay to allow the setoff. A proof of claim would be filed for $500 as secured and $500 as unsecured debt.

---

Setoff, however, has been held not to extend to individual retirement accounts (IRAs). In *In re McDaniel*, 41 B.R. 132 (W.D. Tex. 1984), the court held that an IRA is not a bank's debt to the account holder but rather is a bank's obligation as *trustee* to the account holder.

## Distribution of the Estate

Once the trustee has given secured creditors their collateral or its value and converted the debtor's assets that constitute the estate into cash, the trustee has completed liquidation. Thereafter, the trustee must distribute the estate according to the Bankruptcy Code's provisions (11 U.S.C. § 507).

First, the trustee must pay all "priority claims." These claims include the estate's administrative expenses, wage claims by the debtor's employees, certain unpaid contributions to the debtor's employee benefit plans, payments to individuals of up to $900 for consumer deposits made to the debtor before the bankruptcy filing for consumer services or property which was never received, and tax claims. In addition, "priority claims" can exist for (1) payments the debtor owes to business creditors who extend credit after an involuntary petition is filed but before a trustee is appointed, to allow the debtor to continue doing business, and (2) for certain claims of grain producers and United States fishermen (up to $2,000).

After payment of these priority claims, the trustee will divide the balance of the estate pro rata among the debtor's general unsecured creditors who have filed proofs of claim.

## Discharges

In initiating a bankruptcy, a debtor primarily seeks relief from debt through discharge. **Discharge** is the legal termination of a debtor's responsibility for repayment of debt and is only available to individuals. Corporations and partnerships declaring bankruptcy cannot have their debts discharged. Thus, corporations and partnerships will legally continue to owe debt after their estates have been distributed. But since liquidated corporations and partnerships rarely continue in business, this is unimportant to their creditors, because no assets will be available for repayment of debts.

Given the losses that discharge can cause creditors, it is a privilege extended only to those debtors who are honest and cooperative with the bankruptcy system. In fact, procedures exist to deny discharge to debtors and can be initiated by the court, trustees, creditors, or other interested parties (11 U.S.C. § 727). The Bankruptcy Code provides the following reasons for a denial of discharge to a debtor:

- Within one year before filing a petition, the debtor or someone he or she permitted to do so fraudulently concealed or transferred property of the debtor or, since the filing, property of the estate.

- Without justification, the debtor failed to keep books or records relating to his or her financial history, or concealed, destroyed, or falsified such records. (Fraud is not a necessary element to this reason for denial of discharge; neglect or sloppiness in maintaining records may suffice.)

- The debtor knowingly and fraudulently committed a bankruptcy crime. This includes making a false oath or account in the course of a bankruptcy proceeding, participating in a false claim, giving or receiving a bribe in the course of a bankruptcy proceeding, or withholding records.

- The debtor failed to satisfactorily explain loss of assets.

- The debtor refused to answer questions or obey orders of the bankruptcy court.

- The debtor, during his or her own bankruptcy proceeding or within one year prior to filing the petition, committed any of the above acts in connection with a separate bankruptcy case of an "insider." (An "insider" for this purpose is the same as defined earlier.)

- The debtor was granted a discharge within the six years previous to filing the petition, unless the discharge was pursuant to a Chapter 13 Wage Earner's Plan and a prescribed percentage of unsecured claims was paid.
- The debtor in writing waived his or her right to a discharge according to prescribed code procedures.

*Nondischargeable Debts*

For reasons of public policy, certain types of debt will not be discharged, even when a debtor complies with the requirements for a discharge under the Bankruptcy Code (11 U.S.C. § 523). These debts are summarized as follows:

- most taxes
- debt incurred by fraud, including obtaining credit, property, or services by use of materially false financial statements
- debts not listed in the schedules filed with the bankruptcy petition
- debts arising as a result of the debtor's embezzlement, larceny, or fraud while acting in a fiduciary capacity
- debts to a spouse, former spouse, or child for alimony, maintenance, or support arising out of a divorce decree, separation agreement, or property settlement
- debt for willful and malicious injury caused by the debtor
- fines or penalties assessed against a debtor by a government unit
- certain student loans made, insured, or guaranteed by a government unit or funded through a government or nonprofit corporation
- debt arising from civil judgments for damages done by debtors while driving drunk
- certain debts from a prior bankruptcy filing in which the debtor waived or was denied a discharge

*Case for Discussion*

**KANSAS STATE BANK AND TRUST COMPANY v. VICKERS**

**Facts**

Mr. Vickers filed a petition for relief under Chapter 11 of the Bankruptcy Act. At that time, Vickers owed the Kansas State Bank and Trust Company of Wichita approximately $249,000. Vickers came from a wealthy family and was for many years an outside director of the bank. In the course of his business affairs with the bank, he filed periodic financial statements, including one on May 23, 1973, and one on November 9, 1973. The May 23 statement reported a net worth of $3,711,311 and the November 9 statement reported a net worth of $32,386.

The bank objected to Vickers's discharge from liability for his debt, contending that the May 23 report was false, fraudulent, and made with the intent to deceive the bank. The bank also claimed it relied on the May 23 statement in renewing loans to Vickers on October 1, 1973. In addition, the bank argued that Vickers was acting in a fiduciary capacity as a director when he incurred debts to the bank by fraud, embezzlement, misappropriation, or defalcation. If these allegations were true, the court could not discharge Vickers from his debts under the Bankruptcy Code's exceptions to discharge.

Vickers's financial reverses between May 23 and November 9, 1973, were brought about by unexpected losses in certain real estate ventures. These losses accounted for the discrepancies in the two financial statements. He prepared the November financial statement with the assistance of his attorney, who knew of the real estate losses. Vickers claimed he informed the bank of this matter and yet they still agreed to renew his loan. The bank countered by claiming that it renewed the loans solely based on Vickers's relationship with the bank as a director and in reliance on his written financial statement, which the bank believed was published with intent to deceive.

### Decision
In determining whether sufficient evidence existed to deny a discharge of Vickers's debt, the bankruptcy court noted that the primary purpose of the Bankruptcy Act is to discharge debts of an honest debtor and offer him a fresh start. The court found untrue the bank's charge that Vickers intended to deceive the bank with the May 23 statement because the evidence showed that Vickers suffered subsequent serious financial reverses and informed the bank of his problems. The court thus decided that Vickers did not intentionally make false statements or intend to deceive the bank. Furthermore, the court held that, in this situation, Vickers was simply a borrower of the bank and could not be held to a higher standard because he was a director. *Kansas State Bank*

*and Trust Co. v. Vickers*, 577 F.2d 683 (10th Cir. 1978).

### Questions for Discussion
1. What rules address a bankrupt party's giving false information?
2. Why would the bank want to disallow the discharge of this debt, particularly if Vickers had no assets or sources of revenue?
3. Should the court in this case have held Vickers to a higher standard because he was an outside director of the bank?

---

Of the nondischargeable debts listed previously, the ones most often asserted by banks relate to unscheduled debts and debt incurred by fraud, including the filing of materially false financial statements. Banks and other creditors must make their objections based on debt incurred by fraud within 60 days after the first date set for the meeting of creditors (B. Rule 4007(c)). Once the objection is made, the court will hold a trial at which the creditor can present evidence of fraud.

Banks objecting to a discharge based on fraud as a result of false financial statements must meet certain burdens of proof to succeed. First, the written financial statement used to induce the bank to make a loan must be "materially" false. Second, the debtor must have prepared the statement with the intent to deceive the bank. Third, the bank in making its loan decision must have reasonably relied on the statement (11 U.S.C. § 523(a)(2)(B)).

---

**EXAMPLE** ■ On October 3, 1989, Nick Costello files his petition for bankruptcy and lists in his schedules an unsecured debt to South State Bank for $200,000. Based on an August 2, 1989, financial statement Costello submitted along with his loan request, the bank objects to the discharge. The statement lists a parcel of real estate valued at $25,000, which Costello had sold two months before the August 2 statement. Under cross-examination by Costello's attorney, the bank's loan officer states that his chief reason for making the loan was Costello's good credit history and the cash he had on deposit at the bank and that, without the real estate, the loan would have been made. In this situation, since the bank cannot show "reliance" on the real estate, Costello's debt would be discharged.

Creditors have long objected to abuse of bankruptcy relief by debtors who, on the eve of filing their petitions, engage in spending sprees and then seek the discharge of such debt. Thus, within the category of nondischargeable debts incurred by fraud, a presumption exists that consumer debts owed to a single creditor totaling more than $500 for luxury goods or services purchased within 40 days of filing for bankruptcy, or cash advances made under an open-end consumer credit plan totaling more than $1,000 within 20 days of such filing, were fraudulently obtained. Creditors who formally object to the discharge of consumer debt based on debt or fraud but fail to obtain relief must pay the debtor's expenses and attorney's fees in defending the discharge if the creditor's position was "not substantially jusitified" (11 U.S.C. § 523(d)).

As stated, failure to list a debt in the required schedule can result in its nondischargeability. Debtors cannot pick and choose which debts are to be discharged. They must list them all. The court then uses this list to notify creditors of the existence of the bankruptcy proceeding and the various meetings and deadlines involved, particularly the creditors' deadline for filing proofs of claim and complaints objecting to discharge. Creditors not listed in the required schedule will typically not have their debts discharged. However, if a nonlisted creditor actually knows of the bankruptcy, the debt will be discharged.

---

**EXAMPLE** ■ In the course of contacting Foley about a delinquent payment, Detroit State Bank is informed that he has filed a petition for bankruptcy. Bank personnel confirm the filing with the court but find that the petition does not list the bank as a creditor. The bank, believing its debt will not be discharged, elects not to file a proof of claim. After the bankruptcy is completed, the bank attempts to collect the debt that Foley argues was discharged. Because the bank had actual knowledge of Foley's bankruptcy petition, Foley's debt to the bank was discharged and, by not filing a proof of claim, the bank deprived itself of any pro rata distribution among Foley's general creditors.

---

*Discrimination Based on Discharges*

Any federal, state, or other government agency cannot discriminate against an individual whose debts have been discharged in a bankruptcy proceeding. Thus, drivers who do not pay discharged judgments arising out of traffic accidents cannot be denied licenses nor can students be prohibited from registering for classes where their unpaid tuition debt has been discharged. In addition, no government or private employer may discriminate against an individual because of bankruptcy (11 U.S.C. § 525). However, nothing within the Bankruptcy Code prohibits banks or others from refusing to extend credit to individuals who have had their debts discharged.

---

EXAMPLE ■ Jones applies for a loan at Peoples' Bank and the bank legitimately denies his application based solely on Jones's discharged debts of five years ago.

---

## REHABILITATION

Liquidation of a debtor's assets, distribution of the estate, and discharge of the debts are the objectives of voluntary and involuntary bankruptcies filed under Chapter 7 of the Bankruptcy Code. The code also affords relief for debtors not desiring complete discharge of their debts or loss of all their nonexempt property. Individuals can seek relief under Chapter 13, businesses can use Chapter 11, and farmers can use Chapter 12 of the code.

**Individual Debt Adjustment Plans under Chapter 13**

Chapter 13 **rehabilitation** is often called a **wage earner plan** (11 U.S.C. §§ 1301–30). Chapter 13 permits individuals to repay existing debt according to a court-approved plan, over a period during which creditors can take no collection action against the individual.

Any individual with a stable and regular income may qualify for Chapter 13 relief. That income may come from wages, self-employment, pensions, investments, or other sources. To prevent large sole proprietorships from using Chapter 13, however, debt limitations are placed on individuals seeking this relief. The debt limit for an individual or married couple is $100,000 of unsecured debt, plus secured debt of $350,000 (11 U.S.C. § 109(e)).

*Automatic Stay*  As with a filing under Chapter 7, a filing under Chapter 13 results in an automatic stay that halts creditor collection efforts. If the debt was for consumer purposes and the codebtor is an individual, the stay provisions of Chapter 13 apply to the debtor's cosigners and guarantors as well (11 U.S.C. § 1301) so long as 100 percent payment is proposed.

---

EXAMPLE ■ On April 2, 1989, Hayes files a petition for bankruptcy under Chapter 13. His father had guaranteed one of his consumer debts and had also put up collateral to secure the guaranty. While the stay exists, Hayes's creditors cannot pursue Hayes, his father, or the collateral.

---

For creditors wishing to pursue codebtors, the code provides for specific relief from the stay if the creditor can show potential irreparable harm (11 U.S.C. § 1301(c)).

*Trustees*  As with Chapter 7, the court appoints a trustee in a Chapter 13 proceeding (11 U.S.C. § 1302) who will have responsibilities similar to those of a trustee under Chapter 7. The trustee must investigate the debtor's financial affairs, examine creditor proofs of claim, and make final reports regarding the estate. In addition, the trustee administers the plan approved by the court, including assuring that the debtor makes the required payments. Under Chapter 13, the trustee does not take possession of the debtor's assets.

*The Plan*  The trustee also reviews the Chapter 13 plan proposed by the debtor to determine its feasibility (11 U.S.C. § 1322). The plan must provide for debt repayment within three years, unless the court approves a longer period, but in no case shall the period exceed five years. If the debtor has a principal residence encumbered by a mortgage, its repayment under the plan cannot be any different than that provided by the original debt instruments, except that a default must be cured within a reasonable time. The plan must also include a repayment program that provides first for full payment of all "priority claims" (11 U.S.C. § 1322(a)(2)), as outlined previously in the section entitled "Distribution of the Estate."

Creditors with allowed secured claims must approve the plan and will either receive the collateral or will retain the lien securing the claim, provided that the collateral value is at least equal to the allowed claim. Unsecured creditors must receive in the plan as much as they would receive in a liquidation (11 U.S.C. § 1325(a)(4)). If a debt's original term exceeds the period that the plan is in effect, the debt must only be kept current during the plan's operation (11 U.S.C. § 1322(b)(5)).

As with Chapter 7 proceedings, trustees may assume or reject executory contracts and unexpired leases. The debtor can also propose such assumption or rejection in the plan.

---

EXAMPLE ■ One of Joe Hanson's obligations arises out of a health club membership that requires a monthly payment. The debtor's plan can propose to reject this contract and thereby relieve Hanson of this burden.

---

The plan may also propose the liquidation of some assets to repay debts, as well as their repayment from income (11 U.S.C. § 1322(b)(8)).

After the debtor submits the proposed plan, the court must conduct a hearing to confirm it, at which the trustee, creditors, and other interested parties may make objections to the plan (11 U.S.C. § 1324). Generally, creditors must file written objections with the court prior to the hearing. No creditor's vote is taken at this hearing. To confirm the plan, the court must determine whether it meets the following seven requirements:

■ It must comply with the Bankruptcy Code.

■ It must provide for payment of prescribed fees and charges before confirmation.

- It must be a good faith proposal. Courts have interpreted this requirement to mean that the proposed payments must not abuse the purpose of Chapter 13. This flexible standard results in a case-by-case analysis.

- Unsecured creditors must receive at least what they would be paid under a Chapter 7 proceeding.

- If secured claims are within the plan, the secured creditors have accepted the proposed repayment, have retained their liens, and will receive payments or property the value of which is no less than the amount of the claims, *or* the plan calls for the debtor to surrender the collateral.

- The plan establishes a repayment scheme the debtor will be able to meet and other aspects of the plan are feasible.

- The trustee or any unsecured creditor has no objection, the value of the money or property to be distributed in payment of a claim is no less than the claim, *or* the plan provides that all the debtor's "disposable income" will be applied to make the payments. **Disposable income** is income that is not reasonably necessary for maintenance or support of the debtor and any dependents. If the debtor is a business, then it is the amount not reasonably necessary to continue, preserve, and operate the business (11 U.S.C. § 1325(b)(2)).

## *Discharges*

Once confirmed, the plan binds the debtor and his or her creditors, and the debtor begins to make payments according to the plan. After the plan is completed, the debtor is entitled to a discharge (11 U.S.C. §§ 524(d) and 1328(a)). Even though a debtor has not completed the plan, he or she may nevertheless receive a "hardship" discharge if certain requirements are met (11 U.S.C. § 1328(b)), but such a discharge applies only to unsecured claims.

## Reorganizations under Chapter 11

Chapter 13 **debt adjustment plans** are available only to individuals and sole proprietorships with limited amounts of debt, so Chapter 11 of the Bankruptcy Code provides for rehabilitation of large business entities. Any entity eligible for a liquidation procedure under Chapter 7 qualifies for a **reorganization** proceeding under Chapter 11. Thus, reorganization is unavailable to insurance companies, banks, credit unions, or government entities. In addition, stock and commodity brokers are ineligible for a reorganization under Chapter 11.

Chapter 11 gives a business suffering financial hardship a respite from its creditors in order to reestablish itself on a solid footing. As with other relief under the Bankruptcy Code, a Chapter 11 proceeding begins with the filing of a petition (11 U.S.C. § 301). In addition to the petition, the debtor must submit the same documents required in a Chapter 7 proceeding, plus a list of equity security holders and a list of the 20 largest unsecured claims. If certain criteria are met, creditors may also initiate a reorganization under Chapter 11 (11 U.S.C. § 303(a)).

*Debtors in Possession*

The court does not usually appoint trustees in Chapter 11 proceedings. When none are appointed, the debtor is called a "debtor in possession" (11 U.S.C. § 1101(1)). In Chapter 11 proceedings, a **debtor in possession** has a trustee's rights and powers.

A court, however, can appoint a trustee in a Chapter 11 proceeding upon an interested party's request and after a hearing is held. At the hearing, the requesting party must demonstrate either the debtor's fraud, dishonesty, incompetence, or mismanagement, or that the appointment of a trustee is in the best interests of the debtor's creditors and the estate (11 U.S.C. § 1104).

Once the petition is filed, a first meeting of the creditors is scheduled, which the debtor must attend to answer questions about his or her financial status. The meeting gives the parties the opportunity to discuss the debtor's cash requirements, plans for loans, and repayment of new debt incurred to keep the debtor's business operating.

*Automatic Stays*

For a debtor to rehabilitate its business, it must be able to continue that business without fear that its creditors will take action against its assets. In addition, other entities such as suppliers and banks with which the debtor does business must also have that assurance. As with a Chapter 7 proceeding, an automatic stay goes into effect once a debtor files a Chapter 11 petition. The stay is subject to the same exceptions, "adequate protection" requests, and termination and relief procedures as a stay under Chapter 7.

In a Chapter 11 proceeding, secured creditors are in a different position from those awaiting disbursement in a liquidation. Unless a debtor does not need the secured creditor's collateral to operate its business, the use or availability of that collateral is an integral part of the debtor's rehabilitation. However, the courts have carefully developed rules to assure "adequate protection" of such creditors over the years.

*Operation of the Business*

Under Chapter 11, the debtor in possession is authorized to continue operating the business, and is aided by the automatic stay in retaining assets sufficient to continue that business (11 U.S.C. § 1108). The debtor in possession must report periodically to the court regarding the financial condition of the business. The debtor may make necessary business decisions without the court's approval, so long as he or she acts in the ordinary course of business. The debtor should not take any action outside the ordinary course of business until he or she gives notice to interested parties and provides them with the opportunity for a hearing (11 U.S.C. § 363(b)).

---

EXAMPLE ■ Widget Manufacturing Company is operating under a Chapter 11 proceeding. It continues to manufacture and sell finished widgets, buy raw materials, and enter into contracts. So long as these functions are in the ordinary course of business, the company may continue them without the court's approval. However, if Widget wants to sell one of its three plants, it must provide its creditors an opportunity to be heard.

---

*Creditors' Dealings with Chapter 11 Proceedings*

Once a debtor files a petition under Chapter 11, money in the debtor's accounts becomes the property of the estate. This money is for the debtor's use as the debtor in possession, not for personal use (11 U.S.C. § 363(c)(1)). Because of this, a debtor in possession must typically open new banking accounts.

Chapter 11 debtors also require banks for loans. The debtor in possession may obtain unsecured credit in the ordinary course of business, including loans and purchases on credit. To encourage creditors to deal with Chapter 11 businesses, the Bankruptcy Code provides that prepetition debt is frozen while new debt may be repaid in the ordinary course of business and, if the Chapter 11 is unsuccessful, the new debt will have priority as an administrative expense over prepetition, unsecured debt (11 U.S.C. §§ 507(a)(1) and 503(b)).

EXAMPLE ■ While in a Chapter 11 proceeding, Widget Manufacturing Company asks Acme Metal to sell it raw material with payment due 60 days from delivery. The company also owes Acme a prepetition debt. Acme wants the Chapter 11 proceeding to succeed, enabling Widget to repay its prepetition debt. Given this, and the priority its new credit will receive, Acme will probably make the credit sale to Widget.

*Committees*   Because creditors and equity security holders (which include shareholders) have a great stake in the success of a Chapter 11 proceeding, the code provides for their representation by committee (11 U.S.C. § 1102(a)). Members of these committees represent their class of interested parties and not themselves personally; that is, they have a fiduciary duty to the individuals and entities that their committees are formulated to protect. The committees monitor the ongoing operation of the debtor's business, assist the debtor in possession, negotiate with the debtor to formulate a plan of reorganization, and, if necessary, draft their own plan. Committees may also engage the services of attorneys, accountants, and other professionals to assist them.

*Reorganization Plans*   Within 120 days of commencing a petition for bankruptcy under Chapter 11, a debtor must file a reorganization plan. After that time, any party in interest can propose a plan. Once the debtor's plan is filed, he or she has 60 days in which to have creditors and equity security holders accept it. The court, however, may extend these periods (11 U.S.C. § 1121).

The code also requires that the plan include certain provisions (11 U.S.C. § 1123(a)). The plan must designate classes of claims, such as creditors who have security interests in the same property, unsecured creditors who supplied the debtor with inventory and services, unsecured institutional lenders, shareholders, and bondholders.

Creditors and others whose claims are not impaired by the plan need not be consulted, thus their claims should be listed separately. The plan must also list claimants or interested parties who will be impaired by the plan, the extent of that impairment, and the proposed treatment (11 U.S.C. § 1123(a)). In addition, the plan must specify how its goals will be implemented and describe the steps the debtor will take to place the business in a position to repay creditors, equity security holders, and others.

The debtor must provide copies of the completed plan to interested parties. In addition, the debtor must include a written disclosure with the plan. This statement must provide sufficient information about the debtor's history and present financial condition to enable the parties to make informed judgments about the plan. Before the statement is sent to interested parties, the court must approve it, pursuant to a notice and hearing (11 U.S.C. § 1125(b)).

Once the plan is filed and the court approves the disclosure statement, the debtor or other proponent of the plan seeks its acceptance from interested parties who are impaired by it. The proponent of the plan may modify it to overcome any objections (11 U.S.C. § 1127(a)). The Bankruptcy Code outlines detailed procedures regarding the identity and number of interested parties who must agree to the plan before it is confirmed.

Under Chapter 11, confirmation of a plan cannot occur without notice and a hearing (11 U.S.C. § 1128(a)). In addition, confirmation can occur only after acceptance of the plan by every impaired class or by a **cram down**. In a cram down, the court forces the plan on dissenting classes if at least one impaired class consents to it. The court will do this only if it finds that the plan does not discriminate unfairly and is equitable with respect to each impaired class rejecting the plan (11 U.S.C. § 1129(b)(1)). Either method of acceptance is subject to detailed rules in the code (11 U.S.C. § 1129).

Upon confirmation, the plan fixes the legal rights and obligations of the various parties, and the debtor and interested parties must perform their obligations according to the plan requirements.

## CONCLUSION

Bankruptcy is not new within the scheme of U.S. laws and its legal origins lie within the U.S. Constitution. Over time, bankruptcy has evolved from serving principally as a creditor's tool for collection to providing relief to debtors as well.

Two concepts within the Bankruptcy Code, liquidation and rehabilitation, help to provide that relief to debtors. Those seeking complete relief from their debts submit to liquidation under Chapter 7 of the Bankruptcy Code, while those wishing to retain their nonexempt assets and repay most, if not all, of their debts can seek rehabilitation under Chapter 11 or 13 of the code.

Because banks as creditors continually confront the actual or threatened bankruptcies of their customers, both as borrowers and depositors, bank employees must understand bankruptcy laws in order to assist their banks with the many choices those proceedings provide creditors.

**Questions for Review and Discussion**

1. What authority does the federal government have for enacting bankruptcy laws?

2. How does a debtor initiate a bankruptcy proceeding under Chapter 7?

3. What prevents a creditor from collecting from a debtor or liquidating collateral once the debtor has filed a bankruptcy petition?

4. Who is the trustee?

5. What are exemptions? Give some examples.

6. What is a preference?

7. What happens to a secured creditor's collateral in a Chapter 7 bankruptcy?

8. What is the effect of a discharge?

9. Name two types of debts that are not dischargeable.

10. May a bank refuse to extend credit to an individual whose debts have been discharged?

11. Who may seek rehabilitation under Chapter 13?

12. What is a plan in Chapter 11 and 13 proceedings?

13. What is a "debtor in possession"?

# Federal Regulations Governing Consumer Lending, Privacy, and Electronic Fund Transfers

After studying this chapter, you will be able to

- analyze the scope of the various federal statutes governing consumer credit
- highlight the scope of Regulation Z
- describe disclosures required by the Truth in Lending Act
- differentiate between closed-end and open-end credit
- explain the rescission requirements of the Truth in Lending Act
- determine consumers' rights under the Fair Credit Billing Act
- discuss the civil, regulatory, and criminal penalties for violating various consumer protection statutes
- identify the requirements lessors must meet in leasing goods to consumers
- discuss how the Equal Credit Opportunity Act applies to both consumer and business credit and affects the processing of credit applications and evaluation of loan requests

- determine when the Real Estate Settlement Procedures Act applies to real estate loans
- sum up the requirements of the Fair Credit Reporting Act
- discuss the basic elements of the Fair Debt Collection Practices Act and common-law remedies for abusive debt collection
- describe the Right to Financial Privacy Act and its limited scope
- describe the Electronic Fund Transfer Act and its application
- explain the Credit Practices Rule and its notice-to-cosigner form

No textbook on banking law is complete without some discussion of the laws and regulations governing banks when engaged in consumer lending. Few, if any, consumer loan transactions occur without being affected by laws governing many aspects of the transactions, from loan applications to disclosure of loan terms and retention of records.

The following federal statutes (which deal with consumer lending) are discussed in this chapter:

- Truth in Lending Act
- Fair Credit Billing Act
- Consumer Leasing Act
- Equal Credit Opportunity Act
- Real Estate Settlement Procedures Act
- Fair Credit Reporting Act
- Fair Debt Collection Practices Act

In addition to these federal statutes, the chapter also discusses the federal Right to Financial Privacy Act and the Electronic Fund Transfer Act. Each of these acts has a far-reaching effect on banks and other creditors coming within its scope. Because the acts are so detailed, this chapter only briefly introduces each act, leaving more extensive analysis to other works. These acts also involve numerous regulations that implement the statutory provisions. Although statutes require more time-consuming legislative amendments, regulatory agencies can amend regulations frequently. As a result, regulations change continually and thus must be carefully monitored by bankers and others affected by this area of the law.

Unlike previous chapters in this book, which discussed broad principles of law, this chapter is almost overwhelming in its detail. This reflects the law in this area and the view by Congress that the relationship between creditors and consumers will be subject to precise regulation. In contrast to the laws covering property and contracts, which have been developed over centuries, consumer credit law, at least on the federal level, has developed over the last 30 years.

## TRUTH IN LENDING ACT

The **Truth in Lending Act** was the first significant piece of federal legislation to address consumer credit protection. Until its passage in 1968, only state law protected consumers' credit transactions. Interest rate ceilings (usury laws) were the original credit protection statutes, and nearly every state had some type of structure for rate ceilings.

With the tremendous increase in consumer credit transactions after World War II, the regulation of consumer credit began to receive more attention from the state governments. However, state legislation dealt with this area of law on a piecemeal basis, depending on the type of credit offered and the creditor's and borrower's identities. In many states, this piecemeal approach produced different statutory schemes for retail, automobile, and home-improvement credit, as well as direct lending by financial institutions.

The various state acts gave consumers both substantive and procedural protections. The substantive protections took the form of ceilings on rates that could be charged consumers, prohibitions against certain types of contractual clauses, and "cooling off" periods during which consumers could rescind their agreements. The procedural protections included uniform terms in contracts and uniform methods of calculating the required numerical disclosures.

Reacting to both the lack of consumer protection statutes in some states and the lack of uniformity among those already in existence, Congress passed the Truth in Lending Act (15 U.S.C. § 1601 *et seq.*). The act offers consumers procedural protections through requirements for uniform credit disclosures throughout the United States. It further requires uniform terminology and computation of costs, and simplified disclosures of many of the "fine-print" terms of creditors' documents.

**Regulation Z and Staff Commentary**  Implementing the act itself are the Federal Reserve Board's **Regulation Z** (12 C.F.R. § 226) and an official Federal Reserve Board staff commentary.

**Scope**  The Truth in Lending Act (the act, Regulation Z, and the official staff commentary are hereafter referred to collectively as TILA) is principally a consumer protection law and thus with few exceptions applies only if a credit transaction involves credit for personal, family, or household purposes (12 C.F.R. § 226.1(c)).

---

**EXAMPLE** ■ Frank Joles borrows $10,000 from First Citizens' State Bank to use in his farm operation. For purposes of TILA, Joles is not a consumer because he will not use the loan proceeds for personal, family, or household purposes. Thus, his loan does not come under TILA and the bank need not comply with the act's requirements for this loan.

---

TILA specifically exempts from its requirements credit extensions primarily for business, commercial, or agricultural purposes. Also exempt from TILA provisions are credit extended to government agencies and credit transactions involving securities or commodities accounts conducted by a broker-dealer registered with the federal government. In addition, TILA exempts from its requirements credit transactions in which the amount financed exceeds $25,000 unless the transaction involves a security interest in real property or in personal property used, or expected to be used, as the consumer's principal dwelling (12 C.F.R. § 226.3(b)).

**Requirements**  If a credit transaction comes within TILA, creditors must meet a number of requirements, determined by the type of credit being extended. In setting forth what disclosures creditors need to make to consumers, Regulation Z divides credit into open-end credit and closed-end credit (12 C.F.R. § 226.2(a)(10) and (20)).

Disclosures common to both types of credit are a transaction's "finance charge" (12 C.F.R. § 226.4) and "annual percentage rate" (12 C.F.R. §§ 226.14 and 226.22). These two disclosures are the heart of TILA's objective of uniform disclosure of credit costs. Essentially, the **finance charge** is the cost of consumer credit for the loan disclosed in dollars and cents, while the **annual percentage rate** is the cost of credit disclosed as an annualized percentage rate. In requiring that these charges be calculated and disclosed uniformly, Congress assumed that consumers could make intelligent choices among the terms offered by various creditors.

*Finance Charge*  A loan's finance charge is composed of the various charges a consumer pays for the credit being extended. Regulation Z is very specific about loan finance charges (12 C.F.R. § 226.4), which can include interest, service charges, transaction charges, certain insurance premiums, and loan fees.

---

EXAMPLE ■ Citizens State Bank loans $1,000 to Sam Grabowski to purchase a used car for his family. He is to repay the loan in one payment at the end of one year. The interest rate is 15 percent. In addition, the bank charges Grabowski a $20 loan fee. In this example, Grabowski pays $150 in interest. That figure plus the loan fee of $20 results in a finance charge of $170.

---

*Annual Percentage Rate*  A loan's annual percentage rate is its finance charge expressed as an annualized percentage rate and determined according to calculations strictly defined by Regulation Z. In the previous example, the annual percentage rate of Grabowski's loan is 17 percent. If the finance charge includes any components besides interest, the annual percentage rate will be greater than the interest rate.

## Closed- and Open-End Credit

While the uniform terms "finance charge" and "annual percentage rate" apply to all types of consumer credit disclosures required by TILA, the remaining required disclosures are divided between open-end credit and closed-end credit.

**Open-end credit** involves repeated credit extensions on a revolving basis, whereas **closed-end credit** involves a one-time credit advance. Typical open-end credit programs include credit cards, checking accounts with overdraft privileges, home equity plans, and retail charge accounts.

Any credit extension that does not come within the definition of open-end credit is closed-end credit. Thus, closed-end credit agreements do not normally involve repeated transactions. Closed-end credit can include term, demand, and installment credit instruments. Disclosures provided consumers will vary according to the open-end or closed-end credit plan chosen by the consumer.

### CLOSED-END CREDIT DISCLOSURES

Consumers interested in closed-end adjustable rate mortgages (ARMs) secured by their principal dwellings with terms greater than one year receive a "loan program" disclosure and brochure which in generic terms describes the ARM programs a creditor offers (12 C.F.R. § 226.19(b)). The program disclosure and brochure are provided when the consumer requests an application. The Federal Reserve Board in appendix H to Regulation Z published a model form of this disclosure (see figure 1). The purpose of the loan program disclosure and the Federal Reserve Board's ARM brochure are to give consumers an introduction to ARMs and the specific type of ARM programs offered by a bank.

Consumers who apply for an ARM after receiving a loan program disclosure and brochure, and are approved, will subsequently be treated like applicants for all other types of closed-end consumer credit.

The creditor who enters into a closed-end credit transaction with a consumer must disclose—in addition to the finance charge and annual percentage rate—the amount financed, payment schedule, and identification of any collateral, fees, and other terms prescribed by Regulation Z (12 C.F.R. § 226.18).

Creditors may make closed-end credit disclosures to the consumer at any time before "consummation" of the transaction, except when the

## Figure 1  Model Disclosure Form

### H-14—Variable-Rate Mortgage Sample

This disclosure describes the features of the adjustable-rate mortgage (ARM) program you are considering. Information on other ARM programs is available upon request.

*How Your Interest Rate and Payment Are Determined*

- Your interest rate will be based on an index rate plus a margin.
- Your payment will be based on the interest rate, loan balance, and loan term.
  —The interest rate will be based on the weekly average yield on United States Treasury securities adjusted to a constant maturity of 1 year (your index), plus our margin. Ask us for our current interest rate and margin.
  —Information about the index rate is published weekly in the *Wall Street Journal*.
- Your interest rate will equal the index rate plus our margin unless your interest rate "caps" limit the amount of change in the interest rate.

*How Your Interest Rate Can Change*

- Your interest rate can change yearly.
- Your interest rate cannot increase or decrease more than 2 percentage points per year.
- Your interest rate cannot increase or decrease more than 5 percentage points over the term of the loan.

*How Your Monthly Payment Can Change*

- Your monthly payment can change yearly based on changes in the interest rate.
- For example, on a $10,000, 30-year loan with an initial interest rate of 9.71 percent (the rate shown in the interest rate column below for the year 1987), the maximum amount that the interest rate can rise under this program is 5 percentage points, to 14.71 percent, and the monthly payment can rise from a first-year payment of $85.62 to a maximum of $123.31 in the fourth year.
- You will be notified in writing 25 days before the annual payment adjustment may be made. This notice will contain information about your interest rates, payment amount, and loan balance.

*Example*

The example below shows how your payments would have changed under this ARM program based on actual changes in the index from 1977 to 1987. This does not necessarily indicate how your index will change in the future. The example is based on the following assumptions.

| | |
|---|---|
| Amount | $10,000 |
| Term | 30 years |
| Payment adjustment | 1 year |
| Interest adjustment | 1 year |
| Margin | 3 percentage points |
| Caps | .2 percentage points annual interest rate |
| | .5 percentage points lifetime interest rate |
| Index | Weekly average yield on U.S. Treasury securities adjusted to a constant maturity of one year |

| Year (as of 1st week ending in July) | Index (%) | Margin (percentage points) | Interest Rate (%) | Monthly Payment ($) | Remaining Balance ($) |
|---|---|---|---|---|---|
| 1977 | 5.72 | 3 | 8.72 | 78.46 | 9,927.64 |
| 1978 | 8.34 | 3 | 10.72** | 92.89 | 9,874.67 |
| 1979 | 9.44 | 3 | 12.44 | 105.67 | 9,832.70 |
| 1980 | 8.51 | 3 | 11.51 | 98.79 | 9,776.04 |
| 1981 | 14.94 | 3 | 13.51** | 113.51 | 9,731.98 |
| 1982 | 14.41 | 3 | 13.72*** | 115.07 | 9,683.39 |
| 1983 | 9.78 | 3 | 12.78 | 108.25 | 9,618.21 |
| 1984 | 12.17 | 3 | 13.72*** | 114.96 | 9,554.39 |
| 1985 | 7.66 | 3 | 11.72** | 101.08 | 9,456.03 |
| 1986 | 6.36 | 3 | 9.72** | 88.13 | 9,311.25 |
| 1987 | 6.71 | 3 | 9.71 | 88.07 | 9,151.55 |

To see what your payments would have been during that period, divide your mortgage amount by $10,000; then multiply the monthly payment by that amount. (For example, in 1987 the monthly payment for a mortgage amount of $60,000 taken out in 1977 would be: $60,000 ÷ $10,000 = 6; 6 x $88.07 = $528.42.)

*This is a margin we have used recently; your margin may be different.
**This interest rate reflects a 2 percentage point annual interest rate cap.
***This interest rate reflects a 5 percentage point lifetime interest rate cap.

loan involves a secured loan whose proceeds are used to purchase or construct a borrower's principal dwelling. In that case, an estimated disclosure must be given within three business days of the borrower's credit application. A second, final disclosure must be given before consummation if the annual percentage rate in the first disclosure is not within certain prescribed tolerances (12 C.F.R. §§ 226.17(b) and 226.19(a)). **Consummation** in this context is defined as "the time that a consumer becomes contractually obligated on a credit transaction" (12 C.F.R. § 226.2(a)(13)). Consummation normally occurs at a loan's closing or settlement because that is when the borrower signs a promissory note agreeing to repay an extension of credit.

**EXAMPLE** ■ On October 1, 1989, Joanne Jackson applies for two loans at Wolverine State Bank. One application requests $6,000 to purchase a car for personal use. The other application requests a

$50,000 mortgage loan at a fixed interest rate to purchase a home that will become her principal dwelling.

In this example, the bank must give Jackson a disclosure pertaining to the mortgage application within three business days of October 1. To do this, the bank can either deliver the statement to her or place it in the mail within that period. The only exception to this requirement is when the consummation of the mortgage loan occurs before the three-day period expires. In that case, the bank will give her the disclosure statement pertaining to the home loan at consummation. A disclosure statement pertaining to the car loan would be required at or before that loan's consummation.

---

TILA requires most disclosures for closed-end credit transaction disclosures to be put *within* the so-called **federal box**—the document, or the area within a document, in which all the applicable disclosures are grouped together.

The Federal Reserve Board has issued model federal-box forms and other sample forms as appendix H of Regulation Z. Figure 2 is an example of one of those sample forms.

The disclosures in the federal box may be contained in a separate document or may be included within a document, such as a promissory note, security agreement, or mortgage. Disclosures that are not required to appear in the federal box must appear elsewhere in the loan documentation.

After consummation of a closed-end credit loan, no further disclosures are required unless the loan is an ARM and interest rate changes occur, in which case disclosure must be made before the rate changes (12 C.F.R. § 226.20(c)).

OPEN-END CREDIT DISCLOSURES

As with closed-end credit, the types of disclosures required for open-end credit depend on the type of credit requested. Under the Fair Credit and Charge Card Disclosure Act of 1988, creditors providing or making available unsolicited applications and solicitations for card accounts must provide consumers with generic disclosures providing

Figure 2  Sample Disclosure Form for Installment Loans

```
Friendly Bank & Trust Co.                    Lisa Stone
700 East Street                              22-4859-22
Little Creek, USA                            300 Maple Avenue
                                             Little Creek, USA
```

| ANNUAL PERCENTAGE RATE<br>The cost of your credit as a yearly rate. | FINANCE CHARGE<br>The dollar amount the credit will cost you. | Amount Financed<br>The amount of credit provided to you or on your behalf. | Total of Payments<br>The amount you will have paid after you have made all payments as scheduled. |
|---|---|---|---|
| 12% | $675.31 | $5000- | $5675.31 |

You have the right to receive at this time an itemization of the Amount Financed.
☐ I want an itemization.    ☐ I do not want an itemization.

Your payment schedule will be:

| Number of Payments | Amount of Payments | When Payments Are Due |
|---|---|---|
| 1 | $262.03ᵉ | 6/1/81 |
| 23 | $235.36 | Monthly beginning 7/1/81 |

Late Charge: If a payment is late, you will be charged $5 to 10% of the payment, whichever is less.

Prepayment: If you pay off early, you ☐ may ☐ may not ☐ have to pay a penalty.

Required Deposit: The annual percentage rate does not take into account your required deposit.

See your contract documents for any additional information about nonpayment, default, any required repayment in full before the scheduled date, and prepayment refunds and penalties.

―――――
e means an estimate

basic terms (12 C.F.R. § 226.5(a)). Several model forms for this purpose have been designed by the Federal Reserve Board, including the model shown in figure 3.

In 1988, the Home Equity Loan Consumer Protection Act was passed. Further, 12 C.F.R. § 226.5(b) was added to Regulation Z to implement the Home Equity Act, which applies to all open-end credit plans secured by a consumer's dwelling, including principal dwellings, cottages, and vacation homes.

Figure 3 G-10(A)—Applications and Solicitations Model Form (Credit Cards)

| Annual percentage rate for purchases | _____ % |
|---|---|
| Variable-rate information | Your annual percentage rate may vary. The rate is determined by (explanation). |
| Grace period for repayment of balances for purchases | You have [___days] [until _____] [not less than _____days] [between _____and _____days] [_____ days on average] to repay your balance [for purchases] before a finance charge will be imposed.]<br><br>[You have no grace period in which to repay your balance for purchases before a finance charge will be imposed.] |
| Method of computing the balance for purchases | |
| Annual fees | [Annual] [Membership] fee: $ _____ per year]<br>[(type of fee): $ _____ per year]<br>[(type of fee): $ _____ ] |
| Minimum finance charge | $ _____ |
| Transaction fee for purchases | [$ _____ ] [ _____% of _____ ] |
| Transaction fee for cash advances, and fees for paying late or exceeding the credit limit | Transaction fee for cash advances: [$_____] [_____% of _____]<br>Late-payment fee: [$_____] [_____% of _____]<br>Over-the-credit-limit fee: $_____ |

As with ARMs, this act requires a loan program disclosure to be provided when an application is given to a consumer. This disclosure must be accompanied by another pamphlet developed by the Federal Reserve Board to describe home equity loans. Model "loan program" disclosures have been adopted by the Federal Reserve Board. An example of a disclosure is shown in figure 4.

Any type of open-end consumer credit requires an initial disclosure statement before the consumer makes the first transaction under the terms of the account, and subsequent periodic disclosure statements reflecting transactions in the account during each billing cycle (12 C.F.R. § 226.5(b)).

The objective of the initial disclosure statement for open-end credit is to inform the consumer in advance about the costs and other contractual obligations the consumer will incur if the account is ever used. This disclosure statement cannot provide specific amounts, such

## Figure 4 Sample Loan Program Disclosure

6–1000.71

**G—14A—Home Equity Sample**

IMPORTANT TERMS OF OUR HOME EQUITY LINE OF CREDIT

This disclosure contains important information about our home equity line of credit. You should read it carefully and keep a copy for your records.

*Availability of terms:* To obtain the terms described below, you must submit your application before January 1, 1990.

If these terms change (other than the annual percentage rate) and you decide, as a result, not to enter into an agreement with us, you are entitled to a refund of any fees that you have paid to us or anyone else in connection with your application.

*Security interest:* We will take a mortgage on your home. You could lose your home if you do not meet the obligations in your agreement with us.

*Possible actions:* Under certain circumstances, we can (1) terminate your line, require you to pay us the entire outstanding balance in one payment, and charge you certain fees; (2) refuse to make additional extensions of credit; and (3) reduce your credit limit.

If you ask, we will give you more specific information concerning when we can take these actions.

*Minimum-payment requirements:* You can obtain advances of credit for 10 years (the "draw period"). During the draw period, payments will be due monthly. Your minimum monthly payment will equal the greater of $100 or 1/360th of the outstanding balance plus the finance charges that have accrued on the outstanding balance.

After the draw period ends, you will no longer be able to obtain credit advances and must pay the outstanding balance over 5 years (the "repayment period"). During the repayment period, payments will be due monthly. Your minimum monthly payment will equal 1/60th of the balance that was outstanding at the end of the draw period plus the finance charges that have accrued on the remaining balance.

*Minimum-payment example:* If you made only the minimum monthly payments and took no other credit advances, it would take 15 years to pay off a credit advance of $10,000 at an ANNUAL PERCENTAGE RATE of 12%. During that period, you would make 120 monthly payments varying between $127.78 and $100.00 followed by 60 monthly payments varying between $187.06 and $118.08.

*Fees and charges:* To open and maintain a line of credit, you must pay the following fees to us:

- Application fee: $150 (due at application)
- Points: 1% of credit limit (due when account opened)
- Annual maintenance fee: $75 (due each year)

You also must pay certain fees to third parties to open a line. These fees generally total between $500 and $900. If you ask, we will give you an itemization of the fees you will have to pay to third parties.

*Minimum draw and balance requirements:* The minimum credit advance you can receive is $500. You must maintain an outstanding balance of at least $100.

*Tax deductibility:* You should consult a tax advisor regarding the deductibility of interest and charges for the line.

*Variable-rate information:* The line has a variable-rate feature, and the annual percentage rate (corresponding to the periodic rate) and the minimum payment can change as a result.

The annual percentage rate includes only interest and not other costs.

The annual percentage rate is based on

the value of an index. The index is the monthly average prime rate charged by banks and is published in the *Federal Reserve Bulletin*. To determine the annual percentage rate that will apply to your line, we add a margin to the value of the index.

Ask us for the current index value, margin and annual percentage rate. After you open a credit line, rate information will be provided on periodic statements that we will send you.

*Rate changes:* The annual percentage rate can change each month. The maximum ANNUAL PERCENTAGE RATE that can apply is 18%. Except for this 18% "cap," there is no limit on the amount by which the rate can change during any one-year period.

*Maximum-rate and payment examples:* If you had an outstanding balance of $10,000 during the draw period, the minimum monthly payment at the maximum ANNUAL PERCENTAGE RATE of 18% would be $177.78. This annual percentage rate could be reached during the first month of the draw period.

If you had an outstanding balance of $10,000 at the beginning of the repayment period, the minimum monthly payment at the maximum ANNUAL PERCENTAGE RATE of 18% would be $316.67. This annual percentage rate could be reached during the first month of the repayment period.

*Historical example:* The following table shows how the annual percentage rate and the minimum monthly payments for a single $10,000 credit advance would have changed based on changes in the index over the past 15 years. The index values are from September of each year. While only one payment amount per year is shown, payments would have varied during each year.

The table assumes that no additional credit advances were taken, that only the minimum payments were made each month, and that the rate remained constant during each year. It does not necessarily indicate how the index or your payments will change in the future.

|  | Year | Index (%) | Margin* (%) | ANNUAL PERCENTAGE RATE (%) | Minimum Monthly Payment ($) |
|---|---|---|---|---|---|
| Draw Period | 1974 | 12.00 | 2 | 14.00 | 144.44 |
|  | 1975 | 7.88 | 2 | 9.88 | 106.50 |
|  | 1976 | 7.00 | 2 | 9.00 | 100.00 |
|  | 1977 | 7.13 | 2 | 9.13 | 100.00 |
|  | 1978 | 9.41 | 2 | 11.41 | 105.47 |
|  | 1979 | 12.90 | 2 | 14.90 | 126.16 |
|  | 1980 | 12.23 | 2 | 14.23 | 117.53 |
|  | 1981 | 20.08 | 2 | 18.00** | 138.07 |
|  | 1982 | 13.50 | 2 | 15.50 | 117.89 |
|  | 1983 | 11.00 | 2 | 13.00 | 100.00 |
| Repayment Period | 1984 | 12.97 | 2 | 14.97 | 203.81 |
|  | 1985 | 9.50 | 2 | 11.50 | 170.18 |
|  | 1986 | 7.50 | 2 | 9.50 | 149.78 |
|  | 1987 | 8.70 | 2 | 10.70 | 141.50 |
|  | 1988 | 10.00 | 2 | 12.00 | 130.55 |

*This is a margin we have used recently.    **This rate reflects the 18% rate cap.

as the amount of the finance charge, since no loan or sales transactions have occurred before the statement goes to the consumer. However, it does outline the creditor's method of computing those costs once the account is used and debt is incurred. The initial disclosure statement also includes when a finance charge will be imposed, how it is to be calculated, and a description of fees and collateral.

Once the consumer uses the account, the creditor must make another set of disclosures to the consumer at the end of each billing cycle. Unlike the initial disclosure statement for open-end credit, periodic disclosures reveal the actual costs of the credit used by the consumer. Disclosures in periodic statements include the amount of the debt, how the debt was incurred, payments made on any balances, and the annual percentage rate.

In addition to the disclosures discussed, the regulations implementing the Fair Credit and Charge Card Disclosure Act require additional disclosures if renewal fees are charged or if credit life insurers change (12 C.F.R. § 226.9(e) and (f)).

Additional disclosures are also required for home equity loans. If credit limits are reduced or further credit extensions suspended for the very limited reasons set forth in Regulation Z, the consumer must be notified (12 C.F.R. § 226.9(c)(3)).

## *Rescission*

In enacting the rescission provisions of the Truth in Lending Act, Congress established a policy of protecting consumer residences from liens imposed without the consumers' full understanding of the ramifications of their actions. As provided by TILA, **rescission** is a consumer's ability to terminate a credit transaction unilaterally (that is, without the creditor's consent). Rescission is available to a consumer under TILA only for those credit transactions that result in a security interest (including a mortgage) in real property that is the consumer's principal dwelling or personal property and that are not exempt from Regulation Z (12 C.F.R. §§ 226.15 and 226.23).

Credit extended for nonconsumer purposes, even though secured by a principal dwelling, is not rescindable, and in fact does not even come within the scope of TILA (Regulation Z, commentary paragraphs 15-1 and 23-1). Credit extensions that result in security interests in summer cottages, ski cabins, and other types of secondary or nonprincipal dwellings are not rescindable.

**EXAMPLES** ■ Fred Neale borrows $200,000 from Third National Bank for use in his manufacturing business. As security for the loan, Neale signs a mortgage encumbering his home. Since Neale will use the proceeds of the loan for business purposes, the loan does not come within the scope of TILA, and neither the disclosure nor the rescission requirements of TILA apply.

■ Freda Flower borrows $2,000 from Atlanta State Bank for a vacation. Flower secures the loan with a mortgage on her ski cabin in northern Michigan. While the loan in this situation comes under TILA and thus the bank must provide a disclosure statement to Flowers, the transaction does not involve her principal dwelling and thus the TILA rescission does not apply.

The most noteworthy exception to the rescission requirements of TILA is their inapplicability to "residential mortgage transactions" (12 C.F.R. §§ 226.15(f) and 226.23(f). A residential mortgage transaction

means a transaction in which a mortgage, deed of trust, purchase-money security interest arising under an installment sales contract, or equivalent consensual security interest is created or retained in the consumer's principal dwelling to finance the acquisition or initial construction of that dwelling (12 C.F.R. § 226.2(a)(24)).

**EXAMPLE** ■ Diane Hoffman borrows $20,000 from Montrose National Bank to purchase a mobile home that will be her principal dwelling. At the same time, Francis Blaze borrows $100,000 from Susquehanna State Bank to construct a home that will become his principal dwelling. In neither situation will rescission apply, since both involve financing the acquisition or initial construction of a principal dwelling.

In situations in which TILA rescission rights apply, the creditor must follow precise steps. If open-end credit is involved, the creditor should give a "Notice of Right to Cancel" to consumers when the initial disclosure statement is provided, when a security interest is added or increased to secure an existing open-end plan, and when the debt limit on a plan secured by a principal dwelling is increased (12 C.F.R. § 226.15(a)(b)). Regulation Z provides model forms for notices of the right to cancel that apply to open-end credit (12 C.F.R., appendixes G-5, 6, 7, 8, and 9).

When TILA rescission applies to a closed-end credit transaction, the creditor should give the consumer a "Notice of Right to Cancel" when the loan transaction is consummated. Regulation Z contains model notice forms for closed-end transactions similar to those for open-end transactions (12 C.F.R., appendixes H-8 and H-9).

Once a consumer receives a notice of right to cancel and all TILA disclosures, the consumer has until midnight of the following third business day (including Saturdays) to rescind the credit transaction. Rescission occurs when the consumer returns the applicable portion of the notice form, other writing, or a telegram indicating to the creditor a desire to rescind a credit transaction within the described period. If for any reason the notice of disclosure statement is not given to the consumer or material errors appear in either, the rescission period will run for the earlier of three years or the date the consumer transfers all interest in the property to someone else (12 C.F.R. §§ 226.15(a)(3) and 226.23(a)(3)).

---

**EXAMPLE** ■ Robert Hill borrows $20,000 from Glad National Bank to remodel his home. A mortgage on the home is security for the loan. The loan is closed on November 1, 1987.

Although the loan is subject to the TILA rescission requirement, the bank never gives Hill a notice of the right to cancel. On October 15, 1990, Hill notifies the bank in writing that he wishes to rescind the transaction. In this situation, the consumer may rescind the transaction as long as he still owns the home on October 15, 1990.

---

If a consumer chooses to exercise the right of rescission, the creditor must void the entire credit transaction within 20 days of receiving notice. This includes nullifying the promissory note, discharging the security interest document, and returning all monies received from the consumer, including commitment fees and monies used to pay third parties for appraisals and credit reports. If the creditor has received any payment from the consumer before receiving a notice of rescission, the funds must be returned to the consumer within the 20-day period. If the rescission period is three years, the severity of this requirement can be easily understood (12 C.F.R. §§ 226.15(d) and 226.23(d)). Thus, in the preceding example, Glad National Bank would have to discharge its mortgage on Hill's home, return to him all principal and interest payments it had received, and void its promissory note.

Once the creditor has rescinded its part of the transaction, the consumer must tender to the creditor within a reasonable time the money he or she received. In the previous example, Hill would have to return the $20,000 loan proceeds received from the bank, after it had performed its obligation under the rescission requirements. However, the bank would lose all the interest payments Hill had made.

Consumers may waive the rescission period if a "bona fide personal financial emergency" exists. For example, if a tornado tears the roof off a consumer's home and exposes it to the elements, and the consumer does not have personal funds to make the repairs, a waiver of the rescission period would be appropriate. The waiver must be in writing, dated, and signed by the consumer, with an explanation of the emergency, and must state whether the rescission period is waived or modified. Preprinted waiver forms are specifically prohibited (12 C.F.R. §§ 226.15(e) and 226.23(e)).

## FAIR CREDIT BILLING ACT

With the onset of the computer age in the 1960s came computer billing, which resulted in numerous complaints that creditors were not responding to consumers' problems with billing errors. In 1974, Congress responded with an amendment to the Truth in Lending Act that became known as the Fair Credit Billing Act (15 U.S.C. § 1666 and 12 C.F.R. § 226.13). The **Fair Credit Billing Act** (FCBA) only covers billing errors resulting from consumers' open-end credit transactions. Regulation Z defines **billing error** to include

- periodic statements that misidentify an extension of credit, give insufficient identification, omit necessary information, give erroneous information about amounts or individuals involved, or reflect the use of credit by unauthorized person(s)

- requests for explanation or clarification

- assertions that property or services reflected in a periodic statement or accompanying documents were not delivered or accepted according to an underlying agreement

- failure to deliver a periodic statement within the prescribed time (12 C.F.R. § 226.13(a))

The FCBA provides a procedure for consumers who believe they have experienced a billing error. To preserve rights under FCBA, within 60 days of receiving a periodic statement that includes the alleged billing error, a consumer must notify the creditor of the error in writing (12 C.F.R. § 226.13(b)).

---

EXAMPLE ■ On October 5, 1989, Sam Ford received a periodic statement from the bank pertaining to his overdraft checking account. The statement contained a finance charge for an overdraft check Ford was sure he had not signed. On October 20, Ford sent a written notice of the alleged error to his bank. In this situation, Ford has acted in a timely fashion to allege a billing error, and the bank must comply with FCBA procedures to review the allegation.

---

The first step in a creditor's response to an alleged billing error is a written acknowledgment, within 30 days, to the customer that it has received the notification of billing error. Within two complete billing cycles, but in no case more than 90 days from the date the bank receives notice of the alleged billing error, the dispute must be resolved (12 C.F.R. § 226.13(c)).

Resolution of the alleged billing error may involve any one of the following three possibilities:

- an agreement with the customer that an error has occurred and its correction

- an agreement with the customer that an error has occurred, but a claim that the error is other than the amount alleged by the customer and a corresponding adjustment to the account

- denial that an error has occurred

If the creditor uses either of the latter two responses to resolve the allegation, it must provide a written explanation to the customer and, if the customer so requests, supporting documentation (12 C.F.R. §§ 226.13(e) and 226.13(f)).

During the period after a consumer's notice of billing error has been received and before the resolution procedure is completed, a creditor cannot collect any disputed amounts. Nor may a creditor report to any third parties during this period that the disputed amount is delinquent. If the creditor determines at the conclusion of the resolution procedure that the customer owes all or part of the disputed amount, the creditor can insist on payment of that amount but cannot accelerate the remaining indebtedness (12 C.F.R. § 226.13(d)).

Once the creditor has completed the procedure for resolving a billing error, it has no further obligation to withhold collection efforts, even if the customer is dissatisfied with the creditor's answer. However, if after the resolution procedure is completed the customer notifies the creditor that a dispute still exists, information to that effect must accompany any reports the creditor makes to third parties that the account is delinquent. The creditor must also notify the customer of the name and address of each third party to whom it has reported the delinquency (12 C.F.R. § 226.13(g)).

To assure that customers are aware of their rights under the Fair Credit Billing Act, creditors offering open-end credit must disclose the availability of the procedure for resolving disputes over billing errors. Initial disclosure statements for open-end credit must describe—either within the disclosure statement or in an accompanying document—the billing-error procedure in a form suggested by Regulation Z (12 C.F.R., appendix G-3). To assure that customers continue to understand their rights in resolving disputes over billing errors, creditors must send each customer either a "long" billing-error disclosure form (12 C.F.R., appendix G-3) annually or a "short" billing-error disclosure form (12 C.F.R., appendix G-4) with each periodic statement (12 C.F.R. §§ 226.6(d) and 226.9(a)).

Any creditor who fails to comply with the procedure for resolving billing errors forfeits the right to collect the greater of either the disputed amount or $50 (15 U.S.C. § 1666(e)). In addition, any violation of FCBA billing-error provisions may result in the creditor's liability for further civil and regulatory penalties (discussed later in this chapter).

## Credit Cards

Whether used for consumer, agricultural, or commercial purposes, credit cards come within the scope of TILA (12 C.F.R. § 226.12). Under TILA, a **credit card** is any card, plate, coupon book, or other device presented to obtain money, property, labor, or services on credit (12 C.F.R. § 226.2(a)(15)).

TILA regulates both the issuance of credit cards and a cardholder's liability for their unauthorized use. "Unauthorized use" is the use of a credit card by a person other than the cardholder with no actual, implied, or apparent authority for such use and from which the cardholder receives no benefit. Further, the act permits issuance of credit cards only in response to a request or an application, or as a renewal of an already issued card (12 C.F.R. § 226.12(a)).

**EXAMPLE** ■ Without receiving a request for the application, City State Bank sent an application for its credit card to Juan Carlos. The bank's procedure was legal. It merely sent an unsolicited application to Carlos, which enabled him to request a card if he wished. Had the bank sent Carlos an unsolicited credit card which he could immediately use, it would have violated TILA.

A cardholder's liability for unauthorized use of a credit card cannot exceed the lesser of $50 or the amount of credit obtained with the card before the cardholder notifies the card issuer of the unauthorized use. However, a cardholder's liability is preconditioned upon the card issuer's provision to the cardholder of the following information:

- adequate notice of the cardholder's potential liability for unauthorized use

- an address or telephone number to which notices of unauthorized use, theft, or loss might be reported

- a card that contains a means of identifying the cardholder or authorized user

If any of these three preconditions to a cardholder's liability is not satisfied, the maximum $50 liability cannot be enforced (12 C.F.R. § 226.12(b)(2)).

**EXAMPLE** ■ Joe Barton's credit card was stolen and the thief charged $500 worth of merchandise on it. However, the card issuer had not advised Barton that his liability for unauthorized use could not exceed $50. In this situation, Barton had no liability for the thief's use of his card.

TILA permits cardholders to withhold payment from card issuers for property or services purchased with the card for consumer purposes that turn out to be unsatisfactory. To exercise this right, the consumer cardholder must first attempt to resolve the dispute with the merchant in good faith. However, with limited exceptions, the cardholder cannot withhold payment from a card issuer if the disputed amount is $50 or less, or if the transaction resulting in the dispute occurred outside the cardholder's state or, if in another state, at a location more than 100 miles from the cardholder's address. During any period of dispute, the card issuer cannot report the cardholder as delinquent until the dispute is resolved or judgment is rendered in the card issuer's favor (12 C.F.R. § 226.12(c)).

EXAMPLE ■ Donna Mellon used her bank credit card to purchase an $800 refrigerator from Tower Appliances. After delivery, the refrigerator failed to work properly and Mellon could not obtain any satisfaction from the seller. When her next periodic statement arrived from the bank, she refused to pay the charge for the refrigerator. In this situation, if the bank sues Mellon to collect the $800 debt and any accrued finance charges, she may raise the defective condition of the refrigerator as a defense to payment.

TILA specifically prohibits setoff when a consumer cardholder has incurred a credit-card debt. If a cardholder has incurred the debt for other than consumer purposes, the prohibition against setoff does not apply and, unless state law holds otherwise, the cardholder's deposits may be offset to cure delinquent credit-card debt (12 C.F.R. § 226.12(d)).

Before a 1975 TILA amendment, some card issuers prohibited or limited the ability of merchants and others honoring their credit cards to offer discounts to customers paying with cash. With the 1975 amendment permitting such discounts came a prohibition against card issuers' mandating minimum deposit relationships and the purchase from them of certain tie-in services unessential to the operation of a credit card program (12 C.F.R. § 226.12(f)). TILA continues to prohibit the imposition of a surcharge on a cardholder who elects to use a credit card instead of cash (12 U.S.C. § 1666f(a)(2)).

**Advertising**  TILA's goal of providing consumers with disclosures of credit costs using uniform terminology also applies to the advertising of consumer credit (15 U.S.C. § 1661; 12 C.F.R. §§ 226.16 and 226.24). For TILA purposes, an **advertisement** means any commercial message in any medium that directly or indirectly promotes a credit transaction (12 C.F.R. § 226.2(a)(2)).

The content of advertisements is within the creditor's discretion unless the creditor uses "triggering terms," in which case the advertisement must include certain disclosures. What constitutes a triggering term and the content of the required disclosures will depend on whether the advertisement is for open-end or closed-end credit. Since the use of triggering terms without proper disclosures is a recurrent violation of TILA, creditors and those responsible for their advertising programs should carefully review these TILA requirements.

**Enforcement**  Criminal, civil, and regulatory penalties help to assure compliance with TILA. Criminal penalties must be based upon a showing of willful and knowing violation of either the act or Regulation Z. If such a showing is made, conviction can lead to a fine up to $5,000 or imprisonment for not more than one year, or both (15 U.S.C. § 1611).

Civil penalties are imposed for certain violations of TILA disclosure requirements, as well as for violations of sections of the Fair Credit Billing Act. These civil penalties include actual damages, plus twice the amount of any finance charge (but not less than $100 nor more than $1,000), plus costs of the action and reasonable attorney's fees.

---

EXAMPLE ■ Jane Yeck's loan from Superior State Bank involves a finance charge of $2,500. The disclosure statement given Yeck contains an error that violates TILA. In this situation, Yeck is entitled to at least $1,000 plus her actual costs and fees and, if she can prove actual damages, the bank will be assessed those as well.

---

Class action penalties permit the assessment of damages against a creditor of $500,000 or one percent of the creditor's net worth, whichever is less. Unlike damages in individual actions, class action awards are subject to such mitigating factors as actual damages suffered by the plaintiff, the frequency and persistence of the violations, the creditor's resources, the number of people harmed by the violations, and the extent to which the violations were intentional.

In addition to the mitigating defenses against class actions, creditors may use several other defenses, if applicable, when TILA violations are alleged. The first of these defenses permits a creditor that underdisclosed a charge to escape liability if, within 60 days of discovering its error, it notifies the affected consumer of the error *and* adjusts the consumer's accounts to ensure that he or she will not pay a charge greater than was disclosed.

---

EXAMPLE ■ On May 1, 1989, Acme State Bank gave Henry Filbert a TILA disclosure that stated the loan's annual percentage rate as 3 percent, when in fact it was 13 percent. The bank discovered the error on June 10, 1989. In this situation, if Acme State Bank wishes to use the "60-day defense," it must adjust the account so that it collects no more than the 3 percent annual percentage rate that was disclosed and must then notify Filbert of the error and the adjustment. (See 15 U.S.C. § 1640(b)).

---

The 60-day defense is unavailable if, before the creditor makes the correction, the consumer institutes a court action or gives the creditor written notice of the error.

In addition, a bank or other creditor violating TILA will also escape liability if it can prove that a "violation was not intentional and resulted from a bona fide error notwithstanding the maintenance of procedures reasonably adapted to avoid any such error" (15 U.S.C. § 1640(c)). Examples of bona fide errors are those involving computer malfunctions and clerical or printing errors, but not errors of legal judgment regarding a person's obligations.

Creditors whose actions result from their reliance on Regulation Z, the official staff commentary, or any other rule, regulation, or interpretation of TILA issued by the Federal Reserve Board or its staff are exempt from liability, even if such pronouncements of the board or its staff are later found incorrect (15 U.S.C. § 1640(f)).

If a creditor's disclosure error is within the annual percentage rate or finance charge of a credit extension, TILA prescribes certain tolerances that prevent small calculation errors from being called violations. As long as a disclosure of an annual percentage rate is within ⅛ of 1 percent (¼ of 1 percent for some transactions) of the actual rate, no violation will occur (12 C.F.R. § 226.22). Further, as long as a disclosed finance charge is within $5 of the actual finance charge when the amount of the credit extension is $1,000 or less, and within $10 when the amount financed is more than $1,000, no violation will occur (12 C.F.R. § 226.18, n. 41).

Consumers must file lawsuits alleging TILA violations within one year of the alleged violation. However, if a creditor starts a lawsuit against a consumer, the consumer may "counterclaim" for any TILA violations even if the one-year period has expired if not disallowed by state law (15 U.S.C. § 1640(e)).

---

EXAMPLE ■ On May 2, 1988, Afton National Bank lent Henry Rose $8,000 and on the disclosure statement made an error in the annual percentage rate of ½ of 1 percent. On July 3, 1989, the bank started a lawsuit against Rose for $5,000, the balance due on the then overdue loan. In this situation, Rose could counterclaim for the TILA violation and, unless the bank had one of the defenses outlined earlier, Rose would recover at a minimum twice the loan's finance charge (not less than $100 nor more than $1,000) plus his actual attorney's fees.

---

Regulatory agencies may also impose penalties for TILA violations. The Federal Reserve Board, Federal Deposit Insurance Corporation (FDIC), Comptroller of the Currency, Office of Thrift Supervision, National Credit Union Administration, Civil Aeronautics Board, Secretary of Agriculture, Farm Credit Administration, and Federal Trade Commission all have authority to enforce TILA.

Regulatory agencies have chosen to enforce TILA in various ways. Those that supervise financial institutions conduct compliance exams. Other agencies react to consumer complaints alleging that creditors within their jurisdictions have violated TILA. Still other agencies stress educational programs for the creditors within their jurisdictions. All of the regulatory agencies have restitution powers that enable them to order the creditors within their jurisdictions to return overcharges to consumers. In some cases, these orders have amounted to many thousands of dollars. The restitution procedures of the various agencies mainly address errors in disclosures of annual percentage rates, finance charges, and insurance.

# CONSUMER LEASING ACT

In 1977, TILA was amended to add provisions pertaining to consumer leasing transactions (15 U.S.C. § 1667 *et seq.*) and additional sections were added to Regulation Z to implement those provisions. On April 1, 1982, the provisions of Regulation Z on leasing were deleted and became the entirely new Federal Reserve Board **Regulation M** (12 C.F.R. § 213).

A consumer lease is one in which the terms exceed four months, which involves only personal property as defined by state law, and for which the total contractual obligation does not exceed $25,000. Since only consumer leases come under the act, the lessee must be a natural person using the personal property primarily for a personal, family, or household purpose. Leases for agricultural, business, or commercial purposes do not come under the **Consumer Leasing Act** (12 C.F.R. § 213.2(a)(6); 15 U.S.C. § 1667).

Under this act and regulation, **lessors**—defined as individuals or entities regularly engaged in offering or arranging consumer leases—must make certain disclosures before any consumer lease is consummated (12 C.F.R. §§ 213.2(a)(8) and 213.4). The required disclosures include

- a description of the leased property
- the amount and schedule of lease payments
- fees
- warranties
- security interests and termination provisions
- disclosures regarding responsibility for amounts due when the lease expires

To help lessors, the Federal Reserve Board has accompanied Regulation M with three model forms for lease disclosures, which lessors may adapt to their own use (Reg. M, appendix C).

# EQUAL CREDIT OPPORTUNITY ACT

The **Equal Credit Opportunity Act** (ECOA) is essentially a civil rights act passed to provide access to credit without discrimination based on sex, marital status, race, color, religion, national original, receipt of income from public assistance, and past exercise of a right under the federal Consumer Protection Act (15 U.S.C. § 1691 *et seq.*). The act gave the Federal Reserve Board the authority to promulgate Regulation B to implement the act's provisions (12 C.F.R. § 202 *et seq.*). The Board also issued an official staff commentary.

**Scope**    Unlike statutes discussed earlier, ECOA applies to all types of credit, including consumer and business credit. With the passage of the Women's Business Ownership Act in 1988 and the amendments to Regulation B required by the act, few differences remain in the way creditors can treat consumer and business applicants for ECOA purposes.

The act defines creditors as those who in the course of their business regularly participate in decisions on whether to grant credit. This definition includes creditors' assignees, transferees, and subrogees who participate in such decisions. For limited purposes, the definition of creditors also includes those (such as real estate brokers) who regularly refer people to creditors or offer to select creditors for others (12 C.F.R. § 202.2(1)).

*Case for Discussion*    **SBA v. GUARANTORS**
**Facts**
In January 1987, Melton Meadors, Harold DuCote, and Jay Judd approached the Bargerville State Bank of Indiana for a loan to their lumber business. The bank agreed to make the loan but requested a loan guaranty from the Small Business Association (SBA). SBA reviewed the application and agreed to guarantee the loan.

After considering the loan application, SBA chose to have Meadors, Judd, DuCote, and DuCote's wife sign the required guaranty. This guaranty was a personal pledge to SBA, in case the lumber company defaulted on the loan. When the loan was approved, Meadors was unmarried. Before the loan closing on April 2, 1987, however, Meadors married Betty. SBA did not require her personal guaranty, nor did the bank require her to sign as a prerequisite for disbursing the loan proceeds. However, at the loan closing on April 8, Betty signed the guaranty form.

Later, the lumber company defaulted on its loan and the bank asked SBA to take over the guaranteed portion of the loan. The company's assets were sold, but the proceeds were insufficient to pay off the balance of the loan. SBA is now seeking to collect the deficiency from the guarantors, including Betty.

In court, Betty claims that her signature on the SBA guaranty form was obtained in violation of ECOA and thus is unenforceable. ECOA prohibits a creditor from requiring a spouse's signature on an application for credit if the spouse individually qualified under the creditor's standards for the amount of the credit requested. Meadors, of course, had qualified for the loan on his own credit, since he was not even married to Betty when the bank granted the loan. SBA contends that they did not violate ECOA. They state that Betty was not required to sign the guaranty but voluntarily signed the form.

### Decision

The court rules in favor of SBA. In this case, the court reasons that, even when the creditor does not require the signature of any creditworthy additional party and the spouse accordingly elects to sign as such an additional party, the spouse cannot later raise ECOA as a defense. ECOA is meant to prohibit a spouse from being *required* to sign. When someone voluntarily agrees to sign, ECOA provides no protection.

### Questions for Discussion

1. Describe a situation in which a bank processing an application for business credit might violate ECOA.

2. Describe a situation in which a bank processing an application for consumer credit might violate ECOA.

3. Identify some procedures banks can use to help prevent violations of ECOA.

---

## Applications

ECOA first affects a creditor when it receives an application for credit because the act directly governs the content of an application. Under no circumstances can a creditor seeking information for the purpose of extending credit ask an applicant's race, religion, color, national origin, sex, or family-planning practices and expectations (12 C.F.R. §§ 202.5(d)(3)–202.5(d)(5)). Further, a creditor may ask questions about marital status, age, and public assistance income only under limited circumstances. While the sex of an applicant cannot be asked directly, courtesy titles such as "Ms.," "Mrs.," "Miss," or "Mr." can be used on an application (12 C.F.R. § 202.5(d)(3)).

---

**EXAMPLE** ■ City State Bank has an application form it asks Dave Hayes to complete when he requests a loan to buy a motorcycle. Because the application requests Hayes's sex, it violates ECOA and could subject the bank to civil and administrative penalties.

---

An application for credit may ask an applicant's marital status under limited circumstances including whenever secured credit is requested. In asking for marital status, the application may only use the terms "married," "unmarried," and "separated" (12 C.F.R. § 202.5(d)(1)).

Under ECOA, a creditor may ask for the marital status of an applicant who relies on alimony, child support, or separate maintenance payments to assist in establishing creditworthiness. If the applicant does not want the creditor to rely on such income, the applicant need not reveal that information and the application form must disclose this fact. Birth control practices, family planning, ability to bear children, and child-rearing intentions are additional topics creditors cannot discuss with current or prospective applicants (12 C.F.R. § 202.5(d)(4)).

An application may ask an applicant's age as well as whether any part of his or her income is derived from public assistance. While these questions may be asked, the procedure for credit evaluation set forth in ECOA must weigh the answers carefully (12 C.F.R. § 202.6(b)(2)(iii)).

To help creditors draft application forms that conform to ECOA requirements, the Federal Reserve Board has drafted model application forms for most types of consumer loans and placed them in an appendix to Regulation B. Use of the model forms is discretionary, and the creditor may modify the forms but not their substance.

## Credit Evaluation

Once a creditor receives an application, the evaluation process begins and further ECOA requirements must be met. In deciding whether to extend credit, a creditor may use any information it receives about an applicant from whatever source, so long as the information is not used to discriminate against an applicant on a prohibited basis, namely, on the basis of sex, marital status, race, color, religion, national origin, receipt of income from public assistance, and past exercise of a right under the Consumer Protection Act (12 C.F.R. § 202.6(a)).

ECOA permits creditors, in evaluating applications, to use either an "empirically derived credit system" or a "judgmental system." The former is a credit-scoring system derived by the use of sophisticated statistical information. The latter is any other system a creditor may use to determine an applicant's creditworthiness (12 C.F.R. § 202.2(p)).

For example, if a creditor uses an empirically derived credit-scoring system to determine an applicant's creditworthiness, it may assign constant values to particular age categories. On the other hand, if a creditor uses a judgmental system to decide creditworthiness for applicants 61 years old and younger, it cannot use age in and of itself as a factor as long as the applicant is old enough to enter into a binding contract. However, the creditor can consider age as it relates to other factors, such as an indication of remaining years of employment, life expectancy, length of loan requested, and amount of Social Security or pension income. With either system, it is permissible—though not mandated—for a creditor to consider an applicant 62 years old and older more favorably than younger applicants, based on age (12 C.F.R. §§ 202.2(o) and 202.6(b)(2)(iv)).

---

EXAMPLES ■ Henry Sova, who is 80 years old, applies to First State Bank for a $50,000 mortgage to be repaid over 20 years. Based on its policy of not loaning to anyone over age 70, the bank rejects the application.

In this situation, the bank has violated ECOA. If the bank had turned down Sova's application because actuarial tables showed that he would probably not live long enough to pay off the loan, no violation would have occurred. Under ECOA, life expectancy is a legitimate reason for rejecting a loan application. However, the bank should make an effort to make a counteroffer that will accommodate both Sova's request and its desire to be repaid; one possibility would be to extend the loan Sova wants but to require a three-year balloon payment.

- First National Bank advertises a "Golden Years" program, which includes a credit card with lower interest rates and no fees. To qualify for the program, an applicant must be age 50.

    The bank's program violates ECOA since it offers more favorable credit to those over 49. Had the bank used 62 as the cutoff for the program, it would not have violated ECOA (Regulation B, commentary paragraph 6(b)(2)-1).

---

If an applicant wishes a creditor to consider income from alimony, child support, or separate maintenance payments in its evaluation, the creditor must do so. However, as with any other income, the creditor has the right to weigh its reliability. This may require the creditor to review the court decree ordering payment, the history of the payments, the procedures available to the applicant for compelling payment, and the creditworthiness of the payor (12 C.F.R. § 202.6(b)(5)).

The creditor must also evaluate income from public assistance in the same way as any other income. A creditor may consider how much longer the applicant will qualify for the assistance, which may depend on the ages of the applicant's children as well as on other factors such as the applicant's move to a jurisdiction that may provide fewer benefits. Included within income from public assistance programs are social services benefits, Social Security payments, and unemployment compensation.

---

EXAMPLE ■ Sally Wheat applies for a loan at Centerville Bank. Her only income is the $400 per month she receives in welfare payments for her two children, the oldest of whom will be 18 in one month. At that time, the welfare payments will be reduced to $200 per month. According to the bank's lending criteria, Wheat's income qualifies her for the loan she wants if her income is at least $350 per month. In this situation, the bank may reject Wheat's application, not because her income is derived from public assistance, but because her income will be reduced within the loan repayment period to an amount less than the bank's criteria require.

---

In evaluating an applicant's creditworthiness, the creditor must evaluate part-time employment no differently from full-time employment. An applicant receiving $15,000 per year from part-time employment cannot be evaluated differently from one earning the same amount in a full-time job (12 C.F.R. § 202.6(b)(5)).

In evaluating creditworthiness, creditors normally review an applicant's credit history. To the extent that they consider such a history, ECOA requires creditors to include in the review any earlier credit extensions to the applicant and his or her spouse. However, the weight creditors give such histories may vary, depending on the applicant's input. An applicant has the right to present information to a creditor that joint accounts with a spouse do not accurately reflect the applicant's creditworthiness. For example, a married or divorced woman who had little, if anything, to do with the failure of her current or former husband to repay a joint credit extension has the right to present her case to the creditor evaluating her creditworthiness. On the other hand, when an applicant helped establish a good credit history for a current or former spouse but was not a joint holder of the account, the applicant has the right to ask the creditor to consider that good repayment record in its evaluation (12 C.F.R. § 202.6(b)(6)).

---

*Case for Discussion*

**MILLER v. AMERICAN EXPRESS COMPANY**

### Facts

Bill Miller applied for a bank credit card. When issuing the credit card, the bank offered Bill the option of receiving a supplementary card for Mary, his wife. Since Mary had no credit of her own, Bill thought this was a good idea. According to the bank's rules, Mary was personally liable for all purchases made with her card. Her card had a different number than Bill's and required a separate annual fee. When Bill died unexpectedly, the bank canceled Mary's card without prior notification. The bank did this in accordance with its policy of automatically terminating the account of a supplementary cardholder upon the death of the primary cardholder. Claiming the bank's policy violated ECOA because it discriminated based on marital status, Mary sued the bank. The facts also showed that the bank invited Mary to apply for a new card as a primary cardholder, which she was eventually granted.

### Decision

The court ruled that the bank's policy did violate ECOA regulations because the termination of the supplementary card was based on a change in marital status of a person who was personally liable on an open-end credit card account. However, the court ruled that, under ECOA, it is acceptable for banks to require a reapplication for a credit card after a change in marital status. *Miller v. American Express Co.*, 688 F.2d 1235 (9th Cir. 1982).

### Questions for Discussion

1. What should the bank have done to avoid violating ECOA?
2. What procedures could the bank follow in the future to avoid this kind of ECOA violation?

---

A creditor determining an applicant's creditworthiness may also consider state property laws (12 C.F.R. § 202.6(c)). If laws such as Michigan's dower statute (Mich. Comp. Laws Ann. § 558.1 *et seq.*) or tenancy by the entirety statute (Mich. Comp. Laws Ann. §§ 557.71 and 557.81) or California's community property laws (Cal. Code § 5110), limit a creditor's access to collateralized property upon a default, the creditor can require a nonapplicant spouse to execute instruments that will allow complete foreclosure of the collateral. Essentially, ECOA does permit creditors to treat married applicants differently from unmarried ones if the basis for unequal treatment is state property law.

**EXAMPLE** ■ Joan Hull, a married woman, applies for a $20,000 loan to be secured by a mortgage on real property she owns in her own name in Michigan, where she lives. On the same day, Fred Lake, a married man, applies for the same amount, also to be secured by Michigan real property he owns in his own name. Neither applicant wants his or her spouse to sign any loan documents. Both applicants have sufficient income of their own to repay the loans.

Because each loan is to be secured, the bank may request each applicant's marital status. Since the applicants have sufficient income of their own to repay the loan, the bank cannot request any other person to sign promissory notes. However, because Lake's wife has a dower interest in his property (see chapter 6), the bank can require her signature on the mortgage that is collateral for the loan. In contrast, the bank cannot require Hull's husband to sign the mortgage, since he has no dower interest in her real property. Thus, in this case ECOA permits a creditor to treat a married man differently from a married woman based on state law.

Reviewing an applicant's credit history is an integral part of any credit evaluation. Before ECOA, many married women applicants were unable to furnish separate credit histories. This happened because creditors routinely indexed the credit a woman had obtained jointly with her husband in her husband's name alone. To ensure complete credit histories for married women, ECOA requires creditors who furnish credit information to designate the names of both spouses on accounts for which they are both contractually liable. When furnishing credit information to consumer reporting agencies, creditors must provide the information in such a way that the agencies will also be able to furnish the information in each spouse's name. In addition, creditors responding to inquiries about a married customer's credit record must furnish that information in the name of the spouse about whom the information was requested (12 C.F.R. § 202.10(a)).

## Notification of Credit Decisions

After the creditor receives an application and evaluates the applicant's creditworthiness, the next step is to notify the applicant of its decision. ECOA requires notification within 30 days of the creditor's receipt of a completed application. If a creditor extends the credit to an applicant, no notice other than completing the transaction within the 30 days need be given (12 C.F.R. § 202.9(a)(1)(i)).

If the creditor denies the credit application and the consumer is applying for "consumer credit" (12 C.F.R. § 202.2(h)), the creditor must send a notice of "adverse action" to the applicant within the 30-day period. ECOA prescribes the content of the notice of adverse action and the Federal Reserve Board has drafted model forms to assist creditors in this matter (12 C.F.R. § 202, appendix C). The notice must include

- the denial of the applicant's request for credit
- the name and address of the federal agency regulating the creditor
- a prescribed paragraph summarizing ECOA's purpose and scope
- a statement informing the applicant of the reasons for the credit denial or, if the creditor chooses, informing the applicant that the reasons for denial may be obtained from the creditor

In addition, if the creditor based the denial on information from a third party, this must also be disclosed.

ECOA also requires creditors to give adverse-action notices when they refuse counteroffers, find applications incomplete, or terminate open-end credit accounts. Thus, any consumer whose credit card is terminated or whose overdraft checking plan's credit limit is reduced should receive a notice of adverse action within 30 days of such action (12 C.F.R. §§ 202.2(c)(1)(ii), 202.2(c)(1)(iii), and 202.9(a)(1)(iii)).

If the credit applied for is "business credit," which involves credit primarily for business or commercial (including agricultural) purposes (12 C.F.R. 202.2(g)), the rules governing notification of action taken differ. If the applicant had gross revenues of $1 million or less in its preceding fiscal year and the credit applied for is not trade credit, credit incident to a factoring agreement or similar credit, one set of notification rules apply; other types of business credit require a separate set of notification rules (23 C.F.R. § 202.9(a)(3)).

Creditors wishing to do so may treat all applicants in the same way for notification purposes as they treat consumer purpose applicants.

## *Signature Requirements for Credit-Extension Documents*

If a creditor approves an application for credit or the applicant accepts a counteroffer, the next step in a normal credit transaction is to execute the various documents reflecting the terms of agreement. At this point, ECOA and state laws intertwine to produce complicated results concerning whose signature is required on various documents, including promissory notes, security agreements, or mortgages. Applicants for credit include those actually signing and submitting applications, as well as those who will or may be contractually liable on the extension of credit such as guarantors, sureties, endorsers, and similar parties (12 C.F.R. § 202.2(e)).

A creditor cannot require nonapplicants to sign any document unless their signatures are needed to ensure the creditor's access to real or personal property on which the credit extension depends. Furthermore, state law decides whose signature is needed on which credit-extension document. If an applicant offers property in which a nonapplicant has an interest, either as collateral for a secured loan or as proof of creditworthiness for an unsecured loan, a creditor may require the nonapplicant's signature on whatever documents will assure the creditor's access to that property upon an applicant's default.

State law also determines the type of document the nonapplicant is required to sign. In states recognizing tenancy in common, for example, a nonapplicant joint owner must sign a mortgage if the credit is to be secured by the tenancy-in-common property. However, the creditor cannot require the nonapplicant to sign a promissory note unless the mortgage will be invalid if the nonapplicant is not personally liable for the credit.

The fact that the individual having an interest in the property used by the applicant as collateral or proof of creditworthiness is the applicant's spouse makes no difference in the required signatures, unless state law recognizes a difference. Such a difference would occur in states that recognize dower rights. Creditors in these states must consider the marital status of male applicants when requiring signatures. A single male applicant who offers as collateral real property he alone owns is not required to have any other party sign the credit-extension documents. But a married male applicant in these states is required to obtain his spouse's signature on at least a mortgage to assure the creditor a valid lien.

A common practice among creditors of closed corporations is to require the personal guarantees of shareholders for corporate debt. Before ECOA, many creditors required not only shareholders to sign personal guarantees but also their nonshareholder spouses. ECOA prohibits this practice because, without being justified by state law, it treats shareholders differently based on their marital status.

State laws that are consistent with ECOA and not otherwise exempt from preemption will be preempted unless they extend more protection to the applicant. Through its ability to issue interpretations of ECOA, the Federal Reserve Board is authorized to determine whether ECOA preempts a state law.

## Monitoring Information

ECOA requires creditors to gather and retain certain monitoring information to evidence their compliance with the law (12 C.F.R. § 202.13). Creditors receiving applications to finance the purchase of residential real estate (12 C.F.R. § 202.13(a)) to be secured by a lien on the property are required to ask applicants certain questions, including their race, national origin, sex, marital status, and age. Creditors must use applicants' responses only for monitoring, not for credit evaluation.

The creditor may ignore the monitoring requirements of Regulation B if it is subject to substitute monitoring requirements issued by its regulatory agency. Both the Comptroller of the Currency and the Federal Deposit Insurance Corporation have issued such substitute requirements (12 C.F.R. §§ 27 and 338).

## Special Purpose Credit Programs

"Special purpose credit programs" for economically disadvantaged classes of people, authorized by federal or state law or offered by nonprofit organizations or profit organizations meeting specific criteria, may limit their credit extensions to a particular class of people, sharing one or more of the characteristics that are the basis upon which credit cannot otherwise be denied (12 C.F.R. § 202.8).

EXAMPLE ■ St. Francis Federal Credit Union will extend credit only to its members, who must belong to St. Francis Catholic Church.

Notwithstanding that the credit union will only lend to Catholics, it is not violating ECOA since it is a nonprofit organization offering credit for its members.

**Enforcement**

ECOA violations subject creditors to both regulatory and civil enforcement action. Twelve federal agencies enforce ECOA, including the Comptroller of the Currency, the Federal Reserve Board, the Federal Deposit Insurance Corporation, the Office of Thrift Supervision, and the National Credit Union Administration. To carry out ECOA enforcement, these agencies conduct compliance exams of the various financial institutions within their jurisdictions. If an agency responsible for ECOA compliance cannot ensure compliance from a creditor within its jurisdiction, it may refer the errant creditor's violations to the Attorney General of the United States to institute civil litigation (12 C.F.R. § 202.14(b)).

Civil remedies are also available to individuals harmed by ECOA violations (15 U.S.C. § 1691e). Unlike the Truth in Lending provisions for minimum damages in findings of civil liability, ECOA provides for damages only if plaintiffs can demonstrate actual damages or such grievous conduct by a creditor that punitive damages are justified. Creditors found to have violated ECOA are liable to plaintiffs for actual damages and/or up to $10,000 in punitive damages.

ECOA violations also expose creditors to class actions that, if successful, can result in damages of up to one percent of a creditor's net worth or $500,000, whichever is less. In determining the amount of punitive damages in a class action, the court must look to such mitigating factors as

■ the amount of actual damage sustained by the plaintiff

■ the frequency and persistence of the violations

■ the creditor's resources

- the number of people harmed
- the extent to which the violation was intentional (15 U.S.C. § 1691e(b))

Injunctive relief is another remedy ECOA provides to those seeking to stop an act or practice violating Regulation B (15 U.S.C. § 1691e(c)). Successful private litigants are entitled under ECOA not only to damages and/or injunctive relief but also to their actual costs and reasonable attorneys' fees (15 U.S.C. § 1691e(d)).

Creditors have several defenses to ECOA suits. As with the Truth in Lending Act, creditors relying in good faith on any "official rule, regulation, or interpretation" of the Federal Reserve Board as justification for an action or omission alleged to violate ECOA will not be liable if a court finds that the act or omission did violate ECOA (15 U.S.C. § 1691e(e)).

If a violation of ECOA provisions on notification (12 C.F.R. § 202.9), furnishing of credit information (12 C.F.R. § 202.10), or record retention (12 C.F.R. § 202.12) is unintentional and due to "inadvertent error," a creditor can also escape liability. Inadvertent error does not mean a "good faith attempt to comply with the law" but is narrowly defined as an unintentional "mechanical, electronic, or clerical error" that occurred despite the use of procedures to avoid such errors (12 C.F.R. § 202.2(s)). To assert this defense successfully, the creditor must also prove that it corrected the error as soon as possible.

Normally, ECOA actions must be taken within two years from the violation. However, if during that two-year period a creditor's regulatory agency begins enforcement action or the U.S. Attorney General files suit, a private plaintiff shall have one year from the date when the regulatory enforcement action or civil litigation began to file suit (15 U.S.C. § 1691e).

## REAL ESTATE SETTLEMENT PROCEDURES ACT

The **Real Estate Settlement Procedures Act** of 1974 (12 U.S.C.

§ 2601 *et seq.*) has four specific aims:

- to provide more effective advance disclosures of settlement (closing) costs to home buyers and sellers
- to eliminate certain kickbacks and referral fees
- to limit escrow amounts for taxes and insurance
- to reform local land title recordkeeping

This section will focus on the first three aims of the act. Because of procedural difficulties with the original act, Congress passed the Real Estate Settlement Procedures Act Amendment of 1975, which became effective June 30, 1976. To implement the act's provisions, the secretary of the Department of Housing and Urban Development (HUD) promulgated **Regulation X** (24 C.F.R. § 3500).

**Scope**  RESPA (the act and Regulation X are collectively called RESPA) applies to all "federally related mortgage loans" (24 C.F.R. § 3500.5(a)). Federally related mortgage loans are those secured by first liens whose proceeds are used to finance the transfer of legal title to

- real estate that contains a one- to four-family home
- real estate that contains a mobile home
- real estate that will contain either a mobile home or a one- to four-family home
- a condominium or cooperative unit (24 C.F.R. § 3500.5(b))

The property must be located within a state, the District of Columbia, Puerto Rico, or a U.S. territory or possession.

The mortgage loan must originate with a lending institution that (1) has its deposits insured by an agency of the federal government, (2) is otherwise regulated by the federal government, (3) is a "creditor" as defined by the Truth in Lending Act (15 U.S.C. § 1602(f)), or (4) has some other connection with the federal government as specified by RESPA. Most U.S. bank deposits are insured by an agency of the federal government (the FDIC), are otherwise regulated by the federal government, and are "creditors" as defined by the Truth in Lending Act.

RESPA specifically exempts from its coverage certain other loans, including those for

- the purchase of 25 or more acres
- home improvement, refinancing, or where the proceeds are not used to finance the purchase or transfer of legal title to the property
- assumptions, novations, transfers, or sales subject to a preexisting loan
- construction loans not to be converted to permanent financing
- the purchase of property for resale (24 C.F.R. § 3500.5(d))

The definition of federally related mortgage loans excludes from RESPA's scope such transactions as loans for home improvements, the purchase of vacant property with no intent to build, and the execution of land sales or installment land contracts. However, because RESPA is not limited to protecting consumers, the definition would include federally related mortgage loans for both consumer and business purposes. Thus, a loan for transferring legal title to a four-unit apartment building comes within RESPA.

**Disclosures**  If a transaction comes within RESPA, lenders must meet requirements regarding disclosures in advance of settlement. The first disclosure is the *Special Information Booklet,* which lenders must provide to any person or entity submitting a written application for a federally related mortgage loan (12 C.F.R. § 3500.5(a)). Within three business days of receiving an application, the lender must give the booklet to the applicant. The booklet describes what normally occurs when a buyer of residential real estate enters into a purchase agreement, obtains financing, and completes settlement. The booklet also contains sample forms whose use at settlement is mandated by RESPA.

Within the same three-day period for delivering the *Special Information Booklet,* the lender must also deliver to an applicant a disclosure form entitled, "Good Faith Estimate of Settlement Services" (24 C.F.R. § 3500.7). This disclosure estimates certain settlement charges to the applicant, including loan fees, appraisal fees, credit reports, assumption fees, mortgage insurance premiums, title charges, recording fees, and certain other charges.

The disclosures within the *Special Information Booklet* and the "Good

Faith Estimates of Settlement Services" are those made in advance of settlement, with the intent to encourage applicants to compare various lenders' settlement costs. Except in very limited situations, the third disclosure required by RESPA is the "Uniform Settlement Statement," which the lender must provide to both the borrower (that is, purchaser) and the seller of the subject property (24 C.F.R. § 3500.8). This disclosure reflects the actual, not estimated, settlement costs for both the purchaser and seller. The "Uniform Settlement Statement" lists all costs known to the lender or other party conducting the settlement and must be available for inspection by the borrower one business day before settlement.

At settlement, the disclosure of all costs must be completed and copies delivered to the buyer and seller or their agents, unless the buyer executes a written waiver. In that case, the lender must deliver the disclosure to the parties as soon thereafter as possible. If the lender or other party conducting the settlement does not require the parties to meet, or if the borrower or the borrower's agent is not at settlement, the lender need not give the disclosure at settlement but must deliver it to the buyer and seller as soon thereafter as possible (24 C.F.R. § 3500.10).

## *Kickbacks and Referral Fees*

RESPA very specifically prohibits the giving or receiving of fees, kickbacks, or anything of value for referral of any business incident to or part of a real estate settlement service involving a transaction coming within RESPA (12 U.S.C. § 2607(a)). The Federal Reserve Board has issued several examples of what constitutes a violation of this provision of RESPA.

1. *Facts.* $A$, a provider of settlement services maintains an abnormally large balance in a non-interest-bearing account with $B$, a mortgage lender, pursuant to an understanding that $B$ will refer borrowers of federally related mortgage loans to $A$ for the purchase of settlement services in connection with the settlement of such loans.

*Comments.* Allowing $B$ to use the deposited funds at no interest appears to be a thing of value given by $A$ to $B$ pursuant to an agreement or understanding that business incident to a real estate settlement shall be referred to $A$ in violation of section 8 of RESPA. The maintenance of any accounts reasonably needed by $A$ in the normal course of its business would not be a violation of section 8.

2. *Facts.* B, a lender of federally related mortgage loans, pays A, a real estate agent, a fee of $25 per transaction purportedly for services performed such as arranging for B's appraiser to visit the property. The purported services for which the fee is paid are services that real estate agents frequently perform as part of their services and the fee is really intended to enable B to compensate A for referring potential borrowers to B.

*Comments.* Both A and B are in violation of section 8 of RESPA, since the fee is being paid in compensation for the referral of business rather than for legitimate services actually rendered by B on behalf of A.

7. *Facts.* A, a "mortgage originator" or "mortgage broker," receives loan applications and refers borrowers to lenders for a fee.

*Comments.* If A performs services such as obtaining credit and appraisal information or preparing an application for mortgage insurance or guarantee which are of value to the lender paying the fee, without reference to the referral value of such services, and the fees paid bear a reasonable relationship to the value of such services, the payment of such a fee would not be in violation of section 8 of RESPA (24 C.F.R., appendix B).

## Escrow Limitations

Escrow limitations under RESPA apply not only to settlement but to postsettlement payments. The funds for taxes, insurance premiums, and other charges relating to the property, which are collected at settlement, cannot exceed a certain amount. That amount is what is needed to bring such charges current to the date of the first full loan payment, plus $1/6$ of the amount of taxes, insurance premiums, and other charges to be paid during the 12 months following settlement. After settlement, escrow payments made within the loan's monthly payment also cannot exceed a certain amount. That amount is equal to $1/12$ of the anticipated total taxes, insurance premiums, and other charges coming due within the upcoming year, plus an amount needed to maintain an additional balance not exceeding $1/6$ of the anticipated total of such taxes, insurance, and other charges (12 U.S.C. § 2609).

## Enforcement

The federal regulators with jurisdiction over lenders have generally assumed the responsibility of enforcing RESPA's disclosure requirements. Such regulators as the Comptroller of the Currency, the Federal Deposit Insurance Corporation, the Federal Reserve Board, and the

Office of Thrift Supervision examine financial institutions within their jurisdictions for compliance with RESPA. HUD also processes complaints about alleged RESPA violations. However, RESPA provides no specific regulatory or civil penalties for violations of any of its disclosure or escrow requirements. However, violations of 12 U.S.C. § 2607, for kickbacks and unearned fees, can lead to fines of not more than $10,000 or imprisonment of not more than one year, or both (12 U.S.C. § 2607(d)(1)).

## FAIR CREDIT REPORTING ACT

The **Fair Credit Reporting Act (FCRA)** (15 U.S.C. § 1681) was included as Title VI of the Federal Consumer Protection Act to ensure consumers that records of their credit transactions are both accurate and used only for certain purposes. FCRA has no extensive implementing regulation. The Federal Trade Commission has issued both official interpretations and informal staff opinions that provide guidelines for compliance with FCRA requirements.

**Scope**  FCRA regulates the content, issuance, purpose, and use of "consumer reports." Consumer reports include information that "consumer-reporting agencies" communicate by written, oral, or other methods regarding a consumer's creditworthiness, credit standing, credit capacity, character, general reputation, personal characteristics, or mode of living. This information can be supplied only for permissible purposes that include

- determining a consumer's eligibility for credit or insurance used primarily for personal, family, or household purposes

- determining a consumer's eligibility for employment

- purposes outlined by court order

- purposes to which a consumer agrees in writing

- determining a consumer's eligibility for a license or other benefit granted by a government unit which is required by law to consider an applicant's financial status or responsibility

■ determining a legitimate business need for information in connection with a business transaction involving a consumer (15 U.S.C. §§ 1681a and 1681b)

Besides supplying information for these permissible purposes, consumer-reporting agencies may furnish to government agencies information about a consumer's name, address, former addresses, places of employment, or former places of employment, without the need for the government agency to reveal how the information will be used (15 U.S.C. § 1681f).

**Exempt Reports**

If a report is not the product of a consumer-reporting agency or is not used for one of the purposes listed in the previous section, it is not a "consumer report" and does not come under FCRA. Financial institutions and others who relay their own credit experience with a consumer to third parties are not consumer-reporting agencies and need not comply with FCRA. In addition, commercial credit or insurance transactions are excluded from FCRA requirements.

---

EXAMPLE ■ Drummond National Bank, which is not a consumer-reporting agency, receives an application for a consumer loan from Homer Peabody. The bank contacts Third State Bank and requests any information it has on Peabody. Third State Bank relates its own credit history with Peabody, as well as the content of a credit report in its file from Acme Credit Bureau.

By giving Drummond National Bank information on Peabody contained within the credit report, Third State Bank violated FCRA. Only a consumer-reporting agency can provide such third-party information. However, the information Third State Bank gave Drummond National Bank about its own experience with Peabody did not violate the act.

---

FCRA regulates consumer-reporting agencies' preparation and dissemination of consumer reports, as well as their procedures to assure the accuracy of those reports. The act does not regulate entry into the business of consumer reporting. If addressed at all, the licensing of individuals or entities that wish to start consumer-reporting agencies is left to state law.

**Content of Consumer Reports**

Whether the consumer-reporting agency preparing the report or the report's user would consider the following information relevant, consumer reports cannot relay any of this information except under limited circumstances (15 U.S.C. § 1681c):

- bankruptcies adjudicated (date the order for relief was entered) more than 10 years before the date of the report (Section 313 of the Bankruptcy Reform Act amended FCRA by decreasing the period for reporting bankruptcies from 14 to 10 years.)

- suits and judgments that antedate the report by 7 years or until the applicable statute of limitations has run, whichever period is greater
- tax liens paid more than 7 years before the report
- bad debts more than 7 years old
- records of criminal activities more than 7 years old
- any other adverse information more than 7 years old

These limitations on the content of consumer reports do not apply when the report will be used for a credit transaction involving a principal amount of $50,000 or more or for a position of employment paying $20,000 or more annually.

**Furnishing Consumer Reports**

Consumer-reporting agencies must maintain reasonable procedures to avoid furnishing consumer reports except for the specific purposes previously outlined (15 U.S.C. § 1681e(a)). These procedures must include requirements that users of the reports identify themselves and certify the purposes for which the reports will be used and that they will be used for no other purposes. However, consumer-reporting agencies may respond to a government agency's request for a consumer's name, address, former addresses, employment, and former employment without certification of use (15 U.S.C. § 1681f).

Consumer reports can be prepared without the consent of consumers who are the subject of such reports (15 U.S.C. § 1681b) and, except for "investigative consumer reports" for employment purposes, reports can be furnished to users without notifying consumers. Investigative consumer reports are products of personal interviews with individuals who know of the consumer's character, general reputation, personal characteristics, or mode of living (15 U.S.C. § 1681a(e)).

Because of their extremely subjective and personal nature, investigative consumer reports cannot be ordered (except for purposes of employment for which the consumer has not specifically applied) unless certain disclosures are made to the consumer. The disclosures must be in writing, must be delivered within three days after the report is requested, and must inform the consumer of the right to make a written request for a complete and accurate disclosure of the nature and scope of the requested investigation. If the consumer makes a written request for disclosure, it must be furnished no later than five days after the receipt or submission of request, whichever is later (15 U.S.C. § 1681d). If the person requesting an investigative consumer report satisfies the disclosure requirements, the report can be prepared and furnished, whether or not the consumer consents.

## Consumers' Rights to Review Reports

When consumers so request, consumer-reporting agencies must disclose all information (except medical information) in their files on the consumer at the time of the request, the sources of the information, and the identity of the recipients of any consumer reports furnished within the previous six months (unless the report was requested for employment purposes, in which case the period is two years).

For making these disclosures, consumer-reporting agencies may impose reasonable charges on consumers, as long as the consumers are informed of the charges before disclosure. If a consumer's request for disclosure is made within 30 days after the consumer has been notified that, based on a consumer report, (a) credit, insurance, or employment has been denied the consumer or (b) the consumer's credit rating is in jeopardy, then a consumer-reporting agency may not charge for disclosures (15 U.S.C. § 1681j).

## Disputing the Accuracy of Consumer Reports

FCRA specifically requires consumer-reporting agencies to "follow reasonable procedures to assure maximum possible accuracy of the information concerning the individual about whom the report relates" (15 U.S.C. § 1681e(b)). Furthermore, the act gives consumers the right to dispute the completeness and accuracy of consumer reports directly to the agency. Unless reasonable grounds exist for believing a consumer's dispute to be frivolous or irrelevant, the consumer-reporting agency must reinvestigate and record the current status of the disputed information. If the reinvestigation reveals the disputed information to be inaccurate or no longer verifiable, the consumer-reporting agency must delete that information from the consumer's file.

However, if after reinvestigation the consumer-reporting agency finds the disputed information accurate and verifiable and does not delete it from the consumer's file, the consumer may submit a brief statement describing the dispute for inclusion in the agency's file. If the consumer-reporting agency helps prepare the statement, it may require the consumer to limit the statement to 100 words or less. Once the statement is filed, the consumer-reporting agency must note its existence in subsequent consumer reports, unless the agency reasonably believes the statement to be frivolous or irrelevant.

Whenever a consumer-reporting agency deletes inaccurate or unverifiable information or receives a consumer's statement disputing information in the consumer's file, the agency must clearly and conspicuously disclose to the consumer that, if the consumer requests, the agency will inform those who have received consumer reports (within two years for employment purposes and within six months for all other purposes) that the information has been deleted or is disputed (15 U.S.C. § 1681i). If the consumer than requests that such a notification be sent to previous recipients of credit reports, the consumer-reporting agency can impose a reasonable charge on the consumer for the notification (15 U.S.C. § 1681j).

---

**EXAMPLE** ■ Jeff Helper applies for a loan at Upstate National Bank. The bank rejects his application because of a consumer credit report rating based on several defaulted loans at financial institutions with which Helper has never done business. Helper contacts the consumer-reporting agency that furnished the report and disputes the information in it. In this situation, the consumer-reporting agency must reinvestigate its report and, if the information is inaccurate, it must be deleted. If Helper so requests, the consumer-reporting agency must then inform Upstate National Bank of the deletion.

**Users of Consumer Reports**

The greatest burdens imposed by FCRA fall upon consumer-reporting agencies, but users of consumer reports are also subject to specific sections of the act (15 U.S.C. §1681m).

Unless an investigative consumer report is involved, a consumer need not be notified when a report is prepared or distributed regarding the consumer. However, if a creditor denies or increases the terms for credit or insurance for personal, family, or household purposes, or an employer denies employment, based on a consumer report, the user must notify the consumer of the adverse action and must disclose to the consumer the name and address of the consumer-reporting agency that made the report.

**Enforcement**

Federal regulatory agencies enforce FCRA (15 U.S.C. § 1681s). These agencies include all those that regulate financial institutions.

Consumer-reporting agencies and others who violate FCRA may also come within the Federal Trade Commission's enforcement authority if the agencies commit an unfair or deceptive act or practice that violates the Federal Trade Commission Act. As a result, these agencies may suffer the penalties prescribed for such a violation (15 U.S.C. § 1681s(a)).

Further, consumer-reporting agencies or users of consumer reports, such as banks, that willfully fail to comply with any FCRA requirement are liable for actual damages sustained by a consumer, plus any punitive damages, court costs, and reasonable attorneys' fees (15 U.S.C. § 1681n). If a consumer-reporting agency's or user's FCRA violation is due to negligence rather than willfulness, a court may find the defendant liable for actual damages, costs, and attorneys' fees but not for punitive damages (15 U.S.C. § 1681o).

When an aggrieved consumer initiates a civil action based on a violation of either the disclosure of investigative consumer reports or user requirements of FCRA, no liability exists if the defendant can show that, at the time of the alleged violation, it maintained reasonable procedures to ensure compliance with those FCRA provisions (15

U.S.C. §§ 1681d and 1681m). Defendants may also allege that violations were not due to willfulness or negligence to escape liability.

Any person who knowingly and willfully obtains information under false pretenses about a consumer from a consumer-reporting agency faces criminal penalties of up to $5,000 and/or imprisonment for up to one year. The same penalties exist for any officer or employee of a consumer-reporting agency who knowingly and willfully provides information from the agency's file about an individual to a person not authorized to receive that information (15 U.S.C. §§ 1681q and 1681r).

## FAIR DEBT COLLECTION PRACTICES ACT

Ever-increasing judicial and legislative attention has focused on the abusive practices of creditors and those representing creditors in the collection of overdue debt. On the federal level, consumers' complaints about abusive debt collection methods resulted in the **Fair Debt Collection Practices Act** (15 U.S.C. § 1692). While the act did not authorize any agency to promulgate a broad implementing regulation like the Truth in Lending Act's Regulation Z, it did give the Federal Trade Commission authority to issue a staff commentary (15 U.S.C. §§ 1692k(e) and 1692l(d)).

The Fair Debt Collection Practices Act only applies to "debt collectors" who attempt to or do collect a consumer's actual or alleged debts arising out of transactions conducted primarily for personal, family, or household purposes (15 U.S.C. §§ 1692a(5) and 1692a(6)). Thus, the act excludes from its scope the collection of debt for commercial, business, or agricultural purposes.

Under this act, debt collectors are those who regularly collect or attempt to collect debts owed or due—or asserted to be owed or due—someone other than the debt collector. Creditors collecting their own debts come under this definition only if in their collection efforts they use any name other than their own, which would give a debtor the impression that a third party was attempting to collect the debt.

**EXAMPLE** ■ Almont State Bank instructed its debt collectors (who are employees of the bank), to identify themselves as employees of "Debt Collectors, Inc.," when calling bank customers about overdue debts. In this situation, Almont State Bank brought itself within the Fair Debt Collection Practices Act when its employees spoke to debtors using a name other than that of the bank.

Because those collecting debts owed to themselves do not come within the act's scope, the act excludes numerous entities including banks, savings and loan associations, credit unions, retailers, and charge card associations, unless another name is used. However, if a collector and the debt it is pursuing come within the Fair Debt Collection Practices Act, it must comply with numerous provisions in the act, including those governing communications with debtors and third parties; harassment, abuse, false or misleading representations, and unfair practices; validation of debts; legal actions by debt collectors; and forms.

While most banks do not come within the provisions of the Fair Debt Collection Practices Act, its "laundry list" of prohibited debt collection activities is nonetheless a good guideline for banks in their own debt collection. Included within the acts or practices listed as constituting harassment, abuse, or misrepresentation are the following (15 U.S.C. §§ 1692d, 1692e, and 1692f):

■ the use, or threatened use, of violence or other criminal means to injure the physical person, reputation, or property of any person

■ the use of obscene language in written or oral communication to the debtor

■ the publication of a list of consumers who allegedly refuse to pay debts, except publication to a consumer-reporting agency or to other persons or entities meeting certain specific requirements of the Fair Credit Reporting Act

■ advertising for sale any debt to coerce its repayment

- causing a telephone to ring or engaging any person in telephone conversation repeatedly or continuously with the intent to annoy, abuse, or harass any person at the number called

- except in pursuit of location information, the placement of telephone calls without meaningful disclosure of the caller's identity

- the false representation or implication that the debt collector is an attorney or that any communication is from an attorney

- the representation or implication that nonpayment of any debt will result in the arrest or imprisonment of any person or the seizure, garnishment, attachment, or sale of any property or wages of any person, unless such action is lawful and the debt collector or creditor intends to take such action

- the use or distribution of any written communication that simulates or is falsely represented to be a document authorized, issued, or approved by any court, official, or agency of the United States or any state, or that creates a false impression as to its source, authorization, or approval

- the use of the name of any business, company, or organization other than the true name of the debt collector's business, company, or organization

- the collection of any amount (including any interest, fee, charge, or expense incidental to the principal obligation) unless such amount is expressly authorized by the agreement creating the debt or permitted by law

- a debt collector's solicitation of any postdated check or other payment instrument for the purpose of threatening or instituting criminal prosecution

- the taking of, or threat to take, any nonjudicial action to effect dispossession or disablement of property if (a) no present right to possession of the property claimed as collateral exists through an enforceable security interest; (b) no present intention to take possession of the property exists; or (c) the property is exempt by law from such dispossession or disablement

Unlike the federal Fair Debt Collection Practices Act, state debt collection acts may apply to banks and prohibit many of the acts or practices listed above.

**Enforcement**

Enforcement of the Fair Debt Collection Practices Act is accomplished through administrative, individual, and class civil actions. No criminal penalties are imposed for violating the act.

*Administrative Enforcement*

The Federal Trade Commission has primary responsibility for administrative enforcement of the act. While other government agencies, such as those regulating financial institutions, have authority to enforce the act, most creditors within those agencies' jurisdictions do not regularly collect debts owed parties other than themselves and thus are exempt from the act.

Debt collectors violating provisions of the Fair Debt Collection Practices Act are liable for monetary damages equaling the sum of any actual damages caused by their violations, plus any additional damages up to $1,000 allowed by a court. Debt collectors subjected to successful class actions are liable for the total of all actual damages suffered by each member of the class, plus a class award not to exceed the lesser of $500,000 or one percent of the debt collector's net worth. In addition to actual and statutory damages, debt collectors found liable of violating the act must pay the court costs and attorneys' fees of successful plaintiffs (15 U.S.C. § 1692k).

**Common-Law Remedies**

In addition to the federal and state fair debt collection practices acts, the common law also provides remedies for those damaged by abusive collection practices. Courts have found creditors or their agents liable for damages to debtors for the following reasons:

- invasion of privacy (*Gouldman-Taber Pontiac, Inc. v. Zerbst,* 213 Ga. 682, 100 S.E.2d 881 (1957))

- wounded feelings and marital difficulties (*Freeman v. Busch Jewelry Co.,* 98 F. Supp. 963 (N.D. Georgia 1951))

- intentional infliction of emotional distress (*Long v. Beneficial Finance Co. of N.W., Inc.,* 39 App. Div.2d 11, 330 N.Y.S.2d 664 (1972); "Recovery for Debtor's Emotional Distress," 87 A.L.R.3d 201)

- abuse of process by using the criminal process to collect a debt ("Use of Criminal Process to Collect Debt as Abuse of Process," 27 A.L.R.3d 1202)

## CREDIT PRACTICES RULE

Unlike the various acts discussed so far, the **Credit Practices Rule** is not a statute. Further, this rule was promulgated in two forms: the Federal Trade Commission's rule, which became effective on March 1, 1985, and the Federal Reserve Board's rule, Regulation AA, which became effective January 1, 1986.

The Federal Trade Commission (FTC) adopted its rule pursuant to its authority under the Federal Trade Commission Act to issue rules that define and prevent "unfair or deceptive acts or practices" in or affecting the extensions of credit to consumers.

Because the FTC has no direct authority over banks, they need not comply with its rules. However, the Federal Trade Commission Act provides that, whenever the FTC promulgates a rule prohibiting certain practices as unfair or deceptive, the Board of Governors of the Federal Reserve System must adopt a substantially similar rule. The only exception to this procedure is if the board finds that the prohibited acts or practices, when engaged in by banks, are not unfair or deceptive or that the board's adoption of the rule would seriously conflict with its essential monetary policies.

Since both the FTC's rule (16 C.F.R. § 444) and the board's rule (12 C.F.R. § 227) are nearly the same, the following discussion will not distinguish between them unless necessary.

**Scope**  The Credit Practice Rule applies only to consumers seeking or acquiring goods, services, or money for personal, family, or household use other than for the purchase of real property.

The rule's thrust is threefold: (1) it prohibits the existence or enforcement of certain clauses in loan documents between creditors and consumers; (2) it provides a prescribed notice to cosigners; and (3) it prohibits the pyramiding of late charges.

*Prohibited Provisions*     The rule prohibits the inclusion of the following provisions in a consumer's credit obligation:

- a consumer's confession of judgment or other type of waiver of the right to notice and the opportunity to be heard if the creditor files a suit over the obligation

- assignment of the consumer's wages, unless the consumer can revoke the assignment, it is pursuant to a payroll deduction plan, or it applies only to wages already earned at the time of the assignment

- security in household goods other than that given in connection with the purchase of the goods

---

EXAMPLE
- Sue Conroy applies for a $2,000 loan to purchase new living room furniture. Citizens State Bank agrees to make the loan if Conroy will secure it with the furniture she wants to purchase and her existing furniture and appliances.

   The bank's request for a security interest in the furniture to be purchased is acceptable, but a security interest in the rest of the proposed collateral would violate Regulation AA.

---

*Cosigners*     To ensure that cosigners understand their obligations, a creditor must inform a cosigner of the liability involved before any obligation is incurred. If the creditor is within the FTC's jurisdiction, the notice must be separate from the documents evidencing the debt. If the creditor is a bank, the notice may be either separate from or part of the document evidencing the debt. The text of the notice for banks is as follows:

Notice to Cosigner

You are being asked to guarantee this debt. Think carefully before you do. If the borrower doesn't pay the debt, you will have to. Be sure you can afford to pay if you have to, and that you want to accept this responsibility.

   You may have to pay up to the full amount of the debt if the borrower does not pay. You may also have to pay late fees or collection costs, which increases this amount.

The bank can collect this debt from you without first trying to collect from the borrower. The bank can use the same collection methods against you that can be used against the borrower, such as suing you, garnishing your wages, etc. If this debt is ever in default, that fact may become a part of *your* credit record.

This notice is not the contract that makes you liable for the debt.

For purposes of the rule, a **cosigner** is defined as

a natural person who assumes liability for the obligation of a consumer without receiving goods, services, or money in return for the obligation, or, in the case of an open-end credit obligation, without receiving the contractual right to obtain extensions of credit under the account . . . [and] includes any person whose signature is requested as a condition to granting credit to a consumer, or as a condition for forbearance on collection of a consumer's obligation that is in default. The term does not include a spouse whose signature is required on a credit obligation to perfect a security interest pursuant to state law (12 C.F.R. § 227.12).

If a credit document labels an individual cosigner as something other than "cosigner," that fact is irrelevant as long as the above definition applies.

---

**EXAMPLE** ■ Mike Stack applies at First National for a loan to buy a car. The bank denies his application but indicates that it will approve the application if Stack can find an acceptable cosigner. Stack asks his father-in-law, Larry Hanson, to cosign. The note Hanson signs indicates he is a guarantor.

Before Hanson signs the debt instrument, First National must provide him with the "Notice to Cosigner" since he is not receiving anything of value for his guarantee and the bank requested a cosigner. If Stack had offered Hanson as a cosigner when he made the loan application, or if Hanson were receiving any part of the loan proceeds, the bank would not have to provide the notice.

---

*Unfair Late Charges*   The rule prohibits a creditor coming within its scope from charging or collecting any late charge from a borrower when the only reason for the charge is a previous unpaid late charge.

---

EXAMPLE ■ Kathleen Lieder borrows money from Hyattville State Bank pursuant to an installment loan note that requires monthly payments. The note states that if any payment is made after its due date, Lieder will be charged a $5 late fee. Lieder makes a payment, due February 15, on February 20, and the bank adds a $5 late fee to the amount due. On March 15, Lieder makes her next payment but does not pay the $5 late charge then outstanding. The bank adds another $5 late fee to her debt. This action would violate the rule, even if the bank's loan documents permit such a pyramiding of late charges.

---

## RIGHT TO FINANCIAL PRIVACY ACT

While many bank customers and bankers believe that bank records are a customer's private records which banks can reveal to third parties only with the customer's consent, this is not wholly true. In 1976, the Supreme Court held in *United States v. Miller* (425 U.S. 435 (1976)) that individual customers of financial institutions had no legitimate expectation of privacy for the records of their financial transactions kept by such institutions. Under this decision, government agencies could demand, and financial institutions could reveal, the financial records of individuals without their knowledge or right to question it. In response to the Miller decision and a national concern for financial privacy, Congress passed the **Right to Financial Privacy Act** (12 U.S.C. § 3401).

**Scope**   While the Right to Financial Privacy Act may have responded to concern about the government's intrusion into financial records, it actually does little to hinder such intrusions. The act does not repeal the Miller decision. This decision holds that records at a financial institution are not the private property of its customers which deserve Fourth Amendment protection but rather belong to the institution and may be reviewed by government agencies. Instead, the act uses concepts of disclosure requiring that customers be informed before the government inspects their records at financial institutions.

The act applies only to records of individuals or partnerships composed of five or fewer individuals, collectively referred to as customer(s) (12 U.S.C. § 3401(4)(5)). The act excludes from its scope records of such entities as corporations, trusts, and partnerships of six or more individuals. The act also protects records only at financial institutions, which include banks, thrifts, credit unions, consumer finance institutions, and credit card issuers (12 U.S.C. § 3401(1)).

In addition, the act applies only to requests from federal government agencies or departments (12 U.S.C. § 3401(3)). State and local government agencies do not come under the act and may request customers' financial records within the limits of applicable state laws.

The act's scope is limited to those situations in which a federal government authority desires access to a customer's records for a lawful investigation into possible violation of a criminal or civil law, a regulation, a rule, or an order (12 U.S.C. §§ 3401(3) and 3402).

## Conditions for Gaining Access to Records

If a federal government authority desires access to records under the Right to Financial Privacy Act, it must satisfy one of the following conditions before a financial institution can permit access (12 U.S.C. § 3402):

- The customer has authorized the access requested by the government authority.

- The government authority has obtained an administrative summons or subpoena requiring the financial institution to provide access.

- The government authority has obtained a search warrant.

- A judicial subpoena orders the access desired by the government authority.

- Where no administrative summons or subpoena authority reasonably appears to be available, a government authority has made a formal written request to the customer.

In most situations in which a federal government authority seeks access to a customer's financial records, the authority must provide the customer with a notice before gaining access. Upon application by a government authority, a federal district court may grant a delay of up to 90 days in any notice requirement. To grant a delay, however, the court must find that meeting the act's normal notice requirements will result in one of the following (12 U.S.C. § 3409(a)):

- danger to the life or physical safety of any person
- flight from prosecution
- destruction of or tampering with evidence
- intimidation of potential witnesses
- otherwise threaten serious jeopardy to an investigation or official proceeding, or undue delay to a trial or ongoing official proceeding, to an extent as great as that represented by the preceding reasons for delay of notice

If a government authority seeking records determines that it needs them at once because of imminent danger of physical injury to any person, serious property damage, or flight to avoid prosecution, it may require a financial institution to provide the records without a court order. Within five days of obtaining access to the desired records, however, the government authority must file with the appropriate court a signed, sworn statement describing the grounds for the emergency access. The authority must also thereafter comply with the customer notice requirement (12 U.S.C. § 3414(b)). The act's notice requirements may be ignored by any government authority authorized to conduct foreign intelligence activities and by the Secret Service for the purpose of conducting its protective functions (12 U.S.C. § 3414(a)).

## IRS Summons

If the Internal Revenue Service (IRS) seeks bank records according to procedures outlined in the Internal Revenue Code, it is exempt from the requirements of the Right to Financial Privacy Act (12 U.S.C. § 3413(c)).

Under section 7602 of the IRS Code, the IRS has the power to issue a summons compelling the production of records to anyone, including financial institutions. The act further provides that, once the IRS has served the summons on the record holder or the taxpayer, it must wait for a prescribed period of days before it demands the records from that institution or person. After that period expires and the agency receives no objection from the customer whose records are sought, a bank or other custodian of records may turn the records over to the IRS.

A taxpayer wishing to object to an IRS summons must send a notice of objection to the bank or other party served with the summons. Once the record holder receives the notice of objection to the summons, it must not release the records to the IRS until the agency produces a court order or obtains the taxpayer's written consent.

*Additional Exemptions*

In addition to the exemption for an IRS summons, the act provides exemptions from its certification procedures for requests for customer records by the various federal agencies that regulate banks when the request is made pursuant to their powers of examination, or when insiders are suspected of crimes. Further, the act will not apply if records are sought in accordance with any federal statute or rule (12 U.S.C. § 3413).

**Responsibilities of Financial Institutions**

Besides requiring government authorities to provide certificates of compliance before permitting them access to records protected by the Right to Financial Privacy Act, financial institutions have other responsibilities under the act. A financial institution must record, and the customer is entitled to inspect, information, including the name of each government authority to which the customer's records were disclosed and the date of disclosure (12 U.S.C. §§ 3404(c) and 3413(h)(6)).

The act places few restrictions on financial institutions that wish to notify customers of pending government inquiries into their financial records. The government authority may obtain a court order preventing such notice to customers. However, a financial institution cannot notify customers that a government authority is seeking access to their records when that authority is the Secret Service or Federal Bureau of

Investigation and either is involved in foreign intelligence investigations (12 U.S.C. §§ 3409(b)(1) and 3414(a)(3)). Further, a customer cannot be notified regarding any grand jury subpoena served on the bank in connection with an investigation relating to a possible crime against the bank, other financial institution, or regulatory agency in which the customer is named.

Financial institutions may also seek reimbursement for any reasonably necessary costs directly incurred in responding to the government's requests for customers records, and the Federal Reserve Board has established the rates for such reimbursement (12 U.S.C. § 3415).

**Customers' Challenges of Provisions**

Requiring government authorities to notify customers of pending requests for access to their financial records gives the customers time to challenge such access in federal court (12 U.S.C. § 3410). A customer receiving such a notice may file in federal court a motion that contains an affidavit asserting the reasons the customer believes the records sought are irrelevant to the inquiry described in the notice. The affidavit can also assert that the government authority has not substantially complied with the act. Once a customer does this, the court will order the government authority to respond in a sworn statement. The court may then decide the issue or may order further proceedings, which must be completed within seven days of the filing of the authority's response.

If the court decides that (a) the law enforcement inquiry is demonstrably legitimate, (b) the records sought are relevant to that inquiry, and (c) the government authority has substantially complied with the act's provisions, it will deny the customer's motion and permit the government access to the records.

**Enforcement**

Financial institutions must ensure that the government complies with the act since they will incur civil penalties if they wrongfully permit a government authority access to customers' records. Government authorities violating the act will also incur the same penalties. Those penalties include damages equal to the sum of all the following items (12 U.S.C. § 3417(a)):

- $100 statutory damages without regard to the value of the records involved

- any actual damages sustained by a customer as a result of the wrongful disclosure
- punitive damages if the violation was willful or intentional
- the attorney's fees and costs for the customer

In addition to monetary damages, a plaintiff can seek injunctive relief to force compliance with the act, and, if successful, can also recover attorney's fees and costs (12 U.S.C. § 3418).

## ELECTRONIC FUND TRANSFER ACT

In 1978, Congress passed the **Electronic Fund Transfer Act** (15 U.S.C. § 1693 *et seq.*) and the Federal Reserve Board issued **Regulation E** (12 C.F.R. § 205) to implement the act's provisions. (Hereafter the act and Regulation E are collectively called EFTA.) The Board has also issued an official staff commentary to Regulation E, further explaining the act and regulation.

**Scope** EFTA defines an **electronic fund transfer** as any of the following (15 U.S.C. § 1693a(6)):

The term "electronic fund transfer" means any transfer of funds, other than a transaction originated by check, draft, or similar paper instrument, which is initiated through an electronic terminal, telephonic instrument, or computer or magnetic tape so as to order, instruct, or authorize a financial institution to debit or credit an account. Such term includes, but is not limited to, point-of-sale transfers, automated teller machine transactions, direct deposits or withdrawals of funds, and transfers initiated by telephone. . . .

The act specifically eliminates the following items from its coverage (15 U.S.C. § 1693a(6)(A–E):

- any check guarantee or authorization service which does not directly result in a debit or credit to a consumer's account
- any transfer of funds, other than those processed by an automated clearing house, made by a financial institution on behalf of a consumer

by means of a service that transfers funds held at either Federal Reserve banks or other depository institutions and which is not designed primarily to transfer funds on behalf of a consumer

- any transaction, the primary purpose of which is the purchase or sale of securities or commodities through a broker-dealer registered with or regulated by the Securities and Exchange Commission

- any automatic transfer from a savings account to a demand deposit account pursuant to an agreement between a consumer and a financial institution for a purpose of covering an overdraft or maintaining an agreed upon minimum balance in the consumer's demand deposit account

- any transfer of funds which is initiated by a telephone conversation between a consumer and an officer or employee of a financial institution which is not pursuant to a prearranged plan and under which periodic or recurring transfers are not contemplated

All electronic fund transfers under EFTA must result in a debit or credit to an "account." An **account** is defined as a demand deposit (checking), savings, or other consumer asset account established primarily for personal, family, or household purposes (12 C.F.R. § 205.2(b)). Thus, the scope of EFTA is limited not only to particular types of electronic fund transfers but also to such transfers made by consumers—who are defined as "natural persons" (12 C.F.R. § 205.2(e))—for personal, family, or household purposes.

---

EXAMPLE ■ Widget, Inc., uses an automated teller machine to make an electronic transfer of funds. This transaction does not come under EFTA because it is made by a business.

---

Because of EFTA's limited scope, many electronically facilitated financial services presently lie outside federal legislation. State laws may govern such services but, since little uniformity exists among state electronic fund transfer acts, each must be consulted separately.

**Requirements**  Those offering electronic services coming under the act must comply with EFTA requirements which delineate the rights, liabilities, and responsibilities of consumers who participate in an electronic fund transfer system (15 U.S.C. § 1693).

*Issuance of Access Devices*  To complete most electronic fund transfers under EFTA, a consumer must use an "access device." This device is a card, code, or other means of access to a consumer's account used to initiate electronic fund transfers (12 C.F.R. § 205.2(a)(1)). EFTA limits issuance of access devices.

Access devices that consumers can use without further procedures are considered "validated" and may be issued only if one of the following three conditions is met (12 C.F.R. § 205.5(a)):

- if consumers have made an oral or written request or application for the device

- if issuance of the device renews or substitutes an already existing and accepted access device

- if the issuance renews or substitutes a device issued before February 8, 1979, which has yet to be "accepted," if prescribed written disclosures accompany the renewed or substituted device

*Disclosures*  Like the Truth in Lending Act and its implementing Regulation Z, EFTA emphasizes consumers' understanding their rights and obligations in any agreement coming under the act. Disclosures are required both when consumers enter an agreement and periodically thereafter. The timing of these disclosures is similar to that required in open-end credit arrangements under the Truth in Lending Act.

EFTA provides model disclosure forms that financial institutions may use in whole or in part (12 C.F.R. §§ 205, appendix A, and 205.7(a)). Use of the model forms will protect financial institutions from liability for violating certain provisions of the act (15 U.S.C. § 1693m(d)(2)).

The first disclosure required by EFTA is a written disclosure statement made when a consumer contracts for an electronic fund transfer service or before the first transfer occurs pursuant to such a contract. This disclosure statement must state certain terms and conditions of the contract, as well as the consumer's other rights and liabilities, as dictated by law. This initial disclosure statement should include all of the following (12 C.F.R. § 205.7):

- a summary of the consumer's liability for unauthorized electronic fund transfers

- the telephone number and address of the person or office to be notified when a consumer believes an unauthorized transfer has been or may be made

- the financial institution's business days

- the type of electronic fund transfers that the consumer may make and any limitations on the frequency and dollar amount of transfers

- any charges for transfers or the right to make transfers

- a summary of the consumer's right to receive documentation of electronic fund transfers

- a summary of the consumer's right to stop payment of a preauthorized transfer, and a description of the procedure to be followed to stop such payment

- a summary of the financial institution's liability to a consumer for failure to make or stop transfers

- the circumstances under which a financial institution will disclose information to third parties concerning the consumer's accounts

- a notice explaining EFTA's procedure for resolving errors

- language advising consumers of the advisability of promptly reporting the loss or theft of access devices or unauthorized transfers (This last disclosure is optional.)

After making the initial disclosure statement, financial institutions have an obligation to make various other disclosures, depending on the types of transfers they offer and the frequency with which consumers use them.

If a financial institution offers terminal-connected transfer services, such as automated teller machines or point-of-sale systems, it must disclose to the consumer at the terminal, at the time of the transfer, a summary of the consumer's transaction in the form of a written receipt (12 C.F.R. § 205.9(a)).

For any account to or from which a consumer can make an electronic fund transfer, a financial institution must mail or deliver a periodic disclosure that includes a description of the electronic fund transfers in the consumer's account for the period covered by the disclosure (12 C.F.R. § 205.9(b)). The institution must send periodic disclosures to consumers at least monthly unless no electronic fund transfers have occurred for the account, in which case the institution must make the periodic disclosures quarterly.

## *Preauthorized Credit Accounts*

As the definition of "electronic fund transfers" indicates, third parties' direct deposits into a consumer's account come within EFTA. These deposits are made pursuant to underlying agreements between such third parties and consumers. The best example of such preauthorized credit accounts is the federal government's direct deposit of Social Security payments into consumers' accounts.

### DISCLOSURES FOR PREAUTHORIZED TRANSFERS

If third parties may access a consumer's account only by preauthorized electronic fund transfers, a financial institution has several alternatives to providing the monthly periodic disclosure already described. First, when the account is a passbook, the financial institution need never provide the periodic statement if, to update the consumer's passbook whenever requested, the institution enters (or provides on a separate document) the amount and date of each transfer made after the passbook was last presented (12 C.F.R. § 205.9(c)). Second, if the financial institution does not use passbooks to document the account, it must provide a quarterly, rather than monthly, periodic disclosure statement, whether or not the account is active (12 C.F.R. § 205.9(d)).

Besides periodic disclosures that provide an account history for a particular period, financial institutions must disclose additional information about each preauthorized transfer close to when it occurs.

When the same payor makes a preauthorized transfer to a consumer's account at least once every 60 days, the financial institution must *either* notify the customer orally or in writing that (1) the transfer did occur, within 2 business days of the transfer, or (2) the transfer did not occur, within 2 business days of when the transfer should have occurred, *or* must put the burden on the customer by providing a readily available telephone number the customer can call to ascertain whether the transfer has occurred (12 C.F.R. § 205.10(a)). These disclosures are unnecessary if the payor making the preauthorized transfer notifies the consumer that the transfer has been initiated.

The initial disclosure statement should describe which method a financial institution has chosen to verify preauthorized credit transfers to an account (12 C.F.R. § 205.7(a)(6)). Furthermore, all preauthorized transfers to an account must be credited on the day they are received (12 C.F.R. § 205.10(a)(2)).

Preauthorized electronic transfers from customers' accounts can be made only if a customer has consented to the deductions in writing and if the payee or the financial institution maintaining the account has provided the customer with a copy of the authorization (12 C.F.R. § 205.10(b)).

Once a customer consents to a withdrawal of funds from an account and the amounts transferred do not vary from one transfer to the next, neither the payee nor the financial institution need make further disclosures to the customer, except for the periodic disclosure statement. However, if the amounts do vary from either the immediately preceding deduction or the amount the customer initially authorized, certain requirements must be met. The financial institution or the payee must mail or deliver to the customer a written notice of the amount and transfer date at least 10 days before the scheduled transfer.

The initial disclosure statement must inform customers of their right to receive this disclosure (12 C.F.R. § 205.7(a)(6)). Further, in the initial disclosure statement, the financial institution or payee may inform the customer that, instead of receiving notice each time a varying deduction occurs, the consumer can elect to receive notice only when a transfer falls outside a specific range of amounts, or alternatively only when the transfer differs from the immediately preceding transfer by more than an agreed amount (12 C.F.R. § 205.10(d)).

Checking account service charges, mortgage and other loan payments, savings-to-checking-account transfers, payroll deductions, negotiable order of withdrawal (NOW) or share draft account transfers to savings or share accounts, and transfers from checking accounts to

Christmas club accounts are probably the most common preauthorized transfers to and from customers' accounts. However, these transfers are exempt from the disclosure requirements just described and, in fact, are exempt from EFTA itself, pursuant to an intrainstitutional exemption (12 C.F.R. §§ 205.3(d)(1) and 205.3(d)(3)).

## Stop-Payment Procedures

A customer who wants to stop the payment of a preauthorized transfer from his or her account must follow stop-payment procedures similar to those provided by article 4 of the Uniform Commercial Code for stopping payments of checks (12 C.F.R. § 205.10(c) and U.C.C. § 4-403). Within 3 business days of a scheduled transfer, a customer wishing to stop payment must orally or in writing so notify the financial institution holding the account. If the customer orally notifies the financial institution to stop payment, the institution may also require written confirmation of the order within 14 days of oral notification if the institution provides the customer with an address to which the confirmation can be sent. If a written confirmation is requested, the oral request for stop payment will only bind the institution for 14 days.

A financial institution that fails to honor a consumer's stop payment order is liable to the consumer for all damages its failure proximately caused (15 U.S.C. § 1693h(a)(3)). If a financial institution can demonstrate that its failure to stop payment was unintentional and resulted from a bona fide error, notwithstanding its maintenance of procedures to avoid such error, its liability will be limited to actual damages (15 U.S.C. § 1693h(c)).

Again, the initial disclosure statement should explain a financial institution's stop-payment procedure and liability for failure to stop payment properly (12 C.F.R. §§ 205.7(a)(7) and 205.7(a)(8)).

## Financial Institutions' Liability for Failure to Make Transfers

Besides liability for failure to stop transfers from consumers' accounts, financial institutions are liable to consumers for all damage proximately caused by failure to complete electronic fund transfers to their accounts in accordance with terms and conditions of the accounts, in the correct amounts, or in a timely manner when properly instructed to do so by consumers. However, if a financial institution can demonstrate that any one of the following caused its failure to make an electronic fund transfer, it will incur no liability (15 U.S.C. § 1693h):

- The consumer's account had insufficient funds, except if the financial institution's failure to credit the account caused the insufficiency.

- The funds were subject to legal process or other encumbrance restricting such transfer.

- The transfer would have exceeded an established credit limit.

- An electronic terminal had insufficient cash to complete the transaction.

As with failure to properly stop transfers from an account, if a financial institution demonstrates that its failure to properly complete a transfer to an account was unintentional and resulted from a bona fide error, notwithstanding its maintenance of procedures to prevent such error, it is liable only for actual damages and not for all proximate damages.

In addition to the defense of bona fide error, EFTA provides two additional defenses for financial institutions failing to make transfers to accounts. (These defenses are unavailable to institutions failing to stop transfers from accounts.) First, if an act of God or other circumstance beyond an institution's control caused its failure to make the transfer to an account and the institution exercised reasonable care to prevent such an occurrence and appropriate diligence under the circumstances, the institution will not be liable to a customer for any damages. The second defense to a financial institution's failure to make a transfer to a customer's account is proof that the customer knew of a technical malfunction when attempting to initiate an electronic fund transfer or, in the case of a preauthorized transfer, when such a transfer should have occurred (15 U.S.C. § 1693h(b)).

## Procedures for Resolving Errors

EFTA contains extensive procedures to be followed when a consumer alleges that an error has occurred in an electronic transfer of funds. EFTA defines "error" to include

- an unauthorized or incorrect electronic fund transfer to or from a consumer's account

- the consumer's receipt of an incorrect amount of money or statement from an electronic terminal

- the omission from a periodic statement of an electronic transfer required to be included
- a financial institution's computational or bookkeeping error relating to an electronic fund transfer (12 C.F.R. § 205.11(a)).

To ensure that consumers understand these procedures and their rights, EFTA requires that financial institutions continually notify consumers of this information. This approach of establishing detailed procedures for resolving disputes and then informing consumers of them was patterned after provisions in the Fair Credit Billing Act discussed previously in this chapter.

*Notice of Error*

To require a financial institution to investigate an alleged error in an electronic fund transfer, a consumer must provide the financial institution with oral or written notice of such error. A financial institution must receive this notice no later than 60 days after the institution transmitted the periodic disclosure statement, updated the passbook, or transmitted other documents or information upon which the alleged error is based.

If a consumer gives an oral notice of error to a financial institution, the institution can require written confirmation within 10 business days if, upon receiving the oral notice, it so informs the consumer and provides an address to which the consumer may send the confirmation (12 C.F.R. § 205.11(b)(2)). If the consumer fails to provide timely written confirmation of an oral notice, a financial institution will still need to comply with all EFTA procedures for resolving errors, except the provisional recrediting of accounts (discussed in the next section) (12 C.F.R. § 205.11(c)(3)).

*Investigation of Error*

Upon receiving a valid notice of error, a financial institution must investigate the alleged error to the extent required by EFTA to determine whether an error occurred, and transmit the results of its investigation to the consumer (12 C.F.R. §§ 205.11(c) and 205.11(d)). The financial institution has either 10 business days or 45 calendar days, whichever it wishes, to investigate and determine the merits of the alleged error. However, if the institution chooses to spend 45 calendar days to investigate the alleged error and make a determination, it must provisionally recredit the consumer's account in the amount of the alleged error. The institution must also notify the consumer that it has provisionally recredited the account and the consumer will have full use of the funds during the period of the investigation (12 C.F.R. § 205.11(c)(2)).

*Determination*  If after investigation a financial institution determines that an error occurred, it must correct the error within one business day of its determination, including crediting interest wrongfully withheld and refunding fees or charges wrongfully imposed. The institution must then notify the consumer of the correction (12 C.F.R. § 205.11(e)).

If a financial institution determines that it made no error, it must mail or deliver to the consumer, within three business days of making its determination, a written explanation of its findings. The explanation should include a notice of the consumer's right to request the documents on which the institution based its determination.

A financial institution may reverse any provisional recredits made during the investigation. However, for five business days after giving notice of such reversal, the financial institution must honor checks, drafts, or similar paper instruments, and preauthorized transfers from the account as though the institution had not made the reversal. Along with its notice of reversal, the institution must also notify the customer of its obligation to continue honoring such withdrawals for third parties (12 C.F.R. § 205.11(f)(2)).

If a financial institution completes its investigation and determines that an error other than that alleged by a consumer has occurred, it must follow the same procedure as if no error had occurred (12 C.F.R. § 205.11(f)).

**Customers' Liability for Unauthorized Transfers**  One of the chief concerns of those interested in protecting consumers in the context of electronically facilitated financial services is the extent of consumers' liability for unauthorized electronic fund transfers (12 C.F.R. § 205.6). EFTA defines an "unauthorized electronic fund transfer" as a transfer from a consumer's account (a) that a person other than the consumer initiates without actual authority to do so, and (b) from which the consumer derives no benefit (12 C.F.R. § 205.2(1)).

If an unauthorized transfer is made from a consumer's account, the liability of the consumer, if any, will depend on several factors

- the amount of the unauthorized transfer

- the promptness of the consumer in notifying the financial institution of an unauthorized transfer once the consumer is aware of it

- any extenuating circumstances causing the consumer's delay in notifying a financial institution of an unauthorized transfer

- state law

- agreements between a customer and a financial institution concerning liability

**EXAMPLE** Sam Malone was issued an automated teller machine (ATM) card by First State Bank along with a personal identification number (PIN). So he would not forget the PIN, Malone wrote it on the card, in breach of his account agreement with the bank. Later Malone lost the card, which he reported immediately but not before its finder used it to withdraw $500 from Malone's account at an ATM.

Notwithstanding Malone's negligence and breach of contract in writing the PIN on the card, First State must reimburse him $500.

**Enforcement**  EFTA assigns the administrative enforcement of its provisions to the Comptroller of the Currency, the Board of Governors of the Federal Reserve System, the board of directors of the Federal Deposit Insurance Corporation, the Office of Thrift Supervision, and the National Credit Union Administration Board (12 C.F.R. § 205.13). Each agency oversees compliance by the financial institutions within its jurisdiction.

Not only are financial institutions liable for failure to make electronic fund transfers, as has been discussed (15 U.S.C. § 1693h), but individual and class actions are also available to those damaged by a financial institution's failure to comply with EFTA's other provisions (15 U.S.C. § 1693m).

EFTA provisions for civil penalties are similar to those prescribed for violations of the Truth in Lending Act (15 U.S.C. § 1640). In individual actions, financial institutions violating EFTA are liable to an aggrieved consumer in an amount equal to the sum of any actual damages suffered by the consumer, plus a statutory penalty of no less than $100 and no more than $1,000. The amount of the penalty depends on the nature, frequency, and persistence of the financial institution's noncompliance, and the extent to which it was intentional (15 U.S.C. §§ 1693m(a)(1), 1693m(a)(2)(A), and 1693m(b)(1)).

Financial institutions subjected to class actions are liable for no minimum statutory penalties but could be assessed the actual damages suffered by the class members, plus up to $500,000 or one percent of the institution's net worth. The amount of damages assessed in addition to actual damages will depend on the nature, frequency, and persistence of the institution's noncompliance, the institution's resources, the number of people adversely affected, and the extent to which the noncompliance was intentional (15 U.S.C. §§ 1693m(a)(1) and 1693m(b)(2)).

A financial institution accused of an EFTA violation other than failure to make an electronic fund transfer has three possible defenses. First, if the institution can demonstrate that a violation was unintentional and resulted from a bona fide error, notwithstanding its maintenance of procedures to prevent such error, then the institution will incur no liability even if a violation did occur. Second, if the institution committed the alleged violation in good faith conformity with any rule, regulation, interpretation, or model form of, or with the approval of, the Federal Reserve Board or its authorized officials or employees, no civil penalty may be assessed. The third defense is available for financial institutions if, before the consumer initiates an action, the institution

- notifies the consumer that it is aware of the violation
- corrects the violation by complying with EFTA
- makes an appropriate adjustment to the consumer's account
- pays actual damages or, if the violation arises out of a failure to make a transfer, pays all damages proximately caused by the failure (15 U.S.C. §§ 1693m(c) and 1693m(e))

A consumer who succeeds in an action against a financial institution, is entitled not only to damages but also to costs and reasonable attorney's fees (15 U.S.C. § 1693m(a)(3)). If a consumer is unsuccessful in such an action and a court determines that the consumer brought the action in bad faith or for purposes of harassment, the court must award costs and reasonable attorneys' fees to the financial institution (15 U.S.C. § 1693m(f)). Under EFTA, consumers may file civil actions in any U.S. district court or state court of competent jurisdiction within one year from the date of the alleged violation (15 U.S.C. § 1693m(g)).

## *Criminal Penalties*

Anyone knowingly and willfully violating EFTA can incur a maximum penalty of $5,000 and/or one year in prison. Further, anyone committing specified criminal acts involving any card, code, or other device (other than a check, draft, or similar paper instrument) that may be used to make an electronic transfer of funds may be fined not more than $10,000 and/or sentenced to imprisonment for no more than 10 years (15 U.S.C. § 1693(n)).

## CONCLUSION

Many federal statutes and regulations govern the relationship between banks and their customers. Those statutes (and their corresponding regulations) were summarized in this chapter. Banks and other creditors must ensure that they comply with the provisions of these statutes and regulations.

As the banking industry continues to face an era of dramatic change, understanding the statutes and regulations that govern banks' relations with their customers will grow in importance. Banks that keep abreast of and comply with appropriate statutory and regulatory requirements will have a better chance to thrive in a changing economic and regulatory environment.

## Questions for Review and Discussion

1. Does the Truth in Lending Act apply to business and consumer credit?
2. What disclosure equals the sum of the amount financed and the finance charge?
3. What is the Federal Reserve Board's official staff commentary?
4. What is the difference between closed-end and open-end credit?
5. When must open-end credit disclosures be given?
6. What is the "federal box"?
7. Does rescission apply when a borrower's principal dwelling is used to secure a business debt?
8. What is a "residential mortgage transaction"?
9. When does Regulation M apply to a lease?
10. Does the Equal Credit Opportunity Act apply only to consumer credit?
11. What is a "prohibited basis" for discriminating against any individual in a credit transaction?
12. May a bank deciding whether to grant a credit request consider an applicant's age?
13. Does the Real Estate Settlement Procedures Act apply only to single-family residences?
14. Describe what would be an illegal referral fee under the Real Estate Settlement Procedures Act.
15. When should the disclosure of a "Good Faith Estimate of Settlement Services" be given?
16. May a bank order a consumer report for any purpose?
17. When would the Fair Debt Collection Practices Act apply to a bank?
18. Does the Right to Financial Privacy apply to any request for the records a bank has on its customers?
19. What is a "preauthorized transfer"?
20. What is a "cosigner notice"?

# ANSWERS TO QUESTIONS FOR REVIEW AND DISCUSSION

**Chapter 1**
1. A legislative body can repeal or modify common law by enacting a statute.

2. The impetus for legislation may be members of a legislative body itself or interest groups representing particular aspects of society that lobby for enactment of particular bills.

3. No.

4. Unlike statutes, constitutions are not usually created by legislatures (though some may be amended by legislatures). Instead, a convention is called for the purpose of drafting a constitution, which is then placed before the voters for ratification or rejection.

5. The federal system is composed of the state governments and the national government. The banking industry is subject to both federal and state laws.

6. Regulatory law has its origins in the early English attempts to limit the power of bureaucrats. Agents of the Crown, such as sheriffs, were liable to citizens for damages that occurred when agents acted outside the scope of their authority. Thus, if an official unlawfully trespassed on an individual's property or assaulted a person outside the scope of the official's authority, the individual could resort to the courts. The courts issued writs to control officials' actions, such as writs of mandamus, prohibition, and certiorari. These writs were early forms of "regulations" used to control officials' actions.

**Chapter 2**
1. The Bank of the United States, which was created by the federal government in 1791, was owned and operated by the federal government.

2. The National Banking Act enables national banks to be chartered.

3. The FDIC insures deposits and regulates banks that are not members of the Federal Reserve System.

4. The Comptroller of the Currency has no authority over state-chartered banks.

5. No.

6. No.

7. Yes.

8. No. The U.S. Supreme Court can hear only the following types of cases:

    ■ cases arising under the federal Constitution, the laws of Congress, and treaties

    ■ cases affecting ambassadors and public ministers

    ■ cases of admiralty

    ■ controversies between two or more states and between citizens of different states

9. Attorneys usually are not permitted to represent people in small claims courts.

10. The doctrine of sovereign immunity.

**Chapter 3**

1. A tort harms an individual or a legal entity such as a corporation.

2. No. It is also necessary to show damages.

3. The five essential elements of the tort of deceit are

    ■ a false representation of a material fact made by one person, *A* to another, *B*

    ■ knowledge by *A* that the representation is false

    ■ communication of the representation to *B* with the intention that *B* should rely on the representation when acting upon it

    ■ justifiable reliance by *B* in the truth of the representation

- substantial damage to *B*, proximately caused by reliance on *A's* false representation

4. Publication means that the maker of a defamatory statement (oral or written) must utter it or bring it to the notice of someone other than the defamed person.

5. Larceny occurs when a person takes and carries away the personal property of another with the intent to steal it. Embezzlement occurs when a person in a position of trust fraudulently converts or misappropriates money or property that is in that person's custody by virtue of his or her employment.

6. No. While traditional bribery statutes find criminal liability only where favorable treatment is conditioned upon the actual or promised receipt of a bribe, the Bank Bribery Act prohibits a bank employee from receiving gratuities for any bank-related decisions or activities; that is, there is no need to prove that the banker would not have completed the transaction without the gratuity.

7. A currency transaction report (CTR) is a report that must be filed with the Internal Revenue Service by banks and others who are involved in a transaction where the payment, receipt, or transfer of United States coins or currency is in amounts of more than $10,000.

8. Yes, if the activity falls within the guidelines for filing criminal referrals issued by the federal bank regulatory agencies.

**Chapter 4**

1. A bank dealing with a sole proprietorship may transact business in the same way it does with any individual unless the sole proprietor operates the business under an assumed name. When dealing with a sole proprietorship or other entity using an assumed name, banks should require that the account be opened only in the names of the individuals involved.

    A bank dealing with a corporation should assure itself that the corporation is in fact legally incorporated by asking for and reviewing articles of incorporation. The bank should also be sure that the corporation by itself is creditworthy and, if it is not, obtain a guarantee of its shareholders.

2. *Example of apparent authority.* P (bank president) hires A (new employee) to serve as courier. All prior couriers have been allowed to order lunch at Z's restaurant and charge it to the bank if wearing the bank's courier uniform. P intends to stop this practice but fails to notify Z. When A, in bank uniform, eats a $40 lunch at Z's, P will be liable for payment because Z relied on A's appearance of authority based on P's past conduct.

*Example of actual (implied authority).* P (bank president) employs A (real estate broker) to find a buyer for a foreclosed piece of property. On three separate occasions, X has made similar purchases from P through A. P tells A he would like to receive a minimum of $30,000 for the property. A has found buyers for P for the past 10 years, under an oral arrangement with P, and has always been allowed to enter into a purchase agreement with a prospective buyer if the minimum price in cash were met. X is willing to pay $31,000 cash and enters into a purchase agreement with A. Two weeks later, potential purchaser Q offers P $40,000. Because of prior dealings, A reasonably believed that he was authorized to enter into a contract with X, and P cannot now deny A's implied authority to accept a better deal.

3. In a partnership, a partner can be personally liable for the acts of another partner performed on behalf of the partnership. In a limited partnership, the limited partner is not liable for partnership debt beyond the amount of the limited partner's investment.

4. An intestate estate occurs when the decedent dies without executing a valid will; a testate estate involves a will to be probated.

5. Before dealing with a government entity, a bank should be certain that the proposed transaction is within the power of the individual representing the government entity and that it is within the scope of permitted activities of the government entity, as granted by state and local law.

6. The guardian of the person oversees the physical, emotional, and educational needs of the ward or legally incapacitated person; the guardian of the estate manages the assets of the ward or legally incapacitated person.

7. Yes.

**Chapter 5**
1. Yes.
2. The law may be able to set aside a contract to serve social policy or to prevent acts disruptive or otherwise harmful to society.
3. Yes, unless the inability to understand the contract is due to mental incompetence that makes it impossible for the person to understand in a reasonable manner the nature and consequence of the transaction.
4. The law will excuse payment only if the price is unconscionable.
5. Yes, if one or more of the exceptions to the statute of frauds is present.
6. No. According to the parol evidence rule, however, the oral explanation cannot contradict the written contract.
7. Yes. If a party intentionally fails to perform a contract and knows or should be aware of special circumstances that indicate a greater than normal loss for a breach, there may be liability for consequential damages.

**Chapter 6**
1. Real property is land and anything permanently affixed to it, including buildings and standing trees. Personal property includes all property that is not real property and is usually defined as objects that are movable or intangible.
2. Yes. For example, lumber on a building site is personal property. When it is added to a home on the site, it becomes real property, and when the home is later torn down, the lumber becomes personal property again.
3. The eight ways in which personal property may be acquired are

   - production
   - purchase
   - taking possession
   - finding
   - confusion

- accession
- gift
- inheritance

4. Gifts may be classified as gifts inter vivos or gifts causa mortis.

5. Unless otherwise stipulated in the contract between a bank and its bailor customer, a bank must exercise ordinary care in connection with its safe deposit boxes.

6. The security interest in real estate is called a mortgage.

7. A fee simple absolute estate is the broadest interest anyone may have in real property. It allows the owner to use, abuse, and exclusively possess the property; take its fruits (such as timber and crops); and dispose of it by deed or will without restriction.

8. A life estate for mortgages is not very desirable, since upon the death of the mortgagor the mortgagee's interest terminates.

9. The ownership of land.

## Chapter 7

1. The U.S. Constitution, article I, section 8, gives Congress the power to enact bankruptcy legislation.

2. To initiate a Chapter 7 action, the debtor files a petition in the appropriate federal district bankruptcy court, including information regarding all creditors, the debtor's assets and liabilities, and the debtor's current income and expenses.

3. The automatic stay.

4. The trustee is an officer appointed by the bankruptcy court to represent the estate of the debtor.

5. Exemptions are certain items of property that a debtor is allowed to retain despite filing a bankruptcy petition. In many states, a debtor can choose exemptions allowed under state or federal law, whichever is most beneficial. Examples of federal exemptions include

- up to $7,500 interest in residential property or a burial plot of the debtor or dependent
- up to $1,200 interest in one motor vehicle
- up to $4,000 of interest in household goods; an individual item cannot exceed $200 in value
- up to $500 in jewelry for personal family use
- catch-all provision of $4,150
- up to $750 for tools of trade or professional books
- certain insurance policies
- professionally prescribed health aids
- certain government benefits
- certain other income from insurance, personal injury, or crime-victim awards

6. A preference is a voluntary or involuntary transfer made by an insolvent debtor of the debtor's interest in property to a certain creditor for or on account of an antecedent debt. This transfer is made within 90 days before the debtor files a bankruptcy petition (or within one year if the creditor is an "insider") and allows the creditor to receive more than its Chapter 7 distributive share.

7. The trustee may return a secured creditor's collateral if the debtor has no equity in it, or its value when the trustee sells it. If the trustee wants to use the property for the estate, the secured creditor is entitled to adequate protection.

8. If an individual obtains a discharge, liability for all debts listed on the bankruptcy schedule is discharged, unless the debt is nondischargeable for public policy reasons under section 523 of the Bankruptcy Code.

9. Debts that are nondischargeable include the following:
   - most taxes
   - fraudulently obtained debt

- unlisted debt
- debt through embezzlement, larceny, or fraud as a fiduciary
- certain debts to a spouse and child
- debt for willful and malicious injury caused by debtor
- government fines and penalties assessed against debtor
- certain student loans
- civil judgments against debtor for drunk driving damages
- certain debts from a prior bankruptcy filing

10. Yes.

11. Any individual or sole proprietorship with a stable and regular income from wages, self-employment, pensions, investments, or other sources with no more than $100,000 of unsecured debt and no more than $350,000 of secured debt may seek rehabilitation under Chapter 13.

12. In Chapter 11, the business debtor must file a reorganization plan within 120 days of filing the bankruptcy petition or any party in interest can then file a plan. The plan must designate classes of claims and note who will be impaired by the plan. The Chapter 11 debtor must submit the plan first to the court for its approval of the debtor's disclosure statement, and then to the interested parties. Detailed code rules provide for the procedures to confirm the plan.

    In Chapter 13, the plan is the debtor's proposal for a repayment program, which includes whether the debtor intends to assume or reject certain executory contracts or liquidate certain assets. Although creditors can file written objections to the plan, the court will confirm it if it meets the statutory requirements.

13. A debtor in possession is a Chapter 11 debtor who holds property and maintains accounts for the benefit of the estate, not for personal use.

**Chapter 8**

1. The Truth in Lending Act does not apply to business credit.
2. The total of payments.

3. It is the interpretation by the Federal Reserve Board's staff of regulations that the Board addresses.

4. Closed-end credit is amortizing credit; open-end credit is revolving, self-replenishing credit.

5. If a credit card is involved, disclosure must be given when an application is provided, before the credit is used, and periodically thereafter (usually monthly and when renewed).

   If home equity credit is involved, disclosure must be given when an application is provided, before the first transaction, and periodically thereafter (usually monthly).

   If neither a credit card or home equity is involved, disclosure must be given before the first transaction and periodically thereafter (usually monthly).

6. The federal box is the area in a closed-end credit disclosure where most of the required Truth in Lending disclosures must be made.

7. No.

8. A residential mortgage transaction is a closed-end credit mortgage used to finance the purchase of a borrower's principal dwelling.

9. Regulation M applies to a consumer lease. A consumer lease is one in which the terms exceed four months, involve only personal property as defined by state law, and for which the total contractual obligation does not exceed $25,000. The lessee must be a natural person using the personal property primarily for a personal, family, or household purpose.

10. No. It applies to business credit as well.

11. It is one of the eight bases upon which credit cannot be denied pursuant to the Equal Credit Opportunity Act.

12. Yes. The creditor can consider age as it relates to other factors, such as an indication of remaining years of employment, life expectancy, length of loan requested, and amount of Social Security or pension income.

13. No.

14. If a loan comes within the Real Estate Settlement Procedures Act, a referral fee paid by a bank to an attorney for referring loans to it would be illegal.

15. If a loan comes within the Real Estate Settlement Procedures Act, the good faith estimate should be provided within three business days of receipt of the application.

16. No.

17. The Fair Debt Collection Practices Act applies to a bank if it collects its debts using a name other than its own.

18. No.

19. A "preauthorized transfer" is an electronic funds transfer authorized in advance to recur at substantially regular intervals.

20. A "cosigner notice" is a notice that must be furnished to cosigners of consumer debt pursuant to Federal Reserve Board Regulation AA. The notice explains the cosigners' liability.

# GLOSSARY

**abandonment** Absolute, voluntary, and intentional relinquishment of property—total desertion by its owner.

**acceleration clause** A clause in a loan contract stating that the entire loan balance will become due immediately if a breach of certain conditions stated in the contract occurs.

**acceptance** Occurs in a contractual situation when conditions in the offer have been satisfied.

**acceptor** A person who accepts a bill of exchange.

**access device** A card, code, or other means of access to a consumer's account, which may be used for initiating electronic fund transfers.

**accession** Installation or affixing of one type of personal property item into another, resulting in a new item of personal property.

**account** (1) The credit established under a particular name, usually by deposit, against which withdrawals may be made. (2) A record of the financial transactions affecting the assets, liabilities, income, expenditures, or net worth of an individual or business entity. (3) In the Electronic Fund Transfer Act, a demand deposit, savings deposit, or other asset account established primarily for personal, family, or household purposes.

**account party** A buyer or other person who causes an issuer to open a letter of credit.

**administrator** An individual or trust institution appointed by a court to settle the estate of a person who has died (a) without leaving a valid will, (b) without naming an executor, or (c) leaving an executor who will not serve. (A female is called an administratrix.)

**adverse action** Under the Equal Credit Opportunity Act (ECOA), a creditor who denies a consumer's request for credit is a creditor who takes "adverse action" and must advise the applicant of the reason for denial of the credit.

**adverse possession** An occupation of land inconsistent with the right of the true owner.

**advising bank** A bank that notifies the beneficiary that another bank has issued a letter of credit.

**after-acquired property** Property a debtor acquires as security, after the execution of a mortgage or other form of indebtedness, that additionally secures the indebtedness.

**agency** The relationship between an agent who acts on behalf of another person and the principal on whose behalf the agent acts. *See* fiduciary.

**agent** A person who acts for another person by the latter's authority. The distinguishing characteristics of an agent are (a) that he or she acts on behalf, and subject to the control, of his or her principal; (b) that he or she does not have title to the property of his or her principal; and (c) that he or she owes the duty of obedience to the orders given by his or her principal.

**allonge** Paper attached to a negotiable instrument, used for endorsements when there is no room for them on the instrument itself.

**antedated item** An item bearing a past date.

**appellate court** A court with jurisdiction to hear appeals from trial courts.

**articles of partnership (partnership agreement)** A written agreement between business partners that outlines the provisions of their business arrangement.

**assignment** The transfer by one person to another of the title to property, rights, or other interests.

**attachment** A concept designed to grant a security interest in a debtor's property. It usually occurs when a debtor signs a security agreement or surrenders possession of the property to the creditor.

**bailment** The delivery of personal property by one person, the *bailor*, to another, the *bailee*, for a limited period and for some specific purpose, such as use, repairs, or safekeeping, but without passing title to the property.

**bank holding companies** Companies that own or control banks. Holding companies are permitted to engage in nonbank activities to the extent that those activities relate to providing services to banks, including acting as investment advisers, leasing personal and real property, providing data-processing services, operating insurance agencies, and providing management consulting advice and advertising services.

**bankruptcy** The legal proceedings by which the affairs of an entity unable to meet financial obligations are turned over to a trustee or receiver for administration, in accordance with bankruptcy laws.

**bankruptcy trustee** A person or trust institution that holds the legal title to property for the benefit of someone else. A trustee is responsible for preserving and managing the assets of a trust.

**bearer** A person or company that has physical possession of a check, security, or any negotiable financial instrument with no name entered on it as payee. Any bearer can present such an instrument for payment.

**beneficiary** (1) The person for whose benefit a trust is created. (2) The person to whom the amount of an insurance policy, annuity, or bequest is payable. (3) The ultimate party to be credited or paid as a result of a transfer. (4) The person in whose favor a letter of credit is issued.

**bilateral offer** Offer conditioned upon a promise to be made by an offeree.

**bill of exchange** A draft. A negotiable and unconditional written order, such as a check or trade acceptance, signed and addressed by one person to another. The person who receives a bill of exchange must pay a specified sum on demand or at a specific future time.

**bill of lading** A document in one or more parts, issued by a transportation company, that acknowledges receipt of specified goods for transporting to a specific location and sets forth the contract between the shipper and carrier.

**billing error** An error made by a creditor in the billing of an open-end credit account, the allegation of which by a consumer triggers procedures set forth in the Fair Credit Billing Act.

**blue-sky laws** State laws concerning the registration and issuance of securities. These laws may be different from federal laws and regulations and must be obeyed if a security is to be sold in that state.

**bona fide purchaser** One who, without having received notice of any defect in the title, purchases property in good faith and pays a valuable consideration for the property.

**branch (as defined in the McFadden Act and applicable only to national banks)** Any branch bank, branch office, branch agency, additional office, or any branch place of business located in any state or territory of the United States or District of Columbia at which deposits are received, checks paid, or money lent.

**bribery** The giving or receiving of any undue reward to influence the behavior of the person receiving such award in the discharge of his or her official duty.

**certificate of deposit** (1) A formal receipt for funds left with a bank as a special deposit. Such deposits may bear interest, in which case they are payable at a definite date in the future or after a specified minimum notice of withdrawal; or they may be noninterest bearing, in which case they may be payable on demand or at a future date. These deposits are payable only upon surrender of the formal receipt, properly endorsed. (2) A certificate issued to the owners of bonds or stocks as evidence of the deposit of a stated number of shares or bonds when a corporation is reorganized.

**certificate of incorporation** A certificate issued by a state acknowledging corporate existence.

**certificate of title** A certificate that represents ownership of property, titled according to state or federal law outside the scope of article 9 of the Uniform Commercial Code.

**certified check** A customer's check that has been presented to a bank for authentication and guarantee. By its certification, the bank guarantees that sufficient funds have been set aside from the customer's account to cover the amount of the check when payment is demanded. Legally, with the certification of a check, payment becomes the bank's responsibility.

**check** A commercial demand deposit instrument (a draft) signed by the maker and payable to a person named or to a bearer upon presentation to the bank on which it is drawn.

**clean payment** A payment unencumbered by documents.

**clearing house** (1) An establishment maintained by financial institutions for settling clearing claims. (2) A place where representatives of the banks in the same locality meet daily at an agreed time to exchange checks, drafts, and similar items drawn on each other and to settle the resulting balances. (3) An adjunct to a futures exchange through which transactions executed on the floor of the exchange are settled by matching purchases and sales. A clearing organization is also charged with the proper conduct of delivery procedures.

**close corporation** A corporation whose outstanding stock is held by a few people, often members of a single family. The stock is not available for sale and thus is not traded publicly.

**closed-end credit** A type of credit, usually installment credit, that involves an agreement with a customer specifying the total amount involved, the number of payments, and the due date for each payment.

**collateral** Specific property, securities, or other assets pledged by a borrower to a lender as a backup source of loan repayment.

**collecting bank** Any bank handling an item for collection, except the payor bank.

**commercial letter of credit** An instrument, issued by a bank, that substitutes the bank's credit for that of the buyer of goods. It authorizes the seller to draw drafts on the bank and guarantees payment of those drafts if the stated terms have all been met.

**common law** Body of law originating in medieval England and derived solely from usage, habits, and customs. Decisions in common law became the basis for subsequent decisions.

**common stock** *See* stock.

**community property** Property in which a husband and wife both have an undivided one-half interest by reason of their marital status.

**compensatory damages** Damages that place the injured party in the economic position that he or she would have enjoyed if the breach had not occurred.

**Competitive Equality Banking Act (CEBA)** Legislation enacted by Congress in 1987 significantly affecting the operations of nonbank banks, the powers granted to commercial banks and bank holding companies, and the timeframe during which banks of deposit must make checks available to customers.

**Comptroller of the Currency** An officer of the U.S. Treasury that regulates national banks.

**confirmed letter of credit** A letter of credit issued by the local bank of an importer and confirmed by another bank, usually located in the exporter's country. The second bank's obligation is added to the obligation of the issuing bank to honor drafts and documents presented according to the terms of credit.

**consequential (special) damages** Damages that accrue because of some special or unusual circumstance of the particular contractual relationship of the parties, such as loss of employment, business credit, or customers.

**consideration** Something of value given by one party to another in exchange for a promise or act by another party.

**constitutions** Fundamental laws of states or nations. In the United States, constitutions are created by conventions called for that purpose and ratified by voters, rather than enacted by legislative bodies.

**consumer reports** Information supplied by consumer-reporting agencies regarding consumers' creditworthiness, credit capacity, character, and personal lifestyle.

**contract** An agreement between two or more people to perform, or to refrain from performing, certain acts.

**Consumer Leasing Act (1976)** An act requiring lessors to disclose specified information about payment, trade-in allowances, and estimated value of property at the end of the lease.

**corporate borrowing resolution** A resolution passed by a corporation's board of directors specifying who may sign loan documents on behalf of the corporation. This resolution is then kept in the corporation's loan files at the various lending institutions with which it does business.

**corporation** A business organization that is treated as a single legal entity and is owned by its stockholders, whose liability is generally limited to the extent of their investment. The ownership of a corporation is represented by shares of stock that are issued to people or other companies in exchange for cash, physical assets, services, and good will. The stockholders elect the board of directors, which then directs the management of the corporation's affairs.

**cosigner** A person who signs an instrument along with another and becomes responsible for the obligation.

**court of general jurisdiction** A court having power to entertain any action on the trial level, regardless of the amount, subject matter, or type of relief demanded.

**court of limited jurisdiction** A court that is limited by state constitution or statute to entertain only certain actions. Those limitations are usually stated in terms of subject matter, amount, or type of relief sought.

**cram down** A confirmation of a reorganization plan gained by the court's forcing the plan on dissenting classes of creditors, as long as at least one impaired class consents to the plan and the plan does not discriminate unfairly.

**credit** A right granted by a creditor to defer payment of a debt, to incur debt and defer its payment, or to purchase property or services and defer payment on them. *See* open-end credit and closed-end credit.

**credit card** Any card, plate, coupon book, or other single credit device used, upon presentation, to obtain money, property, labor, or services on credit.

**credit union**  A type of financial institution formed on the basis of a common bond. This institution must be a nonprofit corporation and all profits are distributed among members in proportion to their deposits.

**cumulative voting**  One vote for each share of stock owned, multiplied by the number of directors to be elected. Board members of national banks must be elected by cumulative voting.

**curtesy**  The life estate of a widower in the real property of his wife. Most states have abolished this estate. *See* dower.

**damages**  A pecuniary compensation or indemnity that may be recovered in the courts by any person who has suffered loss, detriment, or injury, whether to his or her person, property, or rights, through the unlawful act, omission, or negligence of another. *See* compensatory damages, consequential (special) damages, punitive (exemplary) damages, incidental damages, and liquidated damages.

**debt**  A sum of money owed to another person.

**deceit**  *See* fraud.

**deed, quit claim**  A deed that transfers only such interest, title, or right a grantor may have in real estate when the conveyance is executed.

**deed, warranty**  A deed that guarantees the seller's right to convey clear title to a piece of property and that guarantees the property is free from debts not specifically disclosed.

**defamation**  The invasion of the interest in one's reputation by the communication of derogatory information to a third person. Oral communication is *slander*; if it is in writing or a permanent embodiment, it is *libel*.

**default**  (1) The failure of a borrower to make a payment of principal or interest when due. (2) The state that exists when a borrower cannot or does not pay bond- and noteholders the interest or principal due. (3) A breach or nonperformance of any of the terms of a note or the convenants of a mortgage. (4) The failure to meet a financial obligation.

**deferred posting**  A method of posting bank transactions to accounts after the day of receipt.

**demand deposit**  Funds that a customer, usually by writing checks or using an automated teller machine, may withdraw from a bank with no advance notice. Checking accounts are the most common form of demand deposits.

**depositary bank**  The first bank to which an item is transferred for collection (including the paying bank).

**discharge** Legal termination of an individual's responsibility for repayment of a debt.

**disaffirmation** Action by a party lacking capacity to enter into a contract to relieve him- or herself from a contractual obligation.

**disclosures** Data that federal or state law require to be given to cardholders regarding the terms of the credit extended. Disclosures must appear on cardholder agreements, monthly (periodic) billing statements, or any documents in which the rates for finance charges are mentioned.

**dividend** A payment made periodically, usually quarterly, by a corporation to its stockholders as a return on investment. Dividends can be paid in cash, stock, or property.

**doctrine of avoidable consequence** *See* mitigation of damages.

**donor, donee** *See* gift.

**dower** The life estate of a widow in the real property of her husband. At common law, a wife had a life estate in one-third (in value) of the real property of her husband if he died without leaving a valid will or she dissented from that will. Many states do not recognize common-law dower. *See* curtesy.

**dragnet clause** Language in a mortgage expressing open indebtedness.

**drawee** The party on whom a draft is drawn and who is directed to pay the sum specified.

**drawer** The party who instructs the drawee to pay funds to the payee.

**easement** An acquired right of use or enjoyment, falling short of ownership, which a person may have in the land of another (for example, one person's right-of-way over another's land).

**electronic fund transfer** Any transfer of funds, other than a transaction originated by check, draft, or a similar paper instrument, which is initiated through an electronic terminal, telephonic instrument, computer, or magnetic tape so as to order, instruct, or authorize a financial institution to debit or credit an account. Such a transfer includes, but is not limited to, point-of-sale transfers, automated teller machine transactions, direct deposits or withdrawals of funds, and transfers initiated by telephone. *See* Regulation E.

**embezzlement (misappropriation of funds)** The fraudulent appropriation to one's own use of funds or other property entrusted to one's care by another.

**empirically derived credit system** A credit-scoring system that evaluates an applicant's creditworthiness. This system primarily allocates points or weights to key characteristics that describe the applicant or various aspects of the transaction.

**endorsement** (1) The signature, placed on the back of a negotiable instrument or in an accompanying power, that transfers the instrument to another party and legally implies that the endorser has the right to transfer the instrument. (2) The placement of an endorsement stamp on bank card sales and credit slips to identify the originating bank and the date processed.

**Equal Credit Opportunity Act (ECOA)** A federal law passed in 1974 requiring lenders and other creditors to make credit equally available without discrimination based on race, color, religion, national origin, sex, age, marital status, receipt of income from public assistance programs, or past exercising of rights under the Consumer Credit Protection Act. The ECOA specifies actions and questions that are prohibited when one is obtaining information on credit applicants.

**estate** The right, title, or interest that a person has in any property, to be distinguished from the property itself. The term is often used to describe decedent's property.

**estate at sufferance** The interest of a tenant who rightfully has possessed land by the permission of the owner but continues to occupy the land after the period for which he or she is entitled.

**estate at will** A lease that continues at the will of the lessor.

**estate for years** A lease that continues for a definite period.

**estoppel** The preclusion of a person from alleging in his or her action what is contrary to his or her previous action or omission.

**executor** A party, frequently a trust company, named in a will to carry out its terms. The executor gathers the assets of the creator of the will; pays all taxes, debts, and expenses; and distributes the net estate as ordered in the will. (A female executor is called an executrix.)

**executory interest** A future estate or interest running in favor of a third person instead of a grantor.

**Expedited Funds Availability Act (EFAA)** A law passed by Congress in 1987 that requires financial institutions to make deposited items available for withdrawal on an expedited basis. Implemented by Regulation CC issued by the Federal Reserve Board, the act also requires lobby notices and special notices to a customer if funds will not be made available on the scheduled basis.

**Fair Credit Billing Act of 1974** An amendment to the Truth in Lending Act, this federal law requires that creditors resolve billing errors in a prescribed manner within a specified period. Lenders must furnish customers a detailed description of their rights and the procedures they must follow to make complaints about billing errors. *See* Regulation Z.

**Fair Debt Collection Practices Act** The federal act that prohibits abusive debt collection practices by those collecting debts for parties other than themselves.

**federal box** A document, or an area within a document of a closed-end credit transaction, where all applicable transaction disclosures are grouped together.

**Federal Deposit Insurance Corporation (FDIC)** The federal regulatory agency for state banks that are not members of the Federal Reserve System. The FDIC insures the savings of bank customers.

**Federal Reserve Board** The federal regulator of state banks that are members of the Federal Reserve System.

**Federal Reserve System** A system created by enactment of the Federal Reserve Act in 1913 to encourage cooperation among all banks, whether state or federal.

**federal system** A system, such as that found in the United States, in which federal and state governments share power.

**fee simple (absolute)** The broadest form and most common kind of real property interest. With this kind of interest, the owner may use, abuse, and exclusively possess the real property; take its profits; and dispose of it by deed or will without restriction. Fee simple absolute provides the safest interest for mortgage purposes.

**fee simple subject to condition subsequent (conditional)** An estate that terminates once a stated event occurs and the owner acts to reenter and repossess the estate.

**fee tail** An estate limited to a person and the heirs of that person's body. Most states have abolished fee tail estates and generally converted them into fee simple estates.

**fiduciary** A person or trust institution charged with the duty of acting for the benefit of another party on matters coming within the scope of the relationship between them. A fiduciary relationship between two parties with regard to a business, contract, or piece of property requires that each party place trust and confidence in the other and exercise a corresponding degree of fairness and good faith. Examples of fiduciary relationships are those between guardian and ward, agent and principal, attorney and client, trustee and beneficiary, and one partner and another.

**financing statement** A statement, filed with the appropriate public official by a creditor, recording a security interest or lien on the debtor's assets.

**fixture** Any personal property so affixed to the land as to become part of the realty.

**float** (1) The difference between deposits credited to an account and the amount of those deposits that has been collected. (2) The difference between amounts credited by the Federal Reserve to depositary institutions and the amount of those items collected by the Federal Reserve. (3) The amount of deposited cash items in the process of collection from drawee banks. (4) The time interval between the creation of a check and its ultimate payment by the bank on which it is drawn. Float is simply a means of quantifying the efficiencies or inefficiencies of the "cash in-cash out" cycle and focusing on the associated opportunities and costs. By minimizing the float associated with collection of accounts receivable and extending the float on the accounts payable side, corporations can increase cash flow and improve their working capital position.

**floating lien** An ongoing security interest in all property, whether acquired before, at the time of, or after perfection.

**forbearance** Refraining from proceeding against a delinquent debtor or in exacting the enforcement of a right.

**foreclosure** A legal procedure undertaken to permit a creditor to take possession of and to sell property that is collateral for a defaulted loan.

**fraud (deceit)** Acts, omissions, or concealments intentionally meant to deprive another of his or her rights.

**freehold estate** A legal estate in land, commonly referred to as an estate of inheritance. The three freehold estates are fee simple, fee tail, and life estate.

**future interest** Any fixed interest except a reversion, with the right of possession and enjoyment postponed until some future date or event occurs.

**gift** voluntary transfer of property by one person (*donor*) to another person (*donee*), who gives no consideration for it.

**gift causa mortis**  A gift of personal property made by a person in expectation of, and contingent on, death, completed by actual delivery of the property and effective only if the owner dies of the expected cause. *Distinguish from* gift inter vivos.

**gift inter vivos**  A gift of property by one living person to another. Actual delivery of the property must be made during the lifetime of the donor and without reference to his or her death. *Distinguish from* gift causa mortis.

**good faith**  A standard of conduct between parties, meaning honesty in fact, in the conduct of a transaction. As an element of a defense to violations under several statutes, a good faith effort to comply means that the defendant did not know about the violation and took reasonable steps to avoid it.

**good faith estimate of settlement services**  A disclosure statement required for loans coming within the Real Estate Settlement Procedures Act (RESPA), giving estimates of an applicant's settlement costs.

**goods**  Any item of merchandise, commodity, etc., having value.

**grantee**  *See* grantor.

**grantor**  A person conveying an interest in real property to another person, the *grantee*.

**guarantor**  A person or legal entity that undertakes responsibility for another party's debt or obligation to perform some specific act or duty. Although the original debtor is responsible for the debt, the guarantor becomes liable in the event of default. The liability of the guarantor is secondary and collateral since it is based on a second, independent undertaking and is not part of the original contract as in *surety*.

**guardian**  A person or trust institution appointed by a court to care for the property, person, or both of a minor or incompetent person. When the guardian's duties are limited to the property, he or she is called a guardian of the property. When the guardian's duties are limited to the person, he or she is called a guardian of the person. If the duties apply to both property and person, he or she is simply called a guardian. *See* ward.

**guardianship by nature**  The relationship of a parent and child. For a guardianship by nature, no court appointment is necessary during the child's minority.

**holding company**  A company that owns stock in other corporations and influences the managerial decisions of those companies.

**holder in due course**  Under the Uniform Commercial Code, a party who accepts an instrument in good faith, for value, and without notice that it has been dishonored, is overdue, or has any claim against it.

**imputed knowledge** Knowledge charged to a person because the facts in question were open to his or her discovery and it was his or her duty to inform him- or herself about them.

**incidental damages** Damages that include expenses incurred as a result of a breach.

**indemnify** To agree to compensate or reimburse an individual or other legal entity in the event of a potential loss.

**infant (minor)** A person not of legal age, which at common law was 21 years but has been changed in some states.

**insider** *See* preference.

**insolvent** Unable to pay one's debt obligations when they become due.

**interest** Money charged as compensation for the loan of money or compensation for forbearance from collecting money owed.

**intermediary bank** A bank between the receiving bank and the beneficiary's bank through which a transfer must pass if specified by the sending bank. In such cases, this is the receiving bank's credit party.

**intestate** Refers to a person who has died without having made and left a valid will.

**issuer** A bank or other person that issues a letter of credit.

**joint tenancy** Ownership of a piece of property shared equally by two or more people, each having full right of usage. If one owner dies, the survivor takes full ownership. *Distinguish from* tenancy in common and tenancy by the entirety.

**junior mortgage** A lien that is subordinate to the claims of the holder of a prior, senior lien.

**larceny** Taking the property of another, without his or her consent and against his or her will, with intent to convert it to the taker's use.

**lessee (tenant)** The party who holds the exclusive right of possession under a valid lease.

**lessor (landlord)** A party who leases property to a tenant.

**letter of administration** A certificate of authority to settle a particular estate issued to an administrator by the appointing court. *Distinguish from* letter testamentary.

**letter testamentary** A certificate of authority to settle a particular estate issued by the appointing court to the executor named in the will. *Distinguish from* letter of administration.

**liability** (1) An amount owed to someone else. (2) A legal obligation to make good some loss or damage that results from an action or transaction.

**libel** *See* defamation.

**license** Temporary authority to do one or more acts on the land of another, without possessing any estate or interest therein.

**lien** A legal claim or attachment filed on record against property, as security for the payment of an obligation. A lien is the guaranteed right of a lender or investor to specific property in case of default.

**life estate** An estate that can never be inherited and ends upon death—either the death of the life tenant or the death of another on whose life the estate is based.

**limited partnership** A type of partnership in which individuals may invest in business without exposure to unlimited liability for the partnership's debts. Limited partners cannot participate in control of the business.

**liquidated damages** Those damages recovered under an advance agreement as to the amount recoverable in case of breach of contract. A contract liquidating damages is enforceable if the amount is reasonable. Otherwise, courts will ignore it and award damages as if the liquidation clause did not exist.

**liquidation** The complex procedure in which a corporation's assets are sold and the net proceeds after all expenses are passed along to creditors, bondholders, and shareholders. Payments are made in accordance with the laws and contracts protecting each class of creditor.

**living (inter vivos) trust** A living, personal trust that becomes operative during the maker's lifetime. *Distinguish from* testamentary trust.

**maker** The party who executes an instrument, such as a check, draft, or note. *Also called* drawer.

**material alteration** An alteration that changes the contract of a party to an instrument.

**mechanic's lien** A lien filed against real property as a result of nonpayment for work performed or materials delivered.

**misappropriation of funds** *See* embezzlement.

**mitigation of damages (Doctrine of Avoidable Consequence)** The obligation of an injured party in a breach-of-contract action to attempt to limit his or her own damages.

**mortgage** An instrument whereby the borrower (*mortgagor*) gives the lender (*mortgagee*) a lien on property as security for the payment of an obligation. The borrower continues to use the property and, when the obligation is fully extinguished, the lien is removed.

**most-favored-lender doctrine** Under the National Banking Act, the ability of national banks to charge the maximum rate of interest allowed to any other state lender located in the same state.

**National Credit Union Administration (NCUA)** An agency of the federal government that regulates federal credit unions and acts as an insuring agency for all deposits in federal credit unions and for deposits in those state-chartered credit unions that opt to join NCUA.

**negligence** Failure to use reasonable care under the circumstances.

**negotiability** The extent to which a financial instrument can be transferred by endorsement.

**negotiable** Transferable by endorsement. Title to a negotiable instrument can be transferred by delivery, without need for further certification. Negotiable instruments must be safeguarded as if they were cash. Bearer securities are automatically negotiable by nature, whereas registered securities can only be rendered negotiable by the completion of a power of assignment.

**negotiable instrument** A written instrument (such as a check, promissory note, draft, or bill of exchange), payable to order or to the bearer. A negotiable instrument is transferred by endorsement and delivery or by delivery alone. It must meet all the requirements of article 3 of the Uniform Commercial Code.

**negotiation** (1) Dealings between parties with the goal of reaching an agreement as to the amount, price, quantity, quality, and other terms of an agreement. (2) The transfer of negotiable instruments.

**note** Written evidence of a debt. A note is an unconditional promise to pay a specified amount to a certain entity on a specified date. (2) A medium-term (1 to 5 or 10 years' maturity) security. (3) Currency.

**novation** The substitution of a new debt or obligation for an existing one.

**offer** A promise conditioned upon a thing to be done by the offeree.

**Office of Thrift Supervision** An arm of the Department of Treasury created under the Financial Institutions Reform, Recovery and Enforcement Act of 1989 to regulate federally chartered savings and loan associations.

**on-us check** A check deposited or otherwise negotiated at the bank on which it is drawn.

**open-end credit** The extension of credit, through bank credit cards or personal lines of credit, that allows customers to continue to add purchases or cash advances to their credit accounts.

**order instrument** An instrument that is payable to a specific person's order.

**overdraft** (1) The amount by which a debit or charge against an account exceeds the balance of the trust account. (2) A negative balance in a depositor's account that results from paying checks for an amount larger than the depositor's collected balance. (3) A check that overdraws an account. Banks are not legally obligated to pay an overdraft.

**parol evidence rule** The rule that states that, where parties have entered into a written contract that reflects their complete statement of the contract, no written or oral evidence of prior understandings or negotiations is admissible to contradict or vary the terms of the written contract.

**partnership** A legal entity composed of two or more people to enable them to carry on business as co-owners for profit.

**partnership agreement** *See* articles of partnership.

**payee** The person named in the instrument as the recipient of the sum shown. Thus, the payee is the party who receives the payment of an instrument.

**payment** A transfer of funds in any form between two parties.

**payor** The party that delivers funds.

**perfected lien** A security interest in an asset that has been properly documented and filed with the appropriate legal authority to protect the claim of the creditor.

**piercing the corporate veil** An action in which shareholders become personally liable for corporate debts, usually arising when a corporate entity has been used to perpetrate a fraud or commit an injustice.

**postdated check** A check bearing a future date.

**power of attorney** (1) A document, witnessed and acknowledged, authorizing the person named in it to act as attorney-in-fact for the person signing the document. (2) The authority to act as an attorney-in-fact. A general power of attorney allows action for the principal in all matters; a special power of attorney limits authority to specified matters.

**preference** (1) An insolvent debtor's transfer of property satisfying debts owed to one or more creditors to the disadvantage of the rest. (2) Under the Bankruptcy Code, a term describing a voluntary or involuntary transfer of an insolvent debtor's interest in property to benefit one creditor over other creditors, the transfer dating within 90 days before the date of filing of the bankruptcy petition. If the transfer occurs between 90 days and one year of that date, the recipient creditor is an "insider."

**preferred stock** *See* stock.

**presenting bank** The bank that forwards an item to another bank for payment.

**principal** (1) A party who appoints another to act on his or her behalf. (2) The actual amount of a deposit, loan, or investment, exclusive of interest charges. (3) The primary borrower on a loan, as opposed to the guarantor. (4) The original amount of an estate or fund together with accretions, which may include income. (5) The individual with primary ownership or managerial control of a business.

**proceeds** The total amount received from the sale, exchange, collection, or other disposition of collateral.

**profit a prendre** A right to take something from the land of another (for example, soil, minerals, or timber).

**promissory estoppel** A doctrine (for the most part, limited in actual application to cases of charitable subscriptions, gratuitous bailments, and parol gifts of land) that states that when a person has changed his or her position in good faith, relying on a promise upon which a reasonable person might be expected to rely, the promisor should be prevented (estopped) from using as a defense the absence of consideration for his or her promise.

**promissory note** A written promise made by one person (the *maker*) to pay a certain sum of money to another person (the *payee*), on demand or at a determinable future date.

**property** Assets subject to ownership. *Real property* is fixed or immovable, while *personal property* is movable.

**prospectus** An official document that must be given to buyers of new issues registered with the Securities and Exchange Commission (SEC). A prospectus is an abstract of the lengthy registration statement filed with the SEC and describes the issuer's products and business, the industries in which it competes, its physical facilities, and its management background. It presents historical financial statements and describes the issue and intended use of the funds to be received. The SEC neither approves nor disapproves the prospectus.

**publicly held corporation** A corporation whose stock is traded in the securities markets and is subject to both federal and/or state securities laws and regulations.

**punitive (exemplary) damages** Damages in excess of compensation, awarded to console the plaintiff and punish the defendant.

**purchase-money security interest** A security interest when the money loaned to the borrower is used to purchase the property that secures the loan.

**quasi contrast** A legal obligation arising out of the receipt of a benefit for which there has been no actual promise to pay, but the retention of which without giving consideration would be unjust.

**quiet enjoyment** A covenant in a warranty deed that gives the right of possession without disturbance caused by defects in title.

**quit claim deed** *See* deed, quit claim.

**ratification** Conduct by a person consistent with the existence of a contract, which could have been avoided. This act must be performed with full knowledge of its ratifying what is known to be voidable.

**Real Estate Settlement Procedures Act (RESPA)** A 1974 federal law requiring lenders to provide home mortgage borrowers with information of known or estimated settlement costs. This act is administered by the Department of Housing and Urban Development and establishes guidelines for escrow account balances and the disclosure of settlement costs.

**recording statutes** State laws governing the registration of all conveyances of all real property.

**redemption** (1) A statutory or contractual right to repurchase or repossess pledged, sold, or mortgaged property within the time and according to statutory or contractual conditions. (2) The right of a party under a disability to redeem or recover property taken from him or her, under color of right during the period of his or her disability. (3) The repaying of principal and interest to retire a security.

**redemption period** The time in which a mortgagor, by paying the amount owed in a foreclosed mortgage, may buy back property. The specific time is subject to estate law.

**regulation** A written rule usually issued by agencies of the executive branch of state and federal governments to implement statutes.

**Regulation B** A Federal Reserve regulation that prohibits creditors from discriminating against credit applicants, establishes guidelines for gathering and evaluating credit information, and requires written notification when credit is denied.

**Regulation CC** A Federal Reserve regulation that covers the availability of funds deposited by customers, disclosures of a bank's policy on availability, and the standards that must be used in endorsing checks.

**Regulation E** A Federal Reserve regulation that establishes the rights, liabilities, and responsibilities of parties in electronic fund transfers, and protects consumers using electronic fund transfer systems.

**Regulation M** A Federal Reserve regulation that implements the consumer-leasing provisions of the Truth in Lending Act.

**Regulation X** A Department of Housing and Urban Development regulation applicable to all federally related mortgage loans.

**Regulation Z** A Federal Reserve regulation that prescribes uniform methods of computing the cost of credit, disclosure of credit terms, and procedures for resolving billing errors on certain credit accounts.

**remainder** A future estate or interest in property that will become an estate or interest in possession, upon the termination of the prior estate or interest created at the same time and by the same instrument as the future estate. *Distinguish from* reversion, which remains in the grantor, while the remainder goes to a grantee.

**rescission** Cancellation of a contract without penalty. Under the Truth in Lending Act, the ability of a consumer to unilaterally terminate a credit transaction, that is, without the creditor's consent.

**restrictive covenants** Limitations imposed on the use of a tract of property to benefit the entire parcel.

**reversion** The interest in an estate remaining in the grantor after a particular interest, less than the whole estate, has been granted by the owner to another person.

**reverter** The interest that the grantor retains in property for which he or she has conveyed an interest less than the whole to another party. If the grantor makes the conveyance subject to a condition that may or may not be broken sometime in the future, he or she retains a *possibility of reverter*.

**right of offset**  The common-law right of a lender to use the balances in any of the customer's accounts as payment for the loan in the event of default.

**Right to Financial Privacy Act**  A federal act limiting the ability of the federal government to gain access to the records of bank customers.

**Rule against Perpetuities**  A rule of common law that makes void any estate or interest in property so limited that it will not take effect or vest within a period measured by a life or lives in being at the time of the creation of the estate, plus 21 years and the period of gestation.

**savings and loan association**  A type of financial institution that traditionally, before passage of the Depository Institutions Deregulation and Monetary Control Act of 1980, limited its activities to the areas of savings deposit accounts and residential mortgages.

**secured creditor**  A creditor whose claim against another person is protected by collateral that he or she holds to ensure the settlement of the claim.

**Securities and Exchange Commission (SEC)**  A government agency that regulates the sale of securities in interstate commerce and through the mail.

**security agreement**  An agreement between a seller and buyer which states that the seller will have a security interest in the goods being traded.

**security interest**  (1) Under Federal Reserve Regulation Z, any interest in property that secures performance of a consumer credit obligation and is recognized by state or federal law. (2) Any interest in property that secures as collateral the payment or performance of an obligation.

**settlor**  A creator of a living trust.

**severalty**  Ownership by one person.

**shareholder derivative suit**  A suit brought by shareholders in the name of a bank against board members and/or officers as individuals.

**sight draft**  A draft that is payable on sight (demand) when presented to the drawee.

**slander**  *See* defamation.

**small loan finance company**  A company chartered exclusively under state law, with no ability to accept deposit accounts. The interest rates charged by a small loan finance company are traditionally higher than those charged by other financial institutions.

**sole proprietorship** The simplest form of business organization, owned and operated by an individual person.

**sovereign immunity** A doctrine that a state cannot be sued against its will.

**special information booklet** A pamphlet given applicants for loans coming within the Real Estate Settlement Procedures Act (RESPA). This pamphlet describes the procedures used when a residential real estate buyer enters into a purchase agreement, obtains financing, and completes settlement.

**specific performance** The actual accomplishment of a contract by the party bound to fulfill it. An action to compel the performance of a contract according to its terms is usually brought when the payment of damages would not adequately compensate the aggrieved party.

**stale check** Any check dated more than a reasonable time (a few months) before presentation. According to the Uniform Commercial Code, a bank is not required to pay on a check (other than a certified check) that is presented more than six months after its date. When a bank receives a stale check, it may call the writer for permission to pay the check or it may return the check.

**standby letter of credit** A letter of credit against which funds can be drawn only if another business transaction is not performed.

**Statute of Frauds** A statute, first enacted in England in 1677, designed to prevent many fraudulent practices by requiring proof of a specific kind, usually in writing, of the important transactions of business.

**statute of limitations** A statute that bars suits upon valid claims after the expiration of a specific period. In most states, there is a 20-year limitation on judgments, a 6-year limitation on contract claims, and a shorter period for tort claims (injuries to people or property).

**statutory law (statutes)** Laws enacted by state legislatures and the U.S. Congress.

**stock** A certificate evidencing ownership in a corporation. The stock of a corporation is usually divided into two classes, common and preferred. *Common stock* represents the basic ownership, usually with a voting privilege, but subordinate to claims of bondholders, creditors, and preferred stockholders. The holder of *preferred stock* enjoys priority as to income and generally as to assets.

**strict liability** Automatic responsibility for certain torts.

**subordination agreement** An agreement between two creditors of a particular borrower whereby one party grants to the other a priority claim to the borrower's assets if default occurs.

**surety** A person or company that, at the request of another, usually called the principal, agrees to be responsible for the performance of some act in favor of a third person if the principal fails to perform as agreed. In suretyship, there is only one contract, making the surety's liability original, primary, and direct. *Distinguish from* guarantor.

**tax lien** A claim against real property for unpaid taxes. Property tax liens usually take precedence over a first mortgage, while other tax liens (income, etc.) do not.

**tenancy by the entirety** A tenancy by a husband and wife in which, except in concert with the other, neither the husband nor the wife has a disposable interest in the property during the other's lifetime. When either dies, the property goes to the survivor. *Distinguish from* joint tenancy and tenancy in common.

**tenancy in common** The joint ownership of property without the right of survivorship, in which each person's interest in a property can be distinguished from the others' interests. *Distinguish from* joint tenancy and tenancy by the entirety.

**tenancy in partnership** The holding of property in a partnership's name.

**testamentary trust** A trust established by the terms of a will to manage assets for a beneficiary. This trust becomes active after the maker's death and settlement of the estate. *Distinguish from* living trust.

**testate** Refers to a person who has died after having made and left a valid will. *Compare with* intestate.

**time draft** A draft that is payable at a fixed or determinable future time.

**tort** A private injury proximately caused by breach of a legal duty arising by operation of law. It can include, but is not limited to, assault; battery; intentional infliction of emotional distress; false imprisonment; trespass to land or goods of another; conversion; injuries by animals or extra-hazardous activities; causing a nuisance, fraud, or misrepresentation; defamation; invasion of privacy; false advertising; and negligent manufacturing of goods. Some torts are also criminal offenses and may be prosecuted.

**transit item** A check drawn on an out-of-town bank.

**trust** A fiduciary relationship in which a person or corporation, the *trustee*, holds the legal title to property, the *trust property*. The trustee is subject to an obligation, enforceable in a court of equity, to keep or use the property for the benefit of another person, the *beneficiary*. *See* living trust and testamentary trust.

**trust property** *See* trust.

**trustee** A person or trust institution that holds the legal title to property for the benefit of someone else. A trustee is responsible for preserving and managing the assets of a trust.

**Truth in Lending Act** The popular name for the Consumer Credit Protection Act of 1969, which applies to all lenders that extend credit to consumers. The act requires disclosure of credit terms (for example, the annual percentage rate and total finance charges) using a standard format. *See* Regulation Z.

**ultra vires act** An act by a corporation's agents, officers, or directors that exceeds the rights of its charter and is thus void.

**unauthorized use** The use of a credit card by a person other than the cardholder—a person who does not have actual, implied, or apparent authority to use the card—and a use from which the cardholder receives no benefit.

**Uniform Commercial Code (UCC)** A coordinated code of laws governing the legal aspects of business and financial transactions in the United States. It regulates such topics as the sale of goods, commercial paper, bank deposits and collections, letters of credit, bulk transfers, and documents of title.

**usury** (1) A higher rate of interest than is allowed by law. (2) The act of charging a higher rate of interest for the use of funds than is legally allowed by a state.

**ward** A person who by reason of minority, mental incompetence, or other incapacity is under a court's protection, either directly or through a guardian. *See* guardian.

**warranty** A guarantee made by a seller for the quality or suitability of the product or service for sale.

**warranty deed** *See* deed, warranty.

**wrongful dishonor** The failure to pay a properly payable item.

**zoning** A government specification for the type of use and density of development for a given piece of property.

# INDEX

Abandonment
   In bankruptcy, 284
   Of property, 208–209
Absolute bar, 9
Acceptance, 214–216
Access device, 27, 364
Accession, 206–207, 211–212
Adequate protection, 283–284
Adjustable-rate mortgages (ARMS), 308
Administrative Procedure Act, 15–17
Administrator, administratrix, 113–114, 116
Adverse action, 337
Adverse possession, 207–208, 249
Advertising, 152
Agency relationship, 63
   "Agency coupled with interest," 74–75
   Agent's authority to act for principals, 66–69
      Actual authority, 67–68
      Apparent authority, 67–68
   Authorized acts, 71
   Creation of, 65–66
   Delegation of authority, 63, 70
   Imputed knowledge, 70
   Liability of
      Agent to principals, 64, 73–74
      Power of attorney, 65
      Principals to agents, 72–73
      Principals to third persons, 64, 70–72
      Ratification, elements of, 69
      Termination of agency, 74–75
      Unauthorized acts, 71
Agent, 63
   Independent contractor, 64
   Master-servant, 63
   Principal-agent, 63–64
American Law Institute, 8
Appellate court, 36–38
Articles of incorporation, 93–95
Articles of partnership, 76–77
Assignment of rights (in contracts), 184–186
Assumed-name certificate, 62

Assumption of risk, 254
Attorney-in-fact, 65
Automatic stay, 268–270, 294, 297

Bailments, 217–221
   Bailee's lien, 221–222
   Common carriers and warehousemen, 224–225
   Consumer leases, 222–224
   Definition, 217
   Degrees of care, 219
   Documents of title, 224–225
   Duties of bailees, 218–221
   Duties of bailors, 221
   Federal Bills of Lading Act, 224
   Interstate Commerce Act, 224
   Safe deposit boxes, 219–221
   UCC, article 7, 205, 224
   United States Warehouse Act, 224
Bank board committees, 106–107
   Audit committee, 106
   Investment/asset-liability committee, 107
   Loan committee, 106–107
   Trust committee, 107
Bank Bribery Act, 50–52
Bank examinations, 24–25
Bank holding company, 25–26, 100
   Affiliates, 100
   Subsidiaries, 100
Bank Holding Company Act, 25, 26, 28–29, 100
Bank of the United States, 19, 20
Bank regulation, 19–40
   Branching, 6, 26–27
      McFadden Act (1927), 6, 27
   Chartering, 22–24
      Qualification, 22
      Revocation, 23
      Termination of deposit insurance, 23
   Courts, role in regulation, 28–38
      Appellate courts, 36–38
      Concurrent jurisdiction, 36

Federal court system, 28–32
   Courts of appeal, 30–32
   District courts, 29–30
   Legislative courts, 29
   Supreme Court, 29
State court system, 32–38
   Courts of appellate jurisdiction, 32
   Courts of general jurisdiction, 32
   Courts of limited jurisdiction, 31, 32–35
     City, county, and district courts, 34
     Courts of claims, 33, 35
     Family courts, 34
     Justice of the peace courts, 33–34
     Magistrate's courts, 33–34
     Small claims courts, 33
     Surrogate, Probate, Orphan's courts, 34–35, 113
Early history, 19–21
   Bank of the United States (1791), 19, 20
   Banking Act (1933), 20
   Comptroller of the Currency, 21
   Examinations, 24–25
   Federal Deposit Insurance Corporation (FDIC), 20
   Federal Reserve Act (1913), 20
   Federal Reserve Board, 13, 21
   Federal Reserve System, 20, 28–29
   *McCulloch v. Maryland* (1819), 19
   National Bank Act (1863–1864), 20
   State regulation, 19
   Financial Institutions Examination Council (1978), 24
   Holding companies—Bank Holding Company Act (1956), 25, 26, 28–29, 100
   *See also* Consumer lending regulations
Banking Act (1933), 20
Bankruptcy, 265–301
   Abandoned property, 208–209
   Automatic stay, 268–270, 294, 297
   Chapter 7 (straight bankruptcy—liquidation), 267–268
   Chapter 11 (reorganization), 267, 296–300
   Chapter 13 (rehabilitation—wage earner plan), 293–296
   Committees, 299
   Constitutional and legislative background, 265–267
   Bankruptcy Code, 266–267
   Bankruptcy Reform Act (1978), 266–267
   National Bankruptcy Act (1898), 266
   Definition, 265
   Discharge, 288–293, 296
     Denial of, 288
     Nondischargeable debts, 289
   Discrimination, 293
   Distribution of estate, 287
   End of stay, 269
   Executory contracts, 282
   Exempt property, 271–272
   History, 265–266
   Involuntary, 267–268
   Liquidation, 267–293
   Payments in the ordinary course of business, 279
   Procedures for filing, 268
   Reaffirmation of debt, 286
   Redemption of personal property, 285–286
   Rehabilitation, 293–300
   Secured creditors, 282–284
     Abandonment, 284
     Seeking adequate protection, 283–284
   Setoff, 286–287
   Trustee, 294
     Appointment by court, 270, 294
     Powers, 273–282, 295
Bankruptcy Code, 266–267
   Chapter 7, 267–268
   Chapter 11, 267, 298–299
   Chapter 13, 293–296
   *See also* Bankruptcy
Bankruptcy Reform Act, 266–267
Bank Secrecy Act, 24, 52–54
Beneficiary, 120
Bilateral contract, 159
Billing error, 320
Blue-sky laws, 98, 104
Bona fide purchaser, 275
Branch bank (McFadden Act), 6, 27
Breach of contract, 192
   *See also* Remedies
Bribery, 50–52

Capacity to contract
   Infants, 131–135
   Intoxication, 139–140
   Mental illness, 135–139

Cease-and-desist powers, 23–24
Certificate of limited partnership, 90
Chapter 7 (straight bankruptcy—liquidation), 267
Chapter 11 (reorganization), 267, 296–300
Chapter 13 (Wage Earner Plan), 293–296
Chartering, 22–24
City courts, 34
Close corporations, 95–97
Closed-end credit, 308–311
Common carriers, 224–225
Common law, 2–5
Community property, 245
Comparative negligence, 45
Compensatory damages, 192–193
Comptroller of the Currency, 13, 21, 55
Concurrent jurisdiction, 36
Concurrent powers, 12
Confusion, 210–211
Consequential (special) damages, 193–194
Conservator, 118
Consideration, 159–166
    Adequacy, 161–163
    Conditional gift, 160–161
    Definition, 159
    Exceptions, 163–166
    Legal detriment, 159–160
    Promissory estoppel, 163, 165
Constitutions, 10–13
Consumer Leasing Act, 328
Consumer Lending, 305–377
    Advertising of consumer credit, 324–325
    Consumer Leasing Act, 328
    Credit cards, 322–324
    Credit Practices Rule, 356–359
    Electronic Fund Transfer Act (EFTA), 364–376
    Equal Credit Opportunity Act (ECOA), 24, 329–341
    Fair Credit and Charge Card Disclosure Act of 1988, 311, 316
    Fair Credit Billing Act of 1974 (FCBA), 319–327
    Fair Credit Reporting Act (FCRA), 346–352
    Fair Debt Collection Practices Act, 352–356
    Home Equity Loan Consumer Protection Act of 1988, 312–315
    Real Estate Settlement Procedures Act (RESPA), 24, 341–346
    Right to Financial Privacy Act, 359–364
    Truth in Lending Act, 1968 (TILA), 37, 305–319
Consumer lending regulations, 305–306
Consumer reports, 346
Consummation, 308–311
Contracts, 129–202
    Assignment of rights, 184–186
    Bilateral, unilateral, 151, 156–157, 159
    Breach, 192
    Definition, 129
    Delegation of duties, 186–188
    Disaffirmance of, 131–132, 138–139, 140
    Elements of, 131–166
        Consideration, 159–166
        Legal capacity, 131–140
        Legality, 140–149
        Mutual assent, 149–159
    Excuses for nonperformance, 178–183, 198–200
        Conditions, 181–183
        Frustration of purpose, 180
        Impossibility (legal and personal), 178–180, 197, 198
        Impracticability, 179
        Substantial performance, 183
    Illegal objectives, 140–149, 179
        Against the public interest, 142–143
        Defrauding or injuring third persons, 143–144
        Harmful to administration of justice, 144
        Harmful to marriage relationship, 144–145
        In unreasonable restraint of trade, 141–142
        Usurious agreements, 146–149
        Violation of statutes, 146
        Wagering agreements, 145–146
    Interpretation of, 175–177
    Legally incapacitated, 117, 131–140, 178–179
        Infants, 131–135
        Intoxicated persons, 139–140
        Mentally ill, 135–139
        Wards with guardians, 117, 135
    Offer and acceptance, 151–156
    Necessaries, 133–134
    Novation, 187, 255
    Parol evidence rule, 173–175

Performance, 177–188
    By third party, 183–188
Quasi contract, 133, 196–202
Ratification of, 132, 137
Remedies for failure to perform, 191–196
    Monetary damages, 191–195
        Compensatory, 192–193
        Consequential (special), 193–194
        Incidental, 194
        Liquidated, 195
        Mitigation of damages (doctrine of avoidable consequence), 195–196
        Nominal, 194
            Punitive (exemplary), 194
        Specific performance, 191–192
    Statute of Frauds, 166–173
    Third-party beneficiaries, 188–191
    Void, voidable, 135–136, 139
Contributory negligence, 44
Conversion. *See* Torts
Corporations, 59, 91–112
    Articles of incorporation, 93–95
    Benefits of incorporating, 92
    Blue-sky laws, 98, 104
    Board of directors, 104–110
        Duties and responsibilities, 107–109
        Election of, 104–106
        Liabilities of, 109–110
    Close corporations, 95–97
    Corporate officers, 110–112
    Definition, 91
    Dividends, 101
    Estates, 112–119
    Government entities, dealing with, 112
    Limited liability, 92–93
    Officers, 110–112
    Organization of, 93–95
        Articles of incorporation, 93–95
        Certificate of Incorporation (Charter), 94
        Model Business Corporation Act, 10, 93
    Prospectus, 98
    Publicly held corporations, 97–99
    Securities Act of 1933, 98
    Securities Exchange Act of 1934, 99
    Shareholders, 92, 100–104
        Liabilities of, 103–104
            Piercing the corporate veil, 104
        Meetings, 100–101
        Rights, 100, 101–103
        Stock transfers, 99–100
            UCC transfers, 100
    Stock, 95
    Ultra vires acts, 102
Cosigner, 358
County courts, 34
Courts of appeals (federal), 30–32
Courts of claims, 33, 35
Courts of general jurisdiction, 32
Courts of limited jurisdiction, 31, 32–35
Courts, role in bank regulation, 28–38
Covenants, restrictive, 250–251
Cram down, 300
Credit card, 322–324
    Unauthorized use, 322–323
Credit Practices Rule, 356–359
    Cosigner liability, 357–358
    Prohibited provisions, 357
    Scope, 356
    Unfair late charges, 359
Creditor, secured, 282–284
Creditor beneficiary, 189
Crimes, 41–42, 49–56
    Bribery, 50–52
    Burden of proof, 42, 43
    Compared with torts, 41–42
    Definition, 41, 49
    Embezzlement, 49–50
    Involving banks, 54
    Larceny, 42, 49
    Money laundering, 49, 52–54
Criminal referral, 54–56
Cumulative voting, 105
Currency and Foreign Transaction Reporting Act. *See* Bank Secrecy Act
Currency transaction report (CTR), 53
Curtesy, 83, 230–231, 236–237
Customer-bank computer terminals (CBCTs), 6

Damages
    Compensatory, 192–193
    Consequential, 193–194
    Incidental, 194
    Limitation, 195–196
    Liquidated, 195
    Nominal, 194
    Punitive, 194
    Types of, 192
Debt adjustment plans, 296

Debt collection, 352–356
  Prohibited practices, 353–355
  See also Fair Debt Collection Practices Act
Debtors in possession, 297, 298
Deceit. See Fraud
Deeds
  Quit Claim, 246–247
  Warranty, 246
Defamation, 46–49
Delegation, 186–188
Depository Institutions Deregulation and Monetary Control Act (DIDMCA), 148, 149
Discharge, 125, 288–293, 296
Disposable income, 296
Distribution of estates in bankruptcy, 287
Dividend, 101–102
Doctrine of avoidable consequence, 195–196
Donor, donee, 213, 214
Dower, 83, 230–231, 236–237
Dragnet clause, 253
Duty of due care, 108
Duty of loyalty, 108

Easements, 237–238
Electronic fund transfer, 364
Electronic Fund Transfer Act, 364–376
  Access devices, 27, 364
    Issuance of, 366
  Consumer liability for unauthorized transfers, 367, 373–374
  Defenses and penalties for failure to comply, 371, 375
  Disclosures to consumers, 366–368
  Enforcement, 374–376
    Criminal penalties, 376
  Financial institutions' liability for failure to make transfers, 370–371
  Procedures for resolving errors, 367, 371–373
    Determination, 373
    Investigation of error, 372–373
    Notice of error, 372
  Scope, 364–365
  Stop-payment procedures, 367, 370
Embezzlement, 49–50
Empirically derived credit system, 332
Equal Credit Opportunity Act (ECOA), 24, 329–341
  Credit applications—prohibited questions, 330–332

Credit evaluations, 332–334
  Credit history, 334, 336
  Empirically derived credit system, 332
  Judgmental system, 332
Credit exemptions, 326, 347–348
  Businesses, 337
  Credit-extension documents—signature requirements, 338–339
  Creditors' defenses, 341
  Enforcement, 340
  Monitoring information, 339
  Notification of credit decisions, 337–338
  Regulation B, 329, 341
Estates, 112–119
  At sufferance, 233
  At will, 233
  Definition, 112
  For years, 232
  Freehold, 227–236
  In bankruptcy, 287
  Intestate, 248
  Nonfreehold (leasehold), 231–236
  Of deceased persons, 113–117
  Of persons subject to guardianships (wards), 117–119
  Periodic, 232
  Testate, 113
  See also Property, Real
Estoppel, 76, 78
  Infants' contracts, 134–135
  Partnership formation by, 76
  Promissory, 163, 165
Executor, executrix, 113–114, 116
Executory contracts, 282
Executory interest, 241
Exemplary (punitive) damages, 194
Express conditions, 181

Fair Credit Billing Act of 1974 (FCBA), 319–327
  Procedure if billing error, 320–322
  Scope, 319–327
Fair Credit Reporting Act (FCRA), 346–352
  Consumer reports, 346
  Consumers' rights to review, 349
  Disputing accuracy of, 349–351
  Furnishing to users, 348–349
  Investigative consumer reports, 348–349
  Users of, 351

Enforcement, 351–352
Exempt reports, 326, 347–348
Scope, 346–347
Fair Debt Collection Practices Act, 352–356
Enforcement, 355
Common-law remedies, 355–356
Federal Trade Commission, 355
Prohibited collection acts, 353–355
Family courts, 34
Federal Bills of Lading Act, 224
Federal box, 311
Federal court system, 28–32
Federal Deposit Insurance Corporation (FDIC), 13, 20
Federal government powers, 11–12
Federal Reserve Act (1913), 20
Federal Reserve Board, 13, 21
Federal Reserve System, 20
Federal Savings and Loan Insurance Corporation (FSLIC), 20–21
Federal Trade Commission (FTC), 355
Federal versus state powers, 19–21
Fee simple, 227–229
Absolute, 227
Conditional, 228–229
Determinable, 228–229
Fee tail, 227, 229
Fiduciary, 73, 118, 143, 289
Financial Institutions Examination Council (1978), 24
Financial Institutions Reform, Recovery and Enforcement Act of 1989 (FIRREA), 20, 24, 109
Forbearance, 125, 146
Foreclosure, 247, 256–258
By advertisement, 256
Judicial, 256
Law day, 256
Redemption, 257–258, 285–286
Strict (common law), 256
Fraud (deceit), 45–46, 143–144
Fraudulent transfers, 279–281
Freehold estate, 227–236
Frustration of purpose, 180
Future interests—Executory interests, possibility, reverter, remainders, reversion, rights of reentry, 235, 239–241

Gift, 213–217
Acceptance, 214–216
Causa mortis, 213, 216
Conditional gift, 160–161
Definition, 213
Delivery, 213–214
Donative intent, 213
Inter vivos, 213
Governments as bank customers, 112
Grantee, 226
Grantor, 226
Guaranties, 126–127
Guardians, 117, 118, 119
Guardianship by nature, 117

Holding company, 25–26, 100

Illegal contracts, 140–149, 179
Implied conditions, 182–183
Implied powers, 11
Impossibility of performance, 178–180
Incidental damages, 194
Independent contractors, 64
Individual customers, 59–61
Infants, 131–135
Inherent powers, 12
Inheritance, 217
Insiders, 93, 277, 278, 288
Interest, 75, 146
Interest groups, 6
Interest rate ceilings, 305
Internal Revenue Service (IRS) summons, 361–362
Interstate Commerce Act (bailments), 224
Intestate, 248

Joint and several liability, 86–87
Joint tenancy, 243–244
Judicial review
Of agency decisions, 28–38
*See also* Courts, Role in bank regulation
Justice of the peace courts, 33–34

Land titles, 260–264
Land use, 250–252
Restrictive covenants, 250–251
Zoning ordinances, 251–252
Landlord. *See* Lessor
Larceny, 49
Law day, 256
Law, sources of, 1–18
Common law, 2–5
Constitutions, priority of, 10
Federal versus state powers, 11–13

Regulations, 13–17
   *Marbury v. Madison,* 14
   Writs of mandamus, prohibition, certiorari, 14
  Regulatory agencies, 14–15
   Administrative Procedure Act, 15–17
  Statutory, 5–7
  Uniform laws, 7–10
   National Conference of Commissioners on Uniform State Laws, 8, 10
   Uniform Commercial Code, 8–10
Leasehold estates, 231–236
Leases, 222–224
Legal detriment, 159–160
Legal entities, 59–128
  Agents, 59, 62–75
  Corporations, 59, 91–112
  Estates, 59
  Government, 59
  Guaranties, 59, 126–127
  Individuals, 59–61
  Married couples, 60–61
  Partnerships, 75–91
  Sole proprietors, 59, 61–62
  Sureties, 59, 123–126
   Suretyship defenses, 124–126
  Trusts, 59, 120–123
Lessee (tenant), 226
Lessor (landlord), 226
Letters of administration, 113, 114
Letters of authority, 113
Letters testamentary, 113
Libel, 46–47
License (in real property), 237–238
Life estate, 229–231
Limited partnerships, 89–91
Liquidated damages, 195
Liquidation, 267–293
  Automatic stays, 268–270
  Debtors' options, 284–287
  Involuntary, 267–268
  Secured creditors, 282–284
  Trustees, 270–284
  Voluntary, 267
Living trust, 121
Lost or mislaid property, 209–210

Magistrate's courts, 33–34
*Marbury v. Madison* (1803), 14
Master-servant, 63
*McCulloch v. Maryland* (1819), 19
McFadden Act (branch bank), 6, 27

Mechanics' liens, 258–260
Merchants' offers, 157
Minors. *See* Infants
Misappropriation of funds, 50. *See also* Embezzlement
Mitigation of damages, 195–196
Model Business Corporation Act, 10, 93
Money laundering, 49, 52–54
Mortgagee, mortgagor, 226, 252–253
Mortgages (property, real), 252–256
  Conveyance of mortgaged property, 253–255
   Assumption of, 254
   Due-on-sale clause, 253
   Novation, 255
   Subject to, 253
  Dragnet clause, 253
  Foreclosure, 256–258
  Junior, 258
  Leasehold, 231–236
  *See also* Real Estate Settlement Procedures Act (RESPA)
Most-favored-lender doctrine, 147
Mutual assent, 149–159
  Manifestation by words, conduct, 150
  Offer and acceptance, 151–156
  Revocation, termination of offer, 156–158
  Under UCC, 155–156
Mutual mistakes of fact, 197, 199–200

National Bank Act (1863–1864), 20
National Banking Act, 147, 148
National Bankruptcy Act of 1898, 266
National Conference of Commissioners on Uniform State Laws, 8, 10
Necessaries, 133–134
Negligence, 44–45
  Defenses, 44
  Elements, 44
Nondischargeable debts, 289
Nonpossessory interests, 236–241
  Dower and curtesy, 230–231, 236–237
  Easements, profits, licenses, 237–238
  Future interests, 239–241
  Rule against perpetuities, 240
Notice, actual and constructive, 90
Notice of right to cancel, 318
Novations, 187, 255

Offer, 151
Offer and acceptance, 151–156
Offeror, 151

Open-end credit, 308, 311–316
Options, 156
Oral promise, 169, 171, 172
Orphan's courts, 34–35

Parol evidence rule, 173–175
Partnerships, 75–91
    Articles of partnership (partnership agreement), 76–77, 81
    Assets of, 82–84
    Authority of partners, 79–82
    Certificate of, 90
    Contributions, income, losses, and management, 84–89
    Definition, 75
    Established by estoppel, 76, 78–79
    Formation, 76–79
    Limited, 89–91
    Partners' authority, 79–82
    Personal liability of partners, 83, 85–87, 89
    Tenancy in partnership, 82
    Uniform Limited Partnership Act, 89–90
    Uniform Partnership Act, 76
Performance, 177–188
Personal property. *See* Property, personal
Piercing the corporate veil, 104
Point-of-sale transfers, 364
Power of attorney, 65
Preauthorized credit accounts, 368–370
Preferences, 276
Principal-agent, 63–64
Priority claims, 287, 295
Probate. *See* Estates
Probate (surrogate's, orphan's) courts, 34–35, 113
Profit a prendre, 238
Profits, 237–238
Promissory estoppel, 163, 165
Proof of claim, 42, 43
Property, 203–264
    Personal, 203–225
        Abandonment of, 208–209
        Acquisition of, 205–217
        Accession, 206–207, 211–212
        Bailments, 217–221
        Confusion, 210–211
        Definition, 203
        Finding, 209–210
        Gift, 213–217
        Inheritance, 217
        Lost or Mislaid, 209–210
        Production, 206–207
        Purchase, 207
        Taking possession of (adverse, nonadverse), 207–209
    Real, 203–204, 225–264
        Acquisition of, 246–250
            Adverse possession, 249
            Gift, 248
            Purchase, 246–248
            Quit claim deed, 246–247
            Warranty deed, 246
            Will or descent, 248–249
        Co-ownership of real property, concurrent estates, 241–245
            Community property, 245
            Severalty, 243–244
            Tenancy, 242–245
                By the entirety, 244–245
                In common, 242–243
                In partnership, 82
                Joint, 243–244
        Definition, 203
        Dower and curtesy, 230–231, 236–237
        Easements, profits, and licenses, 237–238
        Freehold estates, 227–236
            Fee simple absolute, 227
            Fee simple conditional and determinable, 228–229
            Fee tail, 227, 229
        Future interests, 239–241
        Interests, 226
        Land titles, 260–264
            Actual and constructive notice, 90
            Statutes (pure race, notice, notice race), 262–263
        Land use, 250–252
            Nonconforming, 252
            Restrictive covenants, 250–251
            Zoning, 251–252
        Leasehold estates, 231–236
            Adverse possession, 207–208, 249
            Estates—at will, at sufferance, for years, and periodic, 232–234
            Lessor–lessee, 231
            Rights and obligations of lessees, 231
        Life estates, 229–231
            Curtesy, dower, 230–231
            Remainder, 230
        Mechanics' liens, 258–260

Mortgages, 252–256
  Conveyance of mortgaged
    property, 253–255
  Dragnet clause, 253
  Foreclosure, 256–258
Nonpossessory interests, 236–241
  Dower and curtesy, 230–231,
    236–237
  Easements, profits, and licenses,
    237–238
  Future interests, 239–241
  Rule against perpetuities, 240
  Title, 204–205
Prospectus, 98
Publicly held corporations, 97–99
Punitive (exemplary) damages, 194

Quasi contract, 133, 196–202
Quiet enjoyment, 234
Quit claim deed, 246–247

Ratification, 132
  In agency, 133
  In guardianship, 133
  Of infants' contracts, 133
Reaffirmation, 286
Real Estate Settlement Procedures Act
  (RESPA), 24, 341–346
  Aims, 342
  Disclosures required by lenders, 343–345
  Enforcement, 345–346
  Escrow limitations, 345
  Kickbacks and referral fees, 344–345
  Regulation X, 342
  Scope, 342–343
Real property. *See* Property, real
Rebuttable presumption, 9–10
Recording statutes, 262
Redemption, 75, 257–258, 285–286
Redemption period, 285
Regulation B, 329
  *See also* Equal Credit Opportunity Act
    (ECOA)
Regulation E, 364
  *See also* Electronic Fund Transfer Act
    (EFTA)
Regulation M, 328
  *See also* Consumer Leasing Act
Regulations, 13–17, 25–27
Regulation X, 341–346
  *See also* Real Estate Settlement Procedures
    Act (RESPA)

Regulation Z, 306
  *See also* Truth in Lending Act (TILA)
Regulatory agencies, 14–15
Regulatory law, 13–14
Rehabilitation, 293–300
  Chapter 11, 267, 296–300
  Chapter 13, 293–296
Remainder, 239–240
Remainderman, 239
Remedies, 191–196
Reorganization, 267, 296–300
Reorganization plans, 299–300
Rescission, 316–319
  Inapplicability to residential mortgages,
    317
  Notice of right to cancel, 318
Restraint of trade, 141–142
Restrictive covenants, 250–251
Reversion, 239
Reverter, possibility of, 241
Right to Financial Privacy Act, 359–364
  Conditions for gaining access to records,
    360–361
    Certification of compliance, 362
    Notice requirement, 361
  Customers' challenge of provisions, 363
  Enforcement, 363–364
    Civil penalties, 363
    Injunctive relief, 364
  IRS exemption, 361–362
  Responsibilities of financial institutions,
    362–363
  Scope, 359–360
Rule against perpetuities, 240
Rules of contract interpretation, 175–177
  Primary rules, 175–177
  Secondary rules, 177

Safe deposit box, 219–221
Secured creditor, 282–284
  Abandonment, 284
  Seeking adequate protection, 283–284
Security interests, 226
Securities and Exchange Commission (SEC),
  99
Setoff, 9, 286–287
Settlor, 120, 121
Severalty, 243–244
Slander, 46–47
Small claims courts, 31
Sole proprietorships, 64
Sovereign immunity, 13–14, 33, 35

Special (consequential) damages, 193–194
Special Information Booklet (RESPA), 341–346
Special purpose credit programs, 339–340
Specific performance, 191–192
Stare decisis, 3–4
State banking agencies, 22
State court system, 32–38
State government powers, 12–13
Statute of Frauds, 166–173
    Exceptions, 171
    Oral promises to lend money, 171, 172
    Parol evidence rule, 173–175
    Promises, 166–171
        By executors, 166, 168
        Made in consideration of marriage, 166, 167
        Not able to be performed within a year, 166, 169–170
        On behalf of another's duty, 166, 168
    Real estate contracts, 166, 170
    Sales—UCC, 170–171
    Writings that satisfy, 172–173
Statute of limitations, 249
Statutory law, 5–7
Stays, 268–270
    End of, 269
Stock, 95
Stock transfers, 99–100
Straight bankruptcy. *See* Liquidation
Strict liability, 43
Subordination agreement, 338
Substantial performance, 183
Sureties, 59, 123–126
    Subrogation of, 124
    Suretyship defenses, 124–126
Surety bond, 260
Surrogate courts, 34–35

Tenancy, 242–246
    By the entirety, 244–245
    In common, 242–243
    In partnership, 245
    Joint, 243–244
Tenant (lessee), 226
Terminal-connected transfer services, 367
Third-party beneficiaries, 188–191
Title, 224–225
Torts, 41–49
    Burden of proof, 42, 43
    By agent, 70
    By partner, 86
    Defamation, 46–49
    Definition, 41
    Distinguish crime, 41–42
    Fraud or deceit, 45–46
    Negligence, 44–45
    Strict liability, 43
    Tortfeasor, 43
Trust, 59, 120–123
    Banks as trustees, 122, 123, 287
    Beneficiary, 120
    Borrowing power, 123
    Express, 120
    Fiduciary responsibility of trustee, 120, 121
    Inter vivos, 120, 121
    Revocable living, 121
    Settlor, 120, 121, 123
    Testamentary, 120
    Trust property, 120
    Trustee, 120
Trustees, 120, 270–284
    Ability to avoid preferences, 276–279
    As hypothetical bona fide purchasers of real estate, 275–276
    As hypothetical lien creditors, 274–275
    As successors to actual creditors, 276
    Court appointment, 270
    Definition, 270
    Distribution of estates, 287
    In bankruptcy, 270–284
    Of trusts, 120–123
    Payments in the ordinary course of business, 279
    Power to act regarding fraudulent transfers, 279–281
Truth in Lending Act (TILA), 304, 305–319
    Advertisement—"triggering terms," 324–325
    Annual percentage rate, 307
    Closed-end credit, 308–311
    Consumer Leasing Act (1977), 328
    Consummation, 308–311
    Credit cards, 322–324
    Enforcement, 325–327
        60-day defense, 326
    Exemptions, 326
    Fair Credit Billing Act of 1974, 319–327
    Federal box, 311
    Finance charge, 307
    Official staff commentary, 306

Open-end credit, 308, 311–316
Regulation Z, 306
Requirements of creditors, 307
Rescission, 316–319

Ultra vires acts, 102
Unauthorized use (credit card), 322–323
Uniform Commercial Code (UCC), 8–10
    Article 2 (sale of goods), 129–130, 170–171
    Article 4 (bank deposits and collections), 370
    Article 7 (bailment), 205, 224
    Article 8 (corporations), 100
    Article 9 (secured transactions), 9, 256
Uniform laws, 7–10
Uniform Limited Partnership Act, 89–90
Uniform Partnership Act, 76, 245
    *See also* Partnerships
Uniform Settlement Statement, 344

Unilateral contracts, 159
United States Warehouse Act, 224
Usury, 146
    Depository Institutions Deregulation and Monetary Control Act (DIDMCA), 148, 149
    Most-favored-lender doctrine, 147
    National Banking Act, 147, 148
    Penalties for, 148–149

Wage Earner Plan (Chapter 13 bankruptcy), 293–296
Wards, 117, 118, 135
Warehousemen, 224–225
Warranty deed, 246
Will, 115, 116, 248–249
Writs of certiorari, mandamus, and prohibition, 14

Zoning, 251–252

# Additional Publications of Interest from ABA

To order copies, contact your local AIB chapter or call ABA Order Processing at (202) 663-5087.

## Personnel and the Law

A must for anyone who supervises others, this seminar covers every aspect of the employment process from recruitment to discharge. Included are actual legal cases, application exercises, and situation analyses that simulate real-life employment situations.

|  | Order Number | Price | ABA Member Price* |
|---|---|---|---|
| Handbook | 623202 | $ 24.00 | $ 18.00 |
| Leader's Guide | 623203 | $ 38.00 | $ 28.00 |

## Law & Banking: Applications, 1990

An introduction to the laws pertaining to secured transactions, letters of credit, and the bank collection process, this text also discusses check losses and frauds and a broad range of legal issues related to processing checks. Interesting case studies illustrate important legal points related to banking practices.

|  | Order Number | Price | ABA Member Price* |
|---|---|---|---|
| Textbook | 050243 | $ 51.00 | $ 38.00 |
| Instructor's Manual | 250243 | $ 24.00 | $ 18.00 |
| Workbook | 050244 | $ 20.00 | $ 15.00 |

## Banking Terminology

This comprehensive, authoritative dictionary unlocks the language of "bankspeak" and makes it comprehensible to all. It defines clearly and concisely over 5,000 terms and almost 200 acronyms used in the banking and financial services industry.

|  | Order Number | Price | ABA Member Price* |
|---|---|---|---|
| Text |  |  |  |
| (1-4 copies) | 629600 | $ 34.00 | $ 25.00 |
| (5-19 copies) |  | $ 30.00 | $ 23.00 |
| (20 or more) |  | $ 27.00 | $ 20.00 |

## A Legal Guide to Employee Relations

This comprehensive guide covers the legal aspects of the entire employment process from pre-employment tests to termination. Designed for practical application, the text is organized by types of employee-related decisions and problems that a supervisor might encounter. Also addressed are such timely issues as drug testing and layoffs, nondiscrimination laws, affirmative action plans, union and nonunion employee relations, the consequences of litigation, and the effects of decisions on employee morale, productivity, and employer-employee relations.

|  | Order Number | Price | ABA Member Price* |
|---|---|---|---|
| Text | 050250 | $120.00 | $ 90.00 |

*The discounted prices are available to ABA member banks and AIB chapters. All prices are subject to change without notice.

**LAW AND BANKING: PRINCIPLES TEXTBOOK QUESTIONNAIRE**          Date:_____

This questionnaire is designed to get your opinion of the <u>Law and Banking: Principles</u> textbook on which this course is based. This is **NOT** an evaluation of your instructor or experience in class. Please take a few minutes to answer the following questions and return this self-mailing questionnaire. Your comments will be used to improve future editions of this textbook.

I. **About the Textbook**

  Please rate your opinions of the textbook by checking the appropriate comment.

  A. Thoroughness
  ___ Covers too little          ___ Sufficient content          ___ Covers too much

  B. Difficulty of content
  ___ Too difficult          ___ Appropriate          ___ Too easy

  C. Readability (language, style, etc.)
  ___ Easy to read          ___ Fairly readable          ___ Hard to read

  D. Practicality (usefulness to your job)
  ___ Too theoretical          ___ Practical          ___ Not practical but useful

  E. Organization of subjects
  ___ Very well organized          ___ Organized          ___ Not well organized

  F. Textbook's ability to address stated learning objectives
  ___ Always addressed          ___ Mostly addressed          ___ Seldom addressed

  G. Graphics/examples
  ___ Always appropriate          ___ Sometimes appropriate          ___ Seldom appropriate

  H. Overall rating of the text (circle rating)
  Very effective                                                    Ineffective
  5          4          3          2          1

II. **Background Information**

  A. Bank Position: _____

  B. Major Job Responsibility: _____

  C. Asset Size of Bank:
  ___ Under $100m          ___ $100-$500m          ___ $501m-$1bil          ___ Over $1bil

  D. Highest Education Level
  ___ High School          ___ Some College          ___ BA/BS Degree          ___ Advanced

  E. Age:
  ___ Under 25          ___ 25-35          ___ 36-45          ___ Over 45

  F. Years in Banking:
  ___ 0-2          ___ 3-5          ___ 6-10          ___ Over 10

III. **Comments**

  A. What specific suggestions can you make for improving this textbook?




  B. If we may call you for more comments, please provide your name and phone number below:

  Name:_____          Phone Number: _____

FOLD IN HALF AND STAPLE

FOLD HERE

NO POSTAGE
NECESSARY
IF MAILED
IN THE
UNITED STATES

**BUSINESS REPLY MAIL**
FIRST CLASS PERMIT NO. 10579   WASHINGTON, DC

POSTAGE WILL BE PAID BY ADDRESSEE

Educational Development
Education Policy & Development Group

American Bankers Association
1120 Connecticut Avenue, N.W.
Washington, D.C. 20077-5760